Rooted in Barbarous Soil

California History Sesquicentennial Series
Edited by Richard J. Orsi

Rooted in Barbarous Soil

PEOPLE, CULTURE, AND
COMMUNITY IN GOLD RUSH
CALIFORNIA

Editors

KEVIN STARR and RICHARD J. ORSI

Illustrations Editor
ANTHONY KIRK

Associate Editor
MARLENE SMITH-BARANZINI

Published in association with the California Historical Society

UNIVERSITY OF CALIFORNIA PRESS
Berkeley · Los Angeles · London

University of California Press
Berkeley and Los Angeles, California

University of California Press, Ltd.
London, England
© 2000 by the Regents of the University of California

Library of Congress Cataloging-in-Publication Data

Rooted in barbarous soil : people, culture, and community in Gold
Rush California / editors, Kevin Starr and Richard J. Orsi ; illustrations
editor, Anthony Kirk ; associate editor, Marlene Smith-Baranzini.
     p .   cm.—(California history sesquicentennial series ; 3)
  "Published in association with the California Historical Society."
  Includes bibliographical references and index.
  ISBN 0-520-22497-3 (alk . paper) — ISBN 0-520-22496-5 (pbk . :
alk   paper)
     1. California—Gold discoveries—Social aspects.   2. California—
Social conditions—19th century.   3. Frontier and pioneer life—
California.   4. California—Civilization—19th century.   I. Starr,
Kevin.   II. Orsi, Richard J.   III. California Historical Society.
IV. Series.
F865 .R68   2000
979.4'04—dc21   00-022228
                                                            CIP

Manufactured in the United States of America

9 8 7 6 5 4 3 2 1 0

10 9 8 7 6 5 4 3 2 1

The paper used in this publication meets the minimum requirements of
ANSI / NISO Z39 0.48-1992(R 1997) (Permanence of Paper) .♾

Contents

PREFACE

Perhaps never in the time-honored American tradition of frontiering did "civilization" appear to sink so low as in gold-rush California. A mercurial economy swung sharply from boom to bust, and back again, rendering everyone's fortunes ephemeral. A volatile assemblage of transients, nearly all of them men, hailing from diverse cultures, were fixated on "making their pile" and returning home. Competition, jealousy, and racism fueled unprecedented, nearly uncontrollable, individual and mass violence. A collective mentality of self-interest, greed, speculation, and momentary earthly pleasure seemed to call the shots at every turn. Shoddy "instant cities" of wood and canvas burst forth overnight to house and supply the sojourners, then were abruptly abandoned in the mad scramble for gold elsewhere, or were even more quickly consumed by fire or flood, only to be rebuilt to serve until they suffered the same fiery or watery fate a few months or years down the line. Like the people, buildings and even whole communities came and went, often leaving barely a trace on the historical record—"was to have been" cities, Louise Clappe, the famed "Dame Shirley," called them. For more than two years after the gold discovery in early 1848, while its non-Indian population was swelling from ten thousand to more than one hundred thousand, California even lacked a clearly established system of rule and government, save for a hastily contrived martial law haphazardly enforced by undermanned U.S. Army forces.

Yet, in the very midst of turbulence, during the first few months, years, and decades of pioneer California, social and cultural forms emerged, solidified, spread, and took hold. Even from her 1852 vantage point in a rough and fleeting Sierra foothill mining camp, Dame Shirley could see the glimmerings of culture, of order, of permanence, of opportunity. When her husband returned to "the States," Louise Clappe decided to stay and become a pioneer schoolteacher and churchwoman in

San Francisco. What she wrote about herself in her last letter to her sister might also be said about culture in gold-rush California: "The 'thistle-seed' . . . sent abroad its roots right lovingly into this barren soil, and gained an unwonted strength in what seemed . . . unfavorable surroundings."

As civilization agonized its way out of chaos and finally took root in California's "barbarous soil," some of the emerging social and cultural forms were "traditional"— reflective or reminiscent of the many old worlds the settlers had hailed from, particularly the eastern United States, home of the majority. But, in such an unusual natural and social environment—particularly the unprecedented diversity of peoples, cultures, and prior experiences—some distinctive, if not completely unique, California patterns were discernible. In the birth, or rebirth, of pioneer culture, some groups were "losers," including Indians and *californios*—the earlier Spanish/Mexican conquerors of the land. They lost lives, lands, resources, livelihoods, autonomy, cultural dominance, and as in the case of many small native tribes, their very existence as peoples. Some, especially newly arriving settlers from the United States and Europe, and to an extent Latin America and Asia, including the few women pioneers, clearly "won." They secured new opportunities; their populations increased; they assumed political control; and their cultures took root and often flourished. Many, though, such as some Indian communities, Californios, and Mexican immigrants, were often forced to measure "success" as mere survival. The gold-rush winners, the losers, and the many in between, their social and cultural forms, their complex and sometimes contradictory interrelationships, and their legacies to future generations, are the subjects of this volume.

Rooted in Barbarous Soil: People, Culture, and Community in Gold Rush California is the third in the California History Sesquicentennial Series, presented by the California Historical Society—the state's officially designated historical society—and the University of California Press, with the support of California State University, Hayward, and many other partners. Four topical, but interrelated, volumes, issued one per year beginning in winter 1997/98, reexamine the meaning, particularly from today's perspective, of the founding of modern California in the pre-1848 and gold-rush-era experiences. Each of the volumes collects essays by a dozen authors, drawn from the ranks of leading humanists, social scientists, and scientists, reviewing the best, most up-to-date thinking on major topics associated with the state's pioneer period through the 1870s. The authors have been asked to consider, within their area of expertise, the general themes that run through all four volumes: the interplay of traditional cultures and frontier innovation in the creation of a distinctive California society; the dynamic interaction of people and nature and the beginnings of massive environmental change; the impact of the California experience on the nation and the wider world; the shaping influence of pioneer patterns on modern California; and the importance and legacy of ethnic and cultural diversity as a major dimension of the state's history.

The California History Sesquicentennial volumes are published simultaneously as double issues of *California History,* the quarterly of the Historical Society, and as books for general distribution. Each volume is co-edited by Richard J. Orsi, Professor of History, California State University, Hayward, and editor of the quarterly, and a consulting editor who is a leading scholar in the specific field. Volume 1 in the series, *Contested Eden: California before the Gold Rush,* co-edited by Ramón A. Gutiérrez, Professor of Ethnic Studies and History at the University of California, San Diego, and issued in 1997/98, dealt with the social, economic, cultural, political, and environmental patterns of Native American, Spanish, and Mexican California through 1848. Volume 2 in the series, *A Golden State: Mining and Economic Development in Gold Rush California,* co-edited by James J. Rawls, member of the history faculty at Diablo Valley College, and issued in 1998/99, examined the pioneer industry of gold mining, its inception and development, and its impact on the state, the West, and the national and world economies. The present volume, the third in the series, is co-edited by Kevin Starr, State Librarian of California, and focuses on the Gold Rush and the migration and settlement of peoples, cultures, organizations, and institutions. Volume 4, to be co-edited by John Burns, former California State Archivist and State Historian and currently historical consultant with the California Department of Education, will investigate the inception of government and politics—statehood, early constitution-building, law, bureaucracy, and civil rights.

The California Historical Society's issuing of these major sesquicentennial publications is made possible through the contributions of all the Society's members, as well as a host of direct and indirect supporters. Chief among the helping agencies are the University of California Press, the California State Archives, California State University, Hayward, which furnishes ongoing support for editing the quarterly, and the Mericos Foundation of South Pasadena, which has provided a generous grant specifically for the Sesquicentennial Series.

Many individuals have also shared their time, knowledge, energy, and resources. The Historical Society's particular appreciation goes to Mike McCone, its recently retired Executive Director, whose loyalty to the Society and its people, faith in its quarterly, and executive ability that can move mountains made this series and other great things happen for the Historical Society; Lynne Withey, Associate Director of the University of California Press, who has been an indispensable part of the project from the beginning; Mrs. Johan Blokker of the Mericos Foundation, whose belief in and support of the sesquicentennial project has been critical to its success; Dr. Norma Rees, President, and Dr. Frank Martino, Vice President and Provost, of California State University, Hayward, who have provided generous assistance for the Sesquicentennial Series and the general editing office of *California History;* Dr. Kevin Starr, State Librarian of California and preeminent scholar of California culture, whose enthusiastic support of the California History Sesquicentennial Series project as Trustee of the California Historical Society and chair of its Publications Committee was indispensable to the series and whose introductory chapter and creative ideas and editing contributions grace the present volume; Anthony Kirk, illustrations editor, who applied his unequaled knowledge and appreciation of California iconography to discover, edit, caption, and interpret a stunning series of images, in many cases never before published; and Marlene Smith-Baranzini, associate editor of *California History* and true partner-editor in every facet of this volume, this series, and all other undertakings of the quarterly. Other important contributors include assistant editors par excellence Joshua Paddison and Peter Orsi; Liz Ginno, historian and member of the library faculty at California State University, Hayward; and Larry Campbell, Patricia Keats, Scott Shields, Emily Wolff, Bo Mompho, Cristina Magpantay, Kathryn Kowalewski, Jennifer Schaffner, Judith Deaton, and other members of the loyal, dedicated, and professional staff of the California Historical Society, San Francisco.

Our thanks also go to all the individuals and institutions who made it possible to use images from their collections in this work or who provided other valuable assistance. Although space precludes listing all their names, special mention should be made of Dace Taube, curator of the California Historical Society/Title Insurance and Trust Photo Collection, Department of Special Collections, University of Southern California Library; Peter Blodgett, Jennifer Watts, Alan Jutzi, Jennifer Martinez, and Lisa Ann Libby, the Huntington Library; Jack von Euw, Susan Snyder, Richard Ogar, William Roberts, and Walter Brem, the Bancroft Library; Ellen Harding and Gary Kurutz, the California State Library; Harvey L. Jones, Diane Curry, Claudia Kishler, and Jeff Kramm, the Oakland Museum of California; John Cahoon, the Seaver Center for Western History Research, Natural History Museum of Los Angeles County; Susan Klusmire, Colton Hall, City of Monterey; Elisabeth Peters, Montgomery Gallery, San Francisco; Alfred C. Harrison, Jr., and Jessie Dunn-Gilbert, The North Point Gallery, San Francisco; Patty Junker, Fine Arts Museums of San Francisco; John and Joel Garzoli, Garzoli Gallery, San Rafael; David S. Bisol, Santa Barbara Historical Society; Claudine Chalmers; and James Sandos.

One final debt needs acknowledgment: there can be no more talented, exacting, resourceful, dedicated, and collegial editor than Kathleen MacDougall, our project editor at the University of California Press.

Michael Duty   *Richard J. Orsi*
Executive Director,   Professor of History,
California Historical Society   California State University, Hayward
                                        Editor, *California History*

1

Rooted in Barbarous Soil

An Introduction to Gold Rush Society and Culture

Kevin Starr

The morning of Wednesday, July 4, 1849, found the sailing ship *Henry Lee* at 29° 54' latitude, 77° 44' longitude, off the mid-Pacific coast of South America. Aboard were the 122 men of the Hartford Union Mining and Trading Company, bound for the gold fields of California. Organizing themselves as a company in Hartford, Connecticut, in mid-December 1848, the Argonauts had set sail from a pier on the East River, New York City, on the morning of February 17, 1849, on what would prove to be a seven-month and ten-day voyage around Cape Horn to San Francisco. On that Wednesday, July 4th, the men of the Hartford Union Mining and Trading Company, assembled on deck for Independence Day festivities, were enjoying, in the words of one of their members, John Linville Hall of Bloomfield, Connecticut, "fair winds, a gentle sea—bright skies—a bland, delicious air—health—cheerfulness—and peace."[1] The men had awakened to a gunfire salute, the ringing of bells, and drum rolls announcing the dawn of the birthday of the Republic.

How sweet it was! A little more than a month earlier, having sailed past the Falklands, the *Henry Lee* had rounded Cape Horn amidst ferocious storms and gales and freezing weather. As the ship tossed to and fro atop the titanic waves, the men of the Hartford Union Mining and Trading Company had huddled in their cabins throughout the short, short days and long, long eighteen-hour Antarctic nights. Many of them were wondering why they had left Connecticut in the first place. Hall himself was a printer; miraculously enough, he had brought a printing press and type with him aboard the *Henry Lee*, which Captain David Vail allowed him to install in a mid-ship stateroom. There, in the dim light and assisted by two other printers aboard, Hall wrote and produced a journal of the seven-month voyage.

Thus, in this instance, the Gold Rush began to document itself from the day the *Henry Lee* set sail from its pier on the East River. The Gold Rush would be about

Pick in hand, gold pan on his knee, a pistol stuffed in his belt, the
Forty-niner Joseph Sharp confidently stares at us from across a
century and a half of time—one of the tens of thousands of bold
young adventurers who came to gather the golden harvest and
transformed a distant pastoral province into a populous, prosperous, urbanized state. *Courtesy Bancroft Library.*

action—about the sheer physical adventure of it all—but it would also be an enterprise documenting itself all the while in an absolute torrent of letters, journals (including Hall's innovative shipboard publication), newspaper reports, contempora-
neously published books, memoirs (published then or later), sketches, paintings,
daguerreotypes, and later recollections. To borrow historian Louis B. Wright's phrase,
the Gold Rush was about culture on the moving frontier: about the way that Americans imaginatively encountered the gold-rush experience or later remembered it and
how they fashioned these encounters and memories into various forms of popular
culture and art. The scholars represented in this volume, then, are linked to John

Linville Hall across 150 years in their mutual effort to memorialize and make sense of the gold-rush experience.

In his essay "No Boy's Play: Migration and Settlement in Early Gold Rush California," Malcolm Rohrbough analyzes how communities formed and reformed, or formed and dissolved, throughout the entire process of coming to California during the gold-rush years. Comprised as it was of Connecticut Yankees of similar background and values, the Hartford Union and Mining Trading Company represented, perhaps, the tightest possible community en route to California. Each member, after all, had bought into the project as an investor-entrepreneur in a joint-stock company pledged to a communal effort in California and elected their own board of directors and management. Their plan was to sail the *Henry Lee* as close as possible to the gold fields (their knowledge of California's geography was somewhat shaky) and commence mining operations, based out of the ship.

And what could be more communal than the exhilaration of that Fourth of July day on the high seas in the Year of Our Lord 1849 as, at half past ten in the morning, the company assembled on deck of the *Henry Lee* for speeches, readings, the singing of hymns and patriotic songs, and an astonishing twenty-five toasts, "pledged in bumpers of cold water," to the Fourth of July itself, the memory of George Washington, the heroes of 1776, the president and vice-president of the United States, the Army, the Navy, the flag, the genius of liberty, the fair sex, the Hartford Union Mining and Trading Company itself, and Cape Horn ("safely clear of your territories, may we be excused from paying our respects to you again, *old fellow*, especially in the winter"). At mid-point, toast number thirteen was to "California, The El Dorado of our hopes. May we not be disappointed, but find stores of golden treasures to gladden our hearts, and make ample amends for the ills and trials of acquisition. May our families and friends be enabled to rejoice in our success, and all end well."[2]

Alas, such would not be the case. Arriving in San Francisco in September 1849, Captain Vail sailed his ancient 500-ton ship, still supplied with a year and a half of provisions, up the Carquinez Strait to Benicia looking for gold fields within striking distance of the ship. There were none; and within weeks, perhaps even days, the happy band of brothers who had celebrated the Fourth of July on the high seas began to break up into groups and travel by small boats upriver to Sacramento for further deployment into the Mother Lode. It was at Sacramento that the company, faced by the realities of California geography and the difficulties, at the time, of large-scale corporate mining, disbanded; and the men set off, singly or in groups, into the Mother Lode.

Within a year, twelve young men, fully 10 percent of the original company, were dead. Twenty-six had returned to Connecticut with approximately $1,280 each to show for their effort. Seventy-seven were still in California, averaging some $1,239

per man in cumulative earnings. The general average of earned money for the surviving members was $1,116 each. When one deducted the cost of passage and equip-
ment from this sum—and this averaged some $350 per man—it would have been
hard to return to toast number thirteen on the high seas ("May we not be disappointed, but find stores of golden treasures to gladden our hearts, and make ample
amends for the ills and trials of acquisition") without some irony and much sadness.

Hall himself returned to Connecticut in May 1850 and became a minister. The
Henry Lee was towed down to the mudflats off the foot of Washington Street in San
Francisco and turned into a storehouse, soon to be absorbed by the expanding city.
And yet, the themes of Hall's shipboard journal—hope, community, physical challenge and danger, the exhilaration of being young at that epic time and journeying
into El Dorado itself—reverberated, as Rohrbough captures so well in his essay,
throughout the entire gold-rush experience and down into our own era.

There were predominately Connecticut men aboard the *Henry Lee*. Such mono-
ethnicity, however, as Sucheng Chan asserts so well in the essay "A People of Exceptional Character: Ethnic Diversity, Nativism, and Racism in the California Gold
Rush," would not be the case in the Golden State. Living with her physician husband in a log cabin in the Mother Lode settlements of Rich and Indian bars in
March 1852, Louise Amelia Knapp Smith Clappe, writing under the pen name
Dame Shirley, was amazed by the languages she heard all around her. "You will
hear in the same day," Dame Shirley wrote in her Letter Fourteenth, "almost at the
same time, the lofty melody of the Spanish language, the piquant polish of the
French . . . the silver, changing clearness of the Italian, the harsh gangle of the German, the hissing precision of the English, the liquid sweetness of the Kanaka, and
the sleep-inspiring languor of the East Indian."[3]

The Gold Rush, as Dame Shirley was experiencing it, represented an unprecedented instance of internationalism in world history. It can be argued, in fact, that
the California Gold Rush more than any other event up to that time firstly and most
boldly dramatized the increasingly global nature of American society in the nineteenth and twentieth centuries. Aside from the fact that the United States had been
administering California since 1846 as a military territory, it can even be argued
that the Gold Rush, in its first phases at least, was an intrinsically international—
rather than American—event. Eventually, after 1849, California would settle down
as an American state. In the first phases of the Gold Rush, however, the exact future
of this polyglot implosion and explosion of global peoples remained, for the time being, uncertain: which is perhaps why, aside from the immemorial imperatives of
racism, Americans seemed especially anxious, as Sucheng Chan so vividly dramatizes, to establish hegemony over all other peoples in the gold fields through miners'
taxes and other forms of intimidation. Never before in the brief history of the American Republic, then a mere sixty years since the adoption of its Constitution in 1789,

The residents of Sierraville, high in the Northern Mines near Yuba Pass, turn out to have their picture taken, sometime in the 1850s. A supply center more than a gold camp, and later a farming and logging town, Sierraville took on the appearance of a traditional American community—with women and children figuring significantly among the population—earlier than most gold-rush towns, which long remained overwhelmingly masculine in character. *Courtesy Bancroft Library.*

had Americans, at that time still predominately an Anglo-Protestant people, been challenged to deal, simultaneously, with such a variety of races and peoples: not only with every variety of European (including the English and speakers of English from Canada, Australia, and New Zealand), but with large numbers of Asians (Chinese in the main, but also Polynesians from Hawaii, then termed Kanakas, and some Filipinos), as well as Hispanic miners from Mexico, Chile, and Peru—not to mention some 150,000 to 170,000 Native Americans and a small but significant remnant of Spanish-speaking Californios (Spanish, Indian, and African in their blood lines) and African Americans, slave and free, from the eastern states. For a people, the Americans, who had not yet settled the question of slavery (which the rest of the English-speaking world had earlier abolished, at least in theory), and who as a population were aggressively white, aggressively Protestant, and aggressively superior in their racial attitudes, the Gold Rush posed an ecumenical challenge of unprecedented magnitude.

Today, thanks to a quarter of a century of unsentimental and frequently revisionist research, it is easy to see that by and large, as Sucheng Chan's essay as well as those by James A. Sandos ("'Because he is a liar and a thief': Conquering the Residents of 'Old' California, 1850–1880") and Irving G. Hendrick ("From Indifference to Imperative Duty: Educating Children in Early California") so thoroughly document, white Americans miserably failed to respond positively to the possibilities of the multiracial, multiethnic society that had materialized itself in California with, as historian Hubert Howe Bancroft would later put it, such a rapid, monstrous maturity.

The story told by Chan, Sandos, and to a lesser extent by Hendrick, is not a pretty story; but it is a true story, and it must be faced. Native Americans were hunted down like so much vermin, including their extermination by state-supported militia operation. Latino, Chinese, and, in many instances, African American miners were driven from the most promising of the gold fields or otherwise suppressed, beaten, or outright murdered, excluded from the protections of the court system, degraded in their fundamental rights and humanity. In assessing American civilization in that era—which is to say, when judging it from the perspective of the present, for all history is written to some degree or another in the present tense—the patterns of racial and ethnic suppression, so evidenced in the gold-rush story as developed by Chan, Sandos, and Hendrick, must be integrated into the larger pattern of America's two-century-plus struggle with racism and ethnic prejudice.

In one sense, the Gold Rush represented—although it was perhaps not recognized at the time—a wake-up call to the United States that it would at some time in its future have to deal with the global nature of American culture. True, that global nature was unclear in 1849. Indeed, it would still take another fourteen years, until the Emancipation Proclamation of 1863 amidst a terrible Civil War, merely to end—at least formally—the suppression of only one American people, African Americans, through the slavery system. The racial and ethnic sins of the Gold Rush, in other words, were being perpetuated by a people who would soon be laying down the lives of hundreds of thousands of young men and maiming the bodies and spirits of hundreds of thousands of others in, as Abraham Lincoln suggested in his Second Inaugural Address, expiation and atonement for its racial sins. The misbehavior of Anglo-Americans during the Gold Rush against their fellow nonwhite miners and immigrants, in other words, serves as a dark and ominous warning that there was something very wrong in the American national character and only a great Civil War could even begin to set it right.

Even as we assess these sins, however, we can find no point outside of history to judge the frequently depressing behavior of the Forty-niners as far as racial and ethnic matters are concerned. Bearing witness through these essays to a terrible burden of past oppression, we cannot exempt ourselves from continuities and responsibilities of prejudice and racial animosities down to our own time. The Gold Rush shows us clearly for what we were, a nation with strong racist and ethnic prejudices in its heart. The Civil War made us pay dearly for these sins, but bad behavior and the burdens thereof have continued down to the present. Not until all racism and ethnic prejudice is purged from American society altogether should we feel morally superior to the California miners chronicled in this volume. The most egregious forms and possibilities of their misbehavior have been curtailed by a century and a half of struggle, down to the civil rights movement in our own time; but the surviving traces of the Forty-niners' disease—hostility to people who are different, who are the Other—is as lingering and self-evident as today's headlines.

Even today, however—no, especially today, in our postmodernist era, so desperate to reconnect with Native American environmentalism and spirituality—we can feel the horror of the genocide leveled against Native Americans in the gold-rush and frontier eras. Such murderous misbehavior continued across three decades. Bret Harte, for example, was working as a newspaper reporter in Uniontown near Humboldt Bay in 1860 when he went out on the morning of February 26 to cover the handiwork of the four or five men from Eureka who with pistols, rifles, axes, and knives had butchered some sixty peaceable Native Americans, mostly women and children, as they slept in their rancheria outside the town. Horrified by what he saw and fearful of retaliation, Harte could only report it for the San Francisco *Bulletin* under the pseudonym "Eye-Witness."

"A short time after," Harte wrote, "the writer was upon the ground with feet treading in human blood, horrified with the awful and sickening sights which met the eye wherever it turned. Here was a mother fatally wounded hugging the mutilated carcass of her dying infant to her bosom; there a poor child of two years old, with its ear and scalp torn from the side of its little head. Here a father frantic with grief over the bloody corpses of his four little children and wife; there a brother and sister bitterly weeping and trying to soothe with cold water the pallid face of a dying relative. . . . The wounded, dead, and dying were found all around, and in every lodge the skulls and frames of women and children cleft with axes and hatchets, and stabbed with knives, and the brains of an infant oozing from its broken head to the ground."[4]

Here, then, is portrayed a ghastly ground-zero point of racist criminality as seen through the eyes of a talented young writer who wished desperately to see the best in the gold-rush experience and would soon be doing so in a series of short stories that would win him international fame. For the moment, surveying the butchery, he must have seen California, as Henry David Thoreau saw California, as but one step closer to hell.

And yet, even as Chan, Sandos, and Hendrick tell their stories of persecution and suppression—and in the case of the Native Americans, outright genocide, frequently organized and supported by the state—they are also chronicling the foundations of a commonwealth, however flawed; and in that organization of a community were more than a few signs of hope. Of the peoples who came to California, no matter how much they were persecuted, none were driven out, or "ethnically cleansed" in current parlance, although there was more than enough reason for many of them to leave voluntarily in sorrow and revulsion. However clouded and compromised by Anglo-American misbehavior, a DNA code of diversity had once and for all been established for California, and this code would remain in force over the next 150 years until, by the year 2000, California once again echoes, as Dame Shirley first heard it echoing at Rich and Indian bars, with the languages—and the faces, and the hopes—of the entire human race. As Chan suggests, for example, the Gold Rush made of California an Asian place, and this Asian identity could never be erased. In the long run, the Chinese refused to remain victims. Even as they were being persecuted, in fact, as Chan shows, they protested their treatment in the name of the rich and complex civilization that had produced them. In the years that followed, the Chinese helped establish the foundations of California agriculture, achieved the western link of the transcontinental railroad (an example of Chinese engineering comparable to the Great Wall of China itself) and in the Sacramento Valley inaugurated a century-long effort at irrigation and flood control.

And as Sandos suggests, the Hispanic Californians were linked to a civilization that would in time also reclaim California for its own. Here, as in Texas, New Mexico, and Arizona, but with a more immediate and representative clash, were encountering each other two of the three dominant language and cultural groups that, along with the French of Canada and Louisiana, had most successfully colonized the New World. Despite all the negative things that must be chronicled—especially the betrayal represented by the Land Act of 1851, which placed the burden of proof of land ownership upon Hispanic Californians and thus drove so many of them into bankruptcy in the effort to pay their legal bills—the Gold Rush announced to Anglo-America that in its own cloudy and obscure way English-speaking peoples shared the New World with Spanish- and Portuguese-speaking peoples: that the United States was only part of a complex bi-hemispheric mosaic of races, languages, and cultures. The young men of the Hartford Union Mining and Trading Company, indeed all those who sailed to California around the Horn or later via the Isthmus of Panama, touching upon Spanish- and Portuguese-speaking cities, were having their first experience of such pan-American diversity. The most skilled and resourceful miners, moreover, the Chileans, the Peruvians, the Mexicans—people with a centuries-long knowledge of mining—established the mining culture of the

A southern Maidu, or Nisenan, holds a quiver of arrows for a studio portrait, about 1850. It was the near the Maidu village called Cullumah that James Marshall discovered gold in 1848, precipitating a mad rush of fortune seekers who overran Indian lands. The Maidu were among the early miners, though they chiefly worked for whites. With the outbreak of hostilities between the Maidu and Argonauts from Oregon Territory in March 1849, they were the first of the California tribes to suffer from American attitudes toward indigenous peoples, which within a couple of decades would decimate Indian numbers and nearly destroy their cultures. *Courtesy Southwest Museum, Los Angeles, N.24675.*

Gold Rush and taught the Americans how to mine. In southern California especially, Spanish-speaking Californios, who had defeated the American dragoons at
the Battle of San Pascual on December 6, 1846, held onto their way of life well into
the 1870s. One of them, Romualdo Pacheco, served briefly, from February to December 1875, as the twelfth governor of the state and after that went on to Congress.

The Gold Rush, in short, was about the amalgamation, assimilation, and transformation of peoples and cultures as well as it was about the suppression by the
strong of the weak. Women, for example, were still some sixty years from their political emancipation when the Gold Rush broke out; but as Nancy J. Taniguchi
points out in her essay "Weaving a Different World: Women and the California
Gold Rush," the entire epoch is today understood to have been much more feminine
than it was once thought to be. In times past—during, say, the centennial of the
Gold Rush in 1949—the archetypal Forty-niner was depicted as a bearded white
male in middle age wearing Levis and one of those Gabby Hayes hats with the
front brim pinned to the crown. Today, thanks to the research efforts of a generation
of historians, we see the Gold Rush as multiethnic and multicultural and bi-gen-
dered. What stories might be told, for one thing, as Taniguchi suggests, regarding
those women who dressed in men's clothing and, whether passing or being accepted
by men as women of a special sort, took their chances alongside the other miners,
pistols and bowie knives tucked into their belts. There were only a few of these, of
course. Most women, again as Taniguchi depicts them, dressed in skirts and bonnets
as they assisted their men in the mines, or ran boardinghouses, or in the case of
Dame Shirley, achieved one of the first sustained interpretations of life in the mines,
which became in turn one of the platform planks of gold-rush literature.

Later writers, Bret Harte and Hubert Howe Bancroft for example, tended to
perpetuate the myth that all women were treated with respect, even reverence, in
the mining towns and settlements, and even shady ladies were accorded a measure
of respect. Yet the hanging of Juanita in Downieville in July 1850 for stabbing to
death a man who was trying to break into her cabin underscores what is perhaps a
more historic reality: namely, that it was not easy to be a woman in the Gold Rush,
whether a woman were Anglo-American, Mexican, French, African American, or
Chinese. With so few women around, sexual jealousy, followed by communal rage as
in the case of Juanita, could also be an expected response along with the more trum-
peted myth of punctilious chivalry. Women had to take care for their physical safety,
and the court records from the era reveal that many of them suffered one or another
form of assault. Yet the women of the Gold Rush did prevail in a predominately
man's world amidst an overwhelmingly masculine atmosphere; and they prevailed
up and down the social ladder and across ethnic lines. Protestant church ladies
such as Sarah Royce, mother of the future philosopher Josiah, prevailed in keeping
their families together during the long trek across the continent by covered wagon

and in the mines of Grass Valley. Other women, such as Sarah B. Gillespie of the Presbyterian Missionary Church at Macao, China, and Sister Frances Assisium McEnnis of the Sisters of Charity, came specifically for religious purposes. Jewish women tended to their families and saw to the Hebrew education of their children. Then there were the women, such as Mary Jane Megquier and the widow Mary Ball, who kept boardinghouses, or Mary Ellen Pleasant, a free woman of African descent who invested wisely in San Francisco real estate. Sarah Kirby managed the house at the Eagle Theatre in Sacramento, and hundreds of other women made respectable livings in cooking and domestic work, frequently in their own establishments. Elsewhere in the mid-Victorian hierarchy of social status were the women who tended bar or dealt the cards in various establishments. A woman such as actress Lola Montez, onetime mistress to the King of Bavaria, occupied a social niche of her own.

The sheer challenge of California—the physical challenges, the fluid and uncertain nature of society, female minority status compounded by mid-Victorian constraints, the sheer anthropological imbalance of it all—made of many women in California, whatever their background, pragmatic feminists. Eliza W. Farnham, for example, had lived in Illinois with her lawyer-writer-explorer husband Thomas in the early 1840s before removing to New York State, where she served as matron of women at Sing Sing Prison. With the death of her husband in San Francisco in 1849, while he had been exploring the Far West, Eliza Farnham's thoughts turned to California, to which she hoped to travel as escort to a group of respectable unmarried women in search of husbands. California, she and the three compatriots who ultimately sailed with her discovered, was not for the wilting, the neurasthenic, or the overly genteel. A woman who came to California, Farnham wrote in *California, In-Doors and Out; or How We Farm, Mine and Live Generally in the Golden State* (1856), should not expect a life of genteel leisure or even a society that would engage, at this point (of its development), "the higher orders of female intelligence." There was just too much work to do. "The necessities to be served here," Farnham noted, "are physical; washing linen, cleansing houses, cooking, nursing, etc. and I would advise no woman to come alone to the country who has not strength, willingness, and skill for one or other of these occupations; who has not, also, fortitude, indomitable resolution, dauntless courage, and a clear self-respect which will alike forbid her doing anything unworthy herself, or esteeming anything to be so, which her judgement and conscience approve."[5]

Farnham is less than obliquely hinting here that the sexual standards of California—or, at the least, what constituted respectability or acceptability—were different from those of the eastern states. A respectable woman in California, Farnham claimed, "will feel herself in an enemy's country, where she is to watch and ward with tireless vigilance, and live, unless she be very happily circumstanced, alone, entirely alone,

Two miners—one white, one black—work a claim on Spanish Flat in 1852. Most of the adventurers who set out for the new El Dorado were white Americans. But by the date this daguerreotype was made, some two thousand Argonauts of African ancestry had joined in the Gold Rush, which lured adventurers from around the world and created a society of such ethnic and cultural diversity that it was one of the wonders of the day. *Courtesy California State Library.*

and bear her trials in silence. None but the pure and strong-hearted of my sex should come alone to this land."[6]

The fact that a onetime women's matron at Sing Sing penitentiary was so obviously finding California morally compromised must in some way be connected to the flourishing culture of prostitution that prevailed in California during the Gold Rush and through the second half of the nineteenth century. Neither Taniguchi nor any of the other essayists in this volume, however, spend much time on this topic; which is to the good, for the prostitute, especially if she is depicted as having a heart of gold, has been overly sentimentalized in gold-rush and frontier lore. Taniguchi's essay is especially welcomed because it gives us so many more images of prevailing, surviving women to counter prior depictions of prostitution in gold-rush and frontier California, although here too, in the matter of whoredom, there is a valid history, and the story should be told.

On the other hand, there remains the question of sexuality on the gold-rush frontier; and few have treated this topic more tellingly than Susan Lee Johnson, both in her brilliant Yale doctoral dissertation of 1993, the basis of her new study *Roaring Camp: The Social World of the California Gold Rush,* and her essay in this volume, "'My own private life': Toward a History of Desire in Gold Rush California." In *Three Years in California* (1857), the Scottish artist J. D. Borthwick described an evening in San Andreas, Calaveras County, in which the men of this all-male settlement gave themselves a ball, although not one woman was present. For several hours, men danced with men to the music of a fiddle and a flute. Some men played the part of women, and the dance caller announced each movement of the dance as if women were present. Men playing women signified their roles, Borthwick wrote, by wearing "a patch on a certain part of his inexpressibles," which is to say, large squares of canvas attached to the flys of their jeans.[7]

Prior generations of California historians, encountering such passages as this—and there are many in the multitudinous literature of the California Gold Rush—passed them by with hardly a notice or, when they noticed them at all, did so with a faint sense of disquiet. What could all this mean, anyway, and hadn't the historian best be getting on to more properly historical questions? Susan Lee Johnson, by contrast, belongs to a generation of historians for whom the ebb and flow of eros, its feints and masks, are at the very basis of historical experience, especially as sex reveals cultural attitudes and sexual arrangements reveal social power. In her provocative dissertation, "'The Gold She Gathered': Difference, Domination, and California's Southern Mines, 1848–1853," Johnson gathered a potpourri of outright evidence and subtle clues to suggest the intricacies of sexual/power relationships in gold-rush California: between white males and white women (this frequently in fantasy life alone, given the shortage of females in California), between white men and women of color (also frequently a matter of fantasy, but touched by hegemony as well), between white males and available women, white or of color (also frequently a matter of dream wish but sometimes edging into actual activity), between white men and prostitutes, white or of color (and here she adds much new information and interpretation to an already developed field of research); and, most blatant in the matter of power, sexual relations between white men and Native American women, which provide Johnson her most fruitful opportunities for cross-cultural analysis. In one instance, moreover, we find a white miner strongly attracted to an African American woman on the right side of mid-Victorian propriety. Evidence of such situations is very hard to come by on the frontier.

Most dramatically, Johnson chronicles the erotic or semi-erotic ties among Anglo-American miners. These attachments ranged from the stylized sublimation of the all-boy miners' dance to highly emotional friendships charged with homoerotic feeling, to strong suggestions of homosexual behavior and, in one instance, to the even stronger possibility of a lifetime homosexual union. Through a close reading of one miner's diary, moreover, Johnson explores new territory: the inner life of erotic memory and longing (and possible autoerotic release) that constitutes the most subtle topic of all her investigations. The vigorous and virile young men of the Gold Rush, in short, and most of the middle-aged men as well, were swept into California on a vast and powerful tide of eros as well as economic ambition. The assessment of eros as a force in history is only beginning. Provocatively, Johnson brings it to the Mother Lode. Never again, thanks to Johnson, will readers of gold-rush literature pass uncomprehendingly through passages in diaries about all-men dances, daydreams of girls back home, passionate friendships and sleeping partners among men, frequently brutal and sometimes touching encounters across race and ethnicity, voyeurism, and the more garden varieties of sexual expression.

If eros represented a subtle but persistent, and sometimes powerful, force in the Gold Rush, so too did religion. Eros and religion are linked, after all, as profound encounters with the forces of life and death. As Steven M. Avella suggests in his brief but encyclopedic inventory of religious life on the gold-rush frontier, "Phelan's Cemetery: Religion in the Urbanizing West, 1850–1869, in Los Angeles, San Francisco, and Sacramento," the global nature of the Gold Rush was also reflected in the arrival in California during these years of the world's great religions, including the religious practices and sensibilities of Islam, Buddhism, Confucianism, and the other religious practices of the Far East, such as the Chinese devotion to the Queen of Heaven.

Christianity, of course, whether in its Protestant or Catholic variations, held dominance, which can be expected, given the origins of most miners. Next came Judaism. So strong was the Jewish presence, in fact, especially in San Francisco, Stockton, and Sacramento, that frontier California can lay claim to having been uniquely shaped by Jewish values and sensibility, most notably in the city of San Francisco, where Jews from the first constituted an influential elite. But then again: the entire history of the American West demonstrates a special affinity between Jews—old American Sephardics and German immigrants, each of the Reform persuasion—and the frontier. In so many ways, these groups found in the Far West, California especially, their promised land.

Although rarely considered as such, the Gold Rush also represents a key chapter in the history of Protestant-Catholic relations in mid-nineteenth-century America. The Gold Rush came, first of all, at the end of a decade of anti-Catholic agitation leading to the Know Nothing movement. In his *Plea for the West* (1835), New England minister Lyman Beecher cast the entire frontier as a competition between the Protestantism of the Atlantic states, moving West, and the Roman Catholicism of Latin America, moving northward up the continent. At some point, Beecher argued, one or another of these religious forces must prevail. The entire history of Protestantism in California during the Gold Rush and through the 1850s, in fact, can be read as an effort by the largely New England-originated missionaries of the American Home Missionary Society to capture California as a Protestant commonwealth, a New England on the Pacific Coast. As the Reverend Timothy Dwight Hunt put it preaching to the New England Society of San Francisco on the December 22, 1852, anniversary of the landing at Plymouth Rock: "You are the representatives of a land which is the model for every other. You belong to a family whose dead are the pride of the living. Preserve your birth-right . . . Here is our Colony. No higher ambition could urge us to noble deeds than, on the basis of the colony of Plymouth, to make California the Massachusetts of the Pacific."[8]

Roman Catholics, most obviously, had other ideas, as suggested by the Franciscan missions themselves, the early presence of Jesuits in higher education in Santa Clara and San Francisco, the speedy elevation by Rome of San Francisco into an archdiocese, the equally speedy appearance of teaching Dominican sisters in Benicia and nursing Sisters of Charity in San Francisco and elsewhere, and even, as Avella points out, the presence in San Francisco of a Chinese priest fluent in Italian. While Yankee and Southern miners tended to be Protestant, Irish (including the Australian Irish), French, Chilean, Peruvian, and Sonoran miners tended to be Roman Catholic, as were the Californios and some Native Americans, the descendants of the Spanish mission neophytes. For some observers, moreover, California was more than just a place where Catholics could be found; California was, as the Reverend Hugh Quigley, a priest of the Archdiocese of San Francisco writing in the late 1870s put it, a natural melding ground between immigrant and native Catholic peoples.

Avella's central theme, however, is not religious competition or even the nativist *noir* of the First and Second Vigilance Committees, through which Know Nothing and Masonic elements sought to suppress a feared Irish Catholic presence in San Francisco, but the way, rather, religion offered an immediately available matrix for personal and social identification in a ferociously fluid society. Whether in Protestant

No. I.

No. VII.

No. II.

THE MINERS' TEN COMMANDMENTS.

A man spake these words, and said: I am a miner, who wandered "from a way down east," and came to sojourn in a strange land, and "see the elephant." And behold I saw him, and bore witness, that from the key of 't's trunk to the end of his tail, his whole body has passed before me; and I followed him until his huge feet stood still before a clapboard shanty; then with his trunk extended, he pointed to a candle card tacked upon a shingle, as though he would say Read, and I read the

MINERS' TEN COMMANDMENTS.

I.

Thou shalt have no other claim than one.

II.

Thou shalt not make unto thyself any false claim, nor any likeness to a mean man, by jumping one; whatever thou findest on the top above or on the rock beneath, or in a crevice underneath the rock—or I will visit the miners around to invite them on my side; and when they decide against thee, thou shalt take thy pick and thy pan, thy shovel and thy blankets, with all that thou hast, and "go prospecting" to seek good diggings; but thou shalt find none. Then, when thou hast returned, in sorrow shalt thou find that thine old claim is worked out, and yet no pile made thee to hide in the ground, or in an old boot beneath thy bunk, or in buckskin or bottle underneath thy cabin; but hast paid all that was in thy purse away, worn out thy body and thy garments, so that there is nothing good about them but the pockets, and thy patience is likened unto thy garments; and at last thou shalt hire thy body out to make thy board and save thy bacon.

III.

Thou shalt not go prospecting before thy claim gives out. Neither shalt thou take thy money, nor thy gold dust, nor thy good name, to the gaming table in vain; for monte, twenty-one, roulette, faro, lansquenet and poker, will prove to thee that the more thou puttest down the less thou shalt take up; and when thou thinkest of thy wife and children, thou shalt not hold thyself guiltless—but in sane.

IV.

Thou shalt not remember what thy friends do at home on the Sabbath day, lest the remembrance may not compare favorably with what thou doest here.—Six days thou mayest dig or pick all that thy body can stand under; but the other day is Sunday; yet thou washest all thy dirty shirts, darnest all thy stockings, tap thy boots, mend thy clothing, chop thy whole week's firewood, t ke up and bake thy bread, and boil thy pork and beans, that thou wilt not when thou returnest from thy long-tom weary. For in six days' labor only thou canst not work enough to wear out thy body in two years; but if thou workest hard on Sunday also, thou canst do it in six months; and thou, and thy son, and thy daughter, thy male friend and thy female friend, thy morals and thy conscience, be none the better for it; but reproach thee, shouldst thou ever return with thy worn-out body to thy mother's fireside;

and thou shalt not strive to justify thyself, because the trader and the blacksmith, the carpenter and the merchant, the tailor, Jews, and buccaneers, defy God and civilization, by keeping not the Sabbath day, nor wish for a day of rest, such as memory, youth and home, made hallowed.

V.

Thou shalt not think more of all thy gold, and how thou canst make it fastest, than how thou wilt enjoy it, af er thou hast ridden rough-shod over thy good old parents' precepts and examples, that thou mayest have nothing to reproach and stig rise, when thou art left ALONE in the land where thy father's blessing and thy mother's love hath sent thee.

VI.

Thou shalt not kill thy body by working in the rain, even though thou shalt make enough to buy physic and attend sore with. Neither shalt thou k ll thy neighbor's body in a duel; for by "keeping cool," thou canst save his life and thy con-cience. Neither shalt thou destroy thyself by getting "tight," nor "slewed," nor "high," nor "corned," nor "half-seas over," nor "three sheets in the wind," by drinking smoothly down—"brandy slings," "gin cocktails," "whisky punches," "rum-toddies," nor "egg-nogg." Neither shalt thou swallow "mint-juleps," nor "sherry-cobblers," through a straw, nor gurgle from a bottle the "raw material," nor "take it neat" from a decanter; for, while thou art swallowing down thy purse, and thy coat from off thy back, thou art burning the coat from off thy stomach; and, if thou couldst see the bosses and lands, and gold dust, and loose comforts already lying there—"a huge pile"—thou shouldst feel a choking in thy throat; and when to that thou addest the crooked walkings and hiccuping tailings, of lodgings in the gutter, of headings in the sun, of prospect-holes half full of water, and of shafts and ditches, 'rom which thou hast emerged like a d awning rat, thou wilt feel disgusted with thyself, and inquire, "Is thy servant a dog that he doeth these things?" verily I will say, Farewell, old bottle, I will kiss thy gurgling lips no more. And then, slings, cocktails, punches, smashes, cobblers, nogs, toddies, sangarees, and julips, forever farewell. Thy remembrance shames me; henceforth, "I cut thy acquaintance," and I and my children, and my buy's children, and all the unholy catalogue of evils that follow in thy train. My wife's smiles and my children's merry-hearted laugh, shall clas.m and reward me for having the manly firmness and courage to say No. I wish thee an eternal farewell.

VII.

Thou shalt not grow discouraged, nor think of going home before thou hast made thy "pile," because thou hast not "struck a lead," nor found a "rich crevice," nor sunk a hole upon a "pocket," lest in going home thou shalt leave four dollars a day, and go to work, ashamed, at fifty cents, and serve thee right: for thou knowest by staying here, thou in a d strike a lead and if y dollars a day, and keep thy manly self-respect,

and then go home with enough to make thyself and others happy.

VIII.

Thou shalt not steal a pick, or a shovel, or a pan from thy fellow miner; nor take away his tools without his leave; nor borrow those he cannot spare; nor return them broken, nor trouble him to fetch them back again, nor talk with him while his water rent is running on, nor remove his stake to enlarge thy claim, nor undermine his bank in following a lead, nor pan out gold from his "riffle box," nor wash the "tailings" from his sluice's mouth. Neither shalt thou pick out specimens from the company's pan to put them in thy mouth, or in thy purse; nor cheat thy partner of his share; nor stand from thy cabin-mate his gold dust, to add to thine, for he will be sure to discover what thou hast done, and will straightway call his fellow miners together, and if the law hinder them not, they will hang thee, or give thee fifty lashes, or shave thy head and brand thee, like a horse thief, with "R" upon thy cheek, to be known and read of all men, Californians in particular.

IX.

Thou shalt not tell any false tales about "good diggings in the mountains," to thy neighbor, that thou mayest benefit a friend who hath mules and provisions, and tools and blankets, he cannot sell,—lest in deceiving thy neighbor, when he returneth through the snow, with nought save his rifle, he present thee with the contents thereof, and like a dog, thou shalt fall down and die.

X.

Thou shalt not covet unsuitable matrimony, nor covet "single blessedness," nor forget absent maidens; nor neglect thy "first love,"—but thou shalt consider how faithfully and patiently she awaiteth thy return; yea, and covereth each epistle that thou sendest with kisses of kindly welcome—until she hath journeyed to this land of gold, and joined her loving heart to thine. Neither shalt thou covet thy neighbor's wife, nor trifle with the affections of his daughter; yet, if thy heart be free, and thou dost love and covet each other, thou shalt "pop the question" like a man, lest another, more manly than thou art, should step in before thee, and thou love her in vain, and in the anguish of thy heart's disappointment, thou shalt quote the language of the great, and say, "such is life;" and thy future be that of a poor, lonely, despised and comfortless bachelor.

A new Commandment give I unto thee—if thou hast a wife and little ones, that thou lovest dearer than thy life,—that thou keep them continually before thee, to cheer and urge thee onward until thou canst say, "I have enough—God bless them—I will return." Then as thou journiest towards thy much loved home, with open arms shall thy come forth to welcome thee, and falling upon thy neck weep tears of inutterable joy that thou art come; then in the fullness of thy heart's gratitude, thou shalt kneel together before thy Heavenly Father, to thank Him for thy safe return. AMEN—So mote it be.

FORTY-NINE.

No. VIII.

No. IX.

No. III.

No. IV.

No. V. No. VI.

No. X.

After toiling in the mines for a couple of years, the English-born Forty-niner James M. Hutchings wrote and published *The Miners' Ten Commandments*, an immensely popular pictorial letter sheet that began "Thou shalt have no other claim than one." The letter sheet sold nearly a hundred thousand copies the first year and enabled the author, in 1856, to found *Hutchings' California Magazine*, the third in a line of literary journals established in San Francisco. As all observers agreed, no other frontier attracted so many educated men, ensuring an early and profuse flowering of literature in gold-rush California. *California Historical Society, FN-30872.*

or Catholic churches, Jewish synagogues, or the Chinese Joss House in Weaverville, Trinity County, religion offered men and women a long way from home a means of reminding themselves of who they were, where they had come from, and where they might be going. With death so omnipresent in the Gold Rush, it is not surprising that Avella begins his essay with a catastrophe, namely, the explosion of the steamer *Pearl* in Sacramento on January 7, 1854—which killed fifty-five and injured one hundred—and the mass burial that followed. The gold country, Avella suggests, is filled with thousands of tombstones whose inscriptions—name, dates, place of origin, a scriptural citation—are in and of themselves mini-histories of individuals, so many of them so very young, for whom seeking the golden fleece ended in an early grave.

The remaining essays in this volume—dealing with art, literature, education, and popular culture—can be grouped under the category of urbanism. Not that such pursuits were confined exclusively to the urban settlements of the Gold Rush. The Forty-niners painted, wrote, sang, read, or otherwise amused themselves in a variety of circumstances, many of them remote and isolated. Yet as Robert Phelps argues in his essay "'All hands have gone downtown': Urban Places in Gold Rush California," the Gold Rush was not so much a matter of the lone prospector (who, by and large, belonged to a later era) as it was a matter of group effort and group settlement, which is to say, towns and cities of one sort or another, however temporary or ramshackle.

Once again, the Gold Rush brings us face to face with California's enduring DNA code: in this instance, its persistent sub/urbanism, its preference, that is, for urban or suburban density in contrast to the settlement of the vast majority of the population, as was the case elsewhere in the United States, on family farms and in market or semi-industrial towns. For nearly 150 years, beginning most notably with the analytical speculations of Henry George and Josiah Royce in the 1870s and 1880s, commentators have wrestled with this aspect of the California formula: its vast spaces, that is, its baronial landholdings leading to agribusiness, and its clustering of populations in urban and suburban settlements. As Phelps suggests, this tendency was present from the beginning.

For all the rapidity of their formation, moreover, for all their heedless and overnight ambiance, the mining towns of the Gold Rush—not to mention the more established cities of San Francisco, Stockton, Sacramento, and Marysville—were possessed from the start of an intrinsic urbanism of design and social function. This can most easily be seen of San Francisco. Again and again, in the diaries, journals, and books of 1849 and 1850, observers expressed their astonishment at how rapidly San Francisco was developing along classic urban lines. Not only did *New York Tribune* writer Bayard Taylor, author of *Eldorado, or, Adventures in the Path of Empire* (1850), make note of the rising urbanism of San Francisco, he predicted as well that the peninsula south of the city would one day abound in elegant urban villas and even a university (which

Designed in the fashionable Renaissance Revival style by the New York-born architect and Argonaut Gordon Cummings, the four-story Montgomery Block was constructed in San Francisco in 1853 of brick covered with plaster. The most significant building in the American West for some years, it long stood testimony to the riches that flowed from the placer mines of El Dorado and to the taste, talent, and creativity of a frontier society that blossomed overnight and created an astounding legacy of cultural achievement. *Courtesy Bancroft Library.*

forty years later materialized as Stanford). The value of Phelps's essay, however, is not only to emphasize the instant urbanism of San Francisco and the other gold-rush towns en route to becoming cities, but to suggest the urban patterns that can be detected as well in even the most overnight of settlements. Today, the Mother Lode, north and south, abounds with surviving gold-rush towns—Placerville, Georgetown, Sutter Creek, San Andreas, Grass Valley, Murphys, and Nevada City come immediately to mind—still possessed of the ability to surprise and delight visitors by their compact and tidy urbanism, their arrangements of streets, courthouses, and public squares, their picturesque placements. Something like an instinctive capacity for city-making arrived in California with the Gold Rush. Mining, after all, might have begun as a solitary or team pursuit, but it soon emerged into a more corporate enterprise, and that meant cities. And besides: even the most solitary of miners required, now and then in his yearly cycle, hardware and provisions from urban retail outlets, a cooked meal and a hot bath in a settlement hotel or boardinghouse, a glass of whiskey in a main street saloon, or one or another of the creature comforts of city life.

Within such densities of settlement, the arts and pursuits of culture and civilization were most naturally nurtured. From time immemorial, cities and civilization have paced each other, and gold-rush California was no exception. The surprising thing is that it all happened so early, so quickly. Coming to California in search of gold, men and women almost immediately discovered that they must also continue to paint, sing, write, and perform music. In his essay "'As jolly as a clam at high water': The Rise of Art in Gold Rush California," Anthony Kirk dramatizes just how suddenly, vividly, and persistently the Forty-niners produced paintings and, by the early 1850s, were buying and selling imported art as well. The past thirty years have witnessed a virtual explosion of scholarship and criticism regarding American art in California. Most of this scholarship, however, tends to begin only with the 1860s. Kirk, by contrast, places art in the very mines themselves and in the mining camps: sketches, later paintings, rendered with art supplies packed in-country in a leather pouch, drawn by the flickering light of a campfire. Once again, as in so many of these essays, the international theme is struck as Kirk chronicles the many European or European-born artists who found themselves on the gold-rush frontier.

Like Kirk, Michael Kowalewski, in his essay "Romancing the Gold Rush: The Literature of the California Frontier," is dealing with an artistic pursuit, literature that arrived in 1849, gathered momentum throughout the 1850s, and came into its own in the 1860s. First of all, and most basically, there was created a vast and nearly demotic literature of letters, journals, diaries. Americans of any education whatsoever—by which is meant at least a good primary education, with perhaps some high school or academy work—seemed instinctively to write well in the mid-nineteenth century; or so one is tempted to judge when confronted with the overall excellence of this first phase of gold-rush writing. Again and again, the diaries, journals, letters, or other writings of such spontaneously writing Argonauts as William Perkins, William Manly, Mary Jane Megquier, Edward Gould Buffum, and Hinton Rowan Helper assert the skilled utility of good writing in mid-nineteenth-century America. Knowing that what they were experiencing was important, both historically and to themselves, ordinary men and women took up their pens and wrote; and in the humus of this vast and sometimes near-anonymous groundswell of writing were nurtured more formal instances of literature.

But just as a few Forty-niners came to California expressly to paint, some of them—J. Ross Browne, Bayard Taylor, Alonzo Delano, George Horatio Derby, Prentice Mulford, Sam Ward, Joseph Baldwin, and Frank Marryat—seem to have come to California almost deliberately to write about it, then return east or to Europe for further writing opportunities. Figures such as Ferdinand Ewer and John Rollin

Ridge, by contrast, stayed on to function as literary men in a rapidly stabilizing environment. The Georgia-born son of a Cherokee chief and his white wife, Ridge represented an early and most pure instance of the writer—not the miner who wrote, but the writer pure and simple—practicing his calling in California. In this purity of intention, Ridge is joined, almost, by Dame Shirley; yet Ridge's best-known work, *Life and Adventures of Joaquín Murieta* (1855), together with his posthumously collected *Poems* (1868), is possessed of an intensity, a fierceness of literary intention, that raises it a notch or two above Dame Shirley's skillful and revealing vignettes.

Ridge came almost too early, and he certainly died too young. The 1850s, after all, was a decade of fire and iron, not poetry. How poignant it is, a century and a half later, to leaf through issues of *The Pioneer,* a monthly magazine established by Ferdinand Ewer in 1854 to carry the work of men and women "desirous of distinguishing themselves in Poetry and Belles Lettres, and the more flowering paths of literature." It almost boggles the mind to note that frontier San Franciscans, or Californians in general, in that still-unsettled era were capable of taking the time out to read such *Pioneer* articles as "The Anglican Arrangement of Churches in Connection with the Medieval Prototype" or "An Epitome of Goethe's *Faust*"! (Bayard Taylor, incidentally, would later do a grand translation of Goethe's great poem.) In any event, the experiment lasted for twenty-four months. Given the vagaries of magazine publishing in any era, much less the Gold Rush, which had other things on its mind, such staying power only reinforces Kowalewski's central thesis: namely, that literature came early to California, came nearly anonymously in the Gold Rush, and by the 1860s—in the writings of Ina Coolbrith, Charles Warren Stoddard, Bret Harte, in Samuel Clemens/Mark Twain, William Wright/Dan DeQuille, and the other writers of the *Overland Monthly*—was beginning to gain a national audience.

This formula of 1849 beginnings, development in the 1850s, and maturity in the 1860s was characteristic of education as well as art and literature. In this instance, however, California was on the curve or even slightly ahead of the curve; for the notion of tax-supported public schools, in its modern format, did not fully materialize until Boston in the mid-1850s. Irving G. Hendrick is generous in attributing the founding of the state's public schools to the expected cast of characters in his essay "From Indifference to Imperative Duty: Educating Children in Early California"—which is to say, John C. Pelton, the former principal of the Phillips' Free School at Andover, Massachusetts, who arrived in 1849 and established a school in San Francisco; Andrew J. Moulder, a passionate southerner who as state superintendent of public instruction did so much to establish a statewide school system in the late 1850s and 1860s (unfortunately including a strong Jim Crow proviso banning blacks and other people of color from white schools); and the great John Swett, a New Hampshire-born instructor at Girls' High School in San Francisco (now absorbed into Lowell) and later, after 1862, also state superintendent of public instruction.

Credit should also be given, however, to the Reverend Samuel Hopkins Willey, another New Hampshire man, a graduate of Dartmouth and a Presbyterian minister sent to California by the American Home Missionary Society. Arriving in February 1849, Willey lived in Monterey for a number of months before moving to San Francisco in May 1850, where in a carpenter's shop at Second and Minna in the Happy Valley district south of Market he gathered together a small congregation, which eventually established itself on Howard Street. Next on Willey's agenda: a public school. Already, as Willey points out in his autobiography, *Thirty Years in California* (1879), the state legislature had passed a perfectly good school law, but San Francisco had done nothing about it, claiming that there were not enough children of school age in the frontier city to educate. Willey, however, believed that there were up to three hundred schoolchildren in San Francisco. To demonstrate that fact, Willey organized in September 1851 a parade down Montgomery street of some one hundred school-aged children. A few weeks later, on September 25, 1851, the San Francisco Common Council passed its first free-school ordinance. "Ever since," Willey later noted with satisfaction, "the San Francisco schools have fully kept pace, in size and excellence, with the growth of the city itself."[9]

As Gary F. Kurutz demonstrates in his essay "Popular Culture on the Golden Shore," San Franciscans—or Californians, for that matter—needed no such reminder as Willey's parade of children to keep themselves amused. Drawing upon a wide array of contemporary sources, Kurutz depicts the Gold Rush as sport, as entertainment and festival. A rage for amusement, in fact, seemed to pervade gold-rush society, and this love of a good time dovetailed, as in the case of the theater, with parallel efforts to establish high culture. In other instances—the many music hall reviews in San Francisco and throughout the Mother Lode, for example—California was providing the entertainers of that era a venue comparable to the more culturally developed Atlantic East, in profitability, at least, if not in the hardship of being on the road in those mad, mad years of gold fever. Certain amusements—the pitting of bears and bulls against each other, for example—bespoke the underlying barbarity of the era; but against this terrible and degrading spectacle must also be placed the intricate array of drama, musical recitals, vaudeville reviews (to use a term from a later era), and the dazzling presence of such charismatic stage personalities as Lola Montez, Lotta Crabtree, Tom Maguire, Junius Booth, Edwin Forrest, Alexina Baker, Matilda Heron, and Catherine Sinclair. What must it have been like for the miners, so many of whom had not seen a woman for months, to sit in roughly constructed music halls in the mining region or the more elaborate theaters of Marysville, Sacramento, and San Francisco and hear such singers as Elisa Biscaccianti, "the American Thrush," and Kate Hayes, "the Swan of Erin," fill the darkness with the melodious magic of their voices? Kurutz's chapter is proof positive—if any proof were needed—that in the midst of all their trials and tribulations, their hard work, aching

A party of well-dressed tourists poses at Yosemite Valley, surrounded by the magnificent sight of soaring cliffs and great waterfalls. Although the Argonauts developed a resource-based economy that laid waste to mountains and forests and streams, their diaries and letters reveal they also delighted in the wild beauty of the Golden State, and soon Californians were making pleasure jaunts into the countryside, establishing a foundation for a new relationship with nature in the West. As early as 1855 James M. Hutchings organized a tourist party to pursue the truth of stories circulating about astounding natural wonders in an Indian stronghold called Yosemite Valley. *California Historical Society, FN-31529.*

muscles, and frequent disappointments, the miners of the Gold Rush also found time to sing around a campfire, to be lulled into reverie by a violin, a banjo, a concertina, or a harmonica heard after an exhausting day, or to bowl pins in impromptu bowling alleys, to play at cards in their own cabins or at more perilous gambling halls, or crowd into theaters and music halls for an evening of celebrity entertainment, to watch (and to bet on) horse races and cock fights, to drink whiskey alone or in company (and the drinking of too much whiskey gives a disturbing edge to so much discussion of drinking in this era), to organize patriotic parades or impromptu shivarees, or sometimes just to rest by the fire, enjoying a companionable pipe of tobacco and beholding in the flickering flames the images and shadows of the past and of the future, once one has struck it rich.

And so, cumulatively, as this volume indicates, the social and cultural materials of American California were assembled. For better and for worse, the Gold Rush established, once and for all, that California would be an American place. Yet it would be an American place with a difference. California would be international, for one thing, a diverse culture from the start, although that fact frightened and appalled many Americans and drove them to repressive behavior, frequently enacted into law, which burdened the state from the beginning with a legacy of discrimination. More positively, the Gold Rush would give new meaning to the enshrined American imperatives of life, liberty, and the pursuit of happiness. Here too, however, there would be tragedies and paradoxes. The life that beckoned the Forty-niners, the prospect of a better life, a more free and exuberant life, was the very same life that so many of them lost in the mines, and, worse, that they took wholesale from Native Americans by random acts of violence and systematic genocide. The liberty, the exhilarating sense of personal freedom that only such a far-flung frontier could offer, was also the liberty denied to gold-rush immigrants of color. The happiness that was being pursued—so boldly, so joyously, with such zest and exuberance—was also the happiness that so many lost in the gold fields, despite their hopes and dreams, or the happiness that perhaps never once flickered, even momentarily, in the heart of an enslaved Chinese prostitute.

What we think, finally, about the essays in this volume depends, in part, about what we think today, now, of contemporary California and the present-day United States. For some, the Gold Rush is a panorama of delusion, aggression, lies and deceit, broken promises and empty dreams. For those who think this way, those long-ago years continue today in masked but still damaging forms. One hundred and fifty years ago, Henry David Thoreau would have also agreed with such a critique. Yet for those who believe that the California experiment, which is part of the larger American experiment, is of lasting value, the sins of the Gold Rush, while not denied or even forgiven, can be held in equipoise, in mitigating judgment, against all that the

Gold Rush positively achieved. From this perspective, there is a record of accomplishment in these gold-rush years (and in the essays of this volume) that seeks to rescue and make useful the complex, frequently ambiguous legacy of the past. In absolute moral terms, the entire Gold Rush, the whole vast panorama of it—the sailing of ships around the Horn, the crossing of the continent by wagon train, the hives of activity in the Mother Lode, the millions of dollars of wealth extracted, the cities created, the state established—was not worth the wrongful death of one Native American child, such as those butchered children seen on that horrible morning by Bret Harte.

Yet history, which does not proceed according to absolute moral guidelines, has a way of insisting upon tragedy as part of the process of accomplishment. Such positive results do not excuse the sins of the past; yet they do provide a hope that what has been accomplished has been, on balance, worth at the least some of the terrible cost. In and through it all, in and through what has been chronicled in the essays of this volume and the other volumes of the California History Sesquicentennial Series, the commonwealth of California was achieved: with its battered and compromised but enduring legacy, its desperate hope, that ordinary men and women, such as the Forty-niners were, would somehow find on these Pacific shores the raw materials, the physical challenge—and the moral challenge—of a better and more ecumenical American way of life.

NOTES

1. John Linville Hall, *Around the Horn in '49: The Journal of the Hartford Union Mining and Trading Company, December 1848 to September 1849,* with an introduction by Oscar Lewis (San Francisco: The Book Club of California, 1928), 97.

2. Ibid., 100.

3. Louise Amelia Knapp Smith Clappe, *The Shirley Letters: Being Letters Written in 1851–1852 from the California Mines by "Dame Shirley"* [first published serially in *The Pioneer* magazine during 1854–1855], with an introduction by Richard E. Oglesby (Santa Barbara and Salt Lake City: Peregrine Smith, 1970), 109.

4. George R. Stewart, Jr., *Bret Harte, Argonaut and Exile* (Boston and New York: Houghton Mifflin, 1931), 85–86.

5. Eliza W. Farnham, *California, In-Doors and Out; or How We Farm, Mine and Live Generally in the Golden State* (New York: Dix Edwards & Company, 1856), 156.

6. Ibid., 156–57.

7. J. D. Borthwick, *Three Years in California* [1857], with index and foreword by Joseph A. Sullivan (Oakland: Biobooks, 1948), 261–63.

8. Timothy Dwight Hunt, *Address Before the New England Society of San Francisco* (San Francisco, 1853), 20.

9. S. H. Willey, D.D., *Thirty Years in California* (San Francisco: A. L. Bancroft & Co., 1879), 44.

2

No Boy's Play

Migration and Settlement in Early Gold Rush California

Malcolm Rohrbough

On the morning of April 19, 1775, on the green at Concord, Massachusetts, the militia of the New England towns first faced the power of the British Regular Army. Writing a poem more than half a century later to celebrate this dramatic moment, Ralph Waldo Emerson paid tribute to the "embattled farmers," who "fired the shot heard round the world."[1]

Just as the gunfire on Concord Green echoed around the world, so too did James W. Marshall's discovery of January 24, 1848. Marshall's gold flakes set in motion the events that we know as the California Gold Rush. But what events and over what a vast landscape and seascape! The first Forty-niners came from up and down the West Coast, from Sonora and Oregon, and then from the Hawaiian Islands. By the middle of autumn 1848, the news of the gold in California had reached the eastern states, where it rapidly spread from Maine to Mississippi, from Wisconsin to Florida, and eventually around the world. Marshall's gold discoveries launched a thousand ships and hitched a thousand prairie schooners. The overland schooners embarked from county-seat towns and villages across the breadth of the nation, from subsistence farms in the Ohio Valley to the great plantations of the lower Mississippi River Valley. The Gold Rush's appeal was universal, for those who joined the procession in 1849 and over the next dozen years embraced every class, from the wealthy to those in straited circumstances, from every state and territory, including slaves brought by their owners to the gold fields.[2]

The discovery of gold in California was to trigger the greatest mass migration in the history of the young Republic up to that time, some 80,000 in 1849 alone and probably 300,000 by 1854, an immigration largely male and generally young, but not exclusively either, by land across half a continent and by sea over thousands of miles of ocean to new and heretofore unimagined adventure and wealth. And it would become an international event with immigration from all over the world, including farmers from China and lawyers from Paris, miners from Wales and merchants from Chile. California would become in a few short years the most cosmopolitan place in the world, and San Francisco the most cosmopolitan city.[3]

Initially, the arrival of news about the California gold discoveries in the eastern half of the young continental American nation had been greeted with much skepticism, coming from the distant West Coast after a divisive war of conquest. The evidence for the truth of the stories mounted slowly, and the discoveries achieved universal acceptance only with President James K. Polk's message to Congress of December 5, 1848. Polk confirmed the gold in California and added, "The accounts of the abundance of gold in that territory are of such an extraordinary character as would scarcely command belief were they not corroborated by the authentic reports of officers in the public service."[4] The army officer who brought the letters of confirmation had also carried samples of gold, some 220 ounces. On display in the War Department, the gold became a magnet for visitors, officials, and newspaper reporters. The glittering rocks washed away any lingering doubts, and the public gazed with rapt attention at the sparkling specimens. Their wonder would be repeated by a generation of Forty-niners peering at the nuggets in the bottoms of their pans.

Acceptance was soon followed by wild, uninhibited enthusiasm, and the news spread rapidly to the most remote villages of the American Republic. The impact of the news on one tight-knit community may be summarized by the observations of Prentice Mulford on his village of Sag Harbor on Long Island in the autumn months of 1848: "One June morning, when I was a boy, Captain Eben Latham came to our house, and the first gossip he unloaded was that 'them stories about finding gold in Californy was all true.' The report slumbered during the summer in our village, but in the fall it commenced kindling and by winter it was ablaze. Ours was a whaling village. By November 1848, California was the talk of the village, as it was all that time of the whole country. The Gold Fever raged all winter."[5]

This outbreak of what observers like Prentice Mulford called "gold fever" had an immediate impact. Editors scrambled to set the largest headlines and searched reference books for the best analogies to the past, with references to the "El Dorado of the old Spaniards," "the dreams of Cortez and Pizarro," "the Age of Gold," routinely filling the columns of dailies and weeklies.

A wide range of motives drove future Forty-niners who proposed to go to California. Of course wealth was the first and most public. In addition, the prospect of treasure opened by news of these dazzling discoveries at Sutter's Mill offered young people escape from what they thought of as the limited horizons of the village, the farm, or the shop, and the daily demand of labor associated with these places. It was not the young alone, however, who were propelled into motion. Men of all ages and

Wonder and delight spread across the faces of townsfolk as they listen to a newspaper report on the fabulous riches of the new El Dorado in William Sidney Mount's *California News,* painted in 1850. Prentice Mulford, who lived at Sag Harbor, Long Island, not far from the famed artist's community of Stony Brook, remembered that in the summer of 1848 word of the discovery met with only mild interest, but that excitement mounted through the autumn, and by winter "Gold Fever raged" through the village. *Courtesy The Museums at Stony Brook, New York; Gift of Mr. & Mrs. Ward Melville.*

conditions made plans to go to California, and a surprising number of women wished to join them.

From the welter of newsprint and stories passed from one astonished citizen to another (like Captain Eben Latham) emerged two universal truths. First, the gold in California was real and abundant. Among the most astonishing features of the California Gold Rush was that the most outrageous tales of wealth were true. The Golden State—it would join the Union in 1850—produced a seemingly endless flood of gold. While agricultural laborers in the East earned a dollar a day for twelve hours of work in the fields and artisans and craftsmen perhaps a dollar and a half for the same hours, men who were recently farmers and mechanics made sixteen dollars a day washing gravel in the streambeds of California's foothills. In the six years from 1849 to 1855, the Argonauts harvested some $300 million in gold from California.[6]

The second observation that came to enjoy full acceptance was the notion that gold was available to everyone. The California Gold Rush spoke to American values at midcentury: the democratic belief that wealth would be available to all, that success would reward hard work, and that the largest portion of riches would go to those most moral and worthy by the standards of the day. The discovery of gold in 1848 and its wide, indeed universal, accessibility to Americans everywhere was the reincarnation (or the ultimate continuation) of the American dream, the promise of a better life for themselves and their children through hard work. The search for gold in California became the epitome of American economic democracy: anyone with a pick, pan, and shovel could participate, at least in the early years, regardless of wealth, social standing, education, or family name. Hence this greatest bonanza in the history of the young Republic and newly crowned continental nation was open to all.

The appeal was immediate and universal. Everywhere, citizens of the Republic across the breadth of the land pondered the question of whether to join the rush to the West or whether to stay home. The whole family assembled to canvass the issue. This dilemma raised questions about a host of local and family obligations inherently woven into the miniature world of all Americans at midcentury: marital responsibilities and family obligations, in which the opportunity for wealth was measured against long absences that imposed new duties, often with reduced resources. But the prospective Forty-niners cast the opportunities for wealth in California as something that would benefit the entire family and perhaps in a few short months notably enhance its prospects for generations to come.

The gold fever thus began to disrupt families and communities across the nation, in states and in territories, in regions north and south, slave and free, from urban centers to the most remote farming homesteads. Discussions of whether to go, when to go, who would go, who had gone, and why, occupied many long evenings and evoked emotional outpourings. And for those who decided to go, there was the need to raise the funds for the voyage, whether by sea or overland. Many prospective Forty-niners appealed to their families, with visions of wealth to be shared among all members. Young James Barnes of Washingtonville, New York, summed up the pleas of many Argonauts when he wrote, "Father i need thy assistance; dont send your son emty away. . . . i dont ask you to give me the money, only lend it to me until i am able to repay you."[7]

There were other investors outside the family. Two capitalists each put up $2,500 to finance a company of ten from Monroe, Michigan, in exchange "for a quarter share each in the proceeds of the company" for a two-year period. Another man advised his nephew to invest $500 "by fitting out some young man, on whose integrity he could rely and who had no means of going himself—and agree to divide the profits with him." The sum would support "some poor but hardy man" for two years in California with the prospect of a good return for both parties.[8]

Those who determined to go often did so in a "company" with their friends and neighbors. The company was, in truth, often a replica of the local community from which they came. Within the company, an Argonaut might have one or two special friends. One Forty-niner described such a close friendship with the comment, "me and John stick together like wood ticks to a horse."[9] It was a familiar camaraderie; it was also a support network, confronting an unknown adventure of great distances and strange and alien landscape in which the support of friends would be both welcome and necessary.

The company formed and the officers chosen, a period of intense preparation followed. Men who had been tied to labor on farms and in shops suddenly found themselves officers in companies preparing to depart for California. On them fell such solemn duties as victualling, gathering uniforms and arms, and drafting a constitution. The hum and buzz of activity transformed their communities, and they became the envy of all those who had wished to go but decided to remain.[10]

The outbreak of gold fever and the prospect of a large emigration to the West in search of gold was not greeted with universal enthusiasm. Far from it. Among those sometimes ranged in opposition were ministers, who saw the search for gold as mammon triumphant over the family and community. Such views emerged in a sermon preached by the Reverend James Davis of the First Congregational Church in Woonsocket, Rhode Island. His sermon suggested, among other things, the power and influence of the news of gold. The "gold fever," the Reverend Davis intoned, was a national disease, a true epidemic. It should be treated as such. "The excitement is become truly appalling, and reaching not our cities alone, but our villages and towns and shaking every family. There never has been any excitement equal to it within the remembrance of our oldest cities.—War, Pestilence, Famine, the most astonishing discoveries in the arts and sciences . . . the advancement of civilization and Christianity in the subjugation of heathen lands—all these have never filled our land and the minds of our young men with such intense excitement. . . . The gold pestilence which is more terrific than the cholera, threatens to depopulate our land."[11]

Others argued forcefully that the discovery of gold was a blessing, national resources to be used for the national good. It turned out, according to this justification, that those who went to California in search of wealth did not do so as a selfish gesture, but instead they were patriots spreading American civilization and culture to the distant western parts of the new continental nation. These national heroes (and some heroines) would make California an American land, replace Mexican Catholicism with American Protestantism, supplant the Spanish language with English, and supersede Mexican culture with American values and institutions. This new national purpose gave a powerful patriotic dimension to the rush to California, as many editors and public officials commented in offering their blessing to the departing Argonauts.[12]

Finally, there came the partings. These were public with parades and religious services, or private, with a small gathering at the front gate or stoop. In New York City, "the docks are crowded with fathers and mothers, brothers and sisters and sweethearts, and such embracing and waving of handkerchiefs." One departing Argonaut threw his last five-dollar gold piece toward shore, shouting, "I'm going where there is plenty more."[13] And strangers joined the throngs of family members to celebrate the embarkation for this national adventure. In Philadelphia, companies of Argonauts marching to the ships "were greeted with Cheers from different crowds who stood on the wharves to witness our departure."[14]

For many, these were solemn, even sad, occasions. On the crowded wharves of Boston, ministers conducted final services, with sermons appropriate to the anticipated long absences and somber obligations owed family and country. In Prentice Mulford's village of Sag Harbor, Long Island, the departing men and their families filled the church for a special service where they were admonished to behave virtuously, remember the standards and values of their community, and return rich. As a special reward, these leaving Argonauts were then permitted to stay up late with their girls. In Bloomington, Indiana, two thousand people came together to mark the occasion with religious services (a Bible was presented to each member of the departing company) and to sing missionary hymns to the gold companies as the wagons rolled west toward the unknown.[15] These leave-takings lay with a heavy hand on the families and communities from which had departed their young (and sometimes not so young) men for the Golden West. These adventurers left behind spouses, fiancées, children, siblings, parents, and friends. Their absences would change sometimes forever the configuration of their families and communities.

So America went to California in search of gold. The companies went by sailing ship across the seas and around the Horn in 1849; they went by wagon overland from St.

With a shovel over his shoulder and a brace of pistols stuffed in his pocket, Mr. Hexekiah Jeroloman prepares to set off for the gold mines of California in a lithograph published in 1850 by Louis Nagel. Despite the broad humor of the image, the moment of departure was often charged with strong emotions, as the Argonauts took leave of family and loved ones they would not see again for long months or even years. *California Historical Society, FN-28823.*

The Pacific Mail Steamship Company's crack liner *Golden Gate* sails from port in a water-color painting attributed to Charles R. Parsons. Built in 1851 to carry fortune hunters from Panama to California, she was the Pacific Mail's largest ship, capable of comfortably carrying eight hundred passengers. Although the Panama route was expensive, it was the fastest way to reach California. Argonauts could take a steamer from New York to Chagres, cross the isthmus, and, boarding a vessel for California, arrive in the land of gold a little more than a month after leaving home. *Courtesy Huntington Library, San Marino, Calif.*

Joseph or Independence, Missouri, to Placerville (or Hangtown, as the Argonauts affectionately referred to it). Many companies bound for California went by sea, especially those within reach of the Atlantic ports. The journey by sea could begin at any season, anywhere along the coast, and could make the long voyage around Cape Horn or could opt for the shorter route across Panama. The cost was substantial, on the order of $1,000 for individual members of the company. But the conditions were ideal for companies or individuals with investment ambitions. The sailing vessel offered the means to transport equipment and other cargoes for use and for sale. Such companies offered opportunities for absentee investors to buy shares and transport goods for resale in California, opening the Gold Rush as a money-making chance to capitalists who would never leave the comfort of their rooms in Boston or New York.[16]

For those who went by sea, there were several kinds of purchases. For the voyage, the Argonauts needed barrels of beef and ship biscuits, butter and pork, rice and salt. And they needed them immediately and at the most favorable price. In addition, they required personal equipment, clothing, tools, and guidebooks. These items were known collectively as the "kit," and companies along the eastern seaboard from Portland, Maine, to New Orleans, Louisiana, advertised heavily as outfitting centers. To these basic articles might be added special equipment, "goldometers" or gold-digging machines of various kinds, and other exotic technology that immediately appeared on the market. Indeed, the first great bonanza of the California Gold Rush was in the port cities along the Atlantic Coast, where outfitters did a heavy business in outfitting prospective Argonauts and their vessels for the gold fields.[17]

The voyage to California, whether by Cape Horn, or the shorter version by way of Panama, was long, routine, and boring. Energetic, ambitious, and sometimes frantic Forty-niners, anxious to confront the wealth that seemed sure to be theirs, were confined on a ship for several months, powerless to do anything to accelerate the pace of their voyage to the golden port of San Francisco. Many Argonauts kept journals, in search of ways to pass the time and also in response to their sense of the significance of the moment. As relief against boredom, seaborne companies organized communal activities, from military drills to amateur theatricals to practical lectures on the geology of California or the customs of peoples in the ports of call. As the gold fields came closer, company officers prepared their members for debarkation and made necessary arrangements for dividing the company into squads of miners (a final gesture to military organization) and doling out supplies.

Members of the companies, idled by the long voyage, read and talked, smoked and fished. Above all, they gambled. It was something of an irony that, having been warned to hold fast to their traditional values in the face of the temptations of California, they would succumb to games of chance on the voyage there. But they did. Like so much else that would come to be associated with California, upright and God-fearing citizens of the Republic would be seduced by bad habits and sinful activities, and in this case, before they ever washed a single pan of dirt in the diggings.

The long sea voyages invariably generated internal tensions and anxieties, sometimes even open conflict. To begin with, there were variations in accommodations and sometimes in food. Travel by sea to California (whether by Cape Horn or Panama), like sea travel everywhere, had a certain class-conscious element to it. Some could afford better accommodations than others. A few members of the same company brought delicacies for meals, and formed themselves into separate messes to enjoy their special treats. They openly intended to maintain social and economic distinctions between themselves and their fellow company members, as they would have done before the common expedition to California.[18]

Their ocean voyages exposed the seagoing Argonauts to new American places and to foreign cultures. Both often made powerful impressions. Some ships from New England, New York, and Pennsylvania called at Charleston and sometimes New Orleans, and there their passengers had their first encounter with the institution of slavery. By midcentury, slavery had become a dominant influence in American political life. Both Congress and the executive branch were already engaged in the search for an acceptable compromise on the issue of the access of southerners with their slave property to the new territories recently acquired in the war with Mexico. While citizens from the Northeast had heard much about the institution of slavery, few had experienced it firsthand. They now did so. Strolling through the streets of Charleston or New Orleans, they wrote of powerful impressions made by slave auctions.[19]

In the foreign ports of call, whether Panama, Rio de Janeiro, Granada, or Lima, American Protestants had their encounter with a Latin Catholic culture. They were impressed with the landscape and the grandeur of public buildings, especially the cathedrals, and even New Englanders often declared a sense of awe and respect, if not sympathy, for this alien church. The seagoing Argonauts were generally neither impressed by nor sympathetic to the local peoples, however. The Americans deplored local habits that they found lazy or scandalous or both. The universal targets of criticism were music and dancing, especially the enthusiasms of men and women for public entertainments such as the fandango. One Forty-niner expressed shock that men and women bathed together in Granada. Another described Chileans as "a very indolent and idle class of People possessing but little enterprise." And the Americans generally contrasted the beautiful and abundant landscape of Panama with the primitive agriculture and lack of commercial enterprise. Many travelers expressed relief on debarking in San Francisco, not only for the end to the long and boring sea voyage but also for the welcome sight of so many familiar faces and the sound of a familiar language. One Forty-niner wrote of San Francisco streets, "I seemed to feel quite at home among the good honest Saxon countenances . . . everywhere to be seen contrasting favorably with the sallow narrow visaged Spaniards."[20]

Overland travelers faced a formidable journey across half the continent at midcentury. Only a few thousand pioneers had made the trip to Oregon in the previous decade, and these had been farm families headed west in search of land. Never in the history of the Republic had there been a mass migration of tens of thousands overland to the West Coast in a single season. And in the spring and summer of '49, those who made the trek would include city dwellers along with people from small towns and farms, all suddenly caught up the great pioneering challenge of the day. The obstacles included great distances, the monotonous character of much of the landscape, the towering mountain ranges and deserts to be crossed, and fears of attack by Indians.

The migrations of the so-called "overland" Forty-niners shared both similarities and contrasts with those voyaging by sea. Companies were the basic unit of organization here, too, and individuals who went to St. Joseph or Independence, Missouri, without an affiliation always joined a company there. Groups and individuals sought out others with similar origins and values. New Englanders and

The Winter of 1849, a lithograph based on a drawing by the amateur artist Frank Marryat, depicts the raw conditions that greeted Argonauts arriving in the boom town of San Francisco. The Forty-niner William Jewett, who made port in December, wrote that San Francisco was "composed of the greatest conglomeration of trapsticks for the protection of humanity from the elements that the world ever knew." Like countless other gold seekers, he also expressed amazement at how the heavy rains had turned the streets into muddy lagoons. From Frank Marryat, *Mountains and Molehills* (1855). *California Historical Society, FN-31543.*

southerners sought their own kind, of course, but others with special concerns also united. The Sabbath observers joined in companies of those who would stop for a Sunday of rest; temperance men often banded together. Companies going by sea could depart whenever they wished (within limits of weather), and could match the ship to their size and their cargoes. Overland companies had to conform more to size and schedules dictated by the calendar and the nature of the journey. The trek of twenty-two hundred miles overland was a routine enterprise that, at the same time, imposed certain absolute conditions. The travelers had to leave the Missouri River towns late enough in the spring to find grass for their draft animals on the prairies, but early enough so that they could arrive in California before the first heavy snows closed the passes in the Sierra Nevada. In practice, this meant a departure date somewhere around May 15, and arrival at the base of the Sierra before October 1. The companies were cautioned to travel in groups of no more than sixty, for a larger number would tax the available forage and water, and to limit their loads to a minimum in order to protect the energy and health of the draft animals.[21]

Unlike travel by sea, the overland Forty-niners were constantly aware of crowds along the trails and the growing competition for water and grass, and indirectly, to be the first to arrive in the gold country. This sense of rivalry was the stronger because the Argonauts could literally see their competitors ahead and behind them on the trail. "There are thousands of men going along the road; in fact, it looks like the wagons hauling cotton to Macon just after a rise in the staple," wrote one Forty-niner from Alabama. "I believe there are wagons stretching in sight of one another for 500 miles."[22]

Unlike those suffering the boredom of inaction on the sea voyage, the overlanders performed endless daily chores. One Argonaut's observations summarize the accounts of hundreds: "When traveling, we are up at day break; and by the time the horses are fed, curried and harnessed, the breakfast is ready; as soon as that is dispatched, we hitch up and away. At noon—heretofore we have spent no longer time than is just necessary for the horses and ourselves to eat; but when we get to feeding them on grass, a little longer time will be required. In the evening, after stopping, the horses are to offgear, tie up, curry, and fed and water; the tent is to put up—bed clothes to arrange, supper to prepare and eat—which last is not hard to do—by this time it is bed time, and we 'turn in.' Then again, each member of the company comes upon guard duty once every fourth or fifth night."[23] On the trail, for the first time in a society essentially without women, the Argonauts had their first experiences in sewing, washing, and cooking, and they found these new duties awkward and even burdensome. Little did the overland travelers understand that this domestic work on the overland trail was only the beginning of a new range of chores that would confront them in the gold fields.

Unlike those who went by sea, the overland Forty-niners saw themselves as the vanguard of pioneers, a triumphal march of American people and values across the plains, mountains, and deserts that became the standard for the new Golden State. This journey across half the continent with draft animals was the final large-scale reenactment of America's pioneering past that stretched back for a century, to the migration of frontier families across the Appalachians into Kentucky and the Ohio Country. For the Argonauts of '49, it brought them face to face with the fabled symbols of the American West: the huge herds of buffalo, the dangerous Plains Indians tribes (feared but rarely seen), the towering peaks of the Rockies and the Sierra Nevada, the national monuments of Chimney Rock, Fort Laramie, and the Mormon enclave around the Great Salt Lake.

This great overland migration through the varied landscapes and peoples of the American West ended at Placerville in the late summer or early autumn. There, the

The men of the Washington City Company take their ease at a camp on Black Snake Hill, overlooking St. Joseph, Missouri, in a drawing made in May 1849 by J. Goldsborough Bruff, the leader of the party. More than thirty thousand fortune hunters massed along the frontier that momentous spring, impatiently waiting for traveling conditions to improve before heading out across the plains to gather the golden harvest in far-off California. *Courtesy Huntington Library, San Marino, Calif.*

companies generally broke up, as smaller groups of six or eight men banded together and headed for the mines. Placerville merchants did a bonanza business in re-outfitting the newcomers and changing them from transcontinental pioneers into miners. Even those who had brought the proper tools and equipment to California—shovel, pan, pick, tents, blankets, cradle—now had to purchase food and to transport everything to the placers. Supplies for the mines—salt pork, flour, sugar, tea, and coffee—might involve an outlay of one hundred dollars per miner, plus transportation costs of another one hundred.[24]

Arrived in California, the gold seekers found themselves in an alien, new world. It was a world of strangers, not friends and neighbors; it was a world of self-interest, in which individuals had to look out for themselves (hence the great interest in joining together in small groups to mine and to live); it was a world in which prices for staple goods were beyond anything imaginable, and money seemed plentiful and its value diminished. Argonauts from all economic conditions expressed astonishment at the quantities of hard money visible (especially in gambling houses), even passing from hand to hand. "Gold is measured here by bushels and shovel full," wrote one Forty-niner. And another observed, "Money here seems to be of little value, & every person has plenty."[25] This was only one of the many strange qualities of the new land that the voyagers, at last in California, attempted to describe to their disbelieving families and friends at home.

The newly arrived Argonauts—whether by land or by sea—settled in varied places. These destinations included the growing cities of San Francisco, Sacramento, and Stockton; they established themselves in the many small towns and villages dotting the routes to the gold fields or adjacent to the diggings; they went in large numbers into the gold mining country itself. Those who clustered in the cities included professionals such as doctors and lawyers and day laborers who worked on the docks and on the streets. Large numbers also gravitated to the newly energized entertainment industry, which included dance halls, houses of prostitution, and above all, saloons and gambling establishments. These gambling halls were among the most elegant buildings in San Francisco, providing employment for many and making a dramatic impression on the new arrivals in the city. To these groups should be added the laborers in the booming construction industry and the clerks in the numerous merchant houses engaged in importing goods for local consumption and for shipment to the mining camps. Sacramento and Stockton were smaller than San Francisco but no less commercial, for they were the business gateways to the mining camps themselves.[26]

There were hundreds of mining camps in the California gold country. Some were as large as substantial villages; others were simply crossroads with a single street carved out of the forest to accommodate a few stores. These small urban places prospered in proportion to the mines they served. Their commercial establishments included stores for supplies, a boardinghouse, a restaurant or two, perhaps a doctor and a lawyer, a small entertainment place with a bowling alley, and one or more saloons. The sale of liquor was a major business, especially on Sundays. Business in the camps was generally defined by the mining cycle of work, and this included a day of rest and recreation on Sundays. So camps would be crowded on Sundays, from first light to sunset. Since mining was seasonal, closing with the beginning of the rainy season in late November or early December, so too, many camps tended to hibernate during the winter months.[27]

By far the largest number of Argonauts in 1849 and subsequent annual migrations headed directly for the gold fields. There, they mined in small companies, or "messes," of from five to eight. These numbers were most efficient for the mining techniques in use in the early years—the pan, but quickly the cradle and a "long tom"—and for domestic arrangements. The small company was more than simply a matter of economic and domestic convenience; it was also a self-selected group committed to one another in the most personal kind of way. The company as a unit of work and living

An Argonaut and his family pose for a photographer in a gold camp in the rolling foothills of the Sierra Nevada: the simple beginnings of society and community on the California frontier. From a few tents scattered along a stream laden with rich auriferous gravels arose crude settlements, which frequently grew into towns—and often with astonishing speed—as entrepreneurs hastily erected boardinghouses, stores, and saloons to serve the miners. *Unknown artist, daguerreotype, ca. 1850, P1988.1. Courtesy Amon Carter Museum, Fort Worth, Texas.*

offered support in case of sickness and even in case of death. That the sick should be cared for was part of the unwritten contract associated with shared living and working. Every gold seeker could tell stories of individuals taken ill and left to fend for themselves. Occasional accounts of Good Samaritan strangers emerged from the hustle and movement of the Gold Rush, but most Argonauts preferred to rely on carefully chosen companions. Here were the companions who would sit up with the miner taken ill, fetch the doctor, and make the soup. Here, also, were the partners who would close the eyes of the dead man, dress the body and bury it, and handle the estate. And, in a final act, they would communicate with the dead man's family and carry out his last wishes.[28]

The mining company had its origins in a work unit. As early as the summer and fall of 1848, observers had commented on the advantages of working in groups of at least three or four. By the mining season of 1849, mining in groups was universal.

Two miners prepare a meal at their claim on Weaver Creek, not far from Placerville, in one of the many lively, evocative illustrations appearing in *Three Years in California* (1857), a classic account of the Gold Rush by the artist-Argonaut J. D. Borthwick. Life in the diggings invariably took on a communal character, as fortune hunters formed small companies that not only mined together but shared in the domestic responsibilities of cooking, cleaning, and other camp chores. *California Historical Society, FN-30972.*

The work was of the most onerous and repetitive kind. Each day, the members of a mining company trekked to their claim and began a routine of digging, shoveling, carrying, and washing that continued unabated and with little variation throughout the day until dark. In 1849, most companies operated one or more cradles. In a pattern that stretched from one end of the Mother Lode to the other, one man loosened the "dirt," whether by digging or shoveling; a second carried it to the site of the cradle; there, a third washed the materials. The fourth or fifth members of the company would dig or carry. Miners rotated jobs to equalize the work and relieve the monotony. When a company exceeded six or so, it would operate a second cradle.[29]

The basic unit of work in the California Gold Rush—at least for the first half-dozen years—was the human body. The hard, repetitive labor of digging, carrying, and washing was often done in swift, ice-cold, moving water. "You will have to work in water & mud Morning until night it is no boys play," one Forty-niner wrote his parents.[30] Contrasting with the icy water of the snowmelt watercourses was the heat of the summer California sun, beating down on the bars and into the still canyons. The work was exhausting. "Mining is the hardest working imaginable and an occupation which very much endangers health," complained one Argonaut. "A weakly man might about as well to go digging his grave as to dig gold."[31] Under these conditions, the company performed another function: it demanded and received a continuing work commitment on the part of each member. The presence of a member who did not do the expected labor—whether from lack of will or lack of strength made no difference—was a constant source of irritation in a mutually reinforcing group based on equality. So during the long work days that stretched into a long mining season, gold seekers drove themselves forward on a daily basis through a combination of restless energy, hope, self-interest, group loyalty, and sometimes desperation.

The same division appropriate to mining, with its unending physical labor, long hours, and collective work, also helped to define the new living arrangements. For the miners, it was cheaper and more practical to live in groups. From five to eight men would occupy a large tent or cabin as close to the work site as possible, where they would take turns cooking, cleaning, sewing, and making trips to the camps for food and mail. The most important chore was cooking, for it involved all members of the company. The duty of cook rotated on a weekly basis. As all cooks were amateurs, the meals tended to be repetitive. The main evening meal included meat (fresh or preserved), bread or biscuits, and coffee or tea with plenty of sugar. All miners learned how to bake. It was a necessary skill, and most miners later remember their first loaf of bread as vividly as the first sight of buffalo on the plains and gold flakes at the bottom of their cradles.[32]

Through all these frenzied activities, whether in the cities, mining towns and camps, or at the placers themselves, most of the Forty-niners maintained strong ties with their families and communities in the East. Almost all of them, initially at least, fully intended to return home with a full share of California's wealth, to change the future prospects of their family, and to enhance their standing within the family and the community. Their migration overland represented the first steps in a long cycle of adventures in a strange and exotic place and their eventual return home. Their settlement in California completed the first stage of their experiences as the Argonauts of '49.

NOTES

1. The full text of the first verse of Emerson's "Concord Hymn," written in 1837 is:

> By the rude bridge that arched the flood,
> Their flag to April's breeze unfurled,
> Here once the embattled farmers stood
>   And fired the shot heard round the world.

2. Histories of the California Gold Rush stretch from Hubert Howe Bancroft's seven-volume study (1884–1890) to the present time. Three of the most important modern studies are Rodman W. Paul, *California Gold: The Beginning of Mining in the Far West* (Cambridge:

Harvard University Press, 1947); J. S. Holliday, *The World Rushed In: The California Gold Rush Experience* (New York: Simon & Schuster, 1981); and Malcolm J. Rohrbough, *Days of Gold: The California Gold Rush and the American Nation* (Berkeley: University of California Press, 1997).

3. Rohrbough, *Days of Gold,* introduction.

4. Quoted in ibid., 24.

5. Prentice Mulford, *Prentice Mulford's Story: Life by Land and Sea* (New York, 1889), 1.

6. Rohrbough, *Days of Gold,* 3.

7. James Barnes to Jeremiah Barnes, October 21, 1849, Letters, Bancroft Library, University of California, Berkeley. Later correspondence shows that Barnes's father advanced him $150 for the trip.

8. John Cumming has described the Monroe, Michigan, company in *The Gold Rush: Letters from the Wolverine Rangers* (Mount Pleasant, Mich.: The John Cumming Press, 1974), iv–v. David Campbell to his nephew, April 22, 1850, Campbell Family Papers, Special Collections, Perkins Library, Duke University.

9. Charles H. Getzle to James M. Donnelly, May 13, 1849, Kimberly Letters, Chicago Historical Society.

10. See, for example, the correspondence of William A. Pierce, member of the Rhode Island Eagle Trading and Mining Association, to various trading houses, William Pierce Papers, Rhode Island Historical Society, Providence.

11. Rhode Island *Woonsocket Patriot,* February 16, 1849.

12. See, for example, the sermon of Rev. Dr. Edward Beecher in the *Boston Daily Times,* January 29, 1849.

13. Katherine A. White, comp., *A Yankee Trader in the Gold Rush: The Letters of Franklin A. Buck* (Boston: Houghton Mifflin, 1930), 31.

14. John Cowden to Theodore Garretson, March 4–9, 1949, Letters, Beinecke Library, Yale University.

15. Mulford, *Prentice Mulford's Story,* 5; Bloomington *Indiana Tribune & Monroe Farmer,* February 24, 1849.

16. See, for example, the "Constitution of the Bunker Hill Trading and Mining Association" that specified each member of the company could take "one thousand pounds baggage, or the bulk of five barrels in addition to his bedding" (Beinecke Library, Yale University).

17. See, for example, the range of advertisements in the *Boston Daily Journal,* February 5, 1849, and the Boston *Daily Evening Traveller,* March 22, 1849.

18. Rohrbough, *Days of Gold,* 56–58.

19. Ibid., 58.

20. Ibid., 58–61; William Elder to his wife, June 17, 1850, Letters, Bancroft Library.

21. John Unruh's *The Plains Across: The Overland Emigrants and the Trans-Mississippi West, 1840–1860* (Urbana: University of Illinois Press, 1976) is a detailed account of the migration overland.

22. John Milner to his sister, May 18, 1849, Correspondence, Alabama Department of Archives and History, Montgomery.

23. Henry Packer to Mary Elizabeth Judkins, April 30, 1850, Letters, Bancroft Library.

24. Rohrbough, *Days of Gold,* 120.

25. William Daingerfield to his mother, August 10, 1850, Letters, Bancroft Library; Albert G. Osbun, diary, June 16, 1849, Henry E. Huntington Library, San Marino, California.

26. Rohrbough, *Days of Gold,* chap. 10, is an analysis of the urban Forty-niners.

27. Edwin G. Gudde and Elizabeth K. Gudde, *California Gold Camps: A Geographical and Historical Dictionary of Camps, Towns, and Localities Where Gold Was Found and Mined; Wayside Stations and Trading Centers* (Berkeley: University of California Press, 1975), has identified more than 3,500 gold camps, although they were not all in existence at the same time.

28. Rohrbough, *Days of Gold,* 75–78.

29. Ibid., 135–40, describes the mining work routine.

30. F. T. Sherman to his mother and father, November 18, 1849, Correspondence, Chicago Historical Society.

31. William Rothwell to his father, September 15, 1850, Letters, Beinecke Library, Yale University.

32. Rohrbough, *Days of Gold,* 141–44, analyzes domestic arrangements in the gold fields.

3

A People of Exceptional Character

Ethnic Diversity, Nativism, and Racism in the California Gold Rush

Sucheng Chan

Those who marvel (or shudder, as the case may be) at California's current "changing demographics" are off the mark, for California has not just recently become an ethnically diverse state; it has always been one. Even before people from all over the world converged on California during the Gold Rush, this section of the Pacific Coast already had a larger number of Indian tribes, speaking different languages and following disparate cultural practices, than any other region of comparable size in North America. In the eight decades preceding the Gold Rush, the population mix was further diversified by the arrival of Spanish-speaking colonists, a majority of whom were of mixed Spanish, Mexican Indian, and African ancestry but all of whom became Mexican nationals following Mexico's independence from Spain in 1821.[1] Then, after 1848, the influx of aspiring miners and adventurers from the other sections of the United States, from various countries in Europe, as well as from Mexico, Chile, Peru, Canada, Hawaii (at that time an independent kingdom), China, Australia, and New Zealand, turned California's populace into a truly variegated mosaic.

The California Indians and the Californios (people of Spanish and Mexican California) have long been a part of the state's demographic complexity, but the story of these groups, who were California *residents* at the time that the shiny yellow metal was discovered in 1848, is told elsewhere in this volume. This chapter will focus on *immigrants* who arrived during the Gold Rush. The groups selected for study are not necessarily the most numerous ones. Rather, the focus is on those whose presence affected how gold-rush society became stratified. Thus, even though African Americans were U.S. citizens and not immigrants per se, and even though their number in the state was very small until the 1940s, a discussion of their experiences will be included because their situation throws into sharper focus the complex interplay of ethnicity, nativity, and race—three important sorting mechanisms or organizational

44

axes in any society's social structure.[2] A fourth factor, class, will not be considered due to space limitations, while a fifth, gender, is discussed in a separate chapter. Finally, despite the central importance of San Francisco during the gold-rush years, this chapter deals only with the mining areas.

Immigrants and minorities have been treated in writings about the Gold Rush in three bodies of literature: general histories of California, book-length studies of the Gold Rush, and writings on specific ethnic groups who populated the state from 1848 to the early 1860s.[3] The state's pioneer historians—Hubert Howe Bancroft, Theodore Hittell, and Josiah Royce—were quite aware of the injustices perpetrated against Indians, Mexicans, Chilenos, Chinese, and "South Sea Islanders," though they can hardly be considered champions of these nonwhite peoples. Bancroft called the killing and expulsion of nonwhite groups "disgraceful" and "cowardly," while Royce characterized the Gold Rush as a period during which "civilization sometimes seemed to have lapsed into semi-barbarism."[4]

The next generation of writers in the early twentieth century—John McGroarty, Henry Norton, Zoeth Eldredge, and Gertrude Atherton—romanticized the Spanish and Mexican periods by sentimentalizing them on the one hand, and sanitizing their accounts on the other hand. Apart from the Spanish-speaking people, little was said about other ethnic groups, with the exception of the Chinese, whose presence historians were quite aware of.[5] Surveys of California's growth published in the 1920s, 1930s, and early 1940s by Charles Chapman, Robert Cleland, Rockwell Hunt and Nellie Sanchez, and John Caughey—the first professionally trained historians of the Golden State—were more realistic in portraying the oppression of some ethnic groups, but that did not mean the internal histories of immigrant and minority communities were studied on their own terms.[6]

The first author to posit a direct linkage between the multiethnic population that poured into California during and after the Gold Rush and its unusual pattern of cultural, social, political, and economic development was the crusading lawyer and journalist Carey McWilliams. In *California: The Great Exception* (1949), he linked the discovery of gold to the state's demographic composition. California, he said, "has not grown or evolved so much as it has been hurtled forward, rocket fashion, by a series of chain-reaction explosions. . . . It was, of course, the discovery of gold that got California off to a flying start. . . . Not gold alone, but the magic equation 'gold-equals-energy,' is the key to the California puzzle." That energy has also come from its people: "the exceptional character of the population is one of the master keys to the contradictions and paradoxes of the state. Yet, at the same time, the Californians are representative of the American people."[7] Californians represent not a random but, rather, a selective sample of the people from their countries or regions of origin. According to McWilliams, "a selection of this sort tends to *heighten*, to emphasize, the diverse traits and characteristics of the populations from which the migrants have

A daguerreotype of a Chinese man by the early California photographer Isaac Wallace Baker. Although California became ethnically diverse in the eighteenth century with the arrival of Spanish colonists, who included men and women of Spanish, Indian, and African ancestry, the discovery of gold radically changed the composition of California's population, luring fortune hunters from every quarter of the globe and creating a cosmopolitan society without precedent in American history. *Courtesy Oakland Museum of California.*

been drawn." Many newcomers to California abandoned much of their cultural baggage and experimented audaciously with new social forms, in the process endowing the state with its extraordinary dynamism.[8]

A quarter-century would pass before McWilliams's bold thesis would be picked up and elaborated on in the textbooks published during the 1960s and 1970s by Andrew Rolle; Walton Bean; Ralph Roske; William Beck and David Williams; David Lavender; and Edward Staniford.[9] In these works, divergent approaches were used to discuss the experiences of nonwhite minority groups: some authors continued to treat each group in chapters of their own, others to compare them within a single chapter, and yet others to weave their stories into the master narrative. The 1972 work by Lavender was the first California history text to intersperse segments, albeit brief ones, about various nonwhite groups into the main story line, instead of treating them in separate chapters or sections. Furthermore, by noting that a majority of the American stampeders were young, healthy, white, and Protestant—that is, by specifying their age, ethnicity, and religion, however fleetingly—he initiated a historiographical move away from the prevailing tendency to depict the Yankee Argonaut as "universal man" or, more precisely, as the quintessential miner.[10]

The general histories published in the last two decades, which include a number of anthologies, are all liberal in outlook and inclusive in coverage. Many aspects of immigrant and minority life are woven into the larger narrative in the works of Howard DeWitt; Kevin Starr; James Rawls; Richard Rice, William Bullough, and Richard Orsi; Sucheng Chan and Spencer Olin; and David Wyatt.[11] Even these works, however, do not use race, ethnicity, nativity, class, and gender explicitly as categories of analysis in the way that the many New Western Historians have employed such concepts. Practitioners of the New Western History, on the other hand, have paid little attention to the California Gold Rush, so there has been less cross fertilization of ideas among scholars in the two related fields than one might hope for.[12]

In contrast to the general histories of California, works of synthesis on the Gold Rush penned by Owen Coy, John Caughey, Rodman Paul, William Greever, Otis Young, Jr., J. S. Holliday, Paula Marks, and Malcolm Rohrbough contained more material on immigrants and minorities.[13] Of these, Paul's work, *California Gold,* remains seminal more than half a century after its first appearance, not only because the author was fully aware of the multinational origins of the gold-rush population, but also because he recognized the technological contributions that various groups had made to mining. Writing in the 1990s, in *Precious Dust,* Marks told the stories of the African Americans, Australians, British, California Indians, Chilenos, Chinese, Frenchmen, Germans, Irish, and Mexicans quite fully in a chapter entitled "Natives and Strangers." In *Days of Gold,* Rohrbough includes information on fortune hunters from Australia, Great Britain, China, Chile, France, Hawaii, Ireland, Mexico, and Peru, as well as on Native Americans and Californios. But his chapter that focuses on the experiences of these groups, entitled "Threats from Within, Threats from Without: Fear, Hostility, and Violence in the Gold Rush," gives the reader a better picture of what was done to these foreigners and minorities than what mining life was like for them.

An unusual study that taps the multiethnic roots of the Gold Rush is *Bacon, Beans, and Galantines,* a book by Joseph Conlin about the food eaten by the miners, who had no problems crossing ethnic boundaries when it came to their appetites. When they wanted to break their monotonous diet of salted pork or jerked beef, beans, flapjacks, hard biscuits, coffee, and (on Sundays) liquor, they sought out French cuisine, whenever it was available and when they could afford to splurge. The desire for "Frenchy food" was more than a matter of taste preference: eating French food, then, as now, was a sign of wealth and culture. Men who came to seek their fortune welcomed opportunities to display a little of whatever wealth they had acquired. When the miners did not have much to spend but still wanted some variety, they ate Chinese food.[14] Two other important comparative and multiethnic studies of the Gold Rush are a two-part article by Doris Wright published in 1940–41 and a long article by Ralph Roske that appeared in 1963.[15]

In the existing literature on specific ethnic groups, the amount available about a particular group is roughly inversely proportional to its members' degree of visible difference from the traits commonly stereotyped as Anglo-American. Thus, very little has been published about the British or Germans in California, despite their commanding numbers among the state's foreign-born population in the early decades of statehood (see table 3.1). In California, the English-speakers, as well as the Germans (many of whom could speak English, were Protestants, and were considered desirable immigrants—that is, orderly, intelligent, and solid, with "little wish to return to their native country"), were usually treated as honorary Americans. Much more has been written about the French, the European immigrants with the strongest ethnic identity. A sizable corpus is available on California's religiously distinct Jewish immigrants. Though most of the studies on California Jews are more filiopietistic than scholarly, they are nonetheless valuable for recovering that group's history.[16]

The largest amount of ethnic literature has been published about the racially marked groups who appeared during the Gold Rush or shortly thereafter, but as disconnected bodies of writing, these works have seldom been brought into conversation with one another in comparative studies. Most of the studies either focus on the internal dynamics of the groups in question or, when they do examine a particular group's interaction with others, the attention has almost always been on its members' relationship to the Anglo-American majority and not to other immigrant or minority groups. While a significant portion of the works on African Americans in California is about the gold-rush period, relatively few items deal with black mining activities per se. Rather, they focus on the black struggle for civil rights. The writ-

TABLE 3.1

The Most Numerous Foreign-born Groups in California, 1850–1870

Nationality	1850	1860	1870
Chinese	660	34,935	48,790
English	3,050	12,227	19,202
French	1,546	8,462	8,063
German	2,926	21,646	29,699
Irish	2,452	33,147	54,421
Italian	228	2,805	4,660
Mexican	6,454	9,150	8,978

SOURCE: Allyn C. Loosley, *Foreign Born Population of California, 1848–1920* (San Francisco: R & E Research Associates, 1971), 33. Loosley culled his figures from the 1850, 1860, and 1870 U.S. censuses of population for the state of California.

NOTE: The figures for 1850 are undercounts since the census schedules for three populous counties—San Francisco, Santa Clara, and Contra Costa—were lost. Even if the enumerations for those three counties had not been lost, the 1850 figures would still be undercounts, given the transience of the mining population, their scattered and remote locations in the gold country, and the lack of roads.

ings on California's Chinese are voluminous, yet not much attention has been paid to the Chinese as gold miners. The number of studies on gold-rush-era Mexicans, Chilenos, and Peruvians is smaller than might be expected—given their perceived differences from Anglo-Americans—probably because their stay was short: most were driven out of the state within five years of the gold discovery.[17] A recent bibliography of articles from scholarly journals and more popular periodicals compiled by Robert Santos corroborates my own findings regarding the unevenness of ethnic coverage.[18]

The ethnic-specific writings are compensatory in nature: because the general histories of California have not taken notice of the state's immigrants and minorities in a satisfactory way, authors have produced separate works to fill gaps in our knowledge. However, the style and tone of these ethnic-specific writings are quite dated, since many of them were published before the quantitative methods and theoretical assumptions of the new social history became influential. Moreover, they have not been integrated into the general gold-rush historiography. Therefore, they have performed an additive, but not a corrective, function in terms of revising the field.[19] The present essay is a preliminary attempt to move the story of immigrants and minorities from the periphery closer to the center of gold-rush scholarship by placing some commonly known facts into a new framework and reinterpreting their significance and meaning.

GEOGRAPHY, ORDER OF ARRIVAL, AND LOCATIONAL PATTERN

Among the aspiring miners who descended upon California after the gold discovery in early 1848, geographic origin was the most important determinant of their order of arrival, given California's isolation and the difficulty of getting there. That arrival sequence, in turn, affected where miners of various nationalities tended to congregate in the gold country. And where they gathered and in what relative numbers impacted their interaction with the hordes of Americans who began showing up in the spring of 1849 and who overnight became the majority population, not only in terms of numbers, but also in terms of political power, economic control, social dominance, and cultural influence. Finally, the social hierarchy within each ethnic group influenced how the various groups perceived, ranked, and treated one another.

The above aspects of gold-rush society did not remain static. Even though the unprecedented international migration, i.e., the rush per se, lasted only half a dozen years, it can still be divided into three periods: (1) the first mining season of 1848, when surface gold was abundant; (2) the period from 1849 to the early 1850s, which was dominated by labor-intensive placer mining; and (3) the years after 1852, when mining became increasingly industrial and capital-intensive. This periodization scheme is based on three criteria: changes in mining methods and business organization, changes in class relations associated with the respective methods and organizations,[20] and changes in the pattern of race and ethnic relations among the various groups.

In 1848, the state's estimated population included perhaps 150,000 California Indians and between 14,000 and 15,000 non-Indians. Of the latter, slightly more than half were Americans and Europeans who had drifted into Alta California, Mexico's northernmost province, in the quarter century before the discovery of gold. The rest were mixed-blood Californios. California Indians, Californios, and pre-gold-rush settlers from the United States and Europe were the first prospectors to reach the gold fields in mid-1848 after Sam Brannan broadcasted James Marshall's discovery. When the American military governor, Col. Richard Mason, who had taken charge of California after the outbreak of the Mexican-American War, toured the gold country in the summer of 1848, he estimated that half or more of the 4,000-plus miners he saw busy at work were California Indians. Some of them were laboring for Californios or Americans, while others were digging for themselves.

Since trading, whaling, and sea-otter-hunting ships regularly plied the Pacific Ocean during the mid-nineteenth century, news of the gold discovery reached the shores lapped by that body of water before people in the eastern, midwestern, and southern United States or Europe received the same information. Accordingly, the first foreign gold seekers to show up came from lands to the north, south, and west of California rather than to its east. Among the 6,000-plus people who made their way to California in 1848, foreigners outnumbered Americans. The first large contingent of Americans—an estimated 2,000 to 3,000 people—came from Oregon, which was still a territory at the time, while a smaller number came from Hawaii.

James Marshall's find was first publicized in a Hawaiian newspaper, the *Polynesian,* on June 24, 1848, before the news even reached Oregon. The schooner *Louise,* which had left San Francisco for Honolulu on May 31, brought not only the news but also two pounds of gold as proof of its find. By mid-July, signs of "gold fever" had broken out in Honolulu, with as many ships as were available being outfitted for the journey to the Pacific Coast.[21] That summer, a large proportion of the Americans and Europeans residing in the islands, along with scores of native Hawaiians (whom Americans in California called "Kanakas"), sailed for the new El Dorado. The native Hawaiians, though small in number, worked in many locations and were recognizable as a distinct group.[22] In journeying eastward across the Pacific, they were following the footsteps of native Hawaiians who had earlier touched California's shores while working in ships from New England engaged in the hide-and-tallow trade that had flourished during the Mexican period; Hawaiians had also accompanied John Sutter as he established his estate, New Helvetia, in the Sacramento Valley in 1839. A few months after the first exodus from Hawaii, a reverse migration began. As rain and snow fell on California's Sierra Nevada, many miners, including individuals who had not previously lived in the islands, departed for Hawaii to spend the winter months in a warmer clime.

Trade grew along with the movement of people. All available clothing, shoes, raincoats, guns, bullets, gunpowder, knives, cooking utensils, shovels, pickaxes, Irish potatoes, sweet potatoes, sugar, molasses, coffee, and cattle in Hawaii—the dry goods mostly imported from England and the United States, the food grown in Hawaii—were shipped to California for sale at very high prices. The depletion of these goods in the islands caused inflation there. Between 1848 and 1852, Hawaii, along with Oregon, Mexico, and Chile, supplied the bulk of the food eaten in California's gold country. From the mid-1850s onward, however, imported foodstuffs declined in importance as California became increasingly self-sufficient.[23]

Next came thousands of Mexicans and Chilenos and a smaller number of Peruvians. News of California's gold strike first reached Chile on August 18, 1848, when the brig *J.R.S.*—named for its owner, the merchant Juan Ramón Sánchez—docked at Valparaiso after a voyage of sixty-four days from San Francisco. Many of the ship's crew were missing because they had deserted to join the hunt for gold when the ship was anchored in San Francisco Bay. The news did not generate much excitement until the schooner *Adelaide* arrived from California on September 12 with gold dust worth $2,500. Then, when the brig *Correro de Talcahuano* docked on November 3 with another 130 pounds of gold dust, the rush was on.[24] The first forty-five people to depart from Valparaiso were American and English merchants who

had settled in Chile, many of whom had become Chilean citizens and married local women. The English-speaking businessmen owned and operated Valparaiso's
warehouses, hotels, restaurants, saloons, brothels, and gambling parlors. Valparaiso
had become a busy port after legislation was passed in 1835 to make it into a "port of
deposit." Under this arrangement, foreign merchants did not have to pay customs
duty when they unloaded their goods and stored them in the government's warehouses, if such goods were destined for reshipment to other countries. All they had
to pay was a small deposit fee.[25] Such savings made the port popular with foreign
traders. During the Gold Rush, with hundreds of ships from the U.S. East Coast
stopping for fresh water and provisions after rounding Cape Horn, Valparaiso became an even more bustling port of call. Smaller Chilean ports like Talcahuano and
Concepción also prospered in the early 1850s.

There are no reliable statistics on how many people from Chile joined the Gold
Rush, and of those how many were English and American expatriates and how
many were native Chilenos. However, we do know that by July 1849, the government
had issued three thousand passports to California-bound emigrants.[26] In addition,
thousands had left without passports. The number of people who simply departed
became so large that the government decided to abolish the passport law. On July 2,
1849, the *Alta California* reported that 5,677 men and 209 women had arrived by sea
between April 12 and June 30, 1849. Of these, 1,360 men and 70 women had come
from Chile.[27] So, even after the Yankee influx had begun, people from Chile still
comprised almost one-quarter of the total seaborne arrivals.

Like Hawaii, Chile exported many commodities to California: flour, dried beans,
jerked beef, canned sardines, dried fruit, saddles, bridles, spurs, furniture, and even
prefabricated houses.[28] In the early 1850s, an estimated three-fourths of the flour
consumed by the miners came from Chile. But this trade declined as California began growing its own food.

The other sizable group of Latin Americans, Mexicans, traveled mainly overland or by a combination of land and sea routes. Of the 5,000-plus persons who
came overland during the first mining season of 1848, about half were from Oregon
Territory, 200 to 350 were from the United States, and 2,000 to 3,000 were from
Mexico.[29] The latter almost all hailed from the province of Sonora, with smaller
numbers from Sinaloa, Chihuahua, and Durango. While most of them traveled
overland the entire way—following the old Anza Trail to Yuma, then across the
Colorado Desert and through the San Gorgonio Pass to Los Angeles, and up the
coast to the mines—some set sail from the port of Guaymas on the eastern shores
of the Sea of Cortez (also known as the Gulf of California). The first organized
overland caravan left Hermosillo in October 1848, but smaller parties had begun
drifting northward a few months earlier.

Many Sonorans were already familiar with California. During the Spanish period, they had comprised the bulk of the settlers sent north to colonize Alta California. Then they had flocked to Rancho San Fernando in southern California when gold was discovered there in 1842.[30] In the first few months of 1849—that is, before Americans showed up in droves—an additional 6,000 Sonorans found their way to the mines, despite the Mexican government's worries about depopulating the province and thereby leaving the frontier unguarded against Apache raids. Given the relative proximity of their homeland to California, the Sonorans were seasonal migrants: at least half returned home at the end of each mining season.[31]

As in Hawaii and Chile, stores in Sonora were also stripped of their merchandise, which was taken north for sale at great profit. Even more problematic was the departure of thousands of mules—the main mode of transportation in rugged terrain without roads—which were sold in California for many times their price in Mexico. Although thousands of mules from the American Southwest and plains were also eventually driven to California to pull its pack trains, experienced muleteers preferred the sturdier Mexican mules, which were reared for the transportation of goods rather than for use as farm draft animals, as American mules were.

The smallest group of Latin Americans came from Peru. Peruvians first heard about Marshall's find in the late fall of 1848. On October 3, Lt. Lucien Loeser, who was carrying a tea caddy of gold to Washington, D.C., on behalf of Col. Richard Mason, stopped at Payta. Either he or someone else from the *Lambayeque*—the ship that had carried him to Payta—apparently left behind a copy of the newspaper *Californian*, dated August 14, 1848 (the first issue published since the paper's workers had closed shop and left for the mines several months earlier). The *Del Tridente* on October 17 reprinted an article from the *Californian* describing Marshall's find in detail. *El Comercio*, a newspaper in Lima, Peru's capital, then reprinted the *Del Tridente* article on November 6. The news soon reached Callao, located only a few miles from Lima and the chief port for exporting guano. On November 30, the first ship with Peruvian passengers bound for California set sail from Callao.[32] The number of Peruvian gold seekers is even more uncertain than the number of Chilenos and Mexicans, as many Spanish-speaking people were counted as Chilenos in the available statistics of passenger arrivals in San Francisco.

New Zealanders received the news in November 1848 when an American whaler, the *Balfour*, put into port with several newspapers from Hawaii. Australians heard about the strike the following month, when the *Sydney Morning Herald* on December 23 reprinted extracts from Honolulu's *Polynesian* about the discovery. Australians initially were not enthusiastic to join the rush. During the first six months of 1849, only 679 passengers sailed on twenty-five vessels to California. Once news filtered back of Australians who had struck it rich, however, the exodus began in earnest. Thousands left even though newspaper editors intoned against the dangers of depopulating Australia.[33] There were worries about depopulation because the total population of Aus-

tralia at that time—including male and female "convicts under sentence of transportation" but excluding the indigenous Aborigines—was only about 400,000. The
population in New Zealand was less than 30,000 people of European ancestry, not
counting the native Maoris. That is why leaders in both Australia and New Zealand
worried about the impact of the potential loss of manpower on their countries' development. However, they could not stop ships loaded with California-bound passengers
from leaving. The British convicts had been transported from Britain to Botany Bay,
a penal colony set up in Australia. After landing in San Francisco, many acquired
notoriety as the "Sydney Ducks,"[34] even though the penal colony was not in Sydney itself. However, since Sydney was the chief port of embarkation for California,
in the eyes of Americans all Australians came from Sydney. The Australian and New
Zealand migration slowed to a trickle in 1851, when gold was discovered in Australia
itself—in New South Wales—thereby precipitating a reverse flow that included many
non-Australians. But a sufficient number remained in California to comprise 43 percent of the British-origin immigrants in San Francisco when the 1852 state census was
taken.[35] In other words, a sizable fraction of the first gold seekers of British birth to arrive in California came not from Great Britain but from Australia.

Trade between the southern continent and California continued to flourish even
after the emigration stopped. Australia exported a large variety of goods to California, including jerked beef, bacon, lard, butter, cheese, split peas, beer, champagne,
sherry, pharmaceutical drugs, woolen blankets, boots, shoes, nails, axes, window
glass, paint, rope, candles, cooking utensils, and prefabricated wooden houses.[36]

The above, then, were the groups whose arrival predated that of the Forty-niners.
Though the miners, regardless of their national origins, spread themselves out in
search of rich deposits, their locational pattern was not entirely random. Discernible
clusters of people did emerge. For the most part, people from the same national or ethnic origins worked and lived together, although occasionally multinational or multiethnic groupings could be found. The Scottish journalist and artist J. D. Borthwick, for
example, encountered a party of two Americans, two Frenchmen, two Italians, and two
Mexicans led by a German doctor. William Downie, another Scotsman, established
Downieville in Sierra County after prospecting there with a party of seven African
Americans, an Irishman, a Hawaiian, an Egyptian, and several Americans.[37]

The route taken by a particular group to reach the gold fields influenced where its
members tended to gather. Gold-bearing ore could be found in three areas: in the far
north along the Trinity and Klamath rivers and their tributaries, in the Northern
Mines in the Sierra and foothills north of the gold discovery site at Coloma, and in
the Southern Mines in the Sierra and foothills south of Coloma.[38] A significant
number of British Columbians, many of whom were British-born, and Oregonians
dug for the precious metal in the Trinity-Klamath-Shasta region, which they traversed
as they journeyed southward. American Forty-niners who had crossed the Great

The town of Sonora, seat of Tuolumne County, in the Southern Mines, January 1852. Settled in 1848 by Mexicans from the state of Sonora, the famous gold camp was for some time largely Hispanic in population and character, but the imposition of the Foreign Miners' Tax in 1850 drove most of the Sonorans and other Spanish-speaking miners from the diggings. *California Historical Society, FN-31407.*

Plains and the Rocky Mountains dominated the Northern Mines in Plumas, Butte, Sierra, Yuba, Nevada, Placer, El Dorado, and Amador counties because the southern branch of the California Trail cut through the Sierra Nevada at Carson Pass and Donner Pass, which led to the Northern Mines. The largest contingent of Latin Americans prospected in the Southern Mines—in Calaveras, Tuolumne, and Mariposa counties—because as they trekked northward they reached that area first. The 1850 U.S. census counted 159 Chilenos in Calaveras County and 209 in Tuolumne County. The 1852 California state census showed the presence of 1,077 Chilenos in Calaveras County and 443 in Tuolumne County.[39] By the early 1850s, an estimated 12,000 Sonorans and Chilenos were mining in and around Sonorian Town (the name was later shortened to Sonora—the largest mining camp in Tuolumne County, named after its main residents). In addition to Sonora, many other mining camps in the area bore names reflective of their inhabitants' origins, such as Chile Gulch, Chile Bar, Santiago Hill, Spanish Flat, Spanish Bar, and Spanish Dry Diggins.[40]

A second reason that Latin American miners were concentrated in the southern area was that they were the people who knew best how to work the "dry diggings" of the Southern Mines, where relatively little rain fell and the streams were smaller and more often intermittent. Obtaining gold under dry conditions was laborious indeed. The main methods used in placer mining—panning, using the rocker or cradle, the long tom, or flumes and sluices—all required a large amount of water. When water was insufficient, a technique called *aventamiento,* or "dry washing," was used. The miners would dig up the pay dirt, dry it in the sun, and pulverize it into fine gravel. If the lumps were too large or too hard to be broken up manually, they were crushed in a Mexican *arrastre* or a "Chili mill" powered by horses, donkeys, or mules. The mill's enormous stone pieces were hewn out of solid rock by experienced stonecutters. To winnow the gold-bearing sand, the Latinos twirled it in a bowl and tossed the contents high into the air with a circular motion. On a breezy day, the lighter particles of dirt would be blown away by the wind as they fell. When there was no wind, the miners had to use their own powerful breaths. The heavier gold particles dropped directly into a bowl or blanket or cowhide lying on the ground.[41]

Though Latin American miners had also worked claims in the Northern Mines in 1848, after 1849 they became rarer in that region because those who dared to venture into the area were driven away by the newly arrived Americans, British, and Germans, who often acted in concert against them. The only Latin Americans welcomed in the Northern Mines were muleteers, who brought needed supplies even during the foulest weather.

The Chinese—the other major group of trans-Pacific migrants—began drifting in after 1848. There is no reliable evidence on when news of the gold strike first reached China, but it was probably in late 1848, as ships from the United States, England, and Hawaii engaged in the China trade regularly called at Hong Kong, which had been ceded by China to Great Britain at the end of the First Opium War in 1842. Canton, located upriver from Hong Kong, became the chief point of departure for Chinese emigrants to the "Old Gold Mountain"—the Chinese name for San Francisco (in contrast to Australia, the "New Gold Mountain"). According to Bancroft, there were 54 Chinese in California on February 1, 1849, 791 by January 1, 1850, and around 4,000 by the end of 1850.[42] The first arrivals were merchants and artisans who remained in San Francisco to trade. Only when more than 20,000 Chinese landed in 1852 did large crowds of them fan out all over the mining counties, where they became ubiquitous. Thus, their story belongs primarily not to the first two periods of the Gold Rush, but to its third.

FROM ETHNIC CONSCIOUSNESS TO NATIVISM

The various groups of miners were conscious of their ethnicity and drew distinctions between themselves and others by the names they used to refer to one another, by the clothing they wore, and by the religious faiths they professed. Americans lumped all Spanish-speakers together derisively as "greasers," while the latter called Americans and other people of European descent "gringos." The longtime resident Californios, for their part, distinguished themselves from the recently arrived Sonorans, calling the latter *calzoneros blancos* (white breeches) after the Sonorans' flowing white pants.[43] The Sonorans, in turn, could be differentiated from the Chilenos; the former wore long serapes, which differed in color and design from the latter's shorter ponchos. Americans and Europeans, regardless of their former stations in life, all sported the "miners' uniform," consisting of a broad-brimmed slouched hat, a red or blue flannel shirt, a patterned kerchief, blue denim pants, a thick belt to which was attached at least one bowie knife and a pistol, and leather boots. The men also wore beards and were contemptuous of clean-shaven faces. The only European immigrants who did not adopt the miners' uniform were the Jews, who continued wearing their dark suits, which they could do because few of them engaged in mining. Instead, they monopolized the clothing trade. Jewish peddlers and merchants could be found everywhere in the gold country, selling not only clothing but also jewelry, guns, knives, and sundry other articles. The Chinese also had a uniform of their own. Each man shielded himself from the sun with a mat-woven conical hat and wore a dark blue cotton collarless shirt and matching pair of loose pants. Leather boots were the one item of American-made clothing that many Chinese miners bought and wore.

After 1849, when Americans and Europeans overwhelmed the native population and the early immigrants who had come in 1848, new monikers came into use. The French, who began arriving in late 1849, preferred to mingle with the Latin Americans and so they, too, were found in greater numbers in the Southern Mines. Apparently, they felt more comfortable among Catholics who spoke a cognate Romance language than among English-speaking Protestants. Intensely proud of their own language and culture, few Frenchmen tried to master English. For that reason, the Yankees called them *keskydees* because they were often heard asking each other, "Qu'est-ce qu'il dit?" (What did he say?). The Germans were referred to as "Dutch"—a mispronunciation of Deutsch. Actually, the term "Dutchmen" encompassed more than Germans: Yankees used it to refer to all Europeans except for the British, French, and Italians.

Despite their awareness of cultural differences, the miners of different national origins worked amicably alongside one another in the first mining season of 1848. It was a peaceful summer because there was plenty of surface gold to be had and foreign miners numbered only in the thousands. But conditions changed with the coming of the Forty-niners, almost 90,000 of whom poured in that year—about 40,000 by sea and 40,000-plus overland. The seaborne travelers, about three-fifths of whom were Americans and two-fifths foreigners, came by way of the Isthmus of Panama or around Cape Horn (and, after July 1851, over the Isthmus of Tehuántepec in Nicaragua). They began showing up in the early spring. Of the overland adventurers, approximately three-fifths drove wagon trains across the Great Plains and over passes through two forbidding ranges—the Rocky Mountains and the Sierra Nevada. The rest traversed Mexico. Those who crossed the plains did not begin arriving until late summer and early fall because they had not been able to begin their journeys until the spring thaw. About half of the people emerging out of Mexico were Mexicans; the rest were Americans, especially southerners and Texans, who had chosen the southern route. In 1850, about half of those who came by sea had set sail from foreign ports. In the next few years, the proportion of foreigners among the seaborne arrivals declined to between one-fourth and one-third of the total. As these weary fortune hunters made their way to the mines, ethnic consciousness quickly became transformed first into nativism and then into racism. Unlike ethnic consciousness, nativism and racism were and are more than attitudes, feelings, and thoughts. Rather, they were and are often manifested in action—action to discriminate against or harm members of other groups.

As John Higham and Ray Billington have persuasively demonstrated, American nativism—the fear of and hatred toward foreigners—has deep and multifarious roots that stretch back to the Protestant Reformation in Europe. Anti-Catholicism was one of its cornerstones. Then, during the American War of Independence, the burgeoning nationalism felt by Americans made European traditions and institutions suspect, so animosity toward foreigners (initially Europeans) was added to antagonism toward the Pope. Up to the late 1840s, anti-Catholicism was directed mainly against Irish immigrants. Then, in the aftermath of the 1848 revolutions in Europe, tens of thousands of people, especially from Germany and France, fled to the New World to escape the social, economic, and political upheavals that ensued. Radical political ideas came along as part of their cultural baggage. Their presence rekindled anxieties that Americans had harbored since the late eighteenth century over the chaos that might ensue should the status quo be overthrown violently. Anti-radicalism thus emerged as yet another ingredient in the nativist brew. Finally, the belief that the United States's Anglo-Saxon heritage was what gave the nation its greatness added a racialist strain to American nativism.[44]

Among the Argonauts, nativism first reared its ugly head in Panama in January 1849, when General Persifor F. Smith, who was en route to California to assume command of the American military forces there, declared that he would "consider everyone not a citizen of the United States, who enters on public land and digs for gold, as a trespasser." He promised to drive all such trespassers out by force. Inflamed by Smith's words, the hundreds of Americans gathered at the isthmus awaiting passage to the gold fields became further agitated when the first Pacific Mail Steamship Company steamer, the *California*, arrived carrying many Chilenos and Peruvians. When the Forty-niners finally reached the mines after an arduous journey, they were upset to find that Spanish-speaking miners had got there before them and seemed to have found the richest claims. In addition, among the Argonauts were many veterans of the Mexican-American War, who had learned to see Mexicans as enemies. The nationalism and anti-Mexican stereotypes aroused during that conflict added fuel to the fire of nativism.

Because most of the Americans had no experience in gold mining, they were at first glad to learn from the Sonorans and Chilenos. Once they had acquired some knowledge, however, they became jealous of the latter's success. Their nativist sentiments quickly found expression in action. First, the aspiring Yankee miners formed local ad hoc associations and drew up regulations to govern how claims could be made and kept. In general, at each locality, the miners who had congregated there held a meeting to decide what size a claim might be, depending on the auriferous content of the sands and the difficulty of working the ground or riverbank or bed. Each individual could hold only one claim, except for the person who had made the find, who was entitled to two claims. The claims had to be officially recorded with an elected recorder. To hold a claim, a miner had to work it a specified minimum number of days per specified time period. Thus, miners enjoyed only usufructuary rights over their claims, with disputes settled at miners' meetings or by the recorder or alcalde. Such ostensibly democratic rules accorded well with the miners' desire to level social ranks. The miners' uniform also became a useful mechanism for socio-economic leveling: when everyone looked alike, dress could not be used as an emblem of wealth or status. Another practice that facilitated such leveling was the common use of nicknames only, so that anyone who wished to camouflage or disown the identity he or she had possessed "back in the States" could do so.[45]

In the American miners' eyes, however, these egalitarian practices did not apply to foreign "interlopers." Fired by their sense of Manifest Destiny, Yankee miners felt that since the United States had gained possession of California as a result of the nation's victory in the Mexican-American War, all the wealth in the state belonged only to themselves—the land's new masters. In fact, of course, everyone, regardless of national origin, was a trespasser, for the federal government failed to pass any legislation until the 1866 Lode Law to determine how gold might be taken.[46] In the absence of appropriate laws, the assumptions underlying Manifest Destiny determined proprietary rights.

The miners' nativism was a complex phenomenon, for it also contained a strong dose of class antagonism. They scrutinized foreign groups to see whether the members of a particular group worked mainly as lone prospectors, as informal partners, as members of formally constituted joint-stock companies, or in a type of master-servant or master-slave combination. They noticed that some Sonoran and Chileno miners were peons who had been brought to California to dig gold for their *patrones*, while some Californios and pre-gold-rush Anglo-American settlers were using California Indian laborers in the same way.[47] Assuming that such people were incapable of egalitarian relationships, Yankees deemed them unacceptable in the communities springing up in the gold country. By the same logic, Americans from the southern states who had brought their slaves to mine for them were not welcomed either. All "capitalists" and their subservient "cheap labor" were perceived as enemies of "American working men"—something all the Yankee miners considered themselves to be in their present circumstances, when each man was supposed to work his own claim.

The Yankee miners used two methods to drive the foreigners out—physical intimidation and discriminatory rules and laws. Initially, nativist sentiments applied across the board; even the British and Germans experienced antipathy.[48] But once the expulsion campaign began, the English, Irish, and Germans lined up on the side of Americans against the other foreigners, in the process solidifying their own standing as honorary Americans.[49] In contrast, the French encountered hostility partly because of their apparent disinterest in adopting Anglo-American language and culture, partly because they kept mainly to themselves both in San Francisco and in the mines, and partly because of their friendly relations with the Latin American miners. Declared the authors of *The Annals of San Francisco:*

> The French complain that they are not treated so kindly . . . as are the Germans. The reason seems obvious. It is because they do not take the same pains to learn the American language and character. The naturalized Germans are professed and acknowledged brethren; the French—foreign in manner and physical appearance, in thoughts and hopes—can never be considered as such. . . . the wild glorification of Frenchmen to every thing connected with their beautiful France, is often a neglectful insult to the land that shelters them.[50]

In short, Americans found French cultural chauvinism offensive.

As for why the French chose to associate not with Americans but with Mexicans, Chilenos, and Peruvians, no definitive explanation has been given. One possible hypothesis is that, in addition to their shared Catholicism, the social composition of the French miners, as well as the route used by many of them to get to California, may account for their affinity for the Spanish-speakers. Jacques Moerenhout, the French consul at Monterey, first notified the French government of the gold discovery in a letter dated May 15, 1848. Then, on August 17, he sent Paris a long dispatch reporting what he had seen during a six-week tour of the gold country.[51] The first newspaper article on the gold discovery appeared on November 13, 1848, in *Le Journal des Débats*, which reprinted a piece from a New York newspaper.[52] But only after the French press began to publicize President James K. Polk's December 5, 1848, message to the U.S. Congress did the French public begin to believe the news. In January 1849, the first advertisement appeared indicating that a ship, *Le Meuse*, had been chartered to sail for San Francisco on February 15. However, the first

A French miner delightedly discovers an enormous gold nugget in *Travail en Californie,* one of a series of three hand-colored lithographs published about 1850 in Paris. "Upon reaching the diggings," runs the caption, "the workers seize their tools and compete with one another in their search for fortune. Here the rocks raised by the pickax yield gold nuggets; there, with the scraper, the ore is pulverized and the gold gathered—and each day the miners meet with the same good fortune, filling their strongboxes with treasure." Thousands of Gallic Argonauts set off for El Dorado when word of the discovery reached Europe, and by 1854 the population of the state included thirty thousand French-speaking Californians, some of whom had been inspired to leave their native land by images such as this. *Courtesy California State Library.*

sizable group of Frenchmen, numbering about forty people, did not land in San Francisco until September 1849. Between November 1849 and April 1851, more than 4,000 people from France traveled by sea to California, departing from the three main French ports of Le Havre, Bordeaux, and Marseilles and following the Cape Horn route.[53] Three years later, the estimated number of French people in California had risen to between 25,000 and 30,000. These figures are much larger than the 1,546 counted in the 1850 census. The discrepancy can be explained by two facts: (1) most of the French-speaking people came in the early 1850s, after the census was taken, and (2) an estimated two-thirds of them came not directly from France but from Louisiana, Quebec, and French possessions in the Pacific Ocean, such as Tahiti. Thus, the 25,000 to 30,000 figure included all French-speaking people, a large proportion of whom were no longer French nationals or had not been in France for a long time.

Of those who came directly from France, some were scions of aristocratic families, others were middle class, while the majority were poor. The gold discovery coincided with a period of upheaval in France. Louis Philippe, the French monarch, was overthrown in February 1848. Several months later, Louis-Napoléon was elected as president of the Second Republic. Riots erupted periodically. The *petit bourgeois* who owned government bonds lost their savings as bond values plunged. There was fear of an impending famine, as well as of a cholera epidemic. In such troubled times, emigration offered one way to relieve social pressures. The existing French colonies were to be the main emigrant destinations, but soon California was considered another possibility.

To enable those without funds to get to the new El Dorado, eighty-three joint-stock companies—many with alluring names, such as *Le Californienne, L'Aurifère, La Fortune, La Ruche d'Or, L'Eldorado,* and *La Nouveau Monde*—were formed in 1849 and 1850 by promoters with the aim of making money from California gold, a booty for the taking by one and all. A majority of the shareholders were not aspiring miners but speculators, investors who bought shares at prices ranging from five francs to several hundred francs per share. The capital thus raised was to be used to pay the passage of laborers who would go to California to dig for the precious metal. An analysis of extant passenger lists indicated that many of the recruits came from small provincial towns and villages.[54] There were also a significant number of Basques.[55]

In some instances, the emigrants bound themselves to three years of labor in exchange for their transportation. In other cases, emigrants bought shares in the companies in order to acquire the status of *travailleurs associés* (associated workers) instead of being simply contract laborers. The profit-sharing scheme varied from one company to another. A typical division was 40 percent to the shareholders, 40 percent to the mining laborers, and 20 percent to the promoters who had set up the companies. Unfortunately, some of the companies were fraudulent, while others went bankrupt. Not only did the shareholders in those ventures lose all their money, but the would-be miners who landed in California were often left destitute, without money, food, mining tools, and shelter. With no funds, they could not even get their luggage unloaded and ferried to shore because ships had to anchor in San Francisco Bay, rather than dock at a wharf, given the harbor's severely overcrowded conditions. Neither could they afford transportation to the mines. The French consul ended up taking care of many of those who were stuck in San Francisco.[56]

In addition to the joint-stock companies, the French government also got into the act of promoting emigration to California. It became the patron of *La Compagnie des Gardes Mobiles,* which shipped more than 130 former volunteers bearing that name to California. These men had helped to put down riots in 1848 but had become unruly and difficult to control afterwards, so sending them to California was a way to get rid of them. The *gardes mobiles* retained their military organization after their arrival in California. Then, in May 1850, the Paris police authorized a giant lottery called *l'ingot d'or*, with tickets to be sold until November of the following year. The grand prize was a gold nugget worth 400,000 francs (approximately $20,000). Smaller prizes included 244 gold bars and 200 prizes of 1,000 francs each. The lottery was a way to raise money to ship off an anticipated 5,000 "undesirable people," including political radicals, petty criminals, and prostitutes. A total of 3,470 people left by this means.[57]

Since many of the people who came from France directly were either members of the lower class or were middle-class people suffering from downward social mobility, perhaps they had a tendency to identify with others, including the Spanish-speaking groups, who were also down and out.[58] Regardless of what might have been the basis of the bond between French- and Spanish-speakers, notices that appeared in the mining camp of Sonora in May 1850 made it apparent that such a sense of commonality did exist:

> It is time to unite: Frenchmen, Chileans, Peruvians, Mexicans, there is the biggest necessity of putting an end to the vexations of the Americans in California. If you do not intend to allow yourself to be fleeced by a band of miserable fellows who are repudiated by their own country, then unite and go to the camp of Sonora next Sunday: there will we try to guarantee security for us all, and put a bridle in the mouths of that horde who call themselves citizens of the United States, thereby profaning that country.[59]

The Frenchmen and Latin Americans marching into Sonora were delegates representing about five thousand of their compatriots from throughout the Southern Mines, who had met to decide upon a course of action to protest the Foreign Miners' Tax of twenty dollars a month that the California legislature had imposed upon all foreign miners in April 1850. Since most placer miners averaged less than twenty dollars' worth of gold dust a month, the tax would create enormous hardship on those required to pay it. Moreover, though it was supposed to be collected from all foreign miners, in fact, only certain foreigners—primarily French- and Spanish-speakers—bore the brunt of the tax collectors' action. The American miners in the vicinity of Sonora were both affronted and alarmed by the gathering of foreigners—affronted because the Frenchmen, Chilenos, and Sonorans had raised their nations' flags over their camps, and alarmed because they feared an imminent assault from these incensed groups. The Americans gathered about 180 well-armed men and, led by the sheriff of Tuolumne County, confronted the foreign crowd, which dispersed after drafting a memorial to the state governor stating they would be willing to pay a lower tax of four or five dollars a month but objecting to twenty dollars a month, not only because it was too much, but also because it was unjust.[60]

Scholars have offered different explanations with regard to the motives of the legislators who had levied the tax. Leonard Pitt thought its intention was to exploit the foreigners. Richard Peterson argued that it was to exclude them from the gold country altogether. Richard Morefield believed its aim was to remove competition, given the fact that the Sonorans and Chilenos were superior miners.[61] More important than the motives of the legislators, however, was the law's impact: the tax legally sanctioned the anti-foreign violence that had begun to emerge the year before and helped institutionalize a pattern of race relations that has persisted to the present day.

The first nativist acts in the gold fields were resolutions passed by groups of American miners to keep foreigners out. Though these resolutions were passed everywhere in the mining country, the largest number appeared in the Southern Mines, where visible contingents of foreigners had congregated. In the spring of 1849, for example, notices appeared there warning all non-U.S. citizens to leave within twenty-four hours.[62] In late September, miners along the North and South forks of the Stanislaus River resolved that "none but Americans" would be allowed to mine in those areas.[63] A resolution passed in Sonora in July 1850 required all foreigners "not engaged in permanent business and of respectable character" to leave within fifteen days. Those who remained had to turn in their firearms and obtain a permit from a self-styled enforcement committee of American miners.[64]

To enforce these resolutions, American miners often resorted to violence. During April 1849, Mexicans, Chilenos, and Peruvians were ordered to leave the area around Sutter's Mill at Coloma.[65] That summer, Sonorans were driven away from placer claims along the Tuolumne, Stanislaus, and Mokelumne rivers.[66] Mexicans, who were employed by an American named Sherlock, who had discovered the diggings in Mariposa County named after him, were evicted from their grounds when Sherlock was away prospecting elsewhere in the mountains.[67] In mid-December 1849, about one hundred Mexicans were each fined one ounce of gold dust and driven away from the banks of the Calaveras River. According to one American who participated in the action, the next morning "all those concerned went before the Alcalde and received our share of the spoils which we obtained from the Mexicans in the shape of fines."[68] Apparently, some nativist activities brought material rewards.

The Spanish-speaking miners did not always accept such maltreatment passively. In a few instances, as happened at Sonora, they fought back. In December 1849, when American miners in Calaveras County attempted to drive some Chileno miners away, the latter obtained a writ from the authorities to arrest several Americans who they claimed had robbed them of fifteen thousand dollars' worth of gold dust. When no Americans were willing to carry out the order, some eighty Chilenos attacked the Americans, killing two and wounding four. They marched the rest of the Americans back to the Chilenos' own camp. When news of this incident got out, hundreds of enraged and heavily armed Americans swore to "shoot down every one of them on the road." The Americans took eleven Chilenos prisoner. Three of them were shot, the others were flogged, while all Spanish-speaking miners in the locality were banished.[69]

Such nativist actions, which had begun before the Foreign Miners' Tax came into existence, became more frequent after it was levied because it sanctioned the expulsion of foreign miners who could not afford to or who refused to pay the tax. The tax collectors, who could keep three dollars of every twenty they collected, were often aided by bands of armed Americans who "roamed the countryside terrorizing the foreign population." Walter Colton, the American who had served as alcalde of Monterey for three years, noted how some Americans, who had organized themselves into a little "army," marched into Sonora and "liquored up" at the saloons before embarking on their forays.[70] Since tax collecting could be lucrative, impostors sometimes preyed upon the foreign miners. Some of these individuals tore up the receipts that the foreigners had in their possession—proof that they had already paid—and coerced them to pay again. In the minds of the Spanish-speaking miners, these violent attempts to extort and expel them were manifestations of *gringos envidiosos,* jealous white men.

Jacques Moerenhout, the French consul, came to a similar conclusion. He thought Americans were "jealous and angry to see [the gold] fall into the hands of foreigners."[71] French miners, as mentioned above, had protested against the discriminatory Foreign Miners' Tax.[72] The French consul, ever sensitive about French national honor, tried diligently to protect the rights of his compatriots. In the summer of 1852, the claims of some French miners, which had been confiscated, were given back to them following the consul's intervention.[73]

The French consul was not the only diplomat to attempt to do something about these discriminatory actions. The Mexican minister to the United States lodged a complaint with the U.S. secretary of state in Washington, D.C., when English-speaking miners (Americans, Englishmen, and Irishmen) in Mariposa County ordered Mexican miners to leave within twenty-four hours in June 1853. After the Mexicans beat a hasty retreat, taking whatever possessions they could with them, the English-speaking miners auctioned off the Mexicans' ore-bearing grounds and mining equipment for thirteen hundred dollars. With the proceeds, they paid off three hundred dollars' worth of debts owed by the Mexicans to a local merchant and then divided the rest of the take among themselves. Although the State Department did order an investigation upon receiving the Mexican minister's complaint, the U.S. district attorney who looked into the matter concluded he could "find nothing upon which to base a claim of twenty thousand dollars"—the amount the Mexican miners said they had lost.[74] No further action was taken.

American and British miners were successful in these expulsion campaigns; thousands of Latino and French miners left the gold country in 1850, 1851, and 1852.

Some of the Spanish-speakers returned to their native lands while others went to San Francisco, to the smaller towns, or to the rural areas, especially in southern California, to earn a living at menial jobs. Those who remained in mining retreated to more remote areas where they hoped to escape molestation, or they survived by working for American miners or mining companies as low-paid wage laborers. Their status as "cheap labor," however, only served to increase the hostility Anglo-American miners felt toward them.[75] Frenchmen also sought sanctuary in San Francisco, where they specialized in work that enhanced life's comforts. They ran hotels and restaurants, sold French wines, brandies, breads, and condiments, opened department stores that became the mainstays of San Francisco's fashionable set—the City of Paris and the White House—and virtually monopolized bootblacking.

As the economic impact of the immigrant exodus from the Southern Mines became apparent, the class interests of merchants came into play and quickly overrode the miners' nativism. Latino miners had spent whatever gold they had acquired freely. Not only did they gamble away much of their riches, but Mexicans, in particular, tended to buy various merchandise to take back to Mexico at the end of each mining season. Merchants in Stockton—the main distribution point for provisions and other goods destined for the Southern Mines—complained bitterly as these Spanish-speaking customers left. Major suppliers in San Francisco also became concerned. A long editorial in the *Alta California* pinpointed the problems it saw with the Foreign Miners' Tax. The newspaper called the tax

> decidedly unconstitutional, unjust, impolitic, opposed to every principle of our free institutions, behind the age, illiberal and foolish. . . . We have said to the world, we are free, come and enjoy freedom with us. . . . Knowing this, tens of thousands of miners came to California in the full belief that they would not only meet with gold, but far better, justice and kindness. From Mexico and Peru, and Chile they flocked here, better miners than our own people. They dug, they got gold, and they spent it freely. . . . But the iniquitous law was passed. . . . They could not stand it. They left by thousands and tens of thousands. The Southern Mines especially felt the stunning blow. Stockton was knocked completely on the head. . . . The law gave to the unprincipled of our own countrymen and others claiming to be such a wide scope for oppression. . . . Wrongs and robberies led to murders and anarchy, and general prostrations of business. The state has been injured to the value of millions of dollars. . . . While the human devils who hail from the penal colonies are allowed all the rights of our own citizens because they speak the English language, a quiet and laborious people have been driven from among us because they did not speak that language.[76]

In short, the editor's concerns were moral as well as economic. Since the *Alta California* was an influential newspaper, its editorials reflected the perspectives of one of the state's most important opinion-makers.

In light of such criticisms, and because it never raised the vast revenues anticipated, the legislature repealed the first Foreign Miners' Tax in March 1851. A more
reasonable tax of three dollars a month was imposed in May of the following year,
but the Spanish-speaking miners never returned in large numbers. Instead, the second Foreign Miners' Tax found a new target—the Chinese, over 20,000 of whom
landed in California in 1852. Their appearance coincided with a new stage in gold-
rush history, during which placer mining declined and capital-intensive methods of
extracting gold (river, deep shaft or quartz, and hydraulic mining) using wage labor
became ascendant. The egalitarianism that the miners had tried to promote in the
early years gave way to hierarchical class relations. During this same period, the nativism that had been directed against the Latin American and French miners, who
did not speak English and were foreign-born and Catholic, metamorphosed into a
racism against African Americans and Chinese, whose skin color and other pheno-
typical features differed from those of white Anglo-Saxon Protestants.

FROM NATIVISM TO RACISM AND RESISTANCE

"Race" and "racism" are too complex to be discussed at length in this essay. Suffice it
to say that "race" is a concept used to divide groups of human beings into categories
based on perceived differences in their bodies. However, since the divergence within
one "race" can be greater than the disparities among the various "races," there is no
valid biological basis for these racial categories. Nevertheless, race is a powerful concept because it is infused with psychological, social, cultural, and political meaning.
As such, it is an important aspect of a society's structure. Most scholars today would
agree that what "race" signifies is changeable, and is socially constructed and historically determined. "Racism," meanwhile, refers to the ideology used to justify the hierarchical ranking of different "races" at a given time, as well as the concrete practices
employed by one group of human beings to dominate other groups and to discriminate against the latter. In the United States, racial differences have traditionally
been depicted as a black and white dyad, but the arrival of significant numbers of
Chinese in California in 1852 gave race relations there a unique twist.

By 1852, there were over 2,000 persons of African ancestry in California—that
number having grown from only a few dozen in early 1848. Not all were from the
United States. Some had come from Latin America and the various Caribbean islands. Of the American-born, some were enslaved, having been brought from the
southern states by their masters to help dig for gold. En route, these slaves scouted
the terrain, gathered firewood, prepared meals, washed clothes, hitched wagons,
and performed other chores. At least half of the African American Argonauts, however, were free blacks from the northeastern seaboard, especially Massachusetts and
New York, who, like everyone else, came in search of fortune. They traveled via the

same overland and sea routes that other Americans and Europeans took. Their presence was often noted, albeit fleetingly, in the contemporary diaries and journals as well as later reminiscences that have been preserved.[77]

Less well known were the gold seekers of African ancestry from places outside the United States. By the time gold was discovered in California, people of African ancestry had been in the Americas for more than three centuries. Black people had been integral parts of the Spanish expeditions that had explored and colonized Mexico and South America since the early sixteenth century; some had been a part of the colonizing population of California itself from the 1760s. They, along with enslaved or peonized Native Americans, had performed the arduous labor to extract the gold and silver that had enriched Spain's coffers. They had also worked in the haciendas and ranchos that formed the foundation of the Spanish empire's pastoral economy. Yet others had performed domestic service or practiced various skilled trades in the towns.[78] Brazil, Portugal's colony in the Western hemisphere, meanwhile, had received more enslaved Africans than any other single country in the New World—a conservative estimate of over three million people who, after arrival, labored mostly in sugar plantations. Among the first individuals of African ancestry to join the California Gold Rush were sailors from Mexico, Chile, Peru, the Caribbean, and New Bedford (New England's major whaling port); they, like many American and European crews, deserted their ships as soon as the vessels anchored in San Francisco Bay and set off for the gold country.[79]

Like miners of other ethnic or national origins, black miners, though relatively small in numbers, left their marks on the land. In the racist parlance of the day, place names such as Nigger Hill, Nigger Bar, and Arroyo de los Negros attest to not only their presence but also their success, for when a mining camp was named for a particular ethnic group, it generally signaled the luck that miners of that ethnicity had had at that spot. Those enslaved African Americans who managed to find some gold used it to purchase their own freedom, which often cost as much as two thousand dollars, as well as the freedom of their family members left behind. According to the Rev. Darius Stokes, blacks in California sent about three-quarter million dollars to their loved ones in the early 1850s to purchase the latter's freedom.[80]

Some slave owners who did not strike it rich tried to recoup the expenses they had incurred by hiring out or selling their slaves. Thus, from the beginning, both enslaved and free African Americans in California engaged in a diversity of occupations, though most of these were of low status. The individuals who attained middle-class status were those who managed to save enough to open stores, hotels, and restaurants. Since racial segregation was practiced everywhere except in the gambling parlors, blacks had to establish facilities to serve their own people.

According to the 1852 state census, more than 1,000 blacks were found in the mining counties, more than 400 in San Francisco, and 300-plus in Sacramento.

A black miner pauses from his labors with a long tom to pose for a daguerreotype in Auburn Ravine, Placer County, in 1852. By this date two thousand Argonauts of African ancestry had arrived in California, some coming as slaves of southern gold hunters, others as free blacks from the New England states and New York, and still others from the Caribbean and Latin America. *Courtesy California State Library.*

The African American communities in Marysville and Stockton ranked next in size. Nigger Hill, where about 400 miners worked in 1855, contained the largest collection of black miners, but Chinese, Portuguese, and Anglo-American miners could also be found there. Fights occasionally broke out in that multiethnic mining community. In contrast, blacks were not harassed at nearby Massachusetts Flat, which was inhabited by miners of African and Portuguese ancestry from the state after which the locality was named.[81]

There being relatively few African American miners, no organized campaign developed to drive them out of the mines. Just as telling, the individuals who were lynched during the Gold Rush were not blacks but Mexicans and Chilenos and, in one instance, a Frenchman. However, blacks in gold-rush California had to fight larger battles for equality, social justice, and basic human dignity. They struggled to gain freedom from slavery, the right to testify in court, the right to vote, and the right for their children to attend integrated schools.

At the time that California became the thirty-first state, slavery, especially its extension into the territories acquired during America's westward expansion, was the paramount controversy in the nation. In the words of one historian, "California became a centerpiece of national debate and a major factor in the development of sectional discord" during the pre–Civil War era.[82] The reason was that its admission into the union upset the formula that had been established thirty years earlier in the Missouri Compromise—that territories would become states in pairs: one free and one slave, in order to preserve the fragile balance between free and slave states. A problem arose because California was the only state seeking admission in 1850. But its statehood could not wait until another territory was ready because the discovery of gold made Congress eager to incorporate California into the nation. Its entry as a free state was part of the Compromise of 1850, which also made New Mexico a territory and abolished the slave trade in the District of Columbia. To placate the slave-owning states, Congress passed a stringent fugitive slave law.

That national compromise was impelled by the fact that delegates to the 1849 state constitutional convention held at Monterey had already decided that slavery should not be allowed in California. They had opposed the "introduction of domestic slavery into the territory of California" not because they were abolitionists but because the miners did not wish to compete against southerners who might use slave labor to search for gold. More hotly debated was the question of whether or not free blacks should be permitted to enter the state. One delegate who opposed their entry declared that such individuals posed a "threat greater than slavery itself" because they were "idle in their habits, difficult to be governed by the laws, thriftless, and uneducated." Another participant predicted that should free blacks be allowed to seek their fortunes in the mines, "the whole country would be filled with emancipated slaves—the worst species of population—prepared to do nothing but steal, or live upon our means as paupers." But African Americans also had their defenders at the convention: one stated that "free men of color have just as good a right, and ought to have, to emigrate here as white men." Another reminded his fellow delegates of their solemn duty: "We are forming a Constitution for the first State of the American Union on the shores of the Pacific. The eyes of the world are turned toward us." For that reason, he said, the California constitution should be "a model instrument of liberal and enlightened principles." Yet another delegate declared that the proposed exclusion of black people was a "great wrong."[83] After weeks of debate, the provision was voted down due to fears that its inclusion might jeopardize California's statehood when the issue came before Congress.

Admission as a free state and the lack of prohibition against the entry of free blacks, however, did not settle the ambiguous status of those enslaved African Americans who had been brought to California before it became a state. Slave masters continued to claim ownership of their chattel or reneged on promises of manumission,

as illustrated by the Perkins case, which involved three slaves from Mississippi—
Carter Perkins, Robert Perkins, and Sandy Jones—who had been taken to California to help dig for gold. A year later, they were hired out to a doctor, who was told
that should the three men perform their duties faithfully and give their earnings to
their owner, they could be freed. Several months later, their new employer informed
them they had fulfilled their obligations and were free. However, their former master, after returning to Mississippi, changed his mind and decided to reclaim his
"property" and sued to get them back. Using the fugitive slave law that California
had passed in April 1852 (the intention of which was to enable masters to keep
slaves who had been brought into California before it became a state), the three men
were arrested and taken to Sacramento. After a convoluted trial, the court ruled
that the three men were still the property of their former owner. They were remanded to jail to await delivery to the latter.[84]

A more celebrated case involved Archy Lee in 1858. By this time, California's fugitive slave law, which had been renewed annually until 1856, had expired. Two months
after Lee and his master arrived in the state, the latter decided to send the former
home to Mississippi. While in San Francisco awaiting passage, Lee escaped but was
soon apprehended. In the next few months, the African American community rose
up to support his fight for freedom. After winding its way through the lower courts,
the case reached the California Supreme Court, which decided that even though
Lee could not be held according to the (federal) fugitive slave law, "there are circumstances connected with this particular case that may exempt him from the operation
of the rules we have laid down." These circumstances were that Lee's young master
was inexperienced and in poor health and needed his services! Thus, the justices
thought he should be returned to his master. Archy Lee's supporters, however, obtained a new writ of *habeas corpus* and finally succeeded in getting him freed.[85]

The issue that California's African Americans fought hardest for was the right to
testify in court. Being barred from testimony and having to rely on white witnesses
meant that blacks had no recourse against those who robbed or assaulted them. To
gain this right, the black community's leaders held statewide "colored conventions"
in 1855, 1856, and 1857, and launched petition campaigns to influence the legislature.[86]
Though the lawmakers rebuffed their requests, African Americans finally did acquire
the right to testify in 1863, during the Civil War.

Black Californians' struggle for the franchise, however, did not bear fruit until after the Civil War, when the Fifteenth Amendment to the national constitution was
passed in 1870, enabling African Americans around the nation to participate in political elections. Their desire to send their children to integrated schools involved
more local efforts. During the early gold-rush years, there were few black women and
even fewer black children in California (the same demographic imbalance characterized all the other ethnic groups in the state as well). But by the mid-1850s, several

hundred African American children had been born in or brought to California. Their parents had to find ways to educate them, as they were not allowed to attend the public schools. Two means were found: some black churches set up private classes for the children, usually in their basements, while boards of education in San Francisco, Sacramento, and elsewhere allocated funds for the establishment of separate "colored schools." By 1873, twenty-one public "colored schools" existed in the state. Though black parents began protesting segregated schooling in the 1860s, and mounted a legal campaign in 1872 to end it, it was not until the 1890 *Wysinger* v. *Crookshank* decision that California's public schools finally opened their doors to black youth.[87]

In addition to the above inequities sanctioned by law and by common practice, African Americans in California also could not use the same public facilities as whites or serve in the militia and military.[88] Such discrimination was definitely racist and not nativist, for black Californians were not foreigners but Americans. Moreover, what they encountered was not simply prejudice but institutional racism: the major institutions of society—the state legislature, the court system, the state franchise board, various local school boards, the armed services, and municipal governments—all used their power to deny African Californians the rights that other Americans enjoyed, solely on the basis of their purported biological and social defects.

Unlike African Americans, who had been oppressed for centuries but who, as American-born persons, could speak English and were familiar with the U.S. Constitution, the American creed, and everyday social practices, the Chinese who came to California during the Gold Rush had no prior experience as oppressed minorities. Yet, despite the countless charges of unassimilability leveled against them, they fought for the very same civil rights as blacks had done, including the right to testify in court, to earn a living without harassment, to become U.S. citizens, to vote, to attend integrated schools, and to marry individuals of a different race.[89]

That the Chinese should engage in such struggles was unexpected because they supposedly were only crossing the ocean in search of wealth, with no intention of making America their permanent home. Although a significant proportion of the other gold seekers also returned to the places where they had lived before they joined the Gold Rush, and could thus be properly characterized as sojourners, the term "sojourner" has been applied by journalists and historians alike only to the Chinese. Thus, by a single stroke of the pen, these writers have relegated Chinese to the margins of American immigration history by claiming they were not "true" immigrants.[90] This unsubstantiated assertion has been questioned only in recent years, when scholars began to uncover how sophisticated the Chinese in fact were, as they used the American judicial and economic systems to garner some rights, as well as a living, for themselves.[91]

Chinese entered the gold fields just as miners began to abandon placer claims already stripped of easily removable nuggets and gold dust. From 1852 or 1853 onward,

A camp of Chinese miners, as depicted by the Scots artist-Argonaut J. D. Borthwick. Although less than a thousand Chinese had reached *Gum San,* the "Golden Mountain," by 1850, within two years they represented nearly a tenth of the total population of the state. Usually excluded from all but worked-out claims, they nonetheless continued to practice placer mining techniques long after the rise of hydraulic and quartz mining. From J. D. Borthwick, *Three Years in California* (1857). *California Historical Society, FN-31566.*

the Chinese became the main—indeed, in some places, the only—placer miners in the state. An analysis of the manuscript U.S. census schedules for 1860, 1870, and 1880 (the 1850 federal and 1852 state manuscript census schedules were not studied because they are unreliable and illegible on many pages) shows how important mining was as an activity to the Chinese. First, they were heavily concentrated in the mining regions and formed a sizable fraction of the total population there, ranging from 12 to 23 percent in the various counties in 1860, 14 to 22 percent in 1870, and 10 to 20 percent in 1880. In comparison, at no time did they exceed 10 percent of the total population of the state as a whole. Second, of the gainfully employed Chinese enumerated in the mining counties, 80 to 90 percent in all three ore-bearing regions were engaged in mining in 1860. A decade later, 50 percent of Chinese in the Northern Mines were miners, 75 percent were similarly occupied in the Southern Mines, while 87 percent of Chinese in the Klamath-Trinity mining region were likewise prospecting for the shiny metal. In 1880, the respective percentages were 71, 52, and 71 percent.[92]

These figures debunk a second widely held myth about Chinese immigration into the United States: that they were primarily imported as "coolies" (contract laborers) to help build the western half of the first transcontinental railroad. That oft-repeated "fact" simply is not true. Like other groups, including Anglo-Americans, the Chinese were initially lured to California by the discovery of gold; only a decade and a half later did they find work in railroad construction. In fact, gold was such a lodestar for the Chinese that they persisted in mining longer than any other ethnic group. They dug and washed and rocked the picked-over, but still ore-bearing, earth, gleaning whatever residue of gold they could find, until they became too old for that sort of arduous labor. The Chinese miners found by census enumerators in 1900 were all quite old because after the Chinese Exclusion Act was passed in 1882, few young immigrants could come to replenish the aging and dwindling Chinese population.

When the Chinese first appeared in the mining areas, they were tolerated because, as the Mexicans, Chilenos, Peruvians, and French left, they were the only group from whom the new Foreign Miners' Tax could be collected. Such revenue enriched the treasuries of the mining counties until 1870, when the tax was declared unconstitutional. Even more importantly, the Chinese were willing to pay handsome prices for the white miners' "tailings" or worked-out claims. Such an unexpected source of income gave the departing miners a last chance to "raise a stake." Still, Yankee miners complained that "Chinamen are getting to be altogether too plentiful in the country."[93] Attempts were made to expel Chinese from some locations. For example, sixty white miners drove away two hundred Chinese from Mormon Bar on the American River and later another four hundred from Horse Shoe Bar.[94] There were also efforts to exclude the Chinese from Columbia, Rough and Ready, Wood's Creek, Foster's Bar, and Yuba River Camp.[95]

In addition, the state legislature levied a so-called "commutation tax," which required the masters of ships arriving in California ports to submit a list of all foreign passengers and to post a bond of five hundred dollars for each such individual. This bond, however, could be commuted by paying a fee ranging from five to fifty dollars per passenger. Although the Chinese were not explicitly named in this measure, they were, in fact, its main targets. Most of the time, the commutation fee was five dollars, which the shipping companies simply added to the cost of passage and thereby passed on to their Chinese customers.[96]

Despite these hostile acts, Chinese could be found all over the mining regions. Their headquarters was at Chinese Camp in Tuolumne County, which had the largest congregation of Chinese miners in the state and served as the distribution point not only for the Southern Mines but also for all the Chinese mining camps from Plumas County in the north to Mariposa County in the south.[97] There was even a significant number of Chinese miners in the northwestern part of the state, the first contingent of thirty-five having arrived in Siskiyou County in May 1853.[98] This area was so remote that some Chinese found it sufficiently safe to invest in the expensive equipment needed for hydraulic mining—a venture they did not dare undertake in the more populous Northern and Southern Mines, where the chances of their being evicted were higher.

Aside from the mining camps, Chinese also gathered in urban Chinatowns, each of which occupied a small section of towns such as Angels Camp, Auburn, Coloma, Columbia, Coulterville, Grass Valley, Hornitos, Knights Ferry, Mokelumne Hill, Nevada City, Placerville, and Sonora. The Chinatowns contained grocery and dry goods stores, gambling joints, opium dens, brothels, restaurants, and boardinghouses, most of which were housed in shanties. The gambling, opium-smoking, and eating places, as well as the houses of prostitution, were frequented by Chinese and non-Chinese alike.

Chinese in the mining areas earned a living in other ways when they were prevented from mining themselves. As large companies formed to sink deep shafts into the ore-bearing hardrock, which had to be excavated by experienced workers and crushed and processed with heavy machinery, highly skilled miners from Cornwall, England, became the employees of choice. The hardrock miners formed unions and kept the Chinese out, but the latter found work as cooks, wood gatherers, laundrymen, farmers, produce dealers, and herbalists to serve the other miners' needs. (Miners were among the first European Americans to discover the efficacy of traditional Chinese medicine.)

Although the Chinese managed to earn a living, they were abused and discriminated against even more blatantly than blacks, given their larger numbers and consequently the greater threat they were perceived to pose. But, like African Americans, they also fought back. As early as April 1852, Chinese community leaders who had learned English began to protest the negative ways in which their people were being depicted. In a letter to Governor John Bigler, who had made an anti-Chinese statement, Har Wa and Long Achik, two merchants in San Francisco, took exception to his calling all Chinese "coolies." They pointed out that

> there are no Chinese drunkards in your streets, nor convicts in your prisons, madmen in your hospitals, or others who are a charge to your state. They live orderly, work hard, and take care of themselves . . . we are good men; we honor our parents; we take care of our children; we are industrious and peaceable; we trade much; we are trusted for small and large sums; we pay our debts and are honest; and, of course, must tell the truth.[99]

The following month, Norman Asing, another Chinese who was literate in English, sent a second letter to the governor in which he stated:

> we would beg to remind you that when your nation was a wilderness, and the nation from which you sprung *barbarous*, we exercised most of the arts and virtues of civilized life; . . . we are not the degraded race you would make us. . . . You say that "gold, with its talismanic power, has overcome those natural habits of non-intercourse we have exhibited." I ask you, has not gold had the same effect upon your people, and the people

of other countries, who have migrated hither? Why, it was gold that filled your country (formerly a desert) with people, filled your harbors with ships . . . You cannot . . . assert that the cupidity of which you speak is ours alone; . . . Thousands of your own citizens come here to dig for gold, with the idea of returning as speedily as they can.[100]

Chinese not only insisted on their right to be in the United States but soon began to use American institutions, especially the political and judicial systems, to
defend themselves. Thus, in 1853, in response to bills introduced to increase the Foreign Miners' Tax, several Chinese community leaders, accompanied by white attorneys they had hired, met with the state legislature's Committee on Mines and
Mining Interests, during which they rebutted allegations that they were importing
indentured laborers. They supplied information on the Chinese population in the
state and the means by which they had come. Although they did not oppose a reasonable increase in the Foreign Miners' Tax, they did complain about the increasing
violence that Chinese miners were encountering and provided details about numerous physical attacks. They pointed out that the Chinese had no recourse to justice
because the courts would not accept Chinese testimony. The Chinese leaders were
apparently persuasive, for the committee recommended that the Foreign Miners' Tax
be increased by only a dollar a month.[101]

Furthermore, Chinese miners did not hesitate to turn to the local courts when
they were robbed of their gold dust either by other Chinese or by white miners or
when they were evicted from claims they were working.[102] Such action contradicts
the stereotype of them as a people who insulated themselves from the larger society
around them. To handicap them in these legal proceedings, the statute barring Native Americans and African Americans from testifying against whites in California's
courts was formally extended to the Chinese in 1854, in the case of *People* v. *Hall*.[103]
Just as black Californians tried to do, the Chinese fought hard to overturn this prohibition. But they did not succeed until 1872—nine years after blacks had done so.
Not only did it take them longer to achieve this goal, but in 1863 Chinese were additionally barred from testifying in civil cases as well.

Unable to testify in court, "Chinamen are robbed and murdered with impunity,
because they are defenseless and have no remedy," as the *Mountain Democrat* put
it.[104] In a report made by a committee of the state legislature in 1862, it was stated
that eighty-eight Chinese miners were known to have been murdered by whites,
eleven of them by collectors of the Foreign Miners' Tax. The committee concluded
that "it is a well known fact that there has been a wholesale system of wrong and out-
rage practiced upon the Chinese population of this state, which would disgrace the
most barbarous nation upon earth."[105] Only in one instance did the Chinese win a
modest victory with regard to the Foreign Miners' Tax and the physical abuse they
had endured. In 1861, in the case of *Ex parte Ah Pong*, the state supreme court over-

turned a sentence against a Chinese laundryman who had refused to pay the Foreign Miners' Tax, after it was revised to apply to all foreigners living in the mining districts, regardless of their occupation.[106]

Despite the similar injustices they faced, African Americans and Chinese in gold-rush California failed to identify with one another or to join in a common struggle. On the contrary, they showed considerable antipathy to one another. In his letter to Governor Bigler, Norman Asing objected to Chinese being grouped together with blacks:

> you have degraded the Negro because of your holding him in involuntary servitude, and because for the sake of union in some of your states such was tolerated, and amongst this class you would endeavor to place us. . . . Your Excellency will discover, however, that we are as much allied to the African race and the red man as you are yourself, and that as far as the aristocracy of *skin* is concerned, ours might compare with many of the European races.[107]

Neither did the Chinese hesitate to express negative views about California Indians. After the 1854 *Hall* decision, Lai Chun-chuen, a San Francisco Chinese merchant, wrote a letter to Governor Bigler in which he declared:

> your honorable people . . . have come to the conclusion that we Chinese are the same as Indians and Negroes, and your courts will not allow us to bear witness. And yet these Indians know nothing about the relations of society; they know no mutual respect; they wear neither clothes nor shoes; they live in wild places and in caves.[108]

African Americans, for their part, denigrated the "grotesque" appearance of Chinese men, with their queues and "vacant Know Nothing face[s which are] expressive of nothing but stupidity." Echoing the views of white Americans, black Americans faulted the Chinese for being "heathens" and having no "regard for the sanctity of the Christian oath." Philip Bell, a prominent black pioneer newspaper editor in California, urged his readers "not to employ the Chinese nor purchase goods from them."[109] African Americans sought to distance themselves from the Chinese by reminding European Americans that black people were different from the Chinese. As Bell put it, the black American "is a native American, loyal to the Government, and a lover of his country and her institutions—American in all his ideas; a Christian by education, and a believer in the truths of Christianity."[110] In short, African Americans used nativist arguments to elevate themselves vis-à-vis the Chinese. It should be noted, however, that there were also African Americans who sympathized with the Chinese and opposed efforts to exclude them from the country.[111]

Such mutual antagonism between two minority groups indicates how pernicious racism can be in a mixed, fiercely competitive society in which all groups were prone to extreme ethnocentrism. In gold-rush California, not only did racism help whites to justify their oppression of peoples of color, but it also fueled a scramble among the latter for status, opportunities, and white approval—approval to be gained, they thought, by denigrating other nonwhite groups. But that sad history of human failings can also be interpreted dialectically: the struggles for civil rights mounted by Californians of African and Chinese ancestry bear witness to the fact that often it is people who have been most wronged who fight the hardest for liberty and justice. In the case of the Chinese, even though they may have retained their clothing, hairstyle, food preferences, language, religion, and other aspects of daily life—and in that sense did not seem to have assimilated—they, in fact, assimilated to a far greater degree than they have been given credit for, in terms of their fervent desire for fair play and equality. Life (the safety of one's person and the right to earn a living), liberty (the freedom to reside where one wishes, to associate with whomever one wishes, and to say whatever is on one's mind), and the pursuit of happiness (the ability to acquire wealth through honest labor and to partake of human conviviality) are, after all, the very things that define the national identity of the United States. In short, resistance to efforts to *deny* them such basic rights is, in a profound, albeit unconventional, sense, a form of patriotism on the part of American-born blacks, and of assimilation on the part of Chinese immigrants.

CONCLUSION

When we examine the historical experiences of black and Chinese Californians alongside one another, it is apparent that the early 1850s was a period during which racial lines hardened. Those divisions were codified and sanctioned by a series of laws: the 1852 Fugitive Slave Act, the reimposition in 1852 of the Foreign Miners' Tax, the 1852 enactment of a "commutation tax," and the extension of the prohibition against black, mulatto, and Indian testimony to the Chinese in the 1854 *People* v. *Hall* decision. These laws and their official enforcement, as well as de facto implementation through social coercion and even mob violence, all worked to keep Californians of color "in their place." Each discriminatory law and its implementation represented what sociologists Michael Omi and Howard Winant have called a "racial project . . . simultaneously an interpretation, representation, or explanation of racial dynamics, and an effort to organize and redistribute resources along particular racial lines." Cumulatively, such racial projects constitute the process they have called "racial formation," during which "racial categories are created, inhabited, transformed, and destroyed."[112]

One concrete manifestation of racial formation in California was the increasing segmentation of the labor market, in which the more dangerous, menial, and low-paid jobs with little job security and built-in channels for advancement became the province of racial minorities (and of women), while the cleaner, better paid, and more prestigious occupations with greater job security and more possibilities for upward mobility became the preserve of European American men. Thus, while the labor of nonwhite groups was still wanted, their place was now to *serve* the needs of the emerging dominant Anglo-American majority—in contrast to the latter's self-appointed role, which was to own the state's resources, control its decision-making apparatus, dominate all other ethnic groups and women of all backgrounds, and define what was culturally acceptable. This process of stratification had begun during the Spanish and Mexican periods, but it accelerated with the Gold Rush. The creation of such a hierarchy involved five sub-processes vis-à-vis peoples of color: the *exploitation* of their labor, the *denial* of their civil rights, the *aversion* of social contacts with them, the *deprivation* of their chances for upward mobility, and the insistence on *deference* in their behavior toward the European American majority. The rapid emergence of such an unequal society—one that goes against the professed American creed—is one of the darker legacies of the Gold Rush we need to remember as we commemorate its sesquicentennial.

NOTES

1. Manuel P. Servin, "California's Hispanic Heritage: A View into the Spanish Myth," *Journal of San Diego History* 19 (1973): 1–9; Harry Kelsey, "A New Look at the Founding of Old Los Angeles," *California Historical Quarterly* 55 (1976): 327–39; and William Mason, "Tracking the Founders of Los Angeles," *Museum Alliance Quarterly* 6 (Summer 1967): 26–27 and 30.

2. There are many markers of ethnicity. In this chapter, I shall focus on language and religion. Since these two phenomena are also aspects of culture, "ethnicity" and "ethnic identity" will be used interchangeably with "culture" and "cultural identity" in this study.

3. For a fuller historiographical evaluation, see Sucheng Chan, "Immigrants and Minorities in the Historiography of the California Gold Rush" (forthcoming).

4. Hubert H. Bancroft, *California Inter Pocula*, vol. 35 of *The Works of Hubert Howe Bancroft* (San Francisco: The History Co., 1888); Bancroft, *History of California*, vols. 6 and 7 (1884–1890); Theodore H. Hittell, *History of California*, vol. 3 (San Francisco: Pacific Press, 1885–1897); and Josiah Royce, *California from the Conquest in 1846 to the Second Vigilante Committee in San Francisco: A Study of American Character* (1885; New York: Alfred A. Knopf, 1948). Theodore Hittell's brother, John, actually published the first chronicle of the state, but the only immigrant group singled out for special comments were the French: John S. Hittell, *A History of the City of San Francisco and Incidentally of the State of California* (San Francisco: A. L. Bancroft & Co., 1878), 185 ff. Quotes are from Bancroft, *California Inter Pocula*, 236, and Royce, *California*, 357 ff. and 222.

5. John S. McGroarty, *California: Its History and Romance* (Los Angeles: Grafton, 1911), 209–38; Henry K. Norton, *The Story of California: From the Earliest Days to the Present* (1913; Chicago: A. C. McClurg, 1926), 216–17, 228, 288, and 291; Zoeth S. Eldredge, *History of California*, vol. 3 (New York: Century History Co., 1915), chapters 4, 5, and 7 (the reference to Mexicans is on p. 189); and Gertrude Atherton, *California: An Intimate History* (1914; New York: Boni & Liveright, 1927), 123 (the Chinese are covered in chapters 20 and 21).

6. Robert G. Cleland, *A History of California: The American Period* (New York, 1922; New

York: Macmillan, 1927), chapters 17 and 19 (the discussion of foreign miners is on pp. 280–83); Rockwell D. Hunt and Nellie van de Grift Sanchez, *A Short History of California* (New York: Thomas Y. Crowell Co., 1929), 380 and 391; and John W. Caughey, *California* (1940; New York: Prentice-Hall, 1953), chapter 16.

7. Carey McWilliams, *California: The Great Exception* (New York: Current Books, 1949), 25 and 63.

8. Ibid., 86–88.

9. Andrew F. Rolle, *California: A History* (New York: Thomas Y. Crowell Co., 1963); Walton Bean, *California: An Interpretive History* (New York: McGraw-Hill, 1968); Ralph J. Roske, *Everyman's Eden: A History of California* (New York: Macmillan, 1968); Warren A. Beck and David A. Williams, *California: A History of the Golden State* (Garden City: Doubleday, 1972); David Lavender, *California: Land of New Beginnings* (New York: Harper & Row, 1972) and *California: A Bicentennial History* (New York: W. W. Norton for the American Association for State and Local History, 1976); and Edward Staniford, *The Pattern of California History* (San Francisco: Canfield Press, 1975).

10. Lavender, *California: Land of New Beginnings,* see esp. 157, 161, 166, 186, and 209–26.

11. Howard A. DeWitt, *California Civilization: An Interpretation* (Dubuque: Kendall/Hunt, 1979); Howard A. DeWitt, ed., *Readings in California Civilization* (Dubuque: Kendall/Hunt, 1981); Kevin Starr, *Americans and the California Dream, 1850–1915* (New York: Oxford University Press, 1973); James J. Rawls, ed., *New Directions in California History: A Book of Readings* (New York: McGraw-Hill, 1988); James J. Rawls and Walton Bean, *California: An Interpretive History,* 7th ed. (New York: McGraw-Hill, 1998); Richard B. Rice, William A. Bullough, and Richard J. Orsi, *The Elusive Eden: A New History of California,* 2nd ed. (New York: McGraw-Hill, 1996); Sucheng Chan and Spencer C. Olin, eds., *Major Problems in California History* (Boston: Houghton Mifflin, 1997); and David Wyatt, *Five Fires: Race, Catastrophe, and the Shaping of California* (Reading, Mass.: Addison-Wesley, 1997).

12. In Patricia Nelson Limerick, *The Legacy of Conquest: The Unbroken Past of the American West* (New York: W. W. Norton, 1987), and Richard White, *"It's Your Misfortune and None of My Own": A New History of the American West* (Norman: University of Oklahoma Press, 1991)—two works of synthesis that exemplify the "New Western History"—only a few pages in each book are devoted to the Gold Rush. A succinct statement of the New Western Historians' view of race is found in Richard White, "Race Relations in the American West," *American Quarterly* 38 (1986): 396–416.

13. Owen C. Coy, *Gold Days* (San Francisco: Powell, 1929); John W. Caughey, *Gold Is the Cornerstone* (Berkeley: University of California Press, 1948; the paperback edition, published in 1975, appeared under the title *The California Gold Rush*); Rodman W. Paul, *California Gold: The Beginning of Mining in the Far West* (Cambridge: Harvard University Press, 1947); Paul, *Mining Frontiers of the Far West, 1848–1880* (New York: Holt, Rinehart and Winston, 1963); William S. Greever, *The Bonanza West: The Story of Western Mining Rushes, 1848–1900* (Norman: University of Oklahoma Press, 1963); Otis E. Young, Jr., *Western Mining: An Informal Account of Precious-Metal Prospecting, Placering, Lode Mining, and Milling on the American Frontier from Spanish Times to 1893* (Norman: University of Oklahoma Press, 1970); J. S. Holliday, *The World Rushed In: The California Gold Rush Experience, An Eyewitness Account of a Nation Heading West* (New York: Simon & Schuster, 1981); Paula M. Marks, *Precious Dust: The American Gold Rush Era, 1848–1900* (New York: William Morrow, 1994); and Malcolm

J. Rohrbough, *Days of Gold: The California Gold Rush and the American Nation* (Berkeley: University of California Press, 1997).

14. Paul, *California Gold,* 45, 47, 134–37, 142, and 152.

15. Joseph R. Conlin, *Bacon, Beans, and Galantines: Food and Foodways on the Western Mining Frontier* (Reno and Las Vegas: University of Nevada Press, 1986); Doris M. Wright, "The Making of Cosmopolitan California: An Analysis of Immigration, 1848–1870," *California Historical Society Quarterly* 19 (December 1940): 323–43, and 20 (March 1941): 65–79; and Ralph J. Roske, "The World Impact of the California Gold Rush, 1849–1857," *Arizona and the West* 5 (Summer 1963): 187–232.

16. Due to space limitations, writings about the European immigrant groups cannot be cited here. See Chan, "Immigrants and Minorities," for a listing of the available literature. The copious material on the Jews is due partly to the existence of a journal, *Western States Jewish History* (originally called *Western States Jewish Historical Quarterly*).

17. Only a few of the writings about African Americans, Chinese, Mexicans, Chilenos, and Peruvians will be cited below. For fuller listings, see Chan, "Immigrants and Minorities."

18. Robert L. Santos, *The Gold Rush of California: A Bibliography of Periodical Articles* (Denair, Calif.: Alley-Cass Publications, 1998).

19. Corrective in the sense discussed by Jim Sharpe, "History from Below," and Joan Scott, "Women's History," in *New Perspectives on Historical Writing,* ed. Peter Burke (University Park: Pennsylvania State University Press, 1991), 24–41 and 42–66, respectively.

20. For incisive discussions of these changes, see Maureen A. Jung, "Capitalism Comes to the Diggings: From Gold-Rush Adventure to Corporate Enterprise," *California History* 77 (Winter 1998/99): 52–77; and Daniel Cornford, "'We all live more like brutes than humans': Labor and Capital in the Gold Rush," *California History* 77 (Winter 1998/99): 78–104.

21. Seville A. Sylva, *Foreigners in the California Gold Rush* (San Francisco: R & E Research Associates, 1972), 4.

22. Richard Dillon, "Kanaka Colonies in California," *Pacific Historical Review* 24 (February 1955): 17–23.

23. Ralph S. Kuykendall, *The Hawaiian Kingdom, 1778–1854,* vol. 1 (Honolulu: University of Hawaii Press, 1938; 7th printing, 1989), 319–24; and Roske, "World Impact," 189–93.

24. Stephen Giacobbi, *Chile and Her Argonauts in the Gold Rush* (San Francisco: R & E Research Associates, 1974), 8.

25. George E. Faugsted, Jr., *The Chilenos in the California Gold Rush* (San Francisco: R & E Research Associates, 1973), 14.

26. Wright, "Making of Cosmopolitan California," 326.

27. As quoted in Giacobbi, *Chile and Her Argonauts,* 18.

28. Faugsted, *Chilenos in the California Gold Rush,* 19.

29. Wright, "Making of Cosmopolitan California," appendix D, 342.

30. J. M. Guinn, "Early Gold Discoveries in Southern California," *Publications of the Historical Society of Southern California* 3 (1895): 10–16.

31. Wright, "Making of Cosmopolitan California," 324.

32. Jay Monaghan, *Chile, Peru, and the California Gold Rush of 1849* (Berkeley: University of California Press, 1973), 98–101.

33. Charles Bateson, *Gold Fleet to California: Forty Niners from Australia and New Zealand* (East Lansing: Michigan State University Press, 1964), 20–21; and Jay Monaghan, *Aus-*

tralians and the Gold Rush: California and Down Under, 1849–1854 (Berkeley: University of California Press, 1966).

34. Sherman L. Ricards, Jr., and George M. Blackburn, "The Sydney Ducks: A Demographic Analysis," *Pacific Historical Review* 42 (February 1973): 20–31.

35. Robert A. Burchell, "The Gathering of a Community: The British-Born of San Francisco in 1852 and 1872," *Journal of American Studies* 10 (1976): 281.

36. Bateson, *Gold Fleet,* 38.

37. J. D. Borthwick, *Three Years in California* (Edinburgh and London: William Blackwood & Sons, 1857), 239; and Sylva, *Foreigners,* 25.

38. The dividing line between the Northern and Southern Mines was "the ridge on the north side of the north fork of the Mokelumne River" (Theodore H. Hittell, *History of California,* vol. 3, 109). On the Southern Mines, see Roberta E. Holmes, *The Southern Mines of California: Early Development of the Sonora Mining Region* (San Francisco: Grabhorn Press, 1930); William R. Kenny, "History of the Sonora Mining Region of California, 1848–1860" (Ph.D. diss., University of California, Berkeley, 1955); and Elizabeth G. Potter, "Columbia— 'Gem of the Southern Mines,'" *California Historical Society Quarterly* 24 (September 1945): 267–70. On the Northern Mines, see Edmund Kinyon, *The Northern Mines: Factual Narratives of the Counties of Nevada, Placer, Sierra, Yuba, and Portions of Plumas and Butte* (Nevada City: Union Publishing Co., 1949).

39. Carlos U. Lopez, *Chilenos in California: A Study of the 1850, 1852, and 1860 Censuses* (San Francisco: R & E Research Associates, 1973), tables I and II, xvii and xviii.

40. Ibid., xii; and Giacobbi, *Chile and Her Argonauts,* 20.

41. Faugsted, *Chilenos in the California Gold Rush,* 25.

42. Bancroft, *History of California,* vol. 6, 124, note 27.

43. James M. Guinn, "The Sonoran Migration," *Historical Society of Southern California Annual* 8 (1909–1911): 33.

44. Ray Allen Billington, *The Protestant Crusade, 1800–1860: A Study of the Origins of American Nativism* (Gloucester, Mass.: Peter Smith, 1963); and John Higham, *Strangers in the Land: Patterns of American Nativism, 1860–1925* (New Brunswick, N.J.: Rutgers University Press, 1963).

45. Bancroft, *History of California,* vol. 6, 396–402 and 227–28.

46. Richard H. Peterson, *Manifest Destiny in the Mines: A Cultural Interpretation of Anti-Mexican Nativism in California, 1848–1853* (San Francisco: R & E Research Associates, 1975), 36.

47. James J. Rawls, "Gold Diggers: Indian Miners in the California Gold Rush," *California Historical Quarterly* 55 (Spring 1976): 28–45.

48. Helen B. Henniker-Gray, "The Beginnings of Nativism in California, 1848–1852" (M.A. thesis, University of California, Berkeley, 1948), 20, 30, and 31.

49. Theodore H. Hittell, *History of California,* vol. 3, 736.

50. Frank Soulé, John H. Gihon, and James Nisbet, *The Annals of San Francisco* (New York: D. Appleton & Co., 1855), 463–64.

51. Abraham P. Nasatir, *The French in the California Gold Rush* (New York: American Society of the French Legion of Honor, 1934), 7–8.

52. Gilbert Chinard, "When the French Came to California: An Introductory Essay," *California Historical Society Quarterly* 22 (December 1943): 291–92.

53. Wright, "Making of Cosmopolitan California," 71.

54. Chinard, "When the French Came," 307.

55. George Cosgrave, trans., "The French Revolution: Translated from the French of F. Gerstacker's *Scenes de la Vie Californienne*," *California Historical Society Quarterly* 17 (March 1938): 4.

56. Chinard, "When the French Came"; and Henry Blumenthal, "The California Societies in France, 1849–1855," *Pacific Historical Review* 25 (August 1856): 251–60.

57. Chinard, "When the French Came," 311–12; and Blumenthal, "California Societies in France," 258.

58. This statement may seem to contradict Doris Wright's view that the immigrants who came directly from France were "largely from the middle class," with many skilled mechanics and professionals (Wright, "Making of Cosmopolitan California," 72). However, due to the economic losses suffered by many members of the middle class in the aftermath of the 1848 Revolution, even they might have been penurious.

59. Henniker-Gray, "Beginnings of Nativism," 38.

60. Faugsted, *Chilenos in the California Gold Rush*, 42.

61. Leonard Pitt, "The Beginnings of Nativism in California," *Pacific Historical Review* 30 (February 1961): 23–38; Richard H. Peterson, "The Foreign Miners' Tax of 1850 and Mexicans in California: Exploitation or Expulsion?" *Pacific Historian* 20 (Fall 1976): 265–70; and Richard H. Morefield, *The Mexican Adaptation in American California, 1846–1875* (San Francisco: R & E Research Associates, 1971).

62. M. Colette Standart, "The Sonoran Migration to California," *Southern California Quarterly* 58 (Fall 1976): 340.

63. Richard H. Morefield, "Mexicans in the California Mines, 1848–53," *California Historical Society Quarterly* 35 (March 1956): 38.

64. Morefield, *Mexican Adaptation*, 9.

65. Richard H. Peterson, "The Mexican Gold Rush: 'Illegal Aliens' of the 1850s," *The Californians* 3 (May/June 1985): 19.

66. Standart, "Sonora Migration," 340.

67. Peterson, "Mexican Gold Rush," 19; and Morefield, "Mexicans in the California Mines," 38.

68. William R. Kenny, "Mexican-American Conflict on the Mining Frontier, 1848–52," *Journal of the West* 6 (October 1967): 587.

69. Ibid., 587–88; Morefield, *Mexican Adaptation*, 3–5.

70. Kenny, "Mexican-American Conflict," 591.

71. Ibid., 583–84.

72. For an account of a tragicomic incident involving French miners in the vicinity of Sonora, see Cosgrave, "French Revolution."

73. Morefield, *Mexican Adaptation*, 12.

74. George Cosgrave, "A Diplomatic Incident on the Little Mariposa," *California Historical Society Quarterly* 11 (December 1942): 360–61.

75. Winifred Storrs Hill, *Tarnished Gold: Prejudice during the California Gold Rush* (San Francisco: International Scholars Publications, 1990), 27–28.

76. Quoted in ibid., 29–30; and in Henniker-Gray, "Beginnings of Nativism," 41–43.

77. Rudolph Lapp, *Blacks in Gold Rush California* (New Haven: Yale University Press, 1977), 12–48; and B. Gordon Wheeler, *Black California: The History of African-Americans in the Golden State* (New York: Hippocrene Books, 1993), 39–65.

78. Kenneth G. Goode, *California's Black Pioneers: A Brief Historical Survey* (Santa Barbara: McNally & Loftin, 1974), 3–36.

79. Lapp, *Blacks in Gold Rush California,* 49.

80. Goode, *California's Black Pioneers,* 59.

81. Lapp, *Blacks in Gold Rush California,* 52.

82. Ronald C. Woolsey, "A Southern Dilemma: Slavery Expansion and the California Statehood Issue in 1850—A Reconsideration," *Southern California Quarterly* 65 (Summer 1983): 123.

83. Gordon M. Bakken, "Constitutional Convention Debates in the West: Race, Religion, and Gender," *Western Legal History* 3 (Summer/Fall 1990): 229.

84. Ray Albin, "The Perkins Case: The Ordeal of Three Slaves in Gold Rush California," *California History* 67 (December 1988): 214–27 and 187–89.

85. William E. Franklin, "The Archy Case," *Pacific Historical Review* 32 (May 1963): 137–54. For other cases, see Lapp, *Blacks in Gold Rush California,* 126–57.

86. Lapp, *Blacks in Gold Rush California,* 186–238. For the text of the proceedings of these conventions, as well as one held in 1865, see Philip S. Foner and George E. Walker, eds., *Proceedings of the Black State Conventions, 1840–1865,* vol. 2 (Philadelphia: Temple University Press, 1972), 110–205.

87. Charles M. Wollenberg, *All Deliberate Speed: Segregation and Exclusion in California Schools, 1855–1975* (Berkeley: University of California Press, 1976), 8–27.

88. Wheeler, *Black California,* 55.

89. It is outside the scope of this essay to discuss the sustained efforts made by the Chinese to gain civil rights. For a succinct summary, see Sucheng Chan, *Asian Americans: An Interpretive History* (Boston: Twayne Publishers, 1991), 45–61 and 81–100. For a more detailed exposition, see Charles J. McClain, *In Search of Equality: The Chinese Struggle Against Discrimination in Nineteenth-Century America* (Berkeley: University of California Press, 1994).

90. For a discussion of this historiographical issue, see Sucheng Chan, "European and Asian Immigration into the United States in Comparative Perspective, 1820s to 1920s," in *Immigration Reconsidered: History, Sociology, and Politics,* ed. Virginia Yans-McLaughlin (New York: Oxford University Press, 1990), 37–75; and Franklin Ng, "The Sojourner, Return Migration, and Immigration History," *Chinese America: History and Perspectives, 1987* (San Francisco: Chinese Historical Society of America, 1987), 53–72.

91. The two books that point most clearly in this direction are Sucheng Chan, *This Bittersweet Soil: The Chinese in California Agriculture, 1860–1910* (Berkeley: University of California Press, 1986); and McClain, *In Search of Equality.*

92. Chan, *This Bittersweet Soil,* tables 2, 3, 4, and 5, on pp. 48, 54, 62, and 68.

93. Stephen Williams, "The Chinese in the California Mines, 1848–1860" (M.A. thesis, University of California, Berkeley, 1930), 63.

94. Ibid., 66–67.

95. David V. DuFault, "The Chinese in the Mining Camps of California, 1848–1870," *Historical Society of Southern California Quarterly* 41 (1959): 156.

96. McClain, *In Search of Equality,* 12–13.

97. Williams, "Chinese in the California Mines," 75. Also see Irene D. Paden and Margaret E. Schlichtmann, *The Big Oak Flat Road: An Account of Freighting from Stockton to Yosemite Valley* (Oakland: Holmes Book Co., 1959), 67–92; and Anne Bloomfield, Benjamin

F. H. Ananian, and Philip P. Choy, *History of Chinese Camp: Cultural Resources Inventory* (Sonora: Tuolumne County Historical Preservation Review Commission, 1994).

98. Nancy Wey, "Chinese Mining in Siskiyou County, Northern California," *East/West*, October 25, 1978, 7.

99. Har Wa and Long Achik, "The Chinese in California: Letter of the Chinamen to His Excellency Gov. Bigler," *Living Age* 34 (April 29, 1852).

100. Norman Asing, "To His Excellency Governor Bigler from Norman Asing," *Daily Alta California*, May 5, 1855.

101. McClain, *In Search of Equality*, 15–16. In 1855, the tax was raised to six dollars a month, with a provision for augmenting it further by two dollars per year thereafter. However, the 1855 levy was repealed the following year, with the tax set again at four dollars a month.

102. I have found two dozen legal briefs in Nevada County (whose county seat, Nevada City, had the largest Chinatown in the Northern Mines) in which Chinese sued each other as well as whites. I have not written up my findings, but a brief summary of the issues addressed in these cases may be found in McClain, *In Search of Equality*, 295–96, note 122.

103. David Beesley, "More than *People* v. *Hall:* Chinese Immigrants and American Law in a Sierra Nevada Town, 1850–1920," *Locus* 3 (Spring 1991): 123–39; Charles J. McClain, "The Chinese Struggle for Civil Rights in Nineteenth Century America: The First Phase, 1850–1870," *California Law Review* 72 (July 1984): 548–53; and Hudson N. Janisch, "The Chinese, the Courts, and the Constitution: A Study of the Legal Issues Raised by Chinese Immigration to the United States, 1850–1902" (J.D. diss., University of Chicago Law School, 1971), 50–61.

104. Quoted in Janisch, "The Chinese, the Courts, and the Constitution," 60.

105. California State Legislature, "Report of the Joint Select Committee Relative to the Chinese Population of the State of California," *Journals of the Senate and Assembly*, Appendix, vol. 3 (Sacramento: State Printing Office, 1862), 7.

106. McClain, *In Search of Equality*, 24.

107. Asing, "To His Excellency," 127–28.

108. Chun-chuen Lai, *Remarks of the Chinese Merchants of San Francisco, upon Governor John Bigler's Message and Some Common Objections; with Some Explanation of the Character of the Chinese Companies, and the Laboring Class in California* (San Francisco: Whitton, Towne and Co., 1855).

109. Arnold Shankman, "Black on Yellow: Afro-Americans View Chinese-Americans, 1850–1935," *Phylon* 39 (Spring 1978): 2 and 6.

110. As quoted in Leigh Dana Johnsen, "Equal Rights and the 'Heathen Chinee': Black Activism in San Francisco, 1865–1875," *Western Historical Quarterly* 11 (January 1980): 61.

111. David J. Hellwig, "Black Reactions to Chinese Immigration and the Anti-Chinese Movement: 1850–1910," *Amerasia Journal* 6 (1979): 30–31. Also of interest is Dan Caldwell, "The Negroization of the Chinese Stereotype in California," *Southern California Quarterly* 53 (1971): 123–31.

112. Michael Omi and Howard Winant, *Racial Formation in the United States: From the 1960s to the 1990s*, 2nd ed. (New York: Routledge, 1994), 55–56.

4

"Because he is a liar and a thief"

Conquering the Residents of "Old" California, 1850–1880

James A. Sandos

History to the defeated
May say Alas, but cannot help or pardon
      —W. H. Auden, "Spain 1937"

Capitulate or assassinate? Seeking a way to follow the only path he thought honorable and to avoid the act that a majority of his young warriors had demanded of him, Kientipoos, the Modoc war chief known to whites as Captain Jack, began by pressing his alternative plan to Gen. Edward Canby. On Good Friday, April 11, 1873, Canby had come to Jack's stronghold in the lava beds, in remote northeastern California, below Tule Lake, to negotiate peace on Canby's terms. For twenty years white settlers had been moving steadily onto Modoc sacred land. Whites had displaced the Modoc by opening roads, planting 28,000 acres in crops, opening five quartz mines, and logging 4.2 million lumber feet of timber. In the process, whites increased their number to 9,500 against the Modoc population of less than 300. The Modoc retaliated with raids and killing. The U.S. Army, along with volunteers, had fought the Indians and in the early 1860s, forced them onto a reservation to the north with their numerically larger, long-standing enemies, the Klamath. In doing so, the military enforced American Indian policy, which not only removed the Modoc from their territory but also consequently subjected them to death by their reservation neighbors.[1]

Frustrated, Kientipoos and about 150 followers left in April 1870 for their former lands to the south. The Modoc's return enraged worried whites and precipitated new violence. Conflict escalated to the point that General Canby commanded a force of one thousand troopers, Indian scouts, and volunteers when he went to meet Kientipoos. Canby intended that the Modoc immediately surrender and return to their

HARPER'S WEEKLY.

JOURNAL OF CIVILIZATION

Vol. XVII.—No. 853.]   NEW YORK, SATURDAY, MAY 3, 1873.   [WITH A SUPPLEMENT. PRICE TEN CENTS.

Entered according to Act of Congress, in the Year 1873, by Harper & Brothers, in the Office of the Librarian of Congress, at Washington.

THE MODOCS IN THEIR STRONGHOLD.—[See Page 361.]

A sensationalistic rendering of *The Modocs in Their Stronghold* fills the 3 May 1873 cover of *Harper's Weekly*. Defying federal authorities who had forced them to share a reservation with the Klamath, their traditional foes, some fifty Modoc warriors and their families followed the war chief Kientipoos, or Captain Jack, to the wild volcanic terrain of the lava beds bordering Tule Lake. For months they successfully held off a vastly superior force of U.S. Army regulars until, their resistance crushed, they were resettled in the far-off Indian Territory of Oklahoma. *California Historical Society, FN-05449.*

assigned reservation. Canby dismissed as foolish the warning from his Modoc interpreter and cousin of Kientipoos, Winema (little woman-chief), that the Modoc planned to kill him and the other commissioners during the meeting.

Canby began by saying, "I know I will be able to make you see things right today. You will see as I see. Jack, I know that you are a smart man . . . you understand everything good now. The white man's law is straight and strong. What I say is law[.]" Holding up a sagebrush twig, Kientipoos replied that "your law is as crooked as this." But first, Kientipoos tried peace, telling Canby that "If you promise me a home, somewhere in this country, promise me today; although your word is not much good, I am willing to take you at your promise." Canby remained silent. Realizing the futility of talk, Kientipoos said to his braves "ut wih kutt" (let's do it), then drew his revolver, pointed at Canby's face, and squeezed the trigger. Misfire. The second round did not. Canby, struck below the right eye, reeled backward, mortally wounded. Kientipoos had done what his young warriors wanted and in so doing foresaw the consequences for his people: whites would vanquish them. After a long war, Kientipoos was captured, tried, and executed as Captain Jack. The surviving Modoc were resettled in Indian Territory (Oklahoma), where, by the early twentieth century, no full bloods remained and the Army believed that their culture had been extinguished. The Modoc War, 1872–1873, cost the Army its only officer of the rank of general ever killed in the Indian wars (George Armstrong Custer held the rank of lieutenant colonel when he died at the Little Big Horn in 1876), and nearly $1.6 million of today's dollars for each of the five Modoc warriors killed.

Kientipoos and the Modoc represent California Indians' most violent response to American conquest; within their story, in varying degrees, however, lies those of all the other tribes. They are tales of outsiders taking land and game, destroying the ecological basis of Indian life while killing Indians outright if they either objected or did not move out fast enough; of a new legal system that sanctioned the outsiders' behavior; of Indian agents both sincere and corrupt creating a phantom reservation system; and of a confused national Indian policy subverted by local interests. In the words of historian Hubert Howe Bancroft, "the advance of settlement was everywhere marked by a more or less revolting treatment of the natives."[2] While true, we should not let such blanket descriptions of victimization blind us to Indian coping strategies for dealing with this catastrophic change.

Nor were Indians the only older residents of California to suffer devastating consequences from the new American order. Most Californios, whether of native or foreign birth, lost heavily to the newcomers legally, economically, socially, and culturally. While Canby and Kientipoos negotiated in the lava beds, far to the south in San Diego, English-born Juan (John) Forster took to an American court the last Mexican governor of California, Pío Pico—who was also Forster's brother-in-law and

The famed Andrés Pico, scion of an old California family and brilliant commander of the Californios' forces at the Battle of San Pascual, in the early 1850s. Pico and his brother Pío, the last governor of Mexican California, lost enormous land holdings when—like so many other Californios—their lack of business experience, extraordinarily high interest rates, falling cattle prices, and the great drought of the 1860s led them to default on mortgages. *Courtesy Seaver Center for Western Research, Los Angeles County Museum of Natural History.*

godfather—to extinguish Pico's claim to the Santa Margarita Rancho. Forster claimed that Pico had given him full interest in the rancho, today the site of Camp Pendleton, in return for money lent to pay Pico's debts. Pico countered that he had given Forster only one-half interest in the property. Despite the truth of Pico's claims, Forster won and Pico lost the land. Pico survived another twenty years "living off the charity of friends," and died owing his landlady two years' rent.[3]

Many Californios lost their land through carelessness and swindle; Indians were driven out and killed. The suffering of both groups from the influx of settlers invading their spaces was further complicated by the legal entanglement in American courts of their land titles conferred by previous governments. Americans, viewing land ownership differently from Californios and Indians and anxiously seeking to claim land for themselves, impatiently awaited the surveying and parcelization of "vacant" territory, which then could be theirs.

NORTHERN CALIFORNIA INDIANS

Californios exploited the new wealth of the discovery of gold by following their well-established pattern. Utilizing Indians from their ranchos or from adjacent Indian rancherias, Californios supervised Indian labor and reaped the profits while the Indians did the work of panning for gold; in return, Indians received little more than subsistence. Californios such as John Sutter, John Bidwell, James Savage, and Antonio Coronel all used Indian labor to find gold. After a few months local Indian tribes decided to pan on their own. They were, however, generally cheated of the full value of their discoveries. "You know . . . no Christian man is bound to give full value to those infernal red-skins," a store keeper at a trading post on the American River reportedly said. "They are onsoffisticated vagabones and have no more bissiness with money than a mule or a wolf; they've got no religion, and tharfore no consciences, so I deals with them accordin."[4]

When outsiders arrived, many of them took offense at the use of gang-labor because it threatened the interests of individual (and white) effort. Breakdown in cooperation between Indians and whites in mining is generally attributed to men from Oregon Territory, the nearest outsiders to arrive. They quickly made known their displeasure about Californios employing Indians as miners. In March 1849, Oregonian miners entered a southern Maidu village on the American River. In the course of their actions they raped several Indian women; the Maidu men tried to stop it and some were killed. Soon after, five Oregon miners were attacked and killed; their comrades retaliated with another raid in which they killed more than a dozen Indians and captured many more. Seven of the Indian prisoners were taken to Coloma, site of the initial gold discovery, where the Oregonians promptly executed

Indians attack an encampment of miners in a wood engraving from a design by the celebrated gold-rush artist Charles Nahl. Conflict between Argonauts and natives broke out
in the spring of 1849, when, in reprisal for outrages against several of their women, a party
of Maidu killed five miners from Oregon Territory at what would subsequently be called
Murderers Bar, on the American River. Quickly retaliating, the Oregonians hunted down
and slaughtered several Indians, precipitating a series of bloody encounters that drove most
natives from the mines. *California Historical Society, FN-31548.*

them. While the Oregonians did not represent all the white men working claims,
their treatment of Indians led to a tense racial climate in the diggings and ushered
in a period of tolerated abuse and destruction of "diggers." The Coloma tragedy
caused Indians to flee the mines. Whereas when the Oregonians arrived in 1848,
more than half the miners were Indians, following the Coloma incident one observer
noted that Indian labor, "once very useful, and in fact, indispensible . . . has been utterly sacrificed by this extensive system of discrimination and revenge."[5]

While the Indians withdrew their labor, the hostilities begun against them led to
recurring skirmishes. Indians attacked the white men's cattle and hogs, which
ranged upon their land devouring the seeds, grasses, roots, and acorns vital to Indian
survival. Those Indians who could stood their ground in their villages, but since
these were invariably in places well-watered, with good exposure to sun, and pro-

tected against wind and flood, whites coveted them. Fighting back was one option. Augustin Hale, a midwestern emigrant who arrived in the diggings after the Coloma episode in 1849, expressed fear that Indians would steal his animals as they had done to other miners. A year later, after meeting with another group of miners, he wrote in his diary: "This party like all others who have learned from sad experience, positively affirms that it will not do to allow even *one* of them [Indians] to come into camp for they will *surely prove treacherous.*" Despite his admonition, Hale's own experiences proved that Indian-white relations could not be reduced to such a simple formula. When he arrived in Sacramento, he and his companions had "breakfasted on salmon bought of the Indians." At year's end he noted that he "had been sick two months and lived nearly all that time on acorn and beef." The scarcity of wheat flour made its price dearer than many miners could afford. Out of flour, in desperation, and despite the illness plaguing Hale and his party, they nonetheless gathered acorns to make bread. They could only have obtained the knowledge and technique for this process from Indians.[6]

Even as hostilities between Indians and whites spread throughout the mining districts—northern, central, and southern—another set of problems emerged in the area of governmental policy toward native peoples. For nearly two hundred years, first while still British colonies and later as a sovereign nation, the policy of the United States had favored removal: the physical relocation of Indians away from the flow of white settlement. With the conquest of California and its incorporation into the union, federal officials began to rethink the policy of removal. Since Manifest Destiny had carried America from sea to sea, where, then, would the Indians go? Confinement in place for the Indians of the new state—in other words the creation of reservations—emerged as a dominant mode of thinking in Washington. In California, those not directly involved in Indian skirmishing thought the new policy good. Hostile settlers and miners, however, favored continued removal. Newly appointed federal Indian agents and commissioners, therefore, attempted to protect their charges and to negotiate treaties with them in a contentious environment.[7]

An insight into these conflicts comes from the interactions among the pre-American-conquest resident John Bidwell and his Indian neighbors against encroaching miners and settlers. Bidwell had come to California in 1841, worked for Sutter, learned Spanish and the methods for employing Indian labor, and obtained a land grant to the Rancho Chico on the Feather River, site of present-day Chico. When gold was discovered upriver in the Sierra foothills, Bidwell employed Indians to mine for him; he soon extracted more than $100,000 from his operation, known as Bidwell's Bar. Indians had to wade into the cold water to pan and were paid two red calico handkerchiefs a day if they worked well, one if they did not. When the Oregonians objected to his use of Indian labor, Bidwell withdrew from active mining.

John Bidwell poses with Indians from the Yana, Wintun, Maidu, and other tribes at the store and post office on his Rancho Chico, about 1852. Bidwell, who had come to California in 1841 with the first overland emigrant party, employed large numbers of Sacramento Valley natives on his land and tried to protect them from the depredations of miners and of rival Indian tribes. He also worked in the new state legislature to obtain lands for the Indians in return for peace, but, sadly, his efforts had unfortunate consequences. *Courtesy Meriam Library, Special Collections, California State University, Chico, and Bidwell Mansion State Historic Park, Chico.*

He bought more land and gathered Indians together to live on his rancho, both to avoid the attacks of miners and to work for him. Indians who lived in that vicinity mainly came from the tribes of Mechoopda, Wintun, Yana, and Maidu. Bidwell provided them with food, clothing, beads, and protection from whites. Within a few years they had sowed 300 acres of grain and 435 acres of wheat and oats for Bidwell, who in turn prospered further from selling the food and the flour made from his gristmill to miners and settlers.[8]

In late summer 1851, one of the eighteen treaties concluded with California Indians by federal Indian commissioners was signed at Bidwell's ranch. It created reser-

vations in several adjacent areas in which the Indians were to be confined in return
for keeping the peace with whites. The reservations, however, included foothill land,
the prime target of miners, who immediately began encroaching and filing claims.
Hostilities ensued, as they did everywhere in the mining districts where such reservations were created. Newcomers now wanted Indian labor, but on new terms. Miners and settlers took advantage of a law that, ironically, Bidwell had helped to craft.
The 1850 Act for the Government and Protection of Indians, designed to preserve
Indian labor for Californios, allowed whites to take Indians as indentured servants.
Newcomers raided Indian villages to take women as sex slaves and children as servants and workers. These marauders either took Indians for themselves or, in busi-
nesslike fashion, sold their victims to others. Even after the law was repealed during
the Civil War, these kidnapping raids provided constant points of conflict.[9]

Sheltered by their host, Indians at Bidwell's ranch weathered the surrounding
storms of conflict in relative calm until the early 1860s. By then, retaliatory raids by
some Indians finally struck at white children, and the resultant outcry for Indian removal could not be stilled. Bidwell himself reluctantly agreed with the federal sug-
gestion to round up the Indians in his area and remove them 120 miles away to the
reservation at Round Valley. It was a dreadful, but seemingly unavoidable, choice.
The Round Valley Reservation was itself overrun by white squatters, who occupied
about four-fifths of its area. Since many of the whites were single men, the competition, fair and unfair, for Indian women further disrupted Indian life. The widow of
Indian chief Solano, who had seen the despoliation of her own and other native peoples in northern California, later told an interviewer, "I do not like the white man
much because he is a liar and a thief."[10]

Indian removal from Rancho Chico was targeted at the Yana particularly, but the
roundup was so hasty that few if any Yana were included. It was the unlucky Maidu,
Wintun, Mechoopda, and others who became the dispossessed. Gathered together
and escorted by a mixed force of California militia and some federal troops, 461
Indians began an involuntary 120-mile trip down the hot and dusty Sacramento
Valley, then up over the steep Coast Range and down into Round Valley. The lack
of food, disease, and exhaustion that characterized the march killed many. About
277 reached the reservation, many of them sick. Thirty-two more subsequently
died. Some of the more able-bodied fled. It had taken the Indians two weeks to
make the journey; the well-fed and mounted military escort returned to Chico in
just three days.[11]

Initially, the reservations in northern California were no more successful than in
the rest of the state. Reservations failed to keep Indians in or whites out. Despite the
good will and intentions of some of the early Indian agents and subagents, these men
were quickly succeeded by the venal and corrupt, who exploited their positions for
personal profit while failing to feed or protect Indians. Of a total of 3,000 Indians

Maidu headmen with United States Indian commissioners, a poignant image of alien cultures that resonates with failed hopes, broken promises, and, ultimately, the destruction of a native people. *Courtesy George Eastman House, Rochester, N.Y.*

originally under reservation supervision, by the time of the Round Valley removal fewer than 1,000 remained and these were fading quickly into the wild to hide and survive as best they could. And survival was precarious. When whites discovered that the Yana they had wanted to relocate had avoided the roundup, settlers formed volunteer groups to hunt down and kill the natives. At the time of the Gold Rush the Yana had numbered about 1,900. When whites ambushed a remnant group and killed 45 of them in 1867, not enough Yana survived to bury the dead. Over two decades, more than 1,800 Yana died to avenge the deaths caused by them of fewer than 50 whites. Thus within twenty years the Yana numbered less than 100 and went into concealment.[12] The Yahi subtribe had even fewer. Nothing would be heard from them until 1911, when a nearly naked and starving Yana-Yahi man, the last of his tribe, entered the corral of a slaughterhouse in Oroville seeking food. A practitioner of the new discipline of anthropology, Alfred L. Kroeber learned of the "discovery" of this Indian, and Kroeber and his colleagues brought the man to San Francisco for study. They never learned his Indian name and instead called him by the Yana word for man—"Ishi."[13]

Indian population decline had been precipitous under American rule. From about 150,000 native people still living in California at the time of the gold discovery, that number had plummeted to 30,000 in 1860, an 80 percent decline in just twelve years.[14] In the words of historical demographer Sherburne F. Cook, "This desolation was accomplished by a ruthless flood of miners and farmers who annihilated the natives without mercy or compensation."[15] Observers at the time knew that. William Gwin described the plight of California Indians to his colleagues in the U.S. Senate, saying "Their hunting grounds have been destroyed; the rivers where they maintained themselves by fishing the salmon, running through them by the millions, which supported them at certain seasons, are now entirely occupied by miners. The whole of the ground, upon which formerly the trees grew, where they got the acorns they made use of as bread, has been taken up by miners."[16] Added to these causes of Indian decline must be the constant spread of infectious diseases (but without the more severe epidemics of the Spanish and Mexican eras) and the natural causes of age and accident. But it was the unnatural factors, the systematic murders of Indians by whites, that seem to have been the greatest single cause of death after 1848.

Writing at the end of the nineteenth century and lacking the knowledge of more recent human atrocities that the twentieth century would bring, Hubert Howe Bancroft, the first modern historian of California, wrote of this period that "It was one of the last human hunts of civilization, and the basest and most brutal of them all . . . it was not a mark of high merit on the part of the new comers to exterminate them [Indians] so quickly."[17] Whereas historian Frederick Jackson Turner saw the American frontier pushed ever westward by heroic and noble settlers, Bancroft saw a different group in California, one composed of "free trappers, desperadoes, the scum of society, together with unlicensed settlers, knowing no laws and having no protection save of their own devising."[18] Bancroft remarked on the differences in Indian policy between Spain and America but seemed unwilling to draw a comparison to the parallels. Spaniards seeking gold in the Caribbean and more of it in the conquest of the Aztecs, while ruthless in fighting the Indians, did not try deliberately to destroy them. Even though Spaniards regarded Indians as their inferiors, Spaniards nonetheless accepted them and incorporated them as low-caste members of Spanish-created society. Single men seeking gold in California, however, behaved differently. Historian Laurence Hauptman, writing a century after Bancroft, and after carefully examining white behavior in northern California in the 1850s and 1860s, finds that only one word accurately describes what happened to

Indians there: genocide. Using a measured definition of the term, Hauptman concludes that the word can only be precisely used twice in the history of Indian policy in North America, first with the Pequots in Connecticut in the 1630s, and again in northern California in the 1850s and 1860s. In both cases the state supported the murders committed by settlers, whether they organized themselves as militia or acted in informal groups. And in each case the destruction of the Indians, fueled by race hatred, was the goal.[19] From sea to forest, from the Mendocino coast to the lava beds, gold seekers, adventurers, settlers, and thugs carried the destruction of Indians northwest and northeast from the upper mining districts.[20] Fortunately for California Indians, this policy of deliberate genocide was not followed in the rest of the state.

CENTRAL AND SOUTHERN CALIFORNIA INDIANS

Intense but intermittent violence characterized Indian-white relations in the southern mining district, the Sierra foothills south of Coloma. Conflict spread out of the foothills and onto the bottomland of a significant portion of the great Central Valley surrounding Fresno. Federal commissioners continued their negotiations with Indian tribes with the goal of creating reservations. In May 1851, an Indian reservation was created near Fresno; a few days later a small detachment of federal troops established Fort Miller for the protection of Indians and built it with Indian labor. This act initiated in California the military reservation system.[21] But settlers were unhappy with the federal approach. Seeking, and usually finding, support for paramilitary campaigns against Indians from the state legislature, newcomers became progressively more outraged at the treaties the federal representatives concluded with natives they regarded as hostiles. Throughout central and southern California, as well as in the north, from the settlers' viewpoint, the U.S. government's appointees were proposing to *give* land to Indians rather than to extinguish altogether any Indian claim to title.

Acting in good faith, Indian agents in 1851–1852 negotiated eighteen treaties from Humboldt Bay and the Klamath River in the north to Temecula in San Diego County in the south, setting aside as reservation land 7,488,000 acres, or about 7.5 percent of the total state land area. Moreover, nearly 20,000 whites illegally squatting on those reservation lands would have to be removed. Previously favorable public sentiment went sour.[22] The California legislature appointed a special committee to investigate the treaties. In its majority report the committee recommended that the treaties be set aside and all the Indians, save the former mission converts (called neophytes), be removed from the state boundaries. A lone old-time ranchero from the south, J. J. Warner, raised his voice in dissent. Since the Indians had already agreed to the treaties, what right did Americans have to try and annul them unilaterally? "Will it be said," Warner asked, "that while our doors are open to the stranger from the uttermost parts of the earth, we have not spare room for the residence of the once sole inhabitants of our magnificent empire?"[23] State concerns, nonetheless, decisively influenced national policy. In secret executive session, the U.S. Senate rejected the treaties on July 8, 1852 (although that fact was not revealed until more than fifty years later).[24] In August, the Senate, after lengthy debate, agreed to provide $100,000 to purchase food for the Indians who had lost their lands. In the Senate's view, this one-time expenditure of money would buy peace. To ensure that there would be no ongoing relationship, however, the Senate resolution concluded with the following provision: "That nothing herein shall be so construed as to imply the obligation on the part of the United States to feed and support the Indians who have been dispossessed of their lands in California."[25]

The secret rejection of the treaties created further confusion and contention. Reduced to what were no more than temporary reservations, Indians were quickly evicted by white squatters who filed claims to land that Indians thought was theirs, only to learn that it was not. Benjamin D. Wilson, President Millard Fillmore's Indian agent for southern California, in a letter to his subagent, provided the following instructions: "Use all prudent means to protect the Indians, in their rights against impious white men; settle all disputes among themselves; advise with them and encourage them to labor and provide for the maintenance of their families. At present we have no *treaties* to make or supplies to furnish them; our present object is to keep them quiet."[26] With nothing to offer and no power to prevent white encroachment, Indian agents, no matter the nobility of their intentions, were little better than powerless to stop the growing conflict. To calm hostilities, the federal government in 1853 formally imposed a system of military reservations. Utilizing the existing station at Fort Miller as a base, the War Department a year later created Fort Tejon in the Tehachapi Mountains south of the San Joaquin Valley. Eventually five military reservations emerged, but their fates vacillated with federal policy shifts. They were administered by civilian agents who proved mainly to be corrupt, men who charged the government for food and cattle they failed to provide to their charges. Some, like Cave Couts in San Diego County, filed claim and secured title to the very Indian lands they were supposed to protect.[27] Indians with the ability to move away and try something else did so; those who remained were frequently weak and demoralized.

In those areas where Indians proved less contentious, whites used state and local anti-vagrancy laws to control Indian labor. The legislature's 1850 Act for the Government and Protection of Indians also forbade their public loitering and vagrancy. An Indian detained by lawmen, for any reason, and unable to prove employment would be arrested, fined, and if unable to pay, sold at public auction for the fee. For paying the fine, whites could buy an Indian's labor for up to four months. Thus by being indigent, a condition imposed by white invasion and conquest, Indians could be made to work. Intoxicated Indians proved especially vulnerable because whites usually gave them free liquor to initiate the process and did so again after their servitude expired, causing it all to repeat.[28]

Other Indians, including former mission Indians, followed coping strategies of varying effectiveness. In the backcountry inland between Los Angeles and San Diego, Antonio Garra, ex-neophyte from Mission San Luis Rey, led his Cupeño in a tax revolt against an American impost levied on Indians in 1851. Garra sought a pan-Indian effort against the new rulers. His uprising led to the deaths of a few Indians and whites but was crushed by the combined military activity of the Americans and the seizure of Garra by a rival, Juan Antonio, a Cahuilla chief. Juan Antonio then surrendered Garra to the Americans, who tried and executed him. Even Juan Antonio and his Cahuilla suffered from American neglect in maintaining their lands, however. Subsequent white encroachment continued to erode Cahuilla reservations. On the other hand, Manuelito Cota, chief of the Luiseño and later the federal government's appointed chief of the Cupeño following Garra's death, managed to keep Americans sufficiently satisfied that they honored his people's territory, at least until his resignation in 1858. During his tenure the Luiseño, who had farmed land around their central village in Temecula since mission secularization in the 1830s, had become the most prosperous Indians in California. Following Cota's retirement, however, their fortunes declined, slowly at first, then rapidly.[29]

The southern neighbors to the Luiseño, the Diegueño (Kumeyaay), under the leadership of *Capitán* José Panto, struggled to maintain the integrity of their settlement at San Pascual, the site of the only Californio victory over the Americans during the war of 1846–1848. Following American occupation of California, Panto tried to pursue peaceful relations with whites. San Pascual had been organized as a civil pueblo under Mexican rule in the 1830s with an Indian alcalde. The ex-neophytes raised crops and tended cattle, but they also included within their number muleteers, blacksmiths, carpenters, millers, wool-carders, leather-workers, and cheese-makers. In January 1852, Panto signed a treaty of peace and friendship with an American Indian agent and thought his village safe from encroachment as a result. But it was not. In 1856 he complained against white squatters living in the community, but to no avail. Despite assurances that the land had been set aside by executive order as an inviolate reservation, whites continued to move onto Indian land. Apparently through ties of marriage, by 1860 Panto also became headman at the village of Mesa Grande, approximately twelve miles further inland and more remote. As white incursions into San Pascual continued, displacing progressively more Diegueño, many of the Indians sought refuge in Mesa Grande. Panto died in 1874, still fighting white settlement; four years later, it was over. In 1878 "the Superior Court of San Diego County, after hearing the testimony relative to the Indians claim to said land, issued a writ of ejectment in favor of [claimant Perry] Bevington and Deputy Sheriff Ward demolished the Indian huts and moved them off of the land, which land was afterward patented to Perry Bevington."[30] In the phrase of one scholar, white displacement literally pushed Indians "into the rocks" to try and survive.[31]

Compared to northern California, southern California Indians did better in their interactions with whites. The principal reason seems to have been the previous Indian experience with outsiders under Spanish and Mexican rule. Especially for Indians associated with the missions, this background, which included extensive involvement in agriculture, better prepared native peoples to negotiate with, and adapt to, whites than those who had had little or no white contact until the Gold Rush. That southern California was much less affected by the Gold Rush, resulting in a relatively slow influx of new settlers, was also important. In the south, whites at first accepted majority Mexicans, albeit at a step below themselves in their racial hierarchy because Mexicans were mestizos, or racially mixed. Whites also seem to have treated what they perceived as Mexicanized Indians as a type of Mexican—inferior, yes, but people to be dealt with, and perhaps exploited, rather than destroyed.[32] In this context, the Indians surrounding Mission San Fernando fared somewhat better than others in southern California. Indians associated with the mission came from Gabrielino, Chumash, Kitanemak, Tataviam, and Serrano peoples; following mission secularization in the 1830s, they had secured ranchos and villages near the mission. The 1,110- acre rancho of El Escorpión was given in 1845 to Odón Chihuya and two other Indians, who in turn represented upward of thirty more; twenty-one years later the rancho was secured to the Indians by U.S. patent.[33] Through intermarriage of female descendants with French and Basque males, the property eventually became subdivided. Yet El Escorpión represented one of the very few Indian land grants to survive Americanization. Other Indians near the mission settled in the interior along Piru Creek and worked for Californio families as vaqueros and day laborers. One of the important Californio ranchos that continued to maintain an Indian village, drawing native peoples from different tribes, was Rancho Camulos, near present-day Newhall, owned by the Del Valle family. As American intrusion progressed, some San Fernando Indians stayed where they were. Others migrated to the Tejón Ranchería, where although a reservation existed intermittently, cattle ranches needing Indian vaqueros provided continued employment well into the twentieth century.[34] As the cases of El Escorpión and Tejón indicate, the fate of Indians in southern California was linked to that of the Californios through continued contact and work that was different from the north.

The mission of San Fernando, founded in 1797 in the broad valley north of Los Angeles. Descended from neophytes who had labored for the Franciscans, the Indians who inhabited the lands surrounding the old mission had long experience with a conquering race—as well as title to real property in some cases—and fared far better than most natives in the social and cultural turmoil that accompanied the Gold Rush. *California Historical Society, FN-31531.*

THE CALIFORNIOS

American impact on the Californios has been masterfully described by, among others, Robert Glass Cleland, Douglas Monroy, and Leonard Pitt.[35] The Treaty of Guadalupe Hidalgo of 1848, which concluded the Mexican-American War, promised in Article X to respect Mexican land titles, both those that had been perfected under Mexican law and those in the process of being perfected. The U.S. Senate, however, would not accept such a limitation on American authority and so deleted Article X before ratifying the treaty.[36] Those claiming land in California under Spanish or Mexican grants then would have to prove the validity of their titles. On March 3, 1851, Congress created the Board of Land Commissioners to hear such private land claims. The burden of proof lay with the petitioner, meaning that original documents had to be found, copied, notarized, and translated into English to prepare a legal brief to present to the board. American law demanded precise surveys, rather than the general plats, or *diseños*, of Spanish and Mexican usage, and these had to be paid for by the petitioner. To do the work, lawyers and translators had to be hired, depositions taken, and a new legal sea navigated, all at the expense of those who thought they had title. Ultimately, the board heard 809 claims, confirming 604 and rejecting 190 (the rest were withdrawn). Since the board decided finally only *three* of these cases and the rest went to litigation, the final decision lay with higher bodies—district courts, circuit courts, the U.S. Supreme Court. Thus, securing land title was expensive and the process lengthy, taking an average of seventeen years to resolve. Rancheros paid the costs by selling and mortgaging their lands. In the end, 582 private land claims were patented.[37] By then, most of the Californios had lost their land to Americans.

In addition to having to prove their title to the land they occupied, Californios confronted a new problem unknown under Spain or Mexico—land taxes. With statehood, California adopted the general property tax then universal in America, meaning that those owning or claiming to own land in California had to pay annual state and county taxes on it. Failure to pay put the owner in arrears and, if enough time passed, the land could be foreclosed for delinquency. As in defending their land titles, Californios frequently borrowed money to meet these financial obligations, but since interest rates ranged from four to seven percent *a month*, Californios could quickly fall into serious debt. In 1861, for example, Julio Verdugo mortgaged his portion of Rancho San Rafael in Los Angeles County (now Glendale) for $3,445. Paying interest of three percent a month, within eight years his debt had increased to $58,750, and he was landless.[38]

While the question of private legal title dragged through the courts, in time-honored frontier tradition, newcomers squatted on what they regarded as vacant public land, seeking thereby to establish claim to what they wanted to believe was federally held property, which would eventually be open to settlement. When squatting on Indian lands, they frequently prevailed. Politicians appealed to this class for votes since the squatters were numerous and frequently violent. The worst squatter riots erupted in Sacramento, but violence occurred throughout the state. In 1850, squatters rushed in and laid out Oakland on the San Antonio rancho in complete disregard of the Peralta family's rights. In 1853, in Santa Clarita Valley near El Escorpión, northwest of Los Angeles, squatters murdered the owner of Rancho Sespe when he tried to interfere with their claims to land between Santa Paula Creek and Piru Creek. Squatters had become sufficiently powerful that the state legislature passed an act declaring all land to be public until the title could be proven to have passed into private hands. The U.S. Supreme Court eventually declared the statute unconstitutional as a violation of federal authority, but it illustrates squatter power.[39] Squatting also hastened the drive to map the state's lands for division and sale. Surveys by federal, state, and county employees often conflicted because local authorities, eager to get the job done and sell lots, often conducted "saloon surveys" rather than field work. Legal contestation ensued. Yet by 1865, most of California public lands had been plotted. Wetlands, embracing millions of acres of tidelands, salt and fresh marshes, and swamp and overflow lands, which under federal law were subject to transfer to state ownership, proved especially enticing to land speculators.[40] Indians living adjacent to wetlands lost access to food and game. Rancheros frequently found such lands sold from under them. In California, as elsewhere in the world where wetlands were reclaimed, "the poorest landholders and agricultural labourers found their living conditions deteriorating as the loss of their traditional resources through drainage and enclosure led to intensification of economic marginalisation, poverty and landlessness."[41]

Californios held out as long as they did because, initially, the Gold Rush gave their ranching economy, particularly in the south, a boost. In Spanish and Mexican times, cattle had been raised primarily for their low-value hides and tallow. Miners needed beef, however, in addition to the other products, and cattle ranching assumed heretofore unprecedented importance and profitability. With the price of an animal soaring from a few dollars to as high as several hundred dollars a head, herds were gathered from the southern California counties of San Diego, Los Angeles, and Santa Barbara and driven north to market. These cattle drives, led by Californios with Indian vaqueros, took one of two main routes, either up the coast, frequently through the surf and skirting wetlands, or over the Tehachapi Pass into the San Joaquin Valley. Herds going into the valley at the southernmost point assembled at Newhall for the crossing. Once on the valley floor, herders drove their cattle to the east or west before heading north. Along the eastern side in the Sierra foothills, grass and water were more abundant, but there were more tributaries and canyons to cross than on the valley's west side, and the markets of Stockton and Sacramento at trail's end were smaller. The western route, however, meant a difficult and prolonged crossing of the San Joaquin River at its widest point, and the drier region meant less water and grass for the cattle. Proximity to the vast market at San Francisco Bay at its terminus, however, made the route more lucrative. Tens of thousands of cattle yearly made the valley trip.[42] Initially, cattle from what geographer Terry Jordan has called the "Hispanic" ranching system, constituted the vast majority supplied to the mines. But a newer cattle frontier emerged quickly in the central San Joaquin Valley, one Jordan terms the "Anglo Californian" ranching system, dominated by newcomers who replaced Spanish stocks with hardier midwestern bloodlines imported during the 1850s. This newer frontier began to eclipse the southern California ranches by the early 1860s.[43] But in their heyday, Californios of the south made great profits from cattle, profits they spent on gracious living, fancy clothes, silver ornamented saddles, bridles, coats and breeches, and wagers lost on various gaming events, as well as overstocking their ranches.

Both cattle frontiers expanded because of the "no-fence rule," which confirmed older Spanish and Mexican laws privileging the rancher over the farmer. The "open range" philosophy meant that cattle could live off the land. Farmers built fences at their own expense to keep them out, but only if such fences did not obstruct the cattle routes.[44] Cattle drives wrought far-reaching changes to California's environment. Spreading new seeds and animal diseases wherever they went, cattle and horses grazed and trampled the indigenous grasses of coast and valley, setting up conditions for their replacement by hardier and less sweet, invasive European grasses and weeds. Native villages and food sources were disrupted or destroyed by the drives. Environmental degradation accelerated with the twin natural disasters of flood and drought of the early 1860s. In the winter of 1861–62, severe flooding from heavy rains caused thousands of cattle to drown. From 1862 to 1865, severe drought followed the floods, causing hundreds of thousands of cattle to die of starvation and thirst, especially in the south. In Santa Barbara County, 97,000 head of cattle grazed the parched lands in 1863, and by 1865 that number had fallen to 12,100. Surviving cattle everywhere in the south were too weak to make the northbound journey. Loss of income from cattle deaths coupled with ongoing property taxes, the need to litigate to prove their title, and the rapidly falling price of beef caused more and more Californios to lose their land. New and old livestock owners who hung on turned to sheep raising. According to one environmental historian, "this set in motion a pattern of transhumance, or migratory sheep grazing, which virtually devastated the southern Sierra Nevada up to its highest meadows."[45] Sheep grazed grasses even shorter than cattle and enjoyed the same free range as cattle had. Sheep population peaked at six million in 1876, but by then pressures from farmers, who had become more numerous and politically powerful, forced sheepherding out and into the intermountain states. Sheep and cattle raising

The Del Valle family at Rancho Camulos in Ventura County in the late 1880s. Like other Californios, the Del Valles experienced great prosperity in the cattle boom ignited by the Gold Rush, and then suffered from the effects of drought and usurious interest rates. But unlike so many of their friends and neighbors, they managed to keep most of their lands intact, and under the wise guidance of the patriarch Ygnacio, they diversified their holdings and successfully adapted to the new order of American rule and culture. Helen Hunt Jackson spent a few hours at Rancho Camulos one morning in 1882 and later drew heavily upon what she had seen to create the fictional Rancho Moreno in her celebrated romance of old California, *Ramona. California Historical Society, FN-30503.*

had been marginalized. Californio land grants foreclosed by outsiders became parcelized as farms, and this new farming class secured the repeal of the "no-fence" law in 1872, transferring the burden of fencing to the ranchers. Farming would be the immediate agricultural future.[46]

Not all Californios succumbed to the Yankee onslaught. Some of them had sought to join the American union before the war and adapted to changed circumstances afterward. The Del Valle family at Rancho Camulos in the Santa Clarita Valley, for example, made money during the cattle boom and lost heavily from the floods and drought of the 1860s. Ygnacio, the patriarch, saw in these reversals an opportunity to diversify. He borrowed money at high interest rates and planted citrus trees, becoming one of the first in Ventura County to do so. He further invested in nut trees and wine-grape vines. In addition to his twenty-member extended family, Ygnacio also counted two hundred Indians and Mexicans living on his rancho. He sold off other landholdings to consolidate his position at Camulos, and he developed important roles for his sons. Ulpiano and Joventino managed the vineyards, winery, viticulture, and cattle. Reginaldo became a lawyer and politician influential in Los Angeles and capable of managing the family's legal affairs. His brothers proved equally efficient at managing the new economic enterprises that made them similar to American farmers and agriculturalists. The family prospered.[47] Antonio Coronel, close friend of the Del Valles, lived in Los Angeles. He had made money in the mining areas, both with his Indian servants and through bartering with Indians in the gold fields, and had returned south to buy land. His home and some property in Los Angeles he kept, but neither his rancho land claims nor those of his father survived the Land Commission's inspection process. But Coronel remained active in Los Angeles civic life and, among other pursuits, was a school commissioner and a charter member of the Historical Society of Southern California. Coronel continually promoted the retention of Californio customs such as dress, dances, singing, and fiestas.[48] The Pico brothers, Pío and Andrés, also adapted fairly well to the new order. Pío had been the last Mexican governor of the state, and Andrés had led the Californios in defeating the Americans under Stephen Kearny at San Pascual during the war. Afterward both men held political office under the American flag and made and lost money in the cattle boom and bust. Following the downturn, however, neither man moderated his extravagant lifestyle, and the debts mounted. Assumption of their debts for a share of Pío's Santa Margarita rancho by Pío's son-in-law Juan Forster has already been mentioned. The Picos, Coronels, Del Valles, and others of their group saw themselves as Californios, people united by a common language, religion, and shared customs. They saw their ancestry as Spanish, but, on the remote frontier and neglected by Mexico, they mostly identified with their own land, California, and with their group's interests, which differed from Mexico's. Most Californios thought the transfer of their province to the United States to be inevitable. Some thought it desirable.

With the conquest, Americans had to deal with the people who had held political power to effect a smooth transition in rule. Americans, especially southerners, had to confront a disconcerting reality. Some of the mixed-blood Mexicans with whom they would have to work had African ancestry. The Pico brothers were one-eighth African, and Pío visibly reflected it. Andrés did to a lesser extent as well. Whites had to choose: discriminate against potential friends and allies on the basis of skin color or ignore it.[49] Since they called themselves Californios, whites chose to adopt the term as well and to focus on the Spanish ancestry of the Mexican residents, disregarding Mexican antecedents when they could. In the twentieth century, journalist Carey McWilliams called this the "Fantasy Heritage," one that hypocritically ignored the Mexican contribution, past and present, to California.[50] But

The prominent Californio Don Antonio Coronel, dressed in traditional ranchero attire, poses with his wife, Mariana, at their Los Angeles home, *El Recreo*. Adapting easily to American ways, Coronel served as mayor of Los Angeles and later state treasurer, but he cherished his memories of old California, and working to preserve knowledge of days gone by, he assembled a large collection of artifacts and helped to found the Historical Society of Southern California. *Courtesy Seaver Center for Western Research, Los Angeles County Museum of Natural History.*

McWilliams missed the historical point. While Mexicans as Californios preserved and celebrated their culture, whites needed to use the ambiguous construct of "Californio" to avoid the logic of their own racial preferences. Whites, more than Mexicans, constructed this Californio heritage as white European, and then celebrated its accomplishments. Whites did so to curtail the damage to their interests that unbridled racism, with its attendant rejection of the Californios, would have brought them.

CONCLUSION

The story of Indian and Californio response to American conquest reveals that both adversely affected parties played more complex roles than as mere victims of white aggression. Despite the odds against them, and the horrible assault upon Indians, both groups found ways for some of their members to prevail. One of the keys to that success lay in the later protest of activist, Indian reformer, writer, and humanitarian Helen Hunt Jackson. Jackson had written a history of the treaties made and broken by American governments with Indians and published it herself in 1881 as *A Century of Dishonor* and sent a copy, at her expense, to every member of Congress. In recognition of that work, Congress appointed her, along with Abbot Kinney, to investigate the plight of the Mission Indians of southern California. She arrived in the state in 1882 and began her inquiry. In Los Angeles she met Antonio Coronel and his wife and spent many hours in their company. From the Coronels, Jackson learned of Californio culture and history, at least their version of it, and of the different approach to Indians that Spanish-speaking people had adopted. Through the urging of Antonio and through his connections with the family, Jackson visited Rancho Camulos to see the Del Valle family, along with their remaining Indian retainers, at work and play. Together with Kinney she visited many of the Indian villages and reservations set aside for their protection. The more she saw, the more indignant she became.

As a much published writer, she took the lead in writing their final report. Wherever she went she had seen the same story. "From tract after tract of such [ancestral] lands they have been driven out, year by year, by the white settlers of the country," she wrote, "until they can retreat no further; some of their villages being literally on the last tillable spot on the desert's edge or in the mountain fastness." Jackson and Kinney were particularly appalled at the ejection of the Luiseño from Temecula, where they had lived "from time immemorial" and where they had been told annually for twenty years that their lands were secure. "Now [1873], without any previous knowledge by them of any proceedings in court, they [were] ordered to leave their lands and homes." The personal property of the Luiseño had been seized to pay the

cost of the lawsuit. The commissioners recommended the creation of genuine reservations and the removal of all whites from Indian settlements.[51]

Upon her return home to Colorado, Jackson learned that her recommendations
for relief of the Mission Indians had been rejected. Vexed and furious, Jackson decided that, if nonfiction would not bring redress, then she would write a novel. Not
any piece of fiction, this story would be grounded in historical fact and so tender that
it would move the hardest heart to corrective action, just as Harriet Beecher Stowe
had succeeded in doing with *Uncle Tom's Cabin*. Fleeing the distractions of home,
Jackson went to New York, where she wrote with the passion of a woman possessed. The protagonist of her story would be an innocent mixed-blood woman,
while her lover would be pure Luiseño, the son of a chief. Jackson situated her principal character in the home of a Señora Moreno, set in a carefully detailed version of
Californio life drawn from the reminiscences of the Coronels and from the home of
the Del Valles. The travails of the star-crossed lovers would largely be caused by
Americans, cast in Jackson's view as the primary villains. Jackson entitled her novel
after her principal character, *Ramona*. When it appeared in 1884, it caused a sensation, but not in the sense Jackson had intended. Readers responded not to American despoliation of Californios and Indians but to the tragic love story and to the romantic descriptions of bygone, halcyon days filled with dashing *dons* and beautiful
señoritas living in a Spanish arcadia. Jackson died a few months after *Ramona*'s publication, fearing her work had gone for naught.[52]

Jackson, however, did not fail. Despite the massive influx of tourism and subsequent settlement in southern California that her novel generated, she contributed to
a healing of Anglo and Hispanic tensions through the veneration of the Californio
myth. And her close friend in the Indian reform movement, Albert K. Smiley, inspired by her example and motivated by her death, soon secured congressional authorization to adopt her suggestions. Heading a new federal Indian commission,
Smiley set out from his winter home in Redlands in 1891, and laid out the reservation system in southern California that exists today. Of course it was inadequate, but
Indians would cheat the cheaters by turning their marginal, arid lands into gold
through gambling casinos a century later.

NOTES

1. Description of the Modoc War comes from Jeff C. Riddle, *The Indian History of the
Modoc War* (1914; San Jose: Urion Press, 1991), quoted at 90–91; Keith A. Murray, *The Mod-
ocs and Their War* (Norman: University of Oklahoma Press, 1959); and Gregory A. Reed, *An
Historical Geography Analysis of the Modoc Indian War* (Chico: Association for Northern Cal-
ifornia Records and Research, 1991). Cost computation based upon John H. McCusker,
"How Much Is That In Real Money? A Historical Price Index for Use as a Deflator of

Money Values in the Economy of the United States," *Proceedings of the American Antiquarian Society* 101 (October 1991): 297–373.

2. Hubert Howe Bancroft, *History of California*, vol. 7 (Santa Barbara: Wallace Hebberd, 1970; facsimile of 1886 edition), 488, note 21.

3. Paul Bryan Gray, *Forster vs. Pico: The Struggle for the Rancho Santa Margarita* (Spokane: Arthur H. Clark, 1998), passim, quoted at 231.

4. William Kelly, *An Excursion to California over the Prairie, Rocky Mountains, and Great Sierra Nevada . . .* , vol. 2 (London, 1851), 45, cited in James J. Rawls, "Gold Diggers: Indian Miners in the California Gold Rush," *California Historical Quarterly* 55 (Spring 1976): 36.

5. Rawls, "Gold Diggers," 28–45.

6. Diary entries for August 23, 1850, and December 30, November 28, and October 7, 1849; Augustin Hale Collection, Huntington Library, San Marino, California. I thank Peter Blodgett of the Huntington Library for bringing this source to my attention.

7. George Harwood Phillips, *Indians and Indian Agents: The Origins of the Reservation System in California, 1849–1852* (Norman: University of Oklahoma Press, 1997), 3–15 ff.

8. John Bidwell, "Dictation by General John Bidwell," ms, Bancroft Library, University of California, Berkeley (hereinafter "Bidwell Dictation"). In the early 1850s Bidwell had the only gristmill in northern California. See also Dorothy Hill, *The Indians of Chico Rancheria* (Sacramento: Department of Parks and Recreation, 1978), 12–28; and Rockwell D. Hunt, *John Bidwell: Prince of California Pioneers* (Caldwell, Idaho: Caxton Printers, 1942), 133–43.

9. James A. Sandos, "Between Crucifix and Lance: Indian-White Relations in California, 1769–1848," in *Contested Eden: California before the Gold Rush*, ed. Ramón A. Gutiérrez and Richard J. Orsi (Berkeley: University of California Press, 1998), 216–20.

10. Autobiography of Isidora Filomena de Solano, transcribed by Enrique Creel, April 9, 1874, ms, Bancroft Library.

11. Hill, *Indians of Chico Rancheria*, 39–42; Edward D. Castillo, "The Impact of Euro-American Exploration and Settlement," in *Handbook of North American Indians*, vol. 8, *California* (Washington, D.C.: Smithsonian Institution Press, 1978), 107–13.

12. Jerald Jay Johnson, "Yana," *Handbook of North American Indians: California*, 361–69.

13. Theodora Kroeber, *Ishi in Two Worlds: A Biography of the Last Wild Indian in North America* (Berkeley: University of California Press, 1967).

14. Albert L. Hurtado, *Indian Survival on the California Frontier* (New Haven: Yale University Press, 1988), 1. The major source for these figures is the writings of Sherburne F. Cook.

15. Sherburne F. Cook, "Historical Demography," *Handbook of North American Indians*, 93.

16. Senate Debate, May 26, 1860, from the *Congressional Globe*, cited in Robert F. Heizer, ed., *Federal Concern about Conditions of California Indians: Eight Documents* (Socorro, N.M.: Ballena Press, 1979), 46.

17. Bancroft, *History of California*, vol. 7 (San Francisco: The History Co., 1886), 474.

18. Hubert Howe Bancroft, *The Works of Hubert Howe Bancroft*, vol. 38 (San Francisco: The History Co., 1890), 69.

19. Laurence M. Hauptman, *Tribes and Tribulations: Misconceptions About American Indians and Their Histories* (Albuquerque: University of New Mexico Press, 1995), 3–14, 123–27.

20. For original and county boundaries and subsequent adjustments, see Warren A. Beck and Ynez D. Hasse, *Historical Atlas of California* (Norman: University of Oklahoma Press, 1974), 61–64.

21. Phillips, *Indians and Indian Agents,* 99–185.

22. George E. Anderson, W. H. Ellison, and Robert F. Heizer, *Treaty Making and Treaty Rejection by the Federal Government in California, 1850–1852* (Socorro, N.M.: Ballena Press, 1978), 26, 53–54. See also Robert M. Utley, *The Indian Frontier of the American West* (Albuquerque: University of New Mexico Press, 1984), 51–52.

23. California State Journal, 3rd Session, 1852, cited in Anderson, Ellison, and Heizer, *Treaty Making and Treaty Rejection,* 42–44.

24. Robert F. Heizer and Alan F. Almquist, *The Other Californians: Prejudice and Discrimination under Spain, Mexico, and the United States to 1920* (Berkeley: University of California Press, 1971), 76–79.

25. *Congressional Globe,* August 6 and 11, 1852, cited in Anderson, Ellison, and Heizer, *Treaty Making and Treaty Rejection,* 122.

26. Benjamin D. Wilson, Los Angeles, to Cave J. Couts, June 13, 1853, Benjamin Davis Wilson Collection, Huntington Library.

27. Florence C. Shipek, *Pushed into the Rocks: Southern California Land Tenure, 1769–1986* (Lincoln: University of Nebraska Press, 1987), 29.

28. Heizer and Almquist, *Other Californians,* 48–50.

29. George Harwood Phillips, *Chiefs and Challengers: Indian Resistance and Cooperation in Southern California* (Berkeley: University of California Press, 1975), passim, 160–76.

30. Glenn J. Farris, "José Panto: *Capitan* of the Indian Pueblo at San Pascual, San Diego County," *Journal of California and Great Basin Anthropology* 16 (1994): 149–61, quoted at 159.

31. Shipek, *Pushed into the Rocks.*

32. Tomás Almaguer, *Racial Faultlines: The Historical Origins of White Supremacy in California* (Berkeley: University of California Press, 1994), draws his examples of white brutalization of Indians from the northern California experience, implying it was the same for Indians everywhere. Gregorio Mora makes a point very similar to mine in his review of Almaguer's book. See Mora, "New Directions in the Chicano History of California," *Mexican Studies/Estudios Mexicanos* 14 (Summer 1998): 453–56.

33. Crisostomo Perez, *Land Grants in Alta California: A Compilation of Spanish and Mexican Private Land Claims in the State of California* (Rancho Cordova, Calif.: Landmark Enterprises, 1996), 66.

34. John Johnson, "The Indians of Mission San Fernando," in *Mission San Fernando Rey de España, 1797–1997: A Bicentennial Tribute,* ed. Doyce B. Nunis (Los Angeles: Historical Society of Southern California, 1997), 249–90.

35. Robert Glass Cleland, *The Cattle on a Thousand Hills: Southern California, 1850–1880,* 2nd ed. (San Marino, Calif.: Huntington Library, 1951); Douglas Monroy, *Thrown Among Strangers: The Making of Mexican Culture in Frontier California* (Berkeley: University of California Press, 1990); and Leonard Pitt, *The Decline of the Californios: A Social History of the Spanish-Speaking Californians, 1846–1890* (Berkeley: University of California Press, 1966). Unless otherwise specified, my portrait of the era is drawn from these sources.

36. Richard Griswold del Castillo, *The Treaty of Guadalupe Hidalgo: A Legacy of Conflict* (Norman: University of Oklahoma Press, 1990), 46–86, 190.

37. Perez, *Land Grants in Alta California,* 6–8; W. W. Robinson, *Land in California: The Story of Mission Lands, Ranchos, Squatters, Mining Claims, Railroad Grants, Land Scrip, Homesteads* (Berkeley: University of California Press, 1948), 91–109. Robinson's figures differ from those of Perez, but the latter's are unquestionably more reliable.

38. Cleland, *Cattle on a Thousand Hills*, 112.

39. Robinson, *Land in California*, 111–32.

40. François D. Uzes, *Chaining the Land: A History of Surveying in California* (Sacramento: Landmark Enterprises, 1977).

41. Robin A. Butlin and Neil Roberts, eds., *Ecological Relations in Historical Times: Human Impact and Adaptation* (Oxford: Blackwell Publishers, 1995), 8.

42. Siegfried Demke, *The Cattle Drives of Early California* (San Gabriel, Calif.: Prosperity Press, 1985), 9–22.

43. Terry G. Jordan, *North American Cattle-Ranching Frontiers: Origins, Diffusion, and Differentiation* (Albuquerque: University of New Mexico Press, 1993), 241–66.

44. "Laws Concerning Rodeos and Defining the Duties of Judges of the Plains," March 30, 1851, cited in Demke, *Cattle Drives of Early California*, 17. Taken together, these were called the "no-fence" law, repealed in 1872.

45. Raymond F. Dasmann, *California's Changing Environment* (San Francisco: Boyd and Fraser, 1978), 27; Jordan, *North American Cattle-Ranching Frontiers*, 246–48.

46. According to Jordan, *North American Cattle-Ranching Frontiers*, 246–47, the Anglo-Californian cattle frontier moved out of the state and into the Pacific Northwest, Nevada, and Utah.

47. Richard Griswold del Castillo, "The del Valle Family and the Fantasy Heritage," *California History* 59 (Spring 1980): 3–15.

48. Antonio Franco Coronel, *Tales of Mexican California*, trans. Diane de Avalle-Arce (Santa Barbara: Bellerophon Books, 1994), 2–11.

49. This point is thoughtfully discussed in Gray, *Forster vs. Pico*, 51–80.

50. Carey McWilliams, *North from Mexico: The Spanish Speaking People of the United States* (Philadelphia: J. P. Lippincott, 1949), 35–40.

51. Helen Hunt Jackson and Abbot Kinney, *Report on the Condition and Needs of the Mission Indians of California . . . to the Commissioner of Indian Affairs* (Washington, D.C.: Government Printing Office, 1883), 3–31. Jackson noted that the term "Mission Indians" meant all those who had been in the missions or missionized by Franciscans. The Bureau of Indian Affairs, however, used the term to refer to only those Indians in Los Angeles, San Bernardino, and San Diego counties and restricted the tribes further to only the Serrano, Cahuilla, Luiseño, and Diegueño. The Serrano and Cahuilla had only limited mission contact, and all other missionized tribes were excluded. For background on Jackson, see Valerie S. Mathes, *Helen Hunt Jackson and Her Indian Reform Legacy* (Austin: University of Texas Press, 1990); Ronald C. Woolsey, *Migrants West: Toward the Southern California Frontier* (Claremont, Calif.: Grizzly Bear Publishing, 1996), 138–59.

52. James A. Sandos, with the historical architectural assistance of Edna Kimbro, "Historic Preservation and Historical Facts: Helen Hunt Jackson, Rancho Camulos, and Ramonana," *California History* 77 (Fall 1998).

5

"All hands have gone downtown"

Urban Places in Gold Rush California

Robert Phelps

On December 25, 1849, D. D. Demarest found himself in the tiny settlement of San Diego, waiting to resume his journey to the California gold fields. Demarest was a native New Yorker, part of a company of prospective miners who had emerged from the southern overland trail only a week before. The men had expected to continue their overland expedition after a quick re-supply in town, but the locals advised them to sell their animals and "await a chance of passage by sea, as it is impossible to travel up by land at this season." Frustrated by the delay, the men pitched their tents on the east side of Point Loma and waited. San Diego itself was five miles to the northeast, sited on a river "about the size of the Hackensack." Demarest thought the town was "better built" than those he passed on the Rio Grande, with houses "roofed with tiles instead of with mud." In San Diego, the men were able to sell their animals and break up the monotony of frontier life, and Demarest himself spent Christmas Day watching the natives engage in "some fine sport among themselves." Finally, on January 18, 1850, an ocean steamer arrived. It had come from Panama, was full of gold seekers, and it was headed north. The steamer, with the Demarest party aboard, chugged into San Francisco Bay three days later.

Overrun by miners, sailors, and merchants, San Francisco was crowded. The steamer was unable to find a mooring, and the owner of a small boat charged the company two dollars a head to land them on the wharf. Although local saloons were "fitted up in the most showy style," Demarest found San Francisco "nothing but a collection of tents." To the company's dismay, experienced miners recommended that they winter in town. Most boardinghouses resembled "hog pens," and Demarest decided to rent space in a carpenter's shop. Once more disappointed at this "rather long time to be idle," the prospective miners spent the remainder of the winter touring the booming town. Of particular interest were the mission and the

Sacramento Street in San Francisco, looking east from Montgomery Street in the mid-1850s. When the Argonaut D. D. Demarest arrived in January 1850, he dismissed the town as "nothing but a collection of tents." Then overnight, or so it seemed, a great city arose on the shore of Yerba Buena Cove—the metropolis of the Golden State and the financial and cultural center of the American West. Little more than a year after Demarest made his way through the muddy streets of San Francisco, the city had a population of some thirty thousand, and the commerce of its port was exceeded only by that of New York, Boston, and New Orleans. *Courtesy Bancroft Library.*

presidio, remnants of another era when the peninsula served as the northern outpost of Spain's system of defensive settlements.

Demarest and his friends left San Francisco the first week of April, booking passage toward the gold fields on a small sailboat for $35 each. They "had quite a blow in the San Pablo Bay the first night out," but reached Sacramento without incident. There were plenty of saloons and gambling houses in town, but having already wasted valuable time, they were anxious to leave. A few of Demarest's friends hitched a ride on a rowboat headed upriver. The boat belonged to a merchant who had come to Sacramento to purchase goods for his store farther inland. In exchange for rowing both the merchant and his goods thirty-five miles up the Sacramento and Feather rivers, the gold seekers were allowed to return with the boat for the rest of the party. Four days of rowing against the current found Demarest and his friends, now reunited, in Marysville. They returned their borrowed craft, purchased supplies, and then set out for the gold fields, finally ending their journey at the mining camp at Long Bar. It had been nearly a month since the Demarest party had left San Francisco, and almost fourteen months since they had left New York.

Camps like Long Bar were established along branch streams of the Yuba River, where the shifting course of the waters revealed gold-rich sand bars. One of the original camps, founded by Scotsman William Downie and a mining company that included an Irishman, a Native American, a Hawaiian, and ten African Americans, had developed into Downieville, the terminus of a supply system that stretched one hundred miles back to San Francisco. There, miners could find food, the repair or replacement of tools, city newspapers, and most importantly, a mail express service. Consisting of a solitary log cabin only the year before, in the summer of 1850 Demarest found "15 hotels or gambling houses, 4 bakeries, 4 butcher shops." With bedrolls on their backs, the miners of the Yuba made regular trips to Downieville, anxious to take advantage of the goods and services the settlement provided.[1]

The dependence of D. D. Demarest and his fellow gold seekers on the transport, supply, information, and other vital services found in cities and towns confirms the fact that from the time of its inception, California has demonstrated one of its most important contradictions: a physical vastness matched only by an extraordinary level of urbanization.[2] In many ways, the development of urban places in California reflected the larger patterns of city-building in the American West, as mining was the catalyst for the creation of hundreds of frontier settlements throughout the nineteenth century. Yet the appearance of cities and towns in gold-rush California would never have occurred without the miners' reluctance to part with the way of life they had left back home. Far from the popular image of self-reliant frontiersmen, the Americans who traveled to California during the 1850s brought with them a conception of "necessity" that was evolving in a rapidly industrializing nation. They had the habit, in the words of Patricia Limerick, of "celebrating independence while

Miners entertain themselves on a Sunday at Forbestown—or Forbes Diggings, as it was also known—in a spirited drawing done about 1852 by Alonzo Chappel from a daguerreotype. Despite the transient character of life in the diggings, the need for supplies and services created countless camps and towns, making California one of the most urbanized states in the nation. Founded in 1849 near the South Fork of the Feather River and named for Ben Forbes, who established a store here the following year, Forbestown had a population of nearly a thousand by the mid-1850s. *California Historical Society, C. Templeton Crocker Collection, FN-19210.*

relying on a vital connection to the outside world."[3] For the gold seekers, that "vital connection to the outside world" was the network of cities and towns they built on the California frontier. A transient urban system based on the exploitation of inland gold deposits, the patterns of urbanization laid out during the Gold Rush nevertheless provided the template for the state's future urban development.

Urban historians have been at the forefront of an extended reinterpretation of the history of the American West over the last fifty years. As with so many historical subfields, the target for this redirection has been Frederick Jackson Turner, whose celebrated frontier thesis portrayed western cities as the end-product of U.S. territorial advancement and the final stage of American historical development. Turner may have foreshadowed an urban critique of his own paradigm when he noted that the U.S. Census Bureau had declared the frontier closed only a few years before his

acclaimed address at the World's Columbian Exposition in Chicago, the 1893 exhibition itself a testament to the growth of western cities during the second half of the
nineteenth century. However, such was the power of the frontier thesis that it was
not until Americans were faced with the urban problems engendered by the Great
Depression that an extended reevaluation of the historical development of U.S. cities
appeared. Works like Arthur Schlesinger, Sr.'s "The City in American History" and
his later *Rise of the City, 1878–1898,* as well as Lewis Mumford's 1938 classic, *The City
in History,* pointed to the prominent role played by cities on a national scope and
opened the door to an urban reinterpretation of U.S. history.[4] The appearance of corresponding arguments asserting the prominence of the city in the development of the
American West was immediate. Schlesinger himself pointed to "the occupation of
the Great West" as a major catalyst of U.S. urban development, a process grounded
on "the exploitation of natural resources such as the world had never known."[5] Although the historiography of the American city continued to develop after World
War II, Richard Wade's 1959 *The Urban Frontier: The Rise of Western Cities, 1790–1830*
is considered the first comprehensive articulation of the "urban West" perspective.
The argument is simple: towns were the spearhead of the frontier. Writing at a time
when the frontier thesis still held tremendous influence, Wade was cautious, arguing
that while cities represented the "more aggressive and dynamic force" of American
expansion, town and country developed in tandem.[6] The recent rise of both the
New Urban History and the New Western History has strengthened Wade's arguments. Bradford Luckingham's work on the urban Southwest reaffirmed the notion
that cities were a vanguard of American frontier expansion, while Gilbert R. Cruz's
Let There Be Towns rejuvenated the study of the Spanish origins of urban places in
the American borderlands. Lawrence Larsen's *The Urban West at the End of the Frontier* helped place western cities in a broader perspective by arguing that American
frontier settlements represented an extension of the city-building strategies of antiquity. Finally, William Cronon's *Nature's Metropolis* attempted to "stand Turner on
his head" by depicting the frontier as the extension of environmental changes initiated by the economic power of nineteenth-century Chicago.[7]

  Like historians of the American West, scholars of California history have long
appreciated the role of cities and towns in frontier development. The urban nature
of the Gold Rush was instinctively appreciated by amateur historians from the end
of the nineteenth century to the present day. Hubert Howe Bancroft himself lent
much time to recording the rise of the state's cities and towns. That California scholars would write urban histories conforming to national historiographical trends
was natural. Ironically, the emergence of serious scholarly work on California cities
was not initiated by a professional historian, but by Carey McWilliams, a trained
attorney. In an introductory essay for Ray B. West's *Rocky Mountain Cities* and in
McWilliams's own *California: The Great Exception,* both published in 1949, Mc-

Williams proposed that western cities in general, and California cities in particular, were historically more important than their counterparts in the other regions of the United States. Western cities tended to dominate their states' economies and housed a larger proportion of their states' population relative to eastern cities. The attendant rural populations of western states were in fact so negligible that, in effect, western cities and western states were one and the same. This basic recognition of the importance of urban California has had a broad influence. Indeed, Kevin Starr's exhaustive series on the California Dream in many ways follows the tradition set by McWilliams in its emphasis on city culture in the development of the state's unique ideology.[8]

In regard to the Gold Rush itself, San Francisco's status as California's nineteenth-century metropolis made the Bay Area a focal point of study. In *Instant Cities*, Gunther Barth presented San Francisco as a prime example of city-building far in advance of the frontier line. Although Barth argued that the "instant frontier city" was grounded in antiquity, San Francisco was a novel historical variant: an emporium "brought to life by the immediate wealth" of a mining boom "and sustained through the steady need for supplies required by those mining operations."[9] Urban geographers joined in the study of the genesis of gold-rush cities. James E. Vance's *Geography and Urban Evolution in the San Francisco Bay Area* examined the geographic influences that made gold-rush San Francisco a water-transportation-oriented city—the "Venice of the West"—while Mel Scott's *The San Francisco Bay Area* emphasized the early metropolitan nature of the bay community, tracing the development of the region's urban places as an integrated whole. Historian Roger Lotchin complemented such metropolitan approaches with an extensive study of San Francisco itself, downplaying the role of geography and instead focusing on the contingent historical forces that drove the city's growth during the gold-rush era.[10]

Comprehensive studies of the state's cities have not been confined to the San Francisco Bay region. *Southern California: An Island on the Land* (1946), Carey McWilliams's general study of southern California, discussed the social changes unleashed by the Gold Rush in Los Angeles and the smaller communities of the region. While focusing on the development of Los Angeles after the arrival of the railroad, Robert Fogelson's *Fragmented Metropolis* also traced the growth of the city's ranch economy and its role as an agricultural supplier to the state's northern towns during the 1850s and 1860s. John W. Reps's exhaustive work on urban planning on the American frontier provided a rich collection of city biographies that pointed to the importance of urban places in California from Spanish colonization to the end of the nineteenth century. Ralph Mann's intensive study of society and culture in Nevada City and Grass Valley not only provided a glimpse of town life in California during the second half of the nineteenth century, but also reflected the growing belief of historians that the history of the American West was "largely an urban history." Forming a chain of scholarship that addresses the origin and development of great coastal cities, agricultural depots, and ephemeral mining settlements, such diverse studies have made the historiography of urban California, particularly during the Gold Rush, uncommonly rich.[11]

Cities are different things to different people, depending on a myriad of contexts and perceptions. Typically, the dividing line of opinion lies between form and function, as some observers emphasize the built-environment, while others focus on the range of activity contained within a central locality.[12] The U.S. Census Bureau defines "urban" as a place containing 2,500 inhabitants or more. Even by this criteria California was one of the most urban states in the nation by the late nineteenth century. Half of the state's population lived in cities and towns around 1885, at a time when only 35 percent of the total population of the United States was urbanized. As Eric Monkkonen points out, however, such a definition "ignores the hamlets, the places under 2,500 people," which, while not fitting the dichotomous paradigm of "urban" and "rural," were home to people who "certainly had lives that were far less rural than the farmers and farm laborers" of the United States.[13]

For purposes of this overview, we will define an urban place as a center of population, communication, and economic activity whose built-environment is densely arranged relative to its surrounding area. Urban places appear because of the need of an otherwise dispersed population to converge on a central location in order to acquire goods and services. The providers of such items likewise concentrate their activities in a central place because it is where they can reach the largest market and realize economies of agglomeration. However, central places do not exist in isolation, but rather develop in symbiotic relation with other central places. Together, these relations form city systems.

Scholars of city development recognize two basic urban networks. The first network, termed the primate city system, is composed of a single dominant metropolis that contains a disproportionate share of population, economic activity, and political power relative to other central places in a particular region. The commanding influence of the solitary metropolis atrophies the smaller central places within its orbit, thus preventing the appearance of urban rivals. California's central places were enmeshed in such a system during the Spanish and Mexican eras. Although the excellent siting of some of the state's earliest settlements demonstrated the lessons learned in Spain's long tradition of city-building, California's first urban centers were handicapped by their relative isolation from one another and the outside world, the limited nature of their state-delineated functions, and subsequent political decisions that prevented sustained urban growth. The pueblos of Los Angeles and San Jose were required to focus almost exclusively on agricultural pursuits in order to supply nearby presidios, and the development of artisan occupations in both settlements was stunted. Moreover, the export of sea otter pelts to China, a lucrative trade that could

have facilitated the growth of California's coastal communities, was quickly terminated by the protests of those holding a royal charter in Spain's Asian trade.[14]

Unlike the primate system, a rank-order system develops as an expanding population's increasing distance from initial points of convergence generates the establishment of additional central places. Eventually, a dynamic urban network will develop, consisting of a principal regional metropolis that serves an ascending number
of cities, towns, and hamlets, ranked according to a descending range of functions
and population. At the top of the rank-order, the metropolis owes its influence to the
distinct communications' advantages it has over its regional rivals. The metropolis
not only furnishes goods and services required by the population, but might also attract singular activities that are best carried out in one location, be it financial (Wall
Street), professional (Hollywood), or a similar activity. The metropolis serves a number of cities within its orbit, which are the next lower tier of the rank-order. Cities
engage in a range of economic activities, but without the transportation advantages
of the metropolis; they lack the latter's specialized functions, and their growth potential relative to the metropolis is limited. The next functional rank in the network
is the town, settlements that, although more numerous than cities, serve a smaller
population and hence support only a few economic functions. Towns sometimes
exist only to maintain a single activity, mining for example, and town-dwellers must
often journey to the cities to acquire more specialized goods and services. Last in
rank is the hamlet, a small settlement that serves a highly localized area with a very
few basic services such as retailing.[15]

The spread of urban places throughout the United States was characterized by
this rank-order pattern. The lack of the powerful city charters typical of Europe, an
intense spirit of urban boosterism, and the early availability of steam transportation
meant that no single central place could long dominate the nation.[16] New York City
was the metropolis of the eastern seaboard, but its presence could not stifle the
growth of Philadelphia or Boston, or prevent the appearance of Chicago as a rival
metropolis at the end of the nineteenth century. In California before 1848, the independence of the Californios from the rule of Mexico City and the appearance of
a small but aggressive merchant class in such communities as Yerba Buena, later San
Francisco, may have heralded the arrival of a rank-order system. However, the almost
simultaneous discovery of gold at Sutter's Mill with the American conquest of California may have preempted the evolution of a potentially vigorous Californio city
system and instead initiated the rapid development of a rank-order network based
on the provision of goods and services for gold-rush emigrants. Table 5.1 shows that
California's rank-order was an eclectic but interlocking system of ports, mining settlements, and agricultural centers, their size, importance, and economic adaptability
directly related to their proximity to waterborne transportation links.

San Francisco was the metropolis of the gold-rush urban system. The city's

TABLE 5.1

Major Urban Centers in California by Population and Function, 1850–1860

City	Function	Population 1850	Population 1860
San Francisco	Sea port	34,776	56,802
Sacramento	Interior port city	6,820	13,785
Marysville	Interior port city	4,500	4,740
Stockton	Interior port city	n.a.	3,679
Los Angeles	Agricultural center	1,610	4,385
Nevada City	Mining town	2,683	n.a.
Oroville	Mining town	n.a.	2,499
Napa	Agricultural center	159	2,378
Diamond Springs	Mining town	420	2,142
Sonora	Mining town	n.a.	1,960
Placerville	Mining town	n.a.	1,754
Rough and Ready	Mining town	672	1,719
Yreka	Mining town	n.a.	1,631
Santa Rosa	Agricultural center	n.a.	1,623
Mud Springs	Mining town	2,080	1,572
Petaluma	Agricultural center	n.a.	1,505
Monterey	Minor sea port	1,092	n.a.
San Diego	Minor sea port	n.a.	731

SOURCE: *Seventh Census of the United States: 1850. An Appendix, Embracing the Notes Upon the Tables of Each of the States, Etc.* (Washington: Government Printing Office, 1853); Department of the Interior, *Population of the United States in 1860; Compiled from the Original Returns of the Eighth Census* (Washington: Government Printing Office, 1864).

importance in gold-rush trade owed to the simple fact that clipper ships and ocean-going steamers could not negotiate the shallow waters of the state's riverways, and thus passengers and cargo had to be transferred to smaller vessels for the trip inland.[17] Although the limitations of ocean-going craft meant that a major city was certain to appear on San Francisco Bay during the era, geography did not predetermine San Francisco's status as California's nineteenth-century metropolis. During the Mexican War, Edwin Bryant described the town as an isolated backwater, its estimated population of two hundred housed largely in small adobes and wood-framed shelters.[18] The site was impaired by poor climate, a lack of water, inconvenient hills, a mud flat fronting the bay, and the existence of superior inland riverport locations on the *contra costa*, particularly Benicia, which William Tecumseh Sherman described in 1849 as "the best natural site for a commercial city." Instead, San Francisco's preeminence in the state's

San Francisco, Upper California, in 1847, a lithograph published by the New York firm of Sarony and Major. At this date the future metropolis of the Golden State was a wind-blown, scattering village of some four or five hundred souls living in splendid isolation on the far reaches of the American continent. *California Historical Society, C. Templeton Crocker Collection.*

city system is owed to a combination of historical and geographical accident and boosterism. After the American conquest of California, the federal government de-cided to quarter its troops and place its customshouse in the tiny village of Yerba Buena at the tip of the San Francisco peninsula. Favorably positioned as a major re-gional center, Yerba Buena then changed its name to San Francisco in order to iden-tify itself as the primary port on the bay. The strategy was successful. By 1849, as Sher-man observed, every ship that "cleared from any part of the world, knew the name of San Francisco," and made it their ultimate California destination.[19]

San Francisco's growth was also spurred on by the fact that the gold seekers spent an interim of anywhere between a few days and a few months in the city before set-ting out for the gold fields—waiting out a frontier winter they had no desire to chal-lenge, arranging for river transportation, garnering intelligence about the best routes and richest gold fields, or purchasing the seemingly endless array of goods accumu-lating on the city's docks. Virtually every item available in an eastern port city could be had in San Francisco. Typical of the suppliers arriving in the metropolis was the packet ship *Silvie DeGrass,* which in May 1849 advertised among its 164 articles such items as brandy, gin, whiskey, champagne, sugar, molasses, pickles, tomato catsup, playing cards, kino boards, backgammon boards, dominoes, billiard balls, shovels, kettles, cologne water, tea, coffee, stationery, violins, rifles, pistols, sunglasses, cork-screws, rosaries, and crucifixes.[20] As the gold seekers idled in San Francisco, subsidiary industries associated with the carrying trade appeared, initiating a "multiplier effect" that drove the city's growth. Individuals who were perceptive enough to understand that the real money to be made was not in panning for gold, but in pandering to the vices of the gold seekers themselves, opened saloons and gambling houses. Others built hotels and boardinghouses, charged exorbitant rates, and used the profits to build more of them. Merchants, bankers, butchers, bakers, blacksmiths, shopkeepers, shoemakers, expressmen, and a host of other entrepreneurs appeared to supply and serve the gold seekers. Gold was shipped east from San Francisco or minted there into coin, and the express and shipping companies that carried it opened headquarters in the city as well. A U.S. post office added to the importance of the metropolis. San Francisco, whose residents had deserted the city at the start of the Gold Rush, became the permanent site of a rapidly growing population.[21]

Beyond San Francisco, the largest of California's gold-rush cities were the three inland ports of Marysville, Stockton, and Sacramento, as well as the agricultural center of Los Angeles to the south. Though the development of the river cities owed much to the opportunism of local landowners, geography also played a hand, as each was on a strategic position on the Feather, San Joaquin, or Sacramento river. All functioned as the commercial and transport centers for towns and hamlets farther inland. Marysville served the northern settlements, Stockton the southern, Sacramento the central. Like San Francisco, the waterfronts of the inland ports were "piled up with all sorts of goods and provisions for the mines," and all experienced modest versions of the same multiplier effect that built the metropolis.[22] Lacking direct water connections, Los Angeles was the only major settlement outside the immediate geographic zone of the Gold Rush, although the southern city was firmly within the economic orbit of the state's urban system. Southern California was a major source of beef, and the pueblos' rancheros drove their herds to cattle markets in the Sacramento Valley. San Pedro even then served as Los Angeles's rudimentary port, and the federal government established a post office there.[23]

The towns of gold-rush California, the next functional category of the rank-order system, were a diverse lot. Some, like the coastal communities of Monterey and San Diego, were sites that had developed prior to American conquest but maintained specialized economic functions such as whaling, or developed into small way stations for travelers headed to the gold fields. Settlements like San Bernardino, Napa, Santa Rosa, and Petaluma comprised another type of gold-rush town. Some, like tiny San Bernardino, had been established during the Spanish/Mexican colonial era, while others developed after the American conquest. All served as the supply and transport centers for agricultural regions involved in food production for emigrants pouring into the northern part of the state.[24]

The most numerous of California's central places during the Gold Rush were the inland towns and small hamlets that directly served or housed the gold seekers. The

TABLE 5.2
Nevada City, Occupational Make-up, 1850

Occupation	N	Occupation	N
Miners	2,063	Lawyers	8
Auctioneers	2	Magicians	2
Bakers	18	Millwright	1
Barber	1	Painters	2
Blacksmiths	2	Physicians	20
Butchers	14	Sailors	2
Carpenters	29	Servants	4
Clerks	2	Tailor	1
Cooks	3	Tavern keepers	6
Dentist	1	Teamsters	21
Druggist	1	Traders/merchants	215
Engineers	2	Tinner	1
Farmers	2	Town officials	3
Grocer	1	Waiters	4
Laborers	2	Watchmakers	2

SOURCE: U.S. Bureau of the Census, *Schedule of Population for Cities, 1850,* Microfilm Reel 36 (California State Library, Sacramento).

larger towns of Placerville, Sonora, Yreka, and Nevada City typically based their economies on the provision of lodging, general retailing, entertainment, and a small number of specialized services. Table 5.2 shows the diverse occupational makeup of residents of Nevada City, one of California's largest mining towns in 1850. Of Nevada City's 2,683 inhabitants, the occupations of 2,435 could be identified. Miners made up the majority of town residents, with merchants, traders, teamsters, and others engaged in commerce making up the next largest occupational grouping.

Beyond mining and commerce, Nevada City's most important occupational groups were those involved in food preparation and medical care, activities usually associated with women at midcentury. Men made up roughly 90 percent of the state's population during the early 1850s, and hence, the household economy in which women played a vital role was not transported west during the initial stages of the Gold Rush. Male gold seekers were therefore confronted with a dilemma: they could perform the activities usually associated with women themselves, or they could pay someone else to do it. The diaries of many miners suggest their ineptitude in performing such tasks as cooking, washing, sewing, or caring for the sick, and the miners' lack of skill created a massive market for restauranteurs, physicians, launderers, boardinghouse keepers, and other service providers. Old hands who camped near

Coloma were representative in their habit of visiting the town every Sunday "for the express purpose of having one good dinner in a week," and JoAnn Levy's study of women during the Gold Rush found that cooking was profitable employment for female emigrants.[25] This commercialization of the family economy, and the advantage of concentrating these activities in central places, was another impetus to the growth of urban California. In New York State, arguably the most "urban" of states in the antebellum period, there was one baker for every 744 residents in 1850. California's ratio was one to every 351 residents. In the 1850 census, 413 individuals in California listed themselves as cooks, an occupation that does not appear as a separate census category for any other state that year. New York boasted one physician for every 612 state residents, but, while the credentials of its physicians may have been lax, "frontier" California possessed a ratio of one to every 148 residents.[26]

The larger mining towns were linked by dirt trails and river tributaries to the periphery of the urban system, a galaxy of small hamlets and mining camps with names like Angels Camp, Rough and Ready, Jackson, Mokelumne Hill, You Bet, San Andreas, and China Camp. Acting as tiny centers of trade and transitory residence near the gold deposits themselves, most of the hamlets stretched in a broad band from the Merced River north to Lake Almanor, with another concentration based in the north around the Klamath River.[27] Rough and Ready, a mining hamlet of 672 men a few miles east of Nevada City, was a typical mining hamlet. True to a town developing according to a rank-order system, Rough and Ready lacked the specialized services available in Nevada City, things like watch repair, dental care, a druggist, or extensive legal help, although two magicians were present in Nevada City in 1850. However, Rough and Ready had relatively more cooks than Nevada City, and the building trades were stronger in the smaller community as well, the latter probably due to the newness of the settlement and a corresponding flurry of construction activity (see table 5.3). Rough and Ready was also home to sixteen physicians, a ratio of doctors to residents that far outstripped Nevada City, although the hamlet's doctors probably also served miners in the surrounding camps.[28]

The hardships associated with filling the economic void left by women were only matched by a corresponding lack of (or freedom from) family-centered leisure. The difficult nature of placer mining and the need for companionship in a place full of strangers made male-centered leisure an important activity in California's cities and towns. The tavern and other forms of recreation were a ubiquitous feature of frontier life, serving not only as an important place of sociability, but also as a place where one might borrow money, purchase food and supplies, or sleep. San Francisco's saloons were the best built and decorated structures in the city during its early years, and the presence of drinking establishments, gambling houses, and even bowling alleys made people like Chauncey Canfield report in 1853 that Sacramento was "the liveliest place I ever saw."[29] Such services were even more vital in the more isolated

The volunteer firemen of Timbuctoo, Yuba County, strike a pose by the Empire Bakery, about 1857. One of the innumerable gold camps that sprang up in the diggings, Timbuctoo is thought to have been named after an early black Argonaut active in the district. Although a flourishing community for many years, Timbuctoo faded into obscurity before the turn of the century, and all that remains from its glory days are the Wells Fargo Express Office and a few crumbling stone walls. *Courtesy Stephen Anaya Collection. Photograph courtesy Oakland Museum of California.*

inland mining settlements. Nevada City was home to six tavern keepers in 1850, while Rough and Ready was home to fourteen. The relative lack of tavern keepers in Nevada City, as well as its relative want of physicians and cooks, may seem strange in a place otherwise so important commercially, but Nevada City differed from surrounding hamlets in one important respect: Nevada City was home to 43 females over the age of ten, women engaged in the traditional activities of the family economy. Not a single female lived in Rough and Ready when the census taker appeared in early 1850.[30]

Throughout the early years of the Gold Rush, the morphology of California's urban places, their physical form and structure, reflected the expediency of rapid settlement.[31] Since the adoption of the federal Land Ordinance of 1785, which established the surveying of public land in the West into six-mile-square townships divided by lines intersecting true north and south at right angles, most American

TABLE 5.3
Rough and Ready, Occupational Make-up, 1850

Occupation	N	Occupation	N
Miners	360	Miners/traders	2
Sportsmen	16	Painter	1
Bakers	9	Physicians	16
Blacksmiths	5	Ranchers	3
Bricklayer	1	Saddle maker	1
Butchers	12	Sailors	3
Carpenters	38	Shoemakers	2
Clerk	1	Stage drivers	3
Cooks	7	Tailors	2
Coopers	2	Tavern keepers	14
Farmers	8	Teamsters	19
Hotel keepers	2	Traders/merchants	107
Laborers	6	Wagon maker	1
Laddlers	2	Waiter	1
Lawyer	1		

SOURCE: U.S. Bureau of the Census, *Schedule of Population for Cities, 1850,* Microfilm Reel 36 (California State Library, Sacramento).

cities developed along the grid pattern. Such a rectilinear organization of space allowed for the convenient laying out of roads and a rapid subdivision and sale of lots. San Francisco's grid was established by an 1847 survey, commissioned by Yerba Buena that year in order to promote the sale of city lands. Unlike the north-south axis of most of the city's thoroughfares, Market Street and the streets below Market were set at a diagonal to avoid conflict with previously settled land grants and to correspond to the general route of travel between the center of town and the mission, a decision that complicates the city's morphology to this day.[32]

"Though not half the size of San Francisco," Sacramento, D. D. Demarest thought, had "much the same appearance." The only difference of note was that, "instead of hills and a large Bay for surrounding scenery," Sacramento had "a level plain and rivers on two sides." In 1848 John Augustus Sutter, Jr., hired an army topographical engineer to lay out his father's land in anticipation of brisk sales. The resulting town was built on a conventional grid spreading east from the Sacramento River, save for its northern and western borders, which were dictated by the flow of the Sacramento and American rivers. Twelve public squares were placed in regular intervals to break up the grid's monotony, and the city cemetery was prudently located on a small protrusion on the southern fringe of town. Stockton, developed by entrepreneur

Charles M. Weber, was among the best planned gold-rush cities. The town's gridiron was broken up by the intrusion of three main channels linking the city to the
San Joaquin River, enclosed by levees to protect commercial neighborhoods from
flooding. Weber reserved large tracts for public use, and while Sacramento may have
been chosen as the capital, Stockton was able to provide the grounds for the state in-
sane asylum, a coveted prize in an era of minimal public expenditures. Los Angeles
owed its original morphology to the plan developed by Governor Felipe de Neve in
1781, which generally followed the approach to city-building prescribed by Spain's
Law of the Indies, with houses facing a common plaza to facilitate protection and
sociability. By the time of Mexican independence in 1821, a new asymmetrical plaza
had been constructed, surrounded by a church, erratically placed townhouses, and
streets with irregular widths. In 1849, Los Angeles leaders hired Army Lt. Edward
Ord to survey the pueblo and to lay out surrounding land for future development.
Ord's extensions gave Los Angeles a hybrid morphology: a compact but chaotic center encased by American-style gridirons to the southwest and northeast.[33]

The most developed neighborhoods of California's larger cities were usually in
close proximity to the most important economic activities, and over time spread
outward along the path of least resistance. San Francisco's area of initial development
was on the waterfront. At first, vessels had to anchor offshore, the tidal mudflats on
the eastern side of the peninsula preventing their approach. Private businessmen
built an assortment of piers linked by plank walks to solve the problem, the largest
being Long Wharf, which extended two thousand feet to allow the docking of
Pacific Mail Company steamers. Subsequent growth spread along the shore on the
low ground north and south of Market Street.[34] Once the waterfront was largely settled, people began to fill the remaining low-lying land in the crevices between the
slopes and also the mudflats between the piers. Throughout the era, the lowlands
possessed the highest population densities in San Francisco, not only because they
were easier to build on, but also because few streets were planked. Even on level
streets, high boots were needed to avoid sinking in winter mud. Slopes were virtually impossible to traverse.[35] Eventually the hills to the west could not be avoided.
Some of the smaller ones were blasted. People moved up the larger ones. Plank
roads were laid to ease access, and by 1851, neighborhoods began to appear on Russian, Telegraph, and Nob hills. Crowding continued, and by the end of the 1860s the
scarcity of open space was enough of a problem to prompt city leaders to set aside
public land for Golden Gate Park.[36]

Sacramento built up first around Sutter's Fort, near the center of town. To facilitate commerce, "building activity," often in the form of tent raising, then shifted to
the embarcadero at the foot of J Street, just south of where the American River joins
the Sacramento.[37] Settlers were confident in the typicality of the mild winter of
1848–49 and ignored evidence of past flooding. The streets of the city were as poor

TABLE 5.4

Major Urban Centers in California by Population and Function, 1850–1870

City	Function	Population		
		1850	*1860*	*1870*
San Francisco	Sea port	34,776	56,802	149,473
Sacramento	Interior port	6,820	13,785	16,283
Oakland	Interior port	n.a.	1,543	10,500
Stockton	Interior port	n.a.	3,679	10,066
San Jose	Agricultural center	n.a.	n.a.	9,089
Los Angeles	Agricultural center	1,610	4,385	5,728
Marysville	Interior port	4,500	4,740	4,738
Nevada City	Mining town	2,683	n.a.	4,022
Santa Rosa	Agricultural center	n.a.	1,623	2,898
Santa Cruz	Minor sea port	n.a.	950	2,561
San Diego	Minor sea port	n.a.	731	2,300
Napa	Agricultural center	159	2,378	1,879
Placerville	Mining town	n.a.	1,754	1,562
Petaluma	Agricultural center	n.a.	1,505	n.a.
Oroville	Mining town	n.a.	2,499	1,425
Sonora	Mining town	n.a.	1,960	1,322
Rough and Ready	Mining town	672	1,719	1,210
Watsonville	Agricultural center	n.a.	398	1,151
Monterey	Minor sea port	1,092	n.a.	1,112
Yreka	Mining town	n.a.	1,631	1,063
Healdsburg	Agricultural center	n.a.	334	959
Visalia	Agricultural center	n.a.	548	913

SOURCE: Department of the Interior, *Population of the United States in 1860; Compiled from the Original Returns of the Eighth Census* (Washington: Government Printing Office, 1864); Department of the Interior, *Population of the United States in 1870; Compiled from the Original Returns of the Ninth Census* (Washington: Government Printing Office, 1874).

as those of its Bay Area cousin, and Sacramento sidewalks were notorious as "fracture traps" because of the numerous cracks between the plankings.[38]

In spite of the early confidence of its boosters, Sacramento was visited by five major floods between 1850 and 1863, and the city newspaper lamented the misfortune of residents to have been "continually visited with a greater supply of aqueous effusions than were required for any conceivable purposes."[39] Without effective municipal government, private citizens built the city's first levee system. When Sacramento's first mayor was elected under its new articles of incorporation in 1850, the

Steamboats line the waterfront in the lithograph *Sacramento City*, taken from a drawing by Thomas Boyd and published in 1858. The origins of the town date to 1839, when John A. Sutter began work on the fort that became the headquarters of his enormous rancho, Nueva Helvetia, and a famed wilderness outpost. But it was the discovery of gold at Coloma by Sutter's employee James Marshall that gave rise to the "City of the Plain," making it a great river port and entrepôt for the mines, the center of an inland empire. *California Historical Society, FN-30635.*

city came of age: it could borrow money. Funds were used to prevent a recurrence of additional flooding, but the municipal levees could not stop another inundation in 1852. Finally, after the disastrous flood of 1853 threatened to force a mass exodus of local businessmen to rival Sutterville, Sacramento leaders forever changed its physical form by initiating a major program that included road planking, levee improvement and, in a demonstration of the power of municipal government, the raising of I, J, and K streets by three to four feet, at a total cost of $250,000.[40]

Unlike the larger cities of California, most mining towns had a very simple morphology: a single dirt street fronted by businesses and dwellings. As miner John Fletcher described:

> I am at the camp all alone, for all hands have gone downtown. I must give you some description of Nevada City, as it is called, for there is a great many such cities in California. The town has actually got a street in it (though to be sure it is crocked and not very safe for the ox carts which occasionally pass through it). . . . The houses are either

made of canvas or of cedar boards split out instead of sawed and put on rough in the same way clapboards are at home. There are five round tents as large almost as a circus tent occupied entirely as gambling shops and nine out of every ten doors on the street open the way to a liquor bar. There are several tents, camps, and cabins scattered around in the woods. Such is the City of Nevada.[41]

The small size and uncomplicated morphology of California towns was countered by the eclectic origins of gold-rush emigrants, and anyone spending time "downtown" was introduced to the ethnic, racial, and national diversity of the state's population. Indeed, between the end of the Mexican War and 1860, only half of San Francisco's population was American. Roger Lotchin has argued that the American population of San Francisco possessed a general respect for other cultures throughout the 1850s, although such attitudes were tainted by a ranking of the virtues of specific groups and an expectation of eventual assimilation.[42] Tolerance was certainly present, but American cities in the 1850s were walking cities, and their size, made compact because of the lack of commuter transportation services, resulted in a relative integration of residents over space. Yet because of the lack of housing, as well as the notorious conditions of California streets, gold-rush cities were probably even less than walking cities, and San Francisco's relative tolerance may have been reinforced by crowding and the spatial immobility of the population. Even so, California's central places displayed early segregationist impulses. Ralph Mann's study of Grass Valley and Nevada City shows that residents typically sought out men from the same state or region when forming a household. As Mann points out, "camp residents were disposed not only to trust and to associate intimately with men from their own sections of the country, but also to distrust and segregate themselves from natives of other sections."[43] As the Gold Rush wore on, ethnically and class-based neighborhoods began to appear in California's larger cities. San Francisco's Chinese attempted to recreate their homeland around Dupont and Stockton streets. Chileans lived in a tent colony on Telegraph Hill. Americans gradually replicated the class society they had left "back East." San Francisco's middle classes initially clustered around their places of business at the city center, with workers occupying an outer ring just beyond. By mid-decade, the middle classes had deserted their old neighborhoods for the hills to the west. The more prosperous merchants and professionals established elegant homes on Rincon Hill, while the city's Happy Valley section was increasingly occupied by factories and working-class residences. With laborers pouring into the land south of the original settlement, "South of Market"—San Francisco's skid row—owed its origin to the Gold Rush.[44]

Like the morphology of California's smaller communities, gold-rush architecture had an ephemeral quality. Wood and canvas were the most widely used materials in the built-environment in 1849 and 1850. Canvas was used to pitch simple

South Park in San Francisco, looking north toward Rincon Hill, in the mid-1850s—a starkly striking image of the first exclusive neighborhood in California and compelling testimony to the transforming power of gold. Developed in 1854 by the English-born Forty-niner George Gordon and designed by his countryman the civil engineer and architect George H. Goddard, South Park was modeled on the elegant crescents of London and New York. United States Senator William M. Gwin made his home here, as did such other prominent men as Lloyd Tevis, Isaac Friedlander, and Charles Lux. *Courtesy Oakland Museum of California.*

tents, or to cover box frames built with logs or processed lumber. In spite of the primitive quality of the building materials, tent houses gave San Francisco its first panoramic skyline. "Made transparent by the lamps within," the darkness transformed the city's tents into "dwellings of solid light," and the translucent skyline was an early hallmark of all California urban places.[45] "Most every shanty," a Sacramentan reported, was either a "doggery and provisions store, or a provision store," and most were made of canvas. A tent with a "Hospital" sign hung over the flap indicated the presence of a physician. The advantage of such a minimal investment in building materials was described by one Sacramento resident, who remembered that on the same ground where he had shaded his team only hours before "there stood a Baker's shop in full operation selling bread and receiving the money for it!"[46]

The rudimentary nature of the built-environment made life hard in California's urban places. Battered by an undeveloped street system, ramshackle buildings, and the peninsula's cold climate, one merchant complained that "as a residence" San Francisco was "fraught with discomfort. The high winds, and constant dust, together with broken planks," rendered foot travel, "if not dangerous, exceedingly disagreeable." Moreover, San Francisco houses were home to flies "to such an extent that it is impossible to read with any degree of attention. Fleas are so numerous as to be an intolerable nuisance."[47] The city's lodging houses were "barn-like tenements," one miner remembered, "abominable odours arose, and creeping things abounded."[48] To alleviate the lack of structures, captains beached older ships on the bay and riverfronts in San Francisco and Sacramento, converting the hulls into hotels, boardinghouses, and warehouses. By the spring of 1849, however, more substantial structures began to appear in the major cities. Prefabricated buildings, made of sheet metal, iron, or wood, arrived in San Francisco in 1849. The St. Francis Hotel, on the corner of Grant and Clay, was actually a dozen prefabricated cottages joined together side by side or stacked on top of each other.[49] By 1850, Sacramento had "several hundred" permanent structures, "wood, large, commodious, and comfortable," as well as a bowling alley that doubled as a rooming house. The following year the *Sacramento Union* reported lines of "substantial frame houses, and the dwellings of many of the miners are constructed of logs or boards, and the tent is seldom seen."[50]

As wood structures replaced the canvas of the first days of the Gold Rush, California architecture took on a "colonial" quality. Major architectural forms were borrowed from earlier traditions. In Los Angeles and San Diego, where the effects of emigration was minimal, pre–gold-rush architecture remained dominant. Illustrations of Los Angeles in the late 1850s show the prevalence of one-story adobes, walled patios, and outdoor ovens. In the northern part of the state, the "Yankee" origins of many of the gold seekers meant that the New England frame house quickly surpassed the Mediterranean masonry tradition of the Spanish and Mexican colonial eras.[51] The concurrent appearance of the balloon frame in America building practices, which replaced mortises and tenons with nails and two-by-four-inch studs covered by either clapboards or shingles, was ideally suited to rapid house-building in San Francisco and the interior cities.[52]

Due to the state's isolation, there was a significant lag time between the development of architectural innovations in the East and their appearance in California. It took roughly a decade for the stick house, a wood frame structure with front bay windows and steeply pitched gabled roofs, to appear in California after its introduction on the eastern seaboard during the 1850s. By the late 1860s, the common San Francisco townhouse was a flat-roofed stick with an overhanging cornice.[53] In spite of the dominance of American architecture, San Francisco architecture reflected the international origins of its residents throughout the gold-rush era. Classical building designs, particularly examples of Greek Revival, were prominent in the

Los Angeles in the 1850s. The enormous demand for beef cattle created by the Gold Rush brought a wonderful prosperity to the rancheros of El Pueblo, but following hard upon the trail of sudden riches came outlaws, prostitutes, and monte dealers, who gave the dusty cowtown a reputation as one of the toughest and most crime-ridden cities in the American West. *California Historical Society/Title Insurance and Trust Photo Collection, University of Southern California.*

city because, as Harold Kirker points out, it was the only architectural form held in common by San Francisco's competing colonial cultures. Greek and Roman derivatives were the dominant traditions of civic architecture, the best example being San Francisco's second city hall, completed in 1851. The state capitol, occupied in 1869, was similarly derived from a "florid Roman-Corinthian" design.[54]

Since California cities were built overwhelmingly of canvas and wood during the first years of the Gold Rush, fire was an important impetus to the development of the state's architecture. The presence of a masculine culture that valued late nights of heavy drinking illuminated by lantern, and the random tossing of smoldering cigars, exacerbated the threat. Four fires destroyed major portions of San Francisco between 1849 and 1851. A large portion of Marysville burned in 1851. Sacramento, when it was not under water, was visited by five major blazes in the early 1850s. Nevada City burned to the ground for the first time in March 1851, the flames presenting "a spectacle of meteoric splendor seldom equaled." Nevada City residents were generally well armed, and a number of gunpowder-filled structures exploded, "casting flaming timbers, brands, and miss[i]les of all descriptions into the air." Pine trees, interwoven with town buildings, added to the conflagration. Residents finally contained the blaze by tearing down buildings to create a fire break, but only after it destroyed 125 structures, fully half of the town. Nevada City burned to the ground a total of three times during the 1850s.[55]

After each major blaze, individuals in every community used brick in the reconstruction of many buildings, giving an increased sense of permanence to the state's urban places. When fire burst through the windows and doors of masonry structures, landlords began to install locally made iron shutters that doubled as a barrier to burglars. Following the fire of May 1850, San Francisco enacted the state's first building ordinance, prohibiting the construction of cloth structures in the city's commercial district.[56] In spite of the plethora of disasters visited upon California's cities and towns, economics dictated that a booming town would survive. After Nevada City's first great fire, Aaron Augustus Sargent observed that it was "impossible to give a death blow to any point of rendezvous of miners, or miner's supplies, short of an exhaustion of the mines." Like so many gold-rush towns, Nevada City was rapidly rebuilt. Indeed, most inhabitants felt that in the long run, "the fire was a benefit" to the town, "for better buildings and straighter streets resulted from it." Local businessmen "soon forgot their losses in new profits," and by the summer of 1851, Nevada City was as busy as ever. A mud slide swept away a large part of the town in March 1852.[57]

Even as Californians built up their cities and towns, the urban system in which they were enmeshed was in rapid flux. The placer phase of the Gold Rush gave way, and most of the mining hamlets disappeared, the "ghost towns" forming a still-visible skeleton of this ephemeral urban system. All of the mining towns lost population and only the larger towns survived at all. Stockton and Sacramento, too dependent on supplying the dying towns of the southern and central mining districts and the latter devastated by floods as well, witnessed a modest period of growth during the 1860s. Marysville, too far north to tap into the trade associated with the Central Valley's growing agricultural areas, stagnated. Los Angeles, its economy shattered by an oversupply of beef and a terrible drought in the 1860s, struggled as well. Monterey, the provincial capital in Spanish and Mexican California, failed to adjust to the changing reality of competing cities, and saw its population expand by only 600 people between 1870 and 1900.[58]

Yet even with the exhaustion of the gold deposits, the urban dimension of California life was secured. Over the remnants of the gold-rush city system, the transcontinental railroad and the end of California's isolation ushered in a new era of urban development. San Francisco remained the state's major port, its commerce and a growing array of manufacturing establishments providing goods to California's agricultural communities. Oakland boomed as a railroad terminus, and other East Bay communities developed as ferry points and as places of residence and trade.[59] Inland towns continued to grow as supply and transfer points for agricultural products and soon outnumbered the surviving mining towns. Demonstrating the symbiotic relationships inherent in the California city system, much of the agricultural produce found its way to San Francisco and other cities. With the opening of the Santa Fe Railroad, Los Angeles would experience the boom of the 1880s, beginning the reversal of forty years of San Francisco dominance. Great battles would result from this tremendous urban growth into the next century: over possession of water resources, over command of municipal governments, and over the control of city space itself. Rather than representing a break with the past, the hamlets, towns, and cities that have played so important a role in the history of twentieth-century California embody a historical continuity with the world of the Forty-niners. Today, for better or worse, the constancy of city-building in the physical expanse goes on. The modern metropolitan world called California is yet another demonstration of the importance of the urban civilization crafted by the Gold Rush.

NOTES

The author is indebted to Professor Richard Orsi and Professor Judith Stanley of the California State University, Hayward, as well as Professor Eric Monkkonen of the University of California, Los Angeles, and Professor Ronald Tobey of the University of California, Riverside, for their encouragement, support, and generous advice. Thanks are also extended to the staffs of the California State Library and the special collections department of the University of the Pacific Library, who supplied access to their wonderful collections.

 1. Diary of D. D. Demarest, 33–39, Demarest Family Papers, mss. 28, box 1, Holt Atherton Collection, University of the Pacific, Stockton, Calif. For the character of mining in the Yuba camps and a description of the history of Downieville, see Remi Nadeau, *Ghost Towns and Mining Camps of California: A History and Guide* (Santa Barbara: Crest Publishers, 1992), 156–61.

 2. For an excellent overview of the contradictory aspects of the urban West, see Carl Abbott, *The Metropolitan Frontier: Cities in the Modern American West* (Tucson: University of Arizona Press, 1993), xi–xxiii.

 3. Patricia Limerick, *The Legacy of Conquest: The Unbroken Past of the American West* (New York: W. W. Norton, 1987), 18.

 4. For an excellent overview of the urban interpretation of western history, see Gerald D. Nash, *Creating the West: Historical Interpretations, 1890–1890* (Albuquerque: University of New Mexico Press, 1991), 159–95. On the frontier and American historical development, see Frederick Jackson Turner, "The Influence of the Frontier in American History," in his *History, Frontier, Section: Three Essays by Frederick Jackson Turner* (Albuquerque: University of New Mexico Press, 1993). For a general view of the impact of the frontier thesis and its early challengers, see John Higham, *History: Professional Scholarship in America* (Baltimore: Johns Hopkins University Press, 1989), 174–205. For early urban counters to the frontier thesis, see

Arthur M. Schlesinger, Sr., "The City in American History," *Mississippi Valley Historical Review* 27 (June 1940): 43–66, and *Rise of the City, 1878–1898* (New York: Macmillan, 1933); and Lewis Mumford, *The City in History: Its Origins, Its Transformations, and Its Prospects* (New York: Harcourt, Brace and World, 1961).

5. Schlesinger, "The City in American History," 57. For Schlesinger's impact on western urban history, see Nash, *Creating the West*, 37–38.

6. Richard Wade, *The Urban Frontier: The Rise of Western Cities, 1790–1830* (Cambridge: Harvard University Press, 1959), 1. On Wade's impact on western history, see Nash, *Creating the West*, 178.

7. Bradford Luckingham, *Phoenix: The History of a Southwestern Metropolis* (Tucson: University of Arizona Press, 1989); Gilbert R. Cruz, *Let There Be Towns: Spanish Municipal Origins in the American Southwest, 1610–1810* (College Station, Tex.: Texas A&M University Press, 1988); Lawrence Larsen, *The Urban West at the End of the Frontier* (Lawrence, Kan.: Regents Press of Kansas, 1978); William Cronon, *Nature's Metropolis: Chicago and the Great West* (New York: W. W. Norton, 1991).

8. For an example of Bancroft's views of urban California, see Hubert Howe Bancroft, *The Works of Hubert Howe Bancroft*, vol. 35 (San Francisco: The History Company, 1888), 260–93. For McWilliams's views of the urban West, see Carey McWilliams, Introduction to *Rocky Mountain Cities*, ed. Ray B. West (New York: W. W. Norton, 1949), 7–23. For the development of the California Dream within a largely urban context, see Kevin Starr, *Inventing the Dream: California Through the Progressive Era* (New York: Oxford University Press, 1985) and *Material Dreams: Southern California Through the 1920s* (New York: Oxford University Press, 1990). Also see Nash, *Creating the West*, 175–76.

9. Gunther Barth, *Instant Cities: Urbanization and the Rise of San Francisco and Denver* (New York: Oxford University Press, 1975).

10. James E. Vance, Jr., *Geography and Urban Evolution in the San Francisco Bay Area* (Berkeley: Institute of Governmental Studies, 1964), 33–34; Mel Scott, *The San Francisco Bay Area: A Metropolis in Perspective* (Berkeley: University of California Press, 1959); Roger W. Lotchin, *San Francisco, 1846–1856: From Hamlet to City* (Urbana: University of Illinois Press, 1974). Also see William Camp, *San Francisco: Port of Gold* (Garden City, N.Y.: Doubleday and Co., 1947); William Issel and Robert W. Cherny, *San Francisco, 1865–1932: Politics, Power, and Urban Development* (Berkeley: University of California Press, 1986); Dianne Kirkby, "Gold and the Growth of a Metropolis: A Comparative Study of San Francisco and Melbourne, Australia," *Journal of the West* 17 (April 1978): 3–15; and Felix Reisenberg, *Golden Gate: The Story of San Francisco Harbor* (New York: Alfred A. Knopf, 1940).

11. Carey McWilliams, *Southern California: An Island on the Land* (Salt Lake City: Peregrine Smith Books, 1973); Robert Fogelson, *The Fragmented Metropolis: Los Angeles, 1850–1930* (Cambridge: Harvard University Press, 1967); John W. Reps, *Cities of the American West: A History of Frontier Urban Planning* (Princeton: Princeton University Press, 1979); Ralph Mann, *After the Gold Rush: Society in Grass Valley and Nevada City, California, 1849–1870* (Stanford: Stanford University Press, 1982). For overviews of California mining towns during the Gold Rush, see William A. Bullough, "Entrepreneurs and Urbanism on the California Mining Frontier: Frederick Walter and Weaverville, 1852–1868," *California History* 70 (Summer 1991): 162–73; Joseph Henry Jackson, *Anybody's Gold: The Story of California's Mining Towns* (New York: D. Appleton-Century Co., 1941); and Earl Ramey, *The Beginnings of Marysville* (San Francisco: California Historical Society, 1936).

12. For a brief discussion of these two views, see Spiro Kostof, *The City Assembled: The Elements of Urban Form Through History* (London: Thames and Hudson, 1992), 7–8.

13. Eric Monkkonen, *America Becomes Urban: The Development of U.S. Cities and Towns, 1780–1980* (Berkeley: University of California Press, 1988), 85.

14. For Spanish methods of town development in the region, see Cruz, *Let There Be Towns.* For the economic limitations of California towns during the Spanish and Mexican eras, see Steven W. Hackel, "Land, Labor, and Production: The Colonial Economy of Spanish and Mexican California," in *Contested Eden: California Before the Gold Rush,* ed. Ramón A. Gutiérrez and Richard J. Orsi (Berkeley: University of California Press, 1998), 111–46.

15. Monkkonen, *America Becomes Urban,* 45–48.

16. Ibid., 77–81.

17. Roger Lotchin, "San Francisco, 1846–56: The Patterns and Chaos of Growth," in *Cities in American History,* ed. Kenneth T. Jackson and Stanley K. Schultz (New York: Alfred A. Knopf, 1972), 146–47.

18. Edwin Bryant, *What I Saw in California: The Complete Original Narrative and Appendix from the 1849 Appleton Edition in True Facsimile* (Palo Alto, Calif.: Lewis Osborne, 1967), 323–24.

19. William Tecumseh Sherman, "Memoirs of General William T. Sherman," in *Gold Rush: A Literary Exploration,* ed. Michael Kowalewski (Berkeley: Heyday Books, 1997), 151. For the problems of the city site and the efforts of local boosters to overcome them, see Lotchin, "San Francisco, 1846–56: Patterns and Chaos of Growth," 143–46.

20. San Francisco *Alta California,* May 3, 1849, 2.

21. Lotchin, *San Francisco,* 3–29, 45–82.

22. "Rio Rico Mines, Feb. 12, 1850," in *California Emigrant Letters,* ed. Walker D. Wyman (New York: Bookman Associates, 1952), 149. On passenger estimates on the river, see the *Sacramento Union,* September 12, 1851, 2. For an overview of the inland cities' economic functions, see J. S. Holliday, *The World Rushed In: The California Gold Rush Experience, An Eyewitness Account of a Nation Heading West* (New York: Simon & Schuster, 1981), 302–303. On freight activities in Marysville, see the *Sacramento Union,* October 23, 1851, 2. For the history of Sacramento during the period, see V. Aubrey Neasham and James E. Henley, *The City of the Plain: Sacramento in the Nineteenth Century,* ed. Janice A. Woodruff (Sacramento: Sacramento Pioneer Foundation, 1969). For the history of Stockton and surrounding towns during the Gold Rush, see Reps, *Cities of the American West,* 215–19; and Raymond W. Hillman and Leonardo A. Covello, *Cities and Towns of San Joaquin County Since 1847* (Fresno: Panorama West Books, 1985).

23. Fogelson, *Fragmented Metropolis,* 14–15.

24. Scott, *The San Francisco Bay Area,* 39–41.

25. Charles B. Gillespie, "A Miner's Sunday in Coloma," in Kowalewski, *Gold Rush: A Literary Exploration,* 198–203. On the male lack of talent in household endeavors, see Andrew Rotter, "'Matilda for God's Sake Write': Women and Families on the Argonaut Mind," *California History* 58 (Summer 1979): 128–39. On women cooks during the Gold Rush, see JoAnn Levy, *They Saw the Elephant: Women in the California Gold Rush* (Norman: University of Oklahoma Press, 1992), 91–107. On medical care as an aspect of the nineteenth-century household economy, see Susan M. Reverby, *Ordered to Care: The Dilemma of American Nursing, 1850–1945* (Cambridge: Cambridge University Press, 1987), 1–7, 11–16; and Charles E. Rosenberg, *The Care of Strangers: The Rise of America's Hospital System* (New York: Basic Books, 1987), 4.

26. *Seventh Census of the United States: 1850. An Appendix, Embracing the Notes Upon the Tables of Each of the States, Etc.* (Washington, D.C.: Government Printing Office, 1853).

27. For the location of individual mining hamlets, see Erwin G. Gudde and Elisabeth K. Gudde, *California Gold Camps: A Geographical and Historical Dictionary of Camps, Towns, and Localities Where Gold Was Found and Mined; Wayside Stations and Trading Centers* (Berkeley: University of California Press, 1975). For additional descriptions and general histories of the camps, see Nadeau, *Ghost Towns and Mining Camps.*

28. U.S. Bureau of the Census, *Schedule of Population for Cities, 1850,* Microfilm Reel 36, California State Library, Sacramento.

29. Chauncey Canfield, *The Diary of a Forty-Niner* (Stanford: American Book-Strafford Press, 1947), 31. For the role of the tavern in the American West, see Elliot West, *The Saloon on the Rocky Mountain Frontier* (Lincoln: University of Nebraska Press, 1979).

30. U.S. Bureau of the Census, *Schedule of Population for Cities, 1850.*

31. For an excellent overview of the development of urban morphology, see James E. Vance, Jr., *The Continuing City: Urban Morphology in Western Civilization* (Baltimore: Johns Hopkins University Press, 1990).

32. Geoffrey P. Mawn, "Framework for Destiny: San Francisco, 1847," *California Historical Quarterly* 51 (Summer 1972): 165–74. On the dominance of the grid system in U.S. cities west of the Appalachians, see Vance, *Continuing City,* 275–81.

33. Diary of D. D. Demarest, 36; Reps, *Cities of the American West,* 98–101, 195–97, 215, 245–50. Also see Lynn Bowman, *Los Angeles: Epic of a City* (Berkeley: Howell-North Books, 1974), 32–34, 46–51, 141–46.

34. Scott, *San Francisco Bay Area,* 28.

35. Charles Lockwood, "Tourists in Gold Rush San Francisco," *California History* 59 (Winter 1980): 318–19. Lotchin, *San Francisco,* 168–69.

36. Lotchin, *San Francisco,* 14–15. On the development of Golden Gate Park, see Scott, *San Francisco Bay Area,* 52–53.

37. Reps, *Cities of the American West,* 210–11.

38. *Sacramento Union,* October 22, 1851, 2. On the improvement of Sacramento streets, see August 12, 1851, 2.

39. *Sacramento Union,* August 19, 1851, 2. On the flooding of Marysville, see March 8, 1852, 2.

40. Marvin Brienes, "Sacramento Defies the Rivers, 1850–1878," *California History* 58 (Spring 1979): 3–14.

41. John E. Fletcher to Ruth Fletcher, June 20, 1850, John E. Fletcher Correspondence, mss. F613 1849, Holt Atherton Collection, University of the Pacific, Stockton, Calif. For a general history of Nevada City, see Mann, *After the Gold Rush.*

42. Lotchin, *San Francisco,* 100–113.

43. Mann, *After the Gold Rush,* 17–19.

44. Lotchin, *San Francisco,* 3–30, 123–26, 191. Alvin Averbach, "San Francisco's South of Market District, 1850–1950: The Emergence of a Skid Row," *California Historical Quarterly* 52 (Fall 1973): 197–201. Also see Kevin Starr, "'South of Market and Bunker Hill: An Introduction to Neighborhood Histories' by Anne B. Bloomfield and Anastasia Loukaitou-Sideris and Gail Sansbury," *California History* 74 (Winter 1995/96): 370–71; and Anne B. Bloomfield, "A History of the California Historical Society's New Mission Street Neighborhood," *California History* 74 (Winter 1995/96): 372–93.

45. Lockwood, "Tourists in Gold Rush San Francisco," 316.

46. "Sacramento City, Aug. 7, 1849," and "Sacramento City, Aug. 17, 1849," in Wyman, *California Emigrant Letters*, 163–64.

47. "Storeman in San Francisco. St. Joseph Adventure, Oct. 9, 1849," and "Discomforts in San Francisco," in Wyman, *California Emigrant Letters*, 168.

48. William Shaw, "Creeping things abounded," in *San Francisco Memoirs, 1835–1851: Eyewitness Accounts of the Birth of a City*, ed. Malcolm E. Barker (San Francisco: Londonborn Publications, 1994), 169.

49. On the quality of prefabricated houses in San Francisco, see Harold Kirker, *California's Architectural Frontier: Style and Tradition in the Nineteenth Century* (Santa Barbara: Peregrine Smith, 1973), 40–41. On the St. Francis Hotel's construction, see Lockwood, "Tourists in Gold Rush San Francisco," 320.

50. "Rio Saco Mines, Feb. 12, 1850," in Wyman, *California Emigrant Letters*, 165. On housing in Sacramento, see the *Sacramento Union*, August 19, 1851, 2.

51. On the colonial quality of California architecture during the Gold Rush, see Harold Kirker, "California Architecture and Its Relation to Contemporary Trends in Europe and America," *California Historical Quarterly* 51 (Winter 1972): 289–99. Also see the chapter on architecture in the Federal Writers' Project, *California: A Guide to the Golden State* (New York: Hastings House Publishers, 1939), 167–76. For Los Angeles architecture during the 1850s, see Reps, *Cities of the American West*, 250. For additional works on California architecture throughout the nineteenth century, see Joseph Armstrong Baird, Jr., "Architectural Legacy of Sacramento: A Study of 19th Century Style," *California Historical Quarterly* 39 (September 1960): 193–200; Ralph Herbert Cross, *The Early Inns of California, 1844–1869* (San Francisco: Cross and Brandt, 1954); David G. DeLong, ed., *Historic American Buildings: California*, 4 vols. (New York: Garland Publishers, 1980); David Gebhard and Harriette Van Breton, *1868: Architecture in California: An Exhibition Organized by David Gebhard and Harriette Van Breton to Celebrate the Centennial of the University of California* (Santa Barbara: Regents of the University of California, 1968); Donald R. Hannaford and Revel Edwards, *Spanish Colonial or Adobe Architecture of California, 1800–1850* (New York: Architectural Book Publishing Co., 1931); and Harold Kirker, *Old Forms on a New Land: California Architecture in Perspective* (Niwot, Colo.: Roberts Rinehart Publishers, 1991).

52. Kirker, *California's Architectural Frontier*, 59–62.

53. For an overview of the elements of the stick style, see Vincent J. Scully, Jr., *The Shingle Style and the Stick Style: Architectural Theory and Design from Downing to the Origins of Wright* (New Haven: Yale University Press, 1977).

54. Kirker, *California's Architectural Frontier*, 44–85.

55. David Allan Comstock, ed., *1848–1851: 150 Years Ago. Reprint from an account published in 1856. "A Sketch of Nevada County," by Aaron Augustus Sargent* (Nevada City, Calif., 1998), 9–10.

56. Malcolm Edwards, "'Substantial, Fire-Proof Edifices . . .' Made So by the Marvelous Invention of Iron Door and Window Shutters," *California Historical Quarterly* 50 (December 1971): 431–37. On the San Francisco ordinance, see Kirker, *California's Architectural Frontier*, 32. On brick as an impediment to fire, see the *Sacramento Union*, October 25, 1851, 2.

57. Comstock, *1848–1851*, 24–25.

58. On the decline of Monterey, see Barth, *Instant Cities*, 74–75.

59. Vance, *Geography and Urban Evolution*, 33–34.

6

Weaving a Different World

Women and the California Gold Rush

Nancy J. Taniguchi

A woman helped start the rush for gold. That fact was remembered more than twenty-five years later by a feature writer for the San Francisco *Daily Evening Bulletin*, who risked venturing to a hotel in "a quarter where up town ladies seldom visit" for an interview. The lady-like reporter, Mary P. Winslow, there located "Aunty Jenny" (Elizabeth J. Bays Wimmer), former cook for Sutter's workforce at Coloma. She and her husband had arrived in the city in 1874 "in the hope of getting some relief from the society of Pioneers" with the claim that they had Marshall's original gold nugget, plucked from the millrace, in their possession. Winslow invited them to dine, and after dinner, when Wimmer was settled in the largest available rocking chair sucking on her pipe, Winslow allowed the storytelling to begin. Jenny recounted the day when her little son, Martin, came running into the house, calling, "'Here, mother, here's something Mr. Marshall and Pa found, and they want you to put it into the saleratus water to see if it will tarnish.'" Jenny replied, "'This is gold, and I will throw it into my lye kettle . . . and if it is gold it will be gold when it comes out.'" The next morning, after her lye soap was removed and cut, she recalled, "At the bottom of the pot was a double-handful of potash, which I lifted in my two hands, and there was my gold as bright as it could be."[1] True story or not, the nugget (shaped, according to Winslow, like "a piece of spruce-gum just out of the mouth of a school-girl") was not bought by the Society of California Pioneers, but did go on display at the 1893 Chicago World's Fair, a symbol of continuing interest in Aunty Jenny's tale.[2]

By then "her" gold had become the main catalyst of subsequent California history. As Winslow put it, Jenny Wimmer had revealed "this magic instrument that revolutionized the world, gave us the Central Pacific Railroad, Emperor Norton, Bret Harte, *Occident*, the Comstock ledge, [the] Palace Hotel, strawberries and cream the whole year round, Mark Twain, earthquakes, James Lick and King Kaiakaua."[3]

As California transformed, so did the lives of its women. The world of the Indian rancheria and Mexican rancho became surrounded and submerged by Yankee settlement.[4] As the society shifted to one commanded by men from "the States," the position of—and opportunities for—women likewise transformed. Some groups of women were discounted or destroyed, while others arrived, taking advantage of fleeting opportunities, either in traditional or new labor categories largely determined by the desires of the women themselves. But as the Yankee men replicated their past society by bringing "respectable" women from the States, many such possibilities evaporated and society began to harden.

Of course, none of this was anticipated. Jenny Wimmer had not come to Coloma to discover gold. Her specific tasks included cooking and washing laundry for white laborers, as well as caring for the local Indians also in Sutter's employ. Her husband, Peter Wimmer, according to James Marshall, "had charge of the Indians, [and directed] at what particular point to set them to work for the day."[5] In 1855, Jenny and Peter were interviewed for an article in the San Francisco *Daily Herald,* which reported that "Mrs. W., assisted by Martin and Sarah her children, did cooking for the party, and employed her leisure time in making shirts for the Indians."[6]

Then gold was discovered. As the rush started, much of the northern California population flocked to the Mother Lode. The earliest gold seekers often utilized the handiwork of Sierra Indian women in their haste to get rich. As the San Francisco *Californian* reported on August 14, 1848, extractive methods included rockers and long toms. "But far the largest number use nothing but a large tin pan or an Indian basket into which they place the dirt and shake it until the gold gets to the bottom."[7] Indians worked side by side with miners such as Mr. Murphy, who had "a small tribe of wild Indians who gather gold for him . . . in part [due] to the fact that he has married the daughter of the chief—a young woman of many personal attractions."[8] These peaceful, cooperative, sometimes familial relationships foundered in the sea of incoming Argonauts, who routed Indian women from the hills and replaced their beautifully woven baskets with mass-produced products of eastern manufacture. Women's existence disappeared in the stock figure of the lone, unshaven miner with his battered tin pan.

THE UNACCULTURATED

Unacculturated men, fresh from the East, set the tone for gold-rush California due to the sheer weight of numbers. Based on the 1860 census, males outnumbered females in San Francisco by three to two. However, the sex ratio for those under fifteen was about even, so the marriageable population—from fifteen to fifty—faced even more skewed proportions, wherein about 47 percent of the men found no

Eliza Jane Steen Johnson, a native of County Antrim, Ireland, who came to California in the Gold Rush with her husband, John, and opened a dry goods and millinery shop off Portsmouth Square in San Francisco. A strikingly handsome woman, independent-minded and ambitious, she helped make the enterprise a success by modeling clothing for the men who crowded the store. With its overwhelmingly male population, California presented women with both unique opportunities and challenges. *Courtesy Oakland Museum of California; gift of Barbara Smith.*

ready marriage partners. Because so many women stayed in San Francisco because of better amenities, greater work opportunities, or other reasons, the proportion of males to females was even more unbalanced in the diggings.[9] Consequently, men acquired most of the gold. Women had to find ways to earn or extract it from them in order to survive.

Furthermore, although Forty-niners came from all over the globe, the majority were white men from the northern states. Most had been reared with the typical American conventions of the day by good, God-fearing mothers. Their slice of society was preoccupied with the notion of the "separate spheres" in which men went out and swung the ax, killed Indians, engaged in sordid politics, pursued grasping commerce, and gambled for gain, while women, pure vessels of societal morality, stayed home to nurture havens for embattled males when they should be able to return.[10] Before courting such women, some Argonauts resolutely awaited a return to the East, such as avid correspondent Horace Snow, who longed for "old New England and its comely girls!"[11] Like Horace, most male Argonauts believed that slipping into sin, vice, and consorting with "bad" women was the surest road to hell. Not that they did not do such things in faraway California, but they retained ambivalent attitudes about their own behavior and were more or less willing to revert to type when "good" women showed up to demand their conformity. They shared the view of sacred womanhood articulated by pioneer Eliza Farnham, who wrote that "there is no inviolate fireside in California that is not an altar; no honorable woman but is a missionary of virtue, morality, happiness, and peace, to a circle of careworn, troubled, and often, alas, demoralized men."[12] She acted on this perceived need by offering to organize a large-scale emigration of highly respectable women of age twenty-five or older to San Francisco. It was not a success.[13]

Testaments abound to the demoralization she feared. For example, an account of the southern Mother Lode by Mrs. Lee Whipple-Haslam (her first name is unknown) revealed that "in early days I have seen all that made life worth living to a young and handsome man, vibrant with life, destroyed in five minutes, by a man's fists." This observation was occasioned by the attempted seduction of another man's wife. The would-be seducer carried life-long scars of his beating, testimony to the value of at least one gold-rush woman.[14]

Many eastern men who panned streams in the Sierra had little experience with people other than themselves, but the relative lack of women spurred a general openness and curiosity. Around them they found a variety of unfamiliar types—darker, Spanish-speaking, Roman Catholic Mexicans; native peoples as varied as the Hupa, Maidu, and Yokuts; citizens of Pacific nations such as the Chinese, Peruvians, Chileans, and Hawaiians. These people, and especially their women, had no prescribed niche in the Yankee cosmology. Therefore, the Forty-niners' reactions to these "exotics" had to be based on other notions—sometimes race, sometimes religion, sometimes the pure inventiveness born of novelty. This gold-rush multiethnicity and internationalism worked to the disadvantage of some of the women, but opened new possibilities for others, at least until the moral civilizers that the men recognized—their own Yankee women—arrived in force. Then, a newly reconstructed eastern-style society imposed its own dichotomy of femininity, of "good" and "bad" women, a division that superseded lesser concerns of race, class, and ethnicity.

California natives from an interior tribe attend to daily chores in a wood engraving of the mid-1850s. The Gold Rush disrupted traditional patterns of life for Indians throughout California, and within a couple of decades, warfare, disease, and starvation had decreased their numbers by three-quarters or more. Even more than the men, Indian women suffered from the violence and exploitation that marked the era. From John Russell Bartlett, *Personal Narrative of Explorations and Incidents* (1854). *California Historical Society, FN-30529.*

"WRETCHED CREATURES"

Of course, there were exceptions to this acceptance—most persistently in the prejudices against California's earlier inhabitants. Generally, Yankees condemned native Californians without bothering to distinguish one band from another, nor mission ex-neophyte from "gentile." "One fundamental difference between the Hispanic and the Anglo-American cultures," a modern historian noted, "has always been the fact that the former utilized the native as its primary source of labor whereas the latter never did. There simply was no place in the American cosmos for the Indian."[15]

One of the more charitable views of California native women came from "Dame Shirley" in her first letter from Rich Bar in 1851. She admitted that she previously "took" to the Indians portrayed as "glorious forest heroes that live in the Leather Stocking Tales." She consequently noted "the extreme beauty of the *limbs* of the Indian women of California" despite the "haggardness of expression, and ugliness of feature . . . of these wretched creatures."[16]

In general, native people were perceived as not much different from the animals in the forest, and their women, when their gender was even noticed, usually served as objects of prey, derision, or pity. Some locals even took Indian slaves. In 1846, the military commander of California, John Montgomery, found it necessary to extend a proclamation addressed particularly to persons "imprisoning and holding to service Indians against their will . . . [that] the Indian population must not be regarded as slaves."[17] These lofty sentiments were directly countermanded by the state legislature of 1852, which permitted the enslavement of Indian women, men, and children if a small sum be given as a bond to the county justice of the peace against cruel abuse. Indians could also be arrested as vagrants and sold to the highest bidder for up to four months' unpaid labor, their "vagrancy" ensured by the fact that their land was taken up as "unoccupied" by opportunistic pioneers.[18]

To some extent, this picture of absolute destruction is belied by historian Albert Hurtado, who makes specific reference to the survival of Indian women. But while "survival" may have been achieved, it was at a grim cost. In 1853, an official report from El Dorado County noted "open and disgusting acts of prostitution" among Indian women driven by poverty and misery, to the extent that syphilis had proceeded so far in one camp that the women "were unable to walk."[19] Indian women also suffered from rape as well as more generalized violence (murder, burning of their rancherias, destruction of food supplies) that characterized Argonaut-Indian relations as a whole.[20]

Men who married Indians in an attempt to form stable unions could also be discouraged or prevented from doing so, sometimes by social mores, sometimes by government policy. Some Argonauts imported sectional ideas of race that discouraged these unions. For example, William Brewer, a future Yale professor, deprecated "squaw men," equating them with "rank secessionists" and "'poor white trash' from the frontier slave states, Missouri, Arkansas, and Texas."[21] A particularly violent reaction occurred about 1854 among the southern Yokuts. According to Thomas Jefferson ("Uncle Jeff") Mayfield, raised partially among the Yokuts, "the government had been trying to establish Indian reservations on Kings and Fresno Rivers, and a troop of cavalry was attempting to round up all of the Indians of the valley." They rode up to the cabin of a white man named Mann, who had been living with his Indian wife for several years and "demanded the mokee. Mann told them that she was his wife, that he had provided for her for several years, and that he could continue to do so in the future." The expedition's leader demanded that the woman be brought forth, which Mann refused to do. The soldier forced his way into the cabin. "The mokee had crawled under the bed, and the cavalryman started to drag her out. She called to Mann for help. Mann ran to her aid and was shot in the back and killed by one of the troopers outside. The troopers tied the mokee and took her with

A Mexican couple stroll together in an illustration by Charles Nahl that appeared in the March 1857 issue of *Hutchings' California Magazine.* Like the Yankees who visited California during Hispanic days, Argonauts from New England and the Middle Atlantic states frequently responded ambivalently to the Mexican women they encountered in the new El Dorado, taken by their grace and warmth but questioning their virtue. *California Historical Society, FN-31545.*

them and left Mann lying where he had fallen." The Indians later buried him, and Uncle Jeff subsequently saw the woman "many times and heard her tell what happened."[22] Obviously, she survived, but with what future?

LEAD INTO GOLD

The future first intruded as the last lead bullets were fired in the Mexican-American War. Almost simultaneously, gold was discovered, lending credence to the rampant American belief that a benevolent Protestant God assured the "Manifest Destiny" of one nation over another, of Americans over Mexicans. The earliest views of American superiority had been shaped by firsthand accounts such as that of Richard Henry Dana, who described the *Californias'* "fondness for dress . . . [that] is excessive, and is sometimes their ruin. A present of a fine mantle, or of a necklace or pair of earrings gains the favor of the greater part."[23] The war itself had generated a spate of potboiler literature by such famous hacks as Ned Buntline. His formula novels involved heroic American frontiersmen; backward, superstitious Catholic priests; evil, cowardly Mexican men; and breathtakingly beautiful *señoritas* who predictably fell in love with the Yankee frontiersman (and adopted his ways). The American elite as well as the working class gobbled up these accounts, ensuring that many would bring inaccurate, preconceived notions to their encounters with real Mexicans in California.[24] These views differed sharply from actual Californio values, which put strong emphasis on the sanctity of family, maintained a landed elite, supported a traditional mission system, encouraged the inclusion of Indians on ranchos as laborers and as house servants, and carefully chaperoned daughters until an early marriage with a suitably stationed husband.[25] Thus, conflict was inevitable.

The most egregious confrontation occurred in Downieville on July 5, 1851. The account of Major William Downie, for whom the town was named, indicated not only the prevailing racial prejudice but the value placed on women. Downie described a man named Cannon, falling-down drunk after the Independence Day celebration, who smashed through the door of an adobe hut occupied by a Mexican couple. He apparently assaulted the woman, although Downie claimed Cannon only insulted her. The next day, Cannon returned with his male companion of the previous night, supposedly to apologize. Increasingly heated words in Spanish—not understood by the companion—passed between Cannon and the Mexican couple. Suddenly, the woman, Juanita, pulled out a knife and stabbed Cannon to death. The companion rushed back to camp and a lynch mob assembled. Although cries of "Hang the greaser devils!" rang out, the Mexican man was acquitted. Juanita, dressed in her finest, was led to a hastily erected scaffold. "Big" Bill Logan, notorious for administering a vicious flogging a year earlier, was summoned as "it took a man like that to hang a woman." Juanita spoke to "the bloodthirsty mob," explaining why she had killed and that she would do it again. (One wonders how many present understood her.) Then she placed the noose over her own neck and "leaped from the scaffold into eternity. . . . But there was a blot on the fair name of the Yuba which it took years to wash out," concluded Downie.[26]

Perhaps the Yuba River region's notoriety came partly from resultant publicity.[27] A year later, another Hispanic woman died violently with no echoing fanfare. In June 1851, arsonists took flame to San Francisco to facilitate looting. They achieved their ends, as reported by Mary Ball, a widow originally from England who kept an insightful diary. "The robbers were so numerous," she wrote, "that they were allowed to go at large after giving up the articles they had stolen." She also reported the "horror of the night was increased by a man shooting a poor Mexican woman named Carmelita without any cause"; this, while looters went free.[28]

Ball's account of the lack of repercussions for killing a Mexican woman easily squares with the views of William Streeter, an observer of Santa Barbara in the 1850s. He described the Americans: "the majority of these rough, reckless men had little respect for persons or property of the Californians. . . . The generous hospitality of the latter was often repaid with insult . . . This treatment embittered them [the Californios] towards the Americans and together with other causes prevented their reconciliation to American occupation."[29] Similar opinions peppered the testimony of *Californias* interviewed later for Hubert Howe Bancroft's histories. They stressed the centrality of family and importance of familial loyalty. John Sutter was chastised by Rosalia Vallejo de Leese as a man who "left a wife and several children [in Europe and] was living in open concubinage with two black women [Hawaiians] whom he had brought in his vessel from the Sandwich island."[30] Those women who encountered the Bear Flaggers hated and despised them as barbarians assaulting the civilized Californios, and saw the Americans as lacking in virility, both figuratively and literally.[31] Finally, Angustias de la Guerra de Ord asserted, "*La toma del país no nos gustó nada a los californios, y mucho menos a las mujeres.*"[32] Earlier faulty translation rendered an apparent double negative ("*no . . . nada*") into a positive—that is, that the Californios didn't mind the American takeover, and it bothered the women least of all—instead of recognizing the Spanish use of *nada* as emphatic language, equivalent to "they *really* didn't like. . . ." The saying should thus be more properly translated: "The Californios *really* didn't like the [American] takeover [literally, the taking of the country], and the women liked it even less."[33]

Given the already civilized nature of the very *dons* who constituted the main target of Bear Flagger displeasure (headed by John Frémont's prisoners, Mariano and Salvador Vallejo, and Jacob Leese, the husband of Rosalia Vallejo) and their own animosity to the Mexican government, Californios no doubt wondered what the gringos were really after. Diarist Mary Ball, who in 1851 was managing the Oriental Hotel in San Francisco, had this insight: "Julio [July] 15 Martes [Tuesday]. Had a party last night for the Vallejo family who have been some days with us. All the men of the army seem crazy after California Senoritas or their Padres' land, I think too often it must be the land and not the women."[34] Vallejo had his own views of this road to acculturation. Historian Leonard Pitt specified four Yankee-Hispanic unions from southern California and noted that "two of Mariano Vallejo's daughters married Yankees . . . and his son Platón returned from a New York medical school with a bride born in Syracuse."[35] Most *Californias,* however, remained segregated from Yankee society. Besides, most Argonauts anticipated better prospects mining gold.

WOMEN IN THE MINES

From the beginning, women mined. In August 1848, Walter Colton, the alcalde of Monterey, remarked on "a woman, of Sonoranian birth, who has worked in the dry diggings forty-six days, and brought back two thousand one hundred and twenty-five dollars."[36] Touring the gold fields himself, Colton remarked on a nearby discovery, where "a little girl this morning picked up what she thought a curious stone, and brought it to her mother, who, on removing the extraneous matter, found it a lump of pure gold, weighing between six and seven pounds."[37] A general rush for the place ensued. Another Sonoran woman, finding only about a half dollar worth of gold in the bottom of her bowl, "hurled it back again into the water, and . . . strode off with the indignant air of one who feels himself insulted. Poor woman!" he continued. "[H]ow little thou knowest of those patient females, who in our large cities make a shirt or vest for ten cents!"[38] This sad scenario, the result of male control of capital, was soon replicated in California, although at inflated prices.

Intermittently, women still dug gold for themselves and their families. Mining historian Sally Zanjani reported that "the briefest glance at the [1850] census reveals several possible combinations among the gold rush women listed as 'miners'—daughters working with a mother or a father and women on their own as friends working together and as lone teenagers."[39] Almost inevitably came the rumor of a woman who had disguised herself as a man to join her husband in the diggings—perhaps fearing attack from so many lonely males.[40] Two women who reported a pay streak near Marysville earned particular notice because "both . . . were seventy years old."[41] A famous Frenchwoman, who traded homelessness on the streets of Paris for California's opportunities, had arrived in 1850 seeking work as a maid. She soon turned to mining, "cut off her hair, donned men's clothes, took the name of Marie Pantalon, and went prospecting in the gold country."[42]

Women who had first adopted other pursuits soon realized the possibilities of digging their own gold, or at least increasing their proximity to it. For example, by August of 1852, Mary Ball had quit managing San Francisco's Oriental Hotel and had gone north to Barton's Bar. There she boarded miners and dealt with cholera and other illnesses using remedies in Good's *Study of Medicine,* a gift she had received before leaving the East. In October she noted, "I have received over $120 and have as much more on my book for medacine, and no doubt can make more as I get more known. . . . No rest, a man has just come for me to dress his leg."[43]

The Argonaut's willingness to pay well for scarce feminine services could be heightened when a working woman reminded him of female relatives he had left at home with no financial support.[44] An example of this phenomenon was reported by the mystified Louise Clappe (Dame Shirley), who described a widow who had lost her husband to cholera after a few weeks on the trail west. With no one to accompany her back to the States, she pressed on to California with her eight sons and one daughter, the oldest apparently a teenager. "She used to wash shirts, and iron them on a chair—in the open air, of course; and you can fancy with what success. But the gentlemen were too generous to be critical, and as they paid her three or four times as much as she asked, she accumulated quite a handsome sum in a few days. . . . Poor woman! She

A woman joins a party of miners working a long tom at Auburn Ravine in 1852. Women found a range of opportunities for earning money in the diggings, from washing clothes to preparing meals to dealing monte, and despite the hard labor entailed in placer mining, some toiled with pick and shovel and pan alongside men. *Courtesy California State Library.*

told me she seldom gave them as much as they could eat, at any one meal."[45] Her children, with the exception of the eldest, were nonetheless rated "as healthy looking a set of ragged little wretches as ever I saw."[46] Dame Shirley's myopia about the economic difficulties of women alone can be partially excused by her own lack of need to work. Her husband, a doctor, supported her; the cook at the local hotel fixed their meals, and the one time she tried gold panning: "I wet my feet, tore my dress, spoilt a pair of new gloves . . . and lost a valuable breastpin, in this my labor of love."[47]

Poorer women took gold panning much more seriously. Hard-working Mary Ballou, a slightly educated white woman from New Hampshire living at Negro Bar, took a holiday break from her boardinghouse chores to pan. As she wrote home to her sons, "I just washed out about a Dollars worth of gold dust the fourth of July in the cradle so you see that I am doing a little mining in this gold region but I think it harder to rock the [miner's] cradle to wash out gold than it is to rock the cradle for the Babies in the States."[48] California's opportunities always came at a price.

UNPREDICTABLE EXOTICS

The sight of a Frenchwoman in trousers, or two septuagenarians shoveling pay dirt, did not seem so outlandish in a land where "seeing the elephant" (that most exotic of beastly adventures) served as a handy metaphor for life in general. In fluctuating gold-rush society, circumstance and setting, as well as individual taste, dictated the judgments placed on women, particularly where Americans—and Yankee sensibilities—did not dominate. The most Hispanic of the gold-rush settlements, Sonora, had been founded by Mexicans from that state, but had also attracted Peruvians, Chileans, and French, predominately. American diarist William Perkins wrote at length of his experiences there, including one evening when a difference over a game of lansquenet, presided over by a Frenchwoman, led to a cold-blooded murder. He returned to the gaming table, where "the beautiful Mlle. Virginie . . . greeted me with a fascinating smile." After exclaiming "'Ah Monsieur, quel horreur!'" she described recent events "with all the calmness she would have evinced had she been relating a scene from a novel. To me, her delicate white hands seemed smeared with blood and I left in disgust. . . ."[49] Also in Sonora, Englishman Frank Marryat saw "a lady in black velvet who sings in Italian and accompanies herself, and who elicits great admiration and applause on account of the scarcity of the fair sex in this region."[50] In another saloon, Marryat remarked upon "a very interesting and well-looking young girl [who] was attending at a part of the bar where confectionery was sold. I should not have supposed her to have black blood in her veins, but J. B. assured me that she had been a slave, and had been once sold at New Orleans at a very high price."[51] Even a Yankee woman, Elizabeth Gunn, bent somewhat in her social conventions to survive in Sonora's isolation. Seldom able to visit the nearest New England female, who lived five miles away, she made other friends in town. These included Mrs. Yancey from New Orleans, and a Catholic, Mrs. Lane. Even her French neighbor, who supported her mother, younger sister, and brother "by going to the gambling houses and dealing out the cards to the players," did not receive her censure.[52]

The social dynamics of female loneliness also shaped a distinctive future for California's first female Chinese immigrant. Marie Seise arrived in 1848 with the Gillespie family, Hong Kong traders originally from New York.[53] Her name had been acquired upon her marriage to a Portuguese sailor in Macao, who had later been lost at sea. After serving another family, she was hired by Sarah Bentner Gillespie as a personal maid, and grew to live "not . . . as a servant but above a servant—rather as a companion—enjoying her [Sarah's] fullest confidence." The two women were even confirmed together in 1854 in the first such ceremony at San Francisco's Trinity Episcopal Church, kneeling side by side.[54]

Unlike Marie Seise, most gold-rush Chinese women were slaves, procured for prostitution. Long-standing Chinese cultural tradition regarded daughters from an economic perspective. They were valued less than sons because they could not inherit, and left the family that raised them to work in their husband's family upon marriage, essentially providing no return on investment. This imbalance could be corrected, to some extent, if the daughter were sold or bartered to pay family debts, especially if she could, after transferal, earn an income that could be remanded to her family. One of the main ways a daughter could be useful, just as were women of other nations, was through her womanly skills. Daughters could be indentured as *mui tsai*—literally "little sister" in Cantonese—to provide domestic service on a twenty-four-hour basis to a more prosperous Chinese family. Under this system, the girl was supposed to be freed through an arranged marriage at eighteen so she could start her own household.[55] Like Seise, sometimes *mui tsai* were well-treated by their host families, although, in faraway America, if the wife beat them or the husband sexually assaulted them, there was very little recourse.[56] *Mui tsai* could also, despite their original agreement, be sold into prostitution, which made them the slaves of their owners for life.[57]

The combination of Chinese attitudes toward daughters, the sizable influx of Chinese men to *Gum San* ("Gold Mountain"), and the American fascination with exotic women and girls (the ideal age for a Chinese prostitute was said to be fourteen) created a high demand for Chinese prostitution.[58] Ah Toy, San Francisco's most famous Chinese prostitute, had come in 1849 to "better her condition" in this pursuit. Men thronged to gaze on this fascinating creature. In 1849, she charged an ounce of gold dust "to gaze upon her *countenance*," as the newspaper put it, undoubtedly meaning more than just her uncovered face.[59] This fact emerged only because she had filed suit in court against those who paid her in brass shavings instead of gold, a course of action practical only because she was a free woman (not married, indentured, or a slave) and spoke English, a unique combination.[60] She successfully maintained her independent status in court, despite an attempt by local Chinese men who wished to return her to an alleged "husband" in Hong Kong.[61] In 1850, she was again in court as a public nuisance, and in 1851 to repel an attempt by Chinatown leaders to control her and the two other Chinese prostitutes she had recently employed.[62] She relied partly on her beauty to maintain her status, and was appraised by a Frenchman in 1851 as one of the "few girls who are attractive if not actually pretty . . . with her slender body and laughing eyes."[63] Her rivalry with the local Chinese male power structure escalated, especially against Yuen Sheng (also called Norman As-sing), who headed a local benevolent association and protection ring. The men were able to extend their influence, as indicated by the export of eighteen Chinese prostitutes in 1852 to Weaverville, in Trinity County, far up the Sacramento Valley.[64] As their business expanded, the men's power increased vis-à-vis a female independent like Ah Toy. Nonetheless, the growing wealth of the Chinese merchants also opened a new niche for Chinese women in America—as wife. In an example of feminine adaptation to changing society, Ah Toy apparently took this route, settling down with a husband in Santa Clara, where she died in 1928 just short of her hundredth birthday.[65]

EXPANDING ROLES

During the Gold Rush, California was larger than life, in its appetites, its tastes, and its spectacular successes and downfalls. Lola Montez (born Eliza Gilbert in Ireland), the perfect embodiment of risk and the risqué, found a temporary home on the California stage and cut another niche in the edifice of gold-rush California. She arrived in San Francisco in 1853 bearing the reputation of the discarded mistress of the mad king of Bavaria and the title his love-struck highness had bestowed, the Countess of Landsfeld. Her tour de force, the spider dance, both fascinated and repelled, according to Mary Jane Megquier, the wife of San Francisco physician Thomas Megquier and the proprietress of a San Francisco boardinghouse. Megquier wrote that "Lola Montes is making quite a stir here now but many say that her playing is of that character that is not proper for respectable ladies to attend but I do want to see her very much. Mr Clark said that in dancing the spider dance . . . she was obliged to look rather higher than was proper in so public a place."[66] Whether or not Megquier ever attended the performance (she never wrote of it), much of San Francisco did, captivated by Lola's self-constructed identity, and from a desire to be entertained. While Yankee women, especially those without protectors, had to observe proprieties, those truly (or willfully) outside recognized eastern circles had relatively more freedom.

Lola Montez literally capitalized on that freedom, charging five dollars for the best seats in the San Francisco theater, as opposed to only a dollar in New York. From her perch onstage she carried on characteristic chats over the footlights with the front-row patrons, whether they cheered or jeered. Her California sojourn—including additional appearances in Sacramento and throughout the Mother Lode—was capped by a new marriage (she had already had two, and several lovers) and withdrawal to a cottage in Grass Valley after her three-month marital relationship fell apart.[67] There she befriended another future star of the California stage, young Lotta Crabtree, whom Montez allegedly (but not very probably) taught to dance.[68]

Lotta Crabtree was much more of a home-grown entertainer than the divine Montez, and appealed to a different side of the gold-rush culture. While Lola was

As famed for her numerous love affairs as for her talents an actress, Lola Montez met with enormous acclaim when in 1853 she burst onto the San Francisco stage. She caused a sensation with her spider dance, "married" a journalist, and retreated to the mining community of Grass Valley, where she encouraged the young, budding actress Lotta Crabtree. Her stay in California was brief, though, as was her life, and she made her farewell appearance in 1856. *Courtesy Bancroft Library.*

scandalous, Lotta reminded the miners of that little sister or daughter they had left at home. Lotta reportedly made one of her earliest appearances in *The Gaieties, Temple of Mirth and Song,* a "bit" theater managed by Rowena Granice, a hardworking wife saddled with a controlling, alcoholic husband and two young sons. That Granice was able to support her children, defend herself against her husband's financial schemes and physical intimidation, and go on to a respectable career as California's first novelist and as a journalist in Merced County says much for the variety of economic opportunities available to hardworking women of the era.[69]

In California, theater seemed a more natural environment for women than in more staid eastern America, opening another female occupational niche: theater manager. The first to adopt this employment, Sarah Kirby, took over the refurbished Eagle Theatre (renamed the Tehama) near Sacramento's embarcadero. It had flooded out on Christmas Eve 1849, as miners first stood on the benches and then allegedly hung from the balcony to enjoy the performance as the waters rose. By March 1850, when Sarah Kirby took over, the emphasis was on classical plays for respectable women (and men), including *Othello, Richard III,* and *Don Caesar de Bazan.* She also sponsored benefit performances for such causes as the Odd Fellows and Masons Hospital, wedding the slightly shady world of the theater to objectives of good, feminine virtue. When a cholera epidemic closed the Tehama that November, Kirby and her partner, James Stark, traveled to San Francisco and assumed management of impresario Tom Maguire's Jenny Lind Theater. She continued in both arenas despite the devastations of fire, marrying Stark after the death of her first husband, enjoying friendship and some rivalry with other theater managers, spending two theatrical interludes in Australia, and leaving California for good for the New York stage in 1869.[70] Her activities paved the way for other women theater managers, including Laura Keene. Keene served her apprenticeship in Sacramento, Marysville, Stockton, and San Francisco, afterward making a national impact in New York, where she established a respectable niche for "lady managers" at the pinnacle of American theater.[71]

RECOURSE TO RESPECTABILITY

The preoccupation with the "proper" role for respectable women that kept Mary Jane Megquier from guiltlessly viewing Lola Montez came partly from competitive motives. Since "exotics" could generally earn so much more ready money than "good" women (often with less effort), stressing virtues embedded in Yankee mores could help balance the scale. In such circumstances, respectable women carefully policed their own society.

Protected largely by her own respectability, widow Mary Ball, who first operated a San Francisco boardinghouse, took umbrage when one of her boarders "invited a woman called Helen to dine here today. As she is not a respectable woman, I shall not submit to the insult, but go out to dinner." Ball went visiting that evening, and reported that "everyone commends my conduct in reference to Helen, but as it turned out, she did not come." Three days later her boarder and his friend were "still in high indignation at my daring to refuse to countenance a woman that neither would introduce as a companion to their wives."[72] Yet, as will be shown, Ball knew from previous experience with would-be seducers the price exacted for moral laxity.

In a similar situation, highly respectable Sarah Royce had attended a Benevolent Society Ball, organized and "conducted by the ladies of different churches, of which there were, in the city, already four." Although the ladies were bent on diverting the Forty-niners, only wholesome diversions were allowed. Then arrived a "man, prominent for wealth and business-power, bearing upon his arm a splendidly-dressed woman, well known in the city as the disreputable companion of her wealthy escort." The good church ladies sent some "gentlemen" to invite them both to leave. "Of course," she concluded smugly, "there was nothing for him to do but comply; and all went on again pleasantly."[73] Even in gold-rush San Francisco, the force of female moral suasion overruled the world of vice.

The churches to which Royce referred were all of Protestant denominations, led by the Presbyterians. They had organized in May 1849 with six members, including two women, the previously mentioned Sarah B. Gillespie of Hong Kong and Macao, and Ann Hodghton, of the missionary church at Valparaiso, Chile (evidently come to California to save a different sort of heathen).[74] They were quickly followed by the Baptists, Congregationalists, Episcopalians, and Unitarians, involving women throughout.[75] Just as the Gillespies had brought the first Chinese woman to California, the Episcopal minister brought the first woman of African descent, Annie Garrick (later Mrs. Peters), originally of St. Croix, in the Caribbean.[76] Again religion superseded race, adding to gold-rush feminine diversity.

Although the Spanish-speaking Catholics of San Francisco had continued to worship at Mission Dolores, the influx of Irish and French Catholics, particularly the former, led to the establishment of the aptly named St. Patrick's Church in 1851. The attached school and orphanage came under the administration of five Sisters of Charity, led by Sister Frances Assisium McEnnis.[77] While culturally marginalized, the Californios found some stability in religious continuity, supported by women's religious orders.

Despite the presence of Catholic congregations, eastern-based Protestantism became the dominant persuasion in gold-rush California. It prescribed a particular role for women, as noted by the first Presbyterian (and first Protestant) minister in San

Francisco: "not till loved ones are here and the charms of 'sweet, sweet home' adorn the shores of our [San Francisco] bay . . . will men plant and cherish institutions for coming time, and live for the benefit of immediate and remote generations."[78] He need hardly have added that without feminine presence, any chance for "immediate and remote generations" was mighty scant.

While much of gold-rush society might have pined for Christian virtue, the Jewish Argonauts certainly did not. In common with other gold seekers, Jewish men greatly outnumbered Jewish women, but the establishment of religious institutions depended solely on them, the requisite gathering being ten adult males. They shared the common problem of providing future generations, however, and, in the local absence of Jewish females, a man had to send for a wife, "whom he knew only by reputation, or because her brother or friend recommended her, and he did not begrudge either the passage money or the costly outfit."[79] The Jewish women brought into this distinctive society then formed their own separate organizations and, in many cases, established their own institutions for themselves and their children. For example, in 1854, San Francisco supported a Jewish school with forty to fifty students.[80] By 1855, San Francisco's Jewish population had grown enough to support two female societies, the Ladies' United Benevolent Society for so-called Polish Jews (mostly from the Prussian province of Posen) and Der Israelitische Frauenverein for German-speaking Jewish women. Both were allegedly organized to assist poor Hebrew women, but, as historian Rudolf Glanz noted, "It may be assumed that these societies were chiefly social, for . . . there were no Jewish women in want in San Francisco at that time and, indeed, few Jewish women."[81]

Since most of the Jews were merchants and observed a Saturday Sabbath, their stores remained open on Sunday. This practice prompted anti-Semitic rhetoric when a Sunday law for Santa Clara and Santa Cruz counties passed the state assembly in 1855, a bill that reflected moral sensibilities of Protestant women.[82] "There is a similar law in New York and some other Northern States," noted Daniel Levy, probably the leading French Jew in gold-rush California, "but a special clause allows the Jews to keep their establishments open on Sunday, if they observe their Sabbath. The California law does not permit this exception, which at the very least would safeguard the principle of religious freedom."[83]

Disregarding this ideal, other Protestant women brought the Sunday-closing issue to the Mother Lode in 1856. In Columbia, where the Presbyterian minister had so far been ineffectual in this matter, women "passed around a petition and easily collected the signatures of a majority of merchants who promised to observe the [Christian] Sabbath."[84] Among those affected were probably Jewish merchant Benjamin F. Butterfield and his wife, Malvina, in nearby Jamestown. This couple, with their partner, Mr. Klein, must have felt doubly isolated as Protestant values crept deeper into formerly carefree California.[85]

THE VALUE OF DOMESTICITY

Even outside of the churches, the entrenched notion of female purity gave respectable women increased power. Mary Ballou, in Negro Bar, wrote home of her actions when a fight took place in the store (evidently connected to the boardinghouse where she worked). She had never gone in there before, but when she saw one man draw a pistol on another, "I ran into the store and Beged and plead with him not to kill him for eight or ten minutes not to take his life for the sake of his wife and three little children." That night at supper she learned of her own success, as the assailant grumbled that "if it had not been for what that Lady said to him Scheles would have been a dead man."[86] She also described how she earned her money: "the first week earnt 23 dollars sewing for the Spanish Ladies the second week earnt 26 dollars."[87] Eight months later she was given a "present" of a fifty-dollar gold piece for nursing "a French lady one week," and then she went to work in a boardinghouse for one hundred dollars a month for five months. (Her husband made only seventy-five dollars a month at the same establishment.)[88] A similar experience came to the attention of Sarah Royce, who during her 1849 stay in Weaverville was hailed by the only other woman in the camp: "[I]n quite an exultant mood [she] told me that the man who kept the boarding-house had offered her a hundred dollars a month to cook three meals a day for his boarders, that she was to do no dishwashing and was to have someone to help her all the time she was cooking. . . . Her husband, also was highly pleased that his wife could earn so much."[89]

This high value placed on chores that women did for free at home helped many to prosper, although married women who could count on a man to back them up sometimes did better than unmarried ones. Married Mary Jane Megquier wrote to her daughter about a typical day at her San Francisco boardinghouse. It started at "seven o'clock when I get up and fry the potatoes then broil three pounds of steak, and as much liver . . . ," continuing with other great quantities of food for each meal including "lamb . . . beef, and pork, baked, turnips, beets, potatoes, radishes, sallad, and that everlasting soup. . . . [of which] I have cooked every mouthful that has been eaten excepting one day and a half that we were on a steamboat excursion."[90] She also made "six beds every day and do the washing and ironing," although she had the help of another woman who swept, set the table, and washed "the dishes and carpets which have to be washed every day," presumably for wages.[91] By January of 1853, she reported, "[o]n the whole take more money in one month here than I could in the states in two years."[92]

The widow Mary Ball, proprietress of a rival boardinghouse, was not so lucky. She experienced frequent difficulty in collecting debts from her boarders and worried about her reputation when some men (both single and married) made advances toward her and women gossiped about the results. "When I think of this mortifying

The artist-Argonaut Leonardo Barbieri painted Jane Bushton
Allen while on a visit to Monterey in the early 1850s. A native
of England who had gone to live in Australia, she arrived in
1850 at the old Pacific capital, where she supported herself and
her children by running a boardinghouse, an occupation pursued by numerous women in California. It is not unlikely that
Barbieri executed the portrait in exchange for room and board.
Courtesy Colton Hall Museum, City of Monterey.

affair," Ball lamented in one instance, "I am sick at heart, all the women keep as clear
of my parlor as they would of the pest house. I shall never humble myself to them,
for where there is no sin there should be no shame. If I had my money I would not
be here to suffer as I do, and as I have, one month longer."[93] Still unable to collect
some debts, she overcame the gossip and was again mixing socially when in February 1851 she assumed the position of manager at the partially completed Oriental
Hotel. When her chambermaid, Bridget, left for a place in a private home, she
wrote, "I am obliged to sew very late at night to get things for the beds, we have

many more arrivals and not half the necessaries to complete the house."[94] Bridget returned a week later, seeking reinstatement through the good offices of Jane, Ball's assistant, but Ball refused. "Fortunately I got a chambermaid that very morning, so did not want her."[95] Despite all these reported difficulties, at least three independent women were making a respectable living at the Oriental Hotel.

Domestic work offered even more poignant opportunities for African American women. Many of those who came west in the Gold Rush were slaves, although census records remain silent on exact numbers. By mutual agreement, slaveholders sometimes allowed slaves to purchase their "Freedom Papers," after laying up a tidy sum for an indolent master. For example, the slave George Dennis worked as a porter for his white master (and father) in the Eldorado Hotel, "a tent measuring 30 by 100 feet . . . brought from New Orleans." This flimsy San Francisco establishment offered faro and monte tables by day and women by night. George swept up periodically, saving the sweepings, "and at the end of three months, he paid, in five and ten cent pieces, the sum of $1000" for his own bill of sale. When two of his father's gaming partners decided to bring cattle to California from Ohio and offered to fetch George's mother, he paid his father an additional $950 for her purchase. George "rented one of the [Eldorado] gambling tables at $40 per day for the privilege of his mother serving hot meals in the gambling house on it. Eggs were selling at $12 per dozen, apples 25 cents apiece, and a loaf of bread $1. While her expenses were heavy, she averaged $225 a day."[96] One wonders what looks or words passed between her and the father of her son, their former master. The granddaughter of this enterprising woman, later Mrs. Margaret L. Dennis-Benston, became an honors high school graduate, "efficient in the Spanish and Chinese languages, and afterward taught in a private school for Chinese."[97] Such racial intermingling, particularly among people of color, was one of the legacies of gold-rush California.

Domestic skills also benefited Mary Ellen Pleasant, probably the most famous free woman of African descent. She arrived in San Francisco in 1849 with inherited money from the death of her first husband and an enviable reputation as a cook. A group of men seeking to employ her crowded the dock, so she auctioned off her culinary services "with the stipulation that she should do no washing, not even dishwashing." The high bid was $500, "the highest wage paid to a cook, although several others received as much as three hundred dollars a month."[98] She allegedly invested her savings with an accounting firm, West and Harper, and went on to much greater prosperity and influence.[99]

This firm proved particularly sympathetic to African Americans, as illustrated by the enslaved Mrs. Jane Elizabeth Whiting and her three children, brought to San Francisco in 1856. They accompanied their mistress, a Mrs. Thompson, who was going to meet her husband on his ranch in Petaluma, guided by their oldest son,

Howard. The Whitings maintained the fiction that they were free servants all the way across Panama (which would otherwise have granted manumission) but revealed their secret to abolitionists on board the boat steaming up the Pacific Coast. The abolitionists convinced them that since California was a free state, their arrival ensured freedom (a very problematic assertion, at best), and convinced them to be first to disembark. Mrs. Whiting and her children were then hustled to "a colored boarding house . . . which was known as the 'Harper & West Boarding House.' . . . The colored people in San Francisco held a mass meeting and decided to protect them in every way possible." They changed the family name from Whiting to Freeman, found work for the mother, and instructed the children to stay indoors with the shutters closed. But after many long weeks the children ventured outside to play. Another of the former steamer passengers recognized them as the escaped slaves and alerted their mistress, Mrs. Thompson, who had settled on her ranch in Petaluma. Interestingly, she never tried to reclaim them, and "fifteen years afterwards 'Aunt Jane' and her former mistress met on the streets of San Francisco, and recognized each other and talked together, learning that for five weeks, while Mrs. Thompson was in search of these slaves, that they were boarding within a short distance of them all the time."[100]

Other slave women obtained freedom in different ways. Mary Ann Harris worked as a "nurse girl" for a Dr. Ross, who was stationed with his family on Alcatraz Island. She was earning four dollars a month to pay for her freedom when "an old colored woman by the name of Aunt Lucy Evans stole her off the island" and freed her.[101] The most famous of California's enslaved women, Biddy Mason, had to go to court to emancipate herself and her family. In 1850, she had walked all the way from Hancock, Mississippi, behind a caravan of three hundred wagons drawn by oxen (imagine the dust!), driving cattle while minding her own three daughters, Ellen, Ann, and Harriet. After four years of residence in San Bernardino, her owner decided to take his family and slave entourage to Texas, a slave state. They went westward to catch a ship, and had been gone only a few days "when the news reached Los Angeles, through a Mrs. Rowen, of San Bernardino, that these slaves were . . . going back into slavery." The sheriff of Los Angeles County arrested their master. Biddy Mason appeared at the trial not only with her own children but with six of the eight children of her fellow slave—a seventh being at work and the eighth, a newborn babe, lying by the side of her recovering mother. The judge freed all of them, and Mason went on to become a "confinement nurse." She bought property well outside the Los Angeles city limits, but, when the city boomed, sold parcels at a profit and used the proceeds for the good of her race and other downtrodden, including paying "taxes and all expenses on church property to hold it for her people."[102] Her efforts not only ensured the uplift of her race, but added to the weight of Protestantism—no matter how segregated—in changing California.

A DIFFERENT PLACE

Despite the transplantation of so much of Yankee society, certain values were transformed under female direction, as befitted the keepers of the moral flame. Marriage itself became more fleeting, as women, much more often than men, sought to change partners to increase their financial well-being or to unload a vicious spouse. In part, California law allowed easier divorces, and women were not reticent about taking advantage of this opportunity. California joined a group of western states where the overwhelming majority of divorce cases were instigated by wives, and San Mateo and Santa Clara counties led the nation in divorces from 1850 to 1890.[103]

One sensational divorce case highlighted myriad societal changes spawned by the California Gold Rush. In 1899, Lucy Hite sued aging multimillionaire John Hite for divorce, claiming half his property as settlement. This case was unusual because Lucy was a southern Miwok, and Hite's gold-rush fortune was apparently built on the care and goodwill of Lucy and her sister. As the story goes, Argonaut John Hite had survived a snowstorm under the protection of a southern Miwok named Maresa, who, after they became lovers, led him to the gold-bearing waters of the South Fork of the Merced River. When Maresa died, Hite married her sister, Lucy, according to Indian rites. They lived together continuously from 1871 until about 1886 while Hite's fortune swelled. When in 1897 sixty-seven-year-old John Hite "quietly married" a thirty-six-year-old white widow, Lucy took John to court. Despite Lucy's adoption of (out-of-date) American clothing and her long-term association with whites rather than Indians at John's insistence, she was not accepted by most white Californians. With blue tattoos on her chin and forehead, Lucy hardly fit into the society that ate off porcelain plates on linen tablecloths. Although the trial court found for Lucy, the death of the judge led to a retrial and an out-of-court settlement. Lucy withdrew to Indian Peak Ranch above Mariposa in the southern Mother Lode, by then virtually deserted by miners. John died in San Francisco in 1906 on the morning of the earthquake. His remains were incinerated in the ensuing fire along with the funeral parlor that would have buried him, but his heirs haggled over his estate for years. Lucy benefited little and lived simply, returning to her Indian associations and older ways. She wove traditional baskets, some of which now belong to the National Park Service.[104]

The collection and preservation of Lucy Hite's baskets illustrates not only the destruction of the Miwok in absolute numbers, but of much of the culture that they carried. Like other groups present in the California Gold Rush, they still persist, but in altered circumstances. On the coast, Indians had been succeeded by Californios, whose own traditional views and feelings differed widely from those portrayed in American pulp fiction. Both groups foundered under waves of Argonauts—male and female—from almost every continent on earth: adventurers and gamblers; slaves seeking survival, then freedom; artistic nonconformists; hardworking individuals who sometimes chafed against the strait-laced society that they had transplanted to California. This tidal wave of settlement surged first over the Mother Lode, where Jenny Wimmer once sewed shirts for the natives. Indigenous peoples died or were displaced, and the Indian woman's basket became a carefully preserved artifact rather than a utilitarian mining tool.

Women were forced into economic adaptation, as men, specifically Yankees from the eastern states, increasingly monopolized the gold. They ventured various strategies, partly using transplanted tactics, partly through innovation. Increasing numbers of respectable Yankee women stratified and hardened California's once-fluid society based on their own religious and ethical standards, yet many changes could never be reversed. Throughout these events, women acted upon and responded to the Gold Rush in varied, subtle, and significant ways. Weaving women's diversity, adversity, and opportunity into gold-rush California enriches our history even more than did Aunty Jenny's gold.

NOTES

1. Mary P. Winslow, "Mrs. Wimmer's Narrative of the First Piece of Gold Discovered in California, Dec., 1847 [*sic*], From the San Francisco *Daily Evening Bulletin*, December 19, 1874," quoted in Rodman W. Paul, *The California Gold Discovery* (Georgetown, Calif.: The Talisman Press, 1967), 174–76; hereinafter *Discovery*. In Hubert Howe Bancroft, *California Pioneer Register, 1542–1848* (Baltimore: Regional Publishing Company, 1964) 386, Wimmer's full name is noted.

2. Paul, *Discovery*, 177, 46.

3. Ibid., 174.

4. The term "Yankee" is being used throughout this essay in preference to "Anglo" to refer to those who came from the eastern United States.

5. "Marshall's Narrative," in Paul, *Discovery*, 199.

6. "Discovery of Gold at Coloma," San Francisco *Daily Herald*, December 31, 1855, quoted in Paul, *Discovery*, 134.

7. Quoted in Paul, *Discovery*, 73.

8. Walter Colton, *Three Years in California* (Stanford: Stanford University Press, 1949), 277.

9. Michelle Jolly, "Inventing the City: Gender and the Politics of Everyday Life in Gold-Rush San Francisco, 1848–1869" (Ph.D. diss., University of California, San Diego, 1998), 59–62.

10. A very good discussion of these attitudes, based on the works of Alexis de Tocqueville, is found in G. J. Barker-Benfield, *The Horrors of the Half-Known Life: Male Attitudes Toward Women and Sexuality in Nineteenth-Century America* (New York: Harper & Row, 1976), especially 3–57. A historical male view is found in Hubert Howe Bancroft, *California Inter Pocula* (San Francisco: The History Company, 1888), 305–14; hereinafter *California Inter Pocula*.

11. Horace Snow, *"Dear Charlie" Letters* (Mariposa, Calif.: Mariposa Historical Society, 1979), 84.

12. Eliza Woodson Farnham, *California, In-doors and Out* (New York: Dix, Edwards & Co., 1856), 275.

13. Bancroft, *California Inter Pocula*, 312.

14. Mrs. Lee Whipple-Haslam, "Turbulence and evil of every description," in *So Much to Be Done: Women Settlers on the Mining and Ranching Frontier*, ed. Ruth B. Moynihan, Susan Armitage, and Christiane Fischer Dichamp (Lincoln: University of Nebraska Press, 1990), 29.

15. Sherburne F. Cook, "The Destruction of the California Indian," in *Minorities in California History*, ed. George E. Frakes and Curtis B. Solberg (New York: Random House, 1971), 46.

16. "Dame Shirley" (Louise Amelia Knapp Smith Clappe), *The Shirley Letters: Being Letters Written in 1851–1852 from the California Mines*, introduced by Richard E. Oglesby (Salt Lake City: Peregrine Smith, 1992), 13, 12; italics in original.

17. Quoted in Delilah Beasley, *The Negro Trailblazers of California* (Los Angeles, 1919), 68.

18. George H. Tinkham, *Men and Events* (Stockton: Record Publishing Company, 1915), 158; Martha Menchaca, *The Mexican Outsiders* (Austin: University of Texas Press, 1995), 10.

19. Albert L. Hurtado, *Indian Survival on the California Frontier, 1820–1860* (New Haven: Yale University Press, 1988), 179, quoting E. A. Stevenson to Thomas J. Henley, December 31, 1853.

20. See Hurtado, *Indian Survival*, 180–92.

21. Quoted in Hurtado, *Indian Survival*, 176. Hurtado stresses the power of the anti-southern invective, but misses the overtones of racial miscegenation then associated with "degraded" southern society.

22. Frank F. Latta, *Tailholt Tales* (Santa Cruz: Bear State Books, 1976), 93–94.

23. Richard Henry Dana, *Two Years Before the Mast* (New York: Washington Square Press, 1968), 73.

24. Robert W. Johannsen, *To the Halls of the Montezumas: The Mexican War in the American Imagination* (New York: Oxford University Press, 1985), 175–91.

25. Genaro Padilla, "'Yo Sola Aprendi': Mexican Women's Personal Narratives from Nineteenth-Century California," in *Writing the Range: Race, Class, and Culture in the Women's West*, ed. Elizabeth Jameson and Susan Armitage (Norman: University of Oklahoma Press, 1997), 194–95.

26. William Downie, *Hunting for Gold* (Palo Alto: American West Publishing Company, 1971), 147–53.

27. See Albert L. Hurtado, *Intimate Frontiers: Sex, Gender, and Culture in Old California* (Albuquerque: University of New Mexico Press, 1999), 134–36, for a discussion of the publicity and the event's interpretation by historian Hubert Howe Bancroft.

28. Mary Ball, "The Journal of Mary Ball, A California Gold Rush Woman," transcribed and annotated by Norma B. Morris (M.A. thesis, Sonoma State University, 1993), 184.

29. William H. Ellison, ed., "'Recollections of Historical Events in California, 1843–1878' of William A. Streeter," *California Historical Society Quarterly* 18 (March, June, and September 1939): 273, quoted in Albert Camarillo, *Chicanos in a Changing Society* (Cambridge: Harvard University Press, 1979), 18.

30. Quoted in Michelle E. Morton, "Excavating Mexican American Voice in California History: The California Testimonials" (M.A. thesis, University of New Mexico, 1996), 85.

31. On the Bear Flaggers, see the views of Vallejo de Leese in Morton, "Excavating Mexican American Voice," 83–84, 87–88; on fertility, see quotations from Dorotea Valdez and Isidora Filomena de Solano, quoted in ibid., 91, 96.

32. Ord manuscript, 143, quoted in Morton, "Excavating Mexican American Voice," 99.

33. See Padilla, "Yo Sola Aprendi," 198. Revised translation is by the author.

34. Ball, "Journal," 217.

35. Leonard Pitt, *Decline of the Californios: Social History of the Spanish-Speaking Californians, 1846–1890* (Berkeley: University of California Press, 1970), 267–68.

36. Colton, *Three Years in California,* 252–53.

37. Ibid., 292.

38. Ibid., 276.

39. Sally Zanjani, *A Mine of Her Own: Women Prospectors in the American West, 1850–1950* (Lincoln: University of Nebraska Press, 1997), 25.

40. Malcolm J. Rohrbough, *Days of Gold: The California Gold Rush and the American Nation* (Berkeley: University of California Press, 1997), 181.

41. Zanjani, *Mine of Her Own,* 25–26.

42. Ibid.

43. Ball, "Journal," 273.

44. The most comprehensive book on women at home is Linda Peavy and Ursula Smith, *Women in Waiting in the Westward Movement: Life on the Home Frontier* (Norman: University of Oklahoma Press, 1994). Nancy Coffey Heffernan and Ann Page Stecker, in *Sisters of Fortune* (Hanover, N.H.: University Press of New England, 1993), write of a single family.

45. Clappe, *Shirley Letters,* 184.

46. Ibid., 185.

47. Ibid., 74.

48. Mary B. Ballou, *"I Hear the Hogs in My Kitchen"* (New Haven: Yale University Presses, Beinecke, 1962), 11.

49. William Perkins, "Journal," Bancroft Library, University of California, Berkeley, quoted in Elisabeth Margo, *Women of the Gold Rush* (New York: Indian Head Books, 1992; originally published as *Taming the Forty-Niner,* 1955, by Elisabeth Margo Freidel), 50–51.

50. Frank Marryat, *Mountains and Molehills* (Stanford: Stanford University Press, 1952), 235.

51. Ibid., 238.

52. Julie Roy Jeffrey, *Frontier Women: The Trans-Mississippi West, 1840–1880* (New York: Hill and Wang, 1979), 131.

53. Judy Yung, *Chinese Women of America* (Seattle: University of Washington Press, 1986), 14.

54. Carl T. Smith, "The Gillespie Brothers—Early Links Between Hong Kong and California," *Chung Chi Hsiao Kan (Chung Chi Bulletin)* 47 (1969): 28.

55. Judy Yung, *Unbound Feet: A Social History of Chinese Women in San Francisco* (Berkeley: University of California Press, 1995), 37–39.

56. The possibility of sexual assault dogged female servants of all races. See Hurtado, *Intimate Frontiers,* especially 115–28.

57. Yung, *Unbound Feet,* 38–39.

58. Herbert Asbury, *The Barbary Coast: An Informal History of the San Francisco Underground* (New York: Alfred A. Knopf, 1933), 180–81.

59. Quoted in Yung, *Unbound Feet,* 33. Italics in the original.

60. JoAnn Levy, *They Saw the Elephant* (Norman: University of Oklahoma Press, 1992), 167. See also JoAnn Levy's novel based on the life of Ah Toy: *Daughter of Joy* (New York: Tom Doherty Associates, 1998).

61. Yung, *Unbound Feet,* 33; Levy, *They Saw the Elephant,* 166.

62. Benson Tong, *Unsubmissive Women: Chinese Prostitutes in Nineteenth-Century San Francisco* (Norman: University of Oklahoma Press, 1994), 6–8.

63. Albert Benard de Russailh, quoted in Yung, *Unbound Feet,* 33.

64. Tong, *Unsubmissive Women,* 14.

65. Ibid., 11–12.

66. Robert Glass Cleland, ed., *Apron Full of Gold: The Letters of Mary Jane Megquier from San Francisco, 1849–1856* (San Marino, Calif.: Huntington Library, 1949), 80.

67. Janet R. Fireman, "Beautiful Deceiver: The Absolutely Divine Lola Montez," in *By Grit and Grace: Eleven Women Who Shaped the West,* ed. Glenda Riley and Richard W. Etulain (Golden, Colo.: Fulcrum Publishing, 1997), 45–61.

68. Ibid., 62.

69. Jane Kathleen Curry, *Nineteenth-Century American Women Theatre Managers* (Westport, Conn.: Greenwood Press, 1994), 46–48; Delores J. Cabezut-Ortiz, *Merced County* (Northridge, N.C.: Windsor Publications, 1987), 73–75, 78.

70. Curry, *Nineteenth-Century American Women Theatre Managers,* 36–41.

71. Ibid., 45, 51–76.

72. Ball, "Journal," 162, 163.

73. Sarah Royce, *A Frontier Lady* (New Haven: Yale University Press, 1932), 113–14.

74. Frank Soulé, John H. Gihon, and James Nisbet, *The Annals of San Francisco* (New York: D. Appleton & Co., 1854), 690.

75. Ibid., 692–95. Sarah Gillespie shifted her allegiance from the Presbyterians to the Episcopalians as a result of her husband's Episcopal faith, which led to her confirmation, previously recounted. See Smith, "Gillespie Brothers," 28.

76. Beasley, *Negro Trailblazers,* 121.

77. Ibid., 697.

78. [Timothy Dwight Hunt], "Haste to Be Rich," *Pacific* 1, no. 1 (August 1, 1851), quoted in Laurie F. Maffly-Kipp, *Religion and Society in Frontier California* (New Haven: Yale University Press, 1994), 153.

79. Rudolf Glanz, *The Jews of California, From the Discovery of Gold until 1880* (New York: Walson Press, 1960), 112.

80. Glanz, *Jews of California,* 37.

81. Ibid., 35.

82. Ibid., 41.

83. Daniel Levy, "Letters About the Jews of California . . . 1855–1858," trans. Marlene Rainman, *Western States Jewish Historical Quarterly* 3, no. 2 (January 1971): 111.

84. Maffly-Kipp, *Religion and Society,* 160.

85. Glanz, *Jews of California,* 51.

86. Ballou, "I Hear the Hogs in my Kitchen," 11.

87. Ibid., 6.

88. Ibid.

89. Royce, *Frontier Lady,* 83.

90. Cleland, *Apron Full of Gold,* 46.

91. Ibid., 46–47.

92. Ibid., 69.

93. Ball, "Journal," 202.

94. Ibid., 180.

95. Ibid., 181.

96. Beasley, *Negro Trailblazers,* 120.

97. Ibid., 121.

98. Asbury, *Barbary Coast,* 11, quoted in Lynn M. Hudson, "A New Look, or 'I'm Not Mammy to Everybody in California': Mary Ellen Pleasant, Black Entrepreneur," *Journal of the West* 32 (July 1993): 36.

99. Hudson, "A New Look," 36.

100. Beasley, *Negro Trailblazers,* 91–92.

101. Ibid., 91.

102. Ibid., 90–91, 109. See also Joan M. Jensen and Gloria Ricci Lothrop, *California Women: A History* (San Francisco: Boyd and Fraser, 1987), 32.

103. Glenda Riley, *Divorce: An American Tradition* (New York: Oxford University Press, 1991), 90; Robert L. Griswold, *Family and Divorce in California, 1850–1890: Victorian Illusions and Everyday Realities* (Albany: State University of New York Press, 1982), 23–28.

104. Ralph R. Mendershausen, *Treasures of the South Fork* (Fresno: Panorama West Books, 1983), 35–36, 57–70.

7

"As jolly as a clam at high water"

The Rise of Art in Gold Rush California

Anthony Kirk

With a breeze at his back and opportunity before him, William Redmond Ryan rowed out into San Francisco harbor in late April 1849 and, pulling from ship to ship, managed to procure what he had been unable to find anywhere in the raw bustling gold-rush town that was springing up on Yerba Buena Cove: pigments for mixing paints and two or three brushes. The latter, he wrote, were "indifferently adapted for the use I intended to put them to; but in the absence of better, welcome makeshifts." Returning to his lodgings at the Buckland House—a rude, hastily constructed tavern that creaked and groaned with every gust of wind, "as if in the agony of ague"—Ryan hung out a sign emblazoned with a bust of Apollo and symbols of his craft: easel, palette, and brushes. Upstairs, in a corner of the large common room where some twenty men slumbered fitfully at night on the hard, wooden floor, he had fashioned a primitive studio using only his two sea chests, one of them serving as an easel, the other as both seat and table. Here, amid the clutter and confusion—his fellow lodgers occupying themselves with mending clothes, writing letters, repairing saddles, stitching leather pokes—he waited for patrons.[1]

Most of the gold seekers who excitedly coursed the crowded streets below Ryan's studio were young men who intended to make their fortune and then return home to the joyous welcome of family and friends. They and the tens of thousands of Argonauts who followed in their wake were not sturdy pioneers and sagacious empire builders, as local annalists would later proudly proclaim. They had no interest in establishing homesteads, in building communities, in making a better life for themselves on the broad, fertile plains of America's new possession. Their hopes and designs were much simpler, as suggested by a lusty chorus that a century and a half ago boomed through the still night air of the "diggins" outside Nevada City:

On Selby Flat we live in style
Will stay right here till we make our pile.
We're sure to do it after a while,
Then good-bye to Californy.

Though celebrated in song, the miners' naked avarice aroused concern among Californians who held a different vision of this golden land. "Not more than one in a hundred of this immigration," a San Francisco newspaper dourly observed in 1850, "have, on leaving home, had the remotest idea of becoming permanently established in the country, as fixed citizens of the State." The absence of local "domestic relations and attachments" among the Argonauts, it warned, "cannot be regarded with indifference by men who have the real well-being and advancement of the State at heart."[2]

Young and transient, sojourners rather than settlers, with a measure of feckless husbands, smooth confidence men, and genuine desperadoes among them, the Fortyniners would seem unlikely patrons of the arts. They, nonetheless, bought drawings, paintings, and daguerreotypes from the moment of their arrival, revealing through their actions the power of human sentiment and the pervasive sense of history in the making. Countless Argonauts commissioned portraits of themselves to send home to family and loved ones, as they sought to ease the loneliness of months of separation. Many also purchased images of mining camps or other scenes of life in the new El Dorado, commemorating their participation in one of the most thrilling events of all time. Their needs, together with the larger pictorial requirements of a rapidly developing society, stimulated a flowering of art in gold-rush California without precedent on any frontier.

Like the men who thronged the muddy streets outside his San Francisco studio in the spring of '49, William Redmond Ryan was an adventurer. A year prior to the gold discovery, when the drums of war boomed across the land, Ryan had been caught up in the spirit of Manifest Destiny despite British citizenship and filled with romantic notions of life "amidst the wilds and mountains of California," he had come west with Colonel Jonathan D. Stevenson's New York Volunteers to fight the Mexicans. Following his discharge in October 1848, Ryan mined on the Stanislaus River and then wintered in Monterey, where he made an unsuccessful stab at supporting himself as a sign painter before heading up to San Francisco. A portraitist by profession, having "attained some proficiency by years of study and practice," he soon took up his old craft. Not long after hanging a sign outside his studio—probably the first in the mad jumble of tents and flimsy, frame boardinghouses, shops, and saloons destined to emerge as the cultural center of the American West—he was delighted to find himself earning an ounce of gold a day with his brush, as much as a miner might make in twelve hours of hard labor with shovel and pan. His patronage increased so rapidly that he took on a partner, and despite his new friend's love of drink and gaming, the pair prospered beyond expectations. At the onset of summer, Ryan formed a new partnership with a former acquaintance from Stevenson's Regiment, who had "acquired some knowledge of painting" and who proposed they "do business upon a large scale." The two of them constructed a large tent-studio near the waterfront, and they soon, wrote Ryan, "had every reason to rejoice at the success which attended our efforts."[3]

Over the months the pair practiced their craft in a succession of locations. When they could no longer endure the high afternoon winds that violently shook their tent and filled it with swirling clouds of sand and dust, they fitted up a studio in a wooden cottage. The flow of Forty-niners from "the States" and Europe increased week after week that gilded summer, and the press of orders ultimately led the two artists to employ several assistants, as they pursued their art in the exuberant entrepreneurial spirit characteristic of gold-rush California.

Ryan's sole rival in the early months was another British subject, John Prendergast, who had sailed for California from Honolulu when word of the epic discovery circulated through the Sandwich Islands. Prendergast presumably spent time in the diggings, but by the spring of '49 he was busy making drawings and watercolors of San Francisco. Daniel Wadsworth Coit, a representative of the Mexican banking house of Drusina & Co. and a skilled amateur artist, observed Prendergast at work that April and in a letter to his wife expressed amazement that "he gets $25 for his *pencil* sketches which may occupy him a day or two at most." Though Coit dismissed Prendergast's drawings as "neither truthful nor executed with artistic skill," they were, in fact, deftly executed and filled with accurate detail. In some he portrayed a single busy thoroughfare choked with pedestrians and horse-drawn wagons, catching the wonderful vitality of life in frontier San Francisco (figure 1), while in others he showed the magnificent sweep of the city, recording, over the course of several years, the remarkable growth of the city.[4]

Ryan and Prendergast had the field to themselves but briefly. By summer, several of the first artists who had joined in the wild dash from the States were busy with their craft, and at year's end a couple of dozen—including wood engravers and lithographers, as well as painters—could be counted among the residents of San Francisco, Sacramento, and the countless camps scattered through the diggings. By 1853, when placer mining entered into decline, another thirty or more had come west, further enriching the cultural life that had taken root in the Golden State. Like their fellow fortune hunters, they were for the most part young men, in their twenties and thirties, and had traveled from the four quarters of the world. Perhaps half were Americans, nearly all of whom hailed from New England or the Middle Atlantic states, but there were also French, Italian, Cuban, Swiss, and Hungarian nationals among them, reflecting the cosmopolitan character of the great rush. Some lacked training or even much skill as draftsmen, while others enjoyed the benefits of solid

Figure 1. John Prendergast, *Montgomery Street, San Francisco,* 1851. Charcoal and graphite on paper, 7⅛ x 11 in. *California Historical Society; CHS purchase with contributions from Stephen Taber and Alice Whitson, FN-30867.*

academic education and had achieved significant recognition for their work. But regardless of age or nationality, of talent or reputation, they had not come to the land of gold to practice their profession. They were here "to see the elephant."

Such was the case with Samuel S. Osgood, a successful New York portrait painter and a member of the National Academy of Design. In February 1849, two months after President James K. Polk thrilled the nation by confirming tales of an "El Dorado of the Pacific," Osgood kissed his wife a fond farewell and, with snow swirling through the frigid air, boarded the *Crescent City,* the first large steamer filled with fortune hunters to clear for Panama. By April the artist was striding along the road from Sacramento to Coloma, where a year earlier the carpenter James Marshall had caught the gleam of gold flashing in the cold, swift waters of a newly dug tailrace on the American River and, stooping to pluck up several of the dazzling flakes, changed the course of history. Osgood's path across the Central Valley was strewn with wildflowers, "filling the air with delicious fragrance," and he and his companions gathered handfuls of the blossoms and wreathed them 'round their hats, "intoxicated with delight."[5]

Somewhat older than most of the Argonauts, having turned forty the previous year, Osgood held no illusions as to what lay ahead. Even before leaving the comforts of home he had known that to gather the golden harvest he would have to "labor hard—hard as the Irishman who carries the hod or the paver who paves the street." He located a claim on the Middle Fork of the American River, where he mined with a pan and then with a rocker of his own manufacture. At first he suffered in every muscle of his body, but he soon toughened and grew strong, enjoying long nights of deep sleep such as he had not known for years. Through hard work and good luck he frequently washed twenty or thirty dollars of gold a day, and after three months he left the diggings, having made his "pile" and, unlike many miners, not lost it at monte or faro or in drunken dissipation.[6]

Although Osgood enjoyed rare good fortune as a gold hunter, the brevity of his stay in the diggings was typical. Mining was hard, dangerous, and often unrewarding work. To stand in the cold rushing waters of a mountain stream, bent at the waist and endlessly swirling a pan heavy with sand and gravel, or to dig deep into a rocky river bar, shoveling pay dirt into a cradle or long tom hour after hour, as the ascending sun burned ever hotter, required strength and endurance. Frequently a day's labor yielded no more than a dollar or two in dust, and then the weary miner retired to a rude cabin or a tattered tent for an evening meal of salt pork, bread, and coffee before collapsing, exhausted, into bed. Unaccustomed to endless toil and rough conditions, artists rarely mined for more than a single season, concluding, like countless other disappointed fortune hunters, that the practice of their profession was both more congenial and more profitable. Having failed to find the riches that had brought them to California, many headed home to pick up the threads of their old lives. But others lingered on month after month, and some remained to grow up with the country, sojourners become settlers.

Samuel Osgood, for example, found such opportunities for his brush in San Francisco that, despite success in the diggings, he delayed his departure for nearly half a year, finally taking ship for New York on New Year's Day 1850. He charged "California prices" for his portraits, he boasted in a letter home, and by the end of summer he had more than two thousand dollars in commissions awaiting his attention. Bayard Taylor, the chief gold-rush correspondent for the *New York Tribune*, wrote of coming upon him that August "in a studio about eight feet square, with a head of Captain Sutter on his easel." Osgood had first met the lord of New Helvetia on his way to the mines and had been struck by his aristocratic bearing and gracious manner, as had the artist's companions. Sutter was now on his way to the state constitutional convention in Monterey, and though his fortunes were in sad decline, he nonetheless cut a commanding figure. Over the course of several months Osgood made four portraits of him from life, of which the painting reproduced here (plate 1) is especially fine. It exhibits the "ease and strength" contemporaries admired in Osgood's work; and executed on ticking rather than on artist's canvas, it testifies to the curiously congenial companionship of raw conditions and high culture—of Shakespeare performed in rain-soaked tents, of fine champagnes poured in coarse makeshift saloons—that distinguished life in El Dorado. It shows Sutter as a slender, handsome man of forty-five, elegantly dressed in black broadcloth and gleaming linen, his gaze steady and confident—very much "the lion of California," as Osgood called him.[7]

J. D. Borthwick also responded to the rich opportunities to practice art in El Dorado despite good fortune as a gold hunter. But the young Scots, who had succumbed to California fever in the spring of 1850 while living in New York, was single and footloose, a wanderer at heart, and he remained far longer than Osgood, as the seasons passed and turned into years. Borthwick located his first claim a few miles from Placerville, the legendary Hangtown of gold-rush days, and after working it for a spell moved on to try his luck at Coon Hollow and then Weaver Creek, where he mined successfully for a several months. Borthwick was given to drawing in his leisure hours, and his work proved popular with the other miners, who besieged him with requests, particularly on Sundays, the traditional day of rest in the diggings. "Every man," he wrote, "wanted a sketch of his claim, or his cabin, or some spot with which he identified himself; and as they all offered to pay very handsomely, I was satisfied that I could make paper and pencil more profitable tools to work with than pick and shovel."[8]

Over the next two years Borthwick roamed the mining country, from Sonora to Downieville, earning his living as an artist while gratifying his desire to see "all the various kinds of diggings, and the strange specimens of human nature to be found in them." He later described his travels in *Three Years in California* (1857), one of the most insightful and entertaining of all the narratives to emerge from this grand adventure. Among the illustrations from Borthwick's hand that enliven the volume is *A Ball in the Mines* (figure 2), a splendid, vital image that suggests why the artist's sketches were sought after in the diggings. It portrays a dance Borthwick attended one evening at Angels Camp, where, as was usually the case, no women were present. "It was a strange sight," he wrote "to see a party of long-bearded men, in heavy boots and flannel shirts, going through all the steps and figures of the dance with so much spirit, and often with a great deal of grace, hearty enjoyment depicted on their dried-up sunburned faces, and revolvers and bowie-knives glancing in their belts; while a crowd of the same rough-looking customers stood around, cheering them on to greater efforts, and occasionally dancing a step or two quietly on their own account."[9]

Like Borthwick and Osgood, most artists spent a couple of months at hard labor with pick and shovel and pan, and, then, shaking the dust from their clothes, moved on to other pursuits. Some, however, tired of mining in a week or two, and a few never made it to the diggings, precipitously changing their plans in response to the unexpected opportunities for making money that abounded in the land of gold.

Figure 2. John D. Borthwick, *A Ball in the Mines.* Lithograph, from J. D. Borthwick, *Three Years in California,* 1857. *California Historical Society.*

William S. Jewett, a talented New York artist and, like Osgood, a member of the National Academy of Design, arrived in San Francisco in December 1849, and almost at once he was painting portraits and buying real estate. Setting up his easel in "a little room not larger than the one I kep my coal in in N.Y.," he soon had orders from the former commander of the New York Volunteers, Colonel Jonathan D. Stevenson, the prefect of the district, Horace Hawes, and several prominent San Francisco merchants. "I am painting and I am as jolly among them as a clam at high water," he wrote in January 1850 of his popularity among the emerging elite of California society. "I charge from hundred and fifty to eight hundred dollars—shall paint two or three per week if they come fast enough."[10]

A shrewd investor, Jewett speculated in San Francisco real estate when not occupied with portraiture, purchasing one lot for $200 and selling half of it three days later for $250, a transaction typical of those heady days. "I consider this place the greatest field for a good business mind the world affords," he wrote home, "and the worst for an indifferent one." Jewett was not an indifferent businessman, and in February he boasted, "no one who is *any body* thinks of being painted by anyone but W. Jewett," adding that "if Osgood were here now he could stand but little chance with me as I can far excel him on anything." Among the visitors to the artist's studio in 1850 was

Lieutenant Washington A. Bartlett of the United States Navy, who had taken part in the occupation of Yerba Buena during the Mexican War and who subsequently served as the first American alcalde of the sleepy village, which in January 1847 he renamed San Francisco. The elegant portrait that emerged from the sitting (plate 2) shows both Jewett and Bartlett at their best, displaying the artist's strong, expressive brushwork and evoking the lieutenant's serious, high-minded character. The conventional iconography of the work—the lieutenant's dress and pose, the imaginary setting of Doric column, richly upholstered chair, and leaded-glass casement window—reveals, moreover, how quickly the forms and customs, the symbols and imagery traditionally associated with genteel and cultivated society appeared in El Dorado.[11]

Although most of the artists who established themselves in California took up residence in San Francisco, several settled in Sacramento and a few worked in the larger gold camps such as Columbia. Leonardo Barbieri, a well-trained and talented portrait painter, initially followed this pattern, fitting up a studio in San Francisco in December 1849. But early the following year he was off for San Diego, where he executed a charming likeness of Rosario Estudillo Aguirre, the lovely young wife of the wealthy trader and rancher José Antonio Aguirre. Until his departure for Mexico in 1853, Barbieri continued to work chiefly in the Hispanic communities of the state, finding his patrons among the *dons* and *doñas* of old California, who were enjoying the prosperity that flowed from the boom in the cattle industry, brought on by the miners' enormous appetite for beef. Born in the Duchy of Savoy during the brief era of French domination, Barbieri was widely traveled and fluent in Spanish, having spent four years in South America before heading north. By reasons of culture and language and, quite likely, sympathies, he found himself welcome in the homes of the Castros, the Carrillos, the Amestis, the Pachecos, and other prominent Californios, who, with their natural dignity and love of rich display, responded warmly to the artist's elegant style of portraiture. In 1850 Barbieri spent three months in Santa Barbara, producing, among other paintings, a powerful likeness of José Antonio de la Guerra (plate 3). Born in Spain, the son of two distinguished families, de la Guerra had come to Alta California in 1801, fathered nine children, laid claim to several sprawling ranchos, served as commander of the presidio that guarded the district, and made his house a celebrated social center of Santa Barbara. When the grand patriarch donned his finest suit of clothes and velvet house cap to sit for Barbieri, he was in his seventy-first year, a figure seemingly out of an ancient Spanish romance, beloved and respected through the far reaches of southern California, where the traditional seignorial pattern of Hispanic life yet endured.[12]

Not all the artists who joined in the mad rush to El Dorado had the skills of Barbieri or Osgood or Jewett. Some had little or no formal instruction, and their work was, at best, simple and direct, with a rude strength springing from color and design and subject matter. Such is the case with Thomas Moore's painting *E. W. McIlhany, 49er* (plate 4), a flat, linear likeness executed in 1850 at the gold camp of Onion Valley, located high on a tributary of the Middle Fork of the Feather River. Little is known about the artist other than he was a veteran of the Mexican War who in early 1849 set out from his native Virginia with the Charleston Mining Company and on the Fourth of July, filled with patriotism and whiskey, stood on a huge tree stump by the banks of the Green River and delivered a stirring address, periodically firing a small cannon when moved by the sentiments of his oration. Although presumably untrained, Moore imitated an old artistic custom of incorporating an element of his sitter's occupation in the portrait. Behind McIlhany, who had established a store in Onion Valley and ran a packing operation that carried goods to Rich Bar and other remote camps, a train of heavily loaded mules descends a precipitous mountain trail.[13]

Like McIlhany, most of the Argonauts who commissioned drawings or paintings were not as interested in obtaining a work of art as in securing a pictorial record of their California days, either for themselves or for friends and loved ones back home. In the spring of 1850 the Forty-niner Alonzo Delano was able to earn a living as an artist in Marysville, though he possessed only "a little skill in drawing," as he cheerfully admitted himself. Delano, who later established a reputation for his delightfully humorous tales of the Gold Rush written under the pseudonym "Old Block," turned to art after high water on the Feather River brought an end to his company's mining operations, and he found himself "*strapped.*" "For three weeks," he wrote, "I plied my pencil in copying the outre phiz and forms of the long-bearded miners, at an ounce a head, when I found myself the wealthy recipient of four hundred dollars."[14]

Delano's success is not surprising given a story related by J. D. Borthwick, which reveals how easily some of the miners could be pleased. Setting off from Grass Valley House to Foster's Bar one morning, Borthwick was approached by several men who, having seen him drawing the previous evening, asked if he would take their likenesses. Borthwick agreed, and another Argonaut, watching him improve on the looks of the last sitter, "was seized with a violent desire to have his sweet countenance 'pictur'd off' likewise, to send to his wife." Borthwick obligingly began the portrait, amusing himself by making the miner, who was singularly unattractive, "about fifty percent uglier than he really was." To compensate for the cruel caricature, the artist transformed the man's rough clothing into "a very spicy black coat, black satin waistcoat, and very stiff stand-up collars." "The fidelity of the likeness he never doubted," Borthwick wrote, "being so lost in admiration of his dress, that he seemed to think the face a matter of minor importance altogether."[15]

"Gold mining," wrote the wise and witty Dame Shirley to her sister in 1852 from Indian Bar, "is Nature's great lottery scheme." And to a degree the same could be said of the practice of art on the California frontier. Despite the grand success of many artists, fortune failed to smile on others who were equally skilled. In January 1850, in the midst of boasting of the wonderful reception accorded him upon setting up his easel in San Francisco, William Jewett observed, "there are other artists here and do-ing comparably nothing," modestly adding that he was unsure if his own good luck was deserved or not. Charles Nahl, who opened a studio in San Francisco two years later, also made a splash upon his arrival and was soon deluged with commissions. But he, too, noticed that others lacked patronage and wrote home "that an Ameri-can, an English, and a French painter had left this town . . . as they found not enough to do."[16]

For most, failure as an artist was no worse than failure as a miner, a common ex-perience for countless Argonauts. For the young Buckeye E. Hall Martin, however, failure twined with dashed hopes and disillusionment to precede a sad, untimely death, far from family and friends. Martin, who began his career in Cincinnati, was working in New York City when gold fever seized him, and taking passage on the schooner *Panama,* he was among the earliest waves of Forty-niners to set out for California. A fellow voyager long remembered an Argonaut on the vessel who in all likelihood was Martin, recounting that he was "an Artist and a Bohemian, a *bon-vivant,* whose sea-chest was filled with choice cigars and liquors, which rendered the neighborhood of our berth a favorite resort for the 'good fellows' on board." It is unknown if Martin went to the diggings, and if so, if he was successful as a miner, but by late 1849 he was in San Francisco. Establishing a studio in the Ha-ley House, he informed the public that he would "be happy to paint portraits, make sketches in oil of a local character, paint landscapes and sea views, or anything else in the line of his vocation."[17]

But neither in San Francisco nor in Sacramento, where he settled in the summer of 1850, did fortune favor Martin. Though he had exhibited work at both the Amer-ican Academy of the Fine Arts and the American Art-Union in New York, and though his paintings invariably received favorable comment in California newspa-pers, he had trouble securing patronage. Gradually sinking into poverty, he fell be-hind in his rent and occasionally went without meals. He was, as well, often ill and frequently tormented by melancholia. One bleak day, facing eviction from his rooms and overcome by despair, he wrote out his will and penned a scathing farewell to "The Fine Arts and their Sacramento Patrons." A friend came to his aid, paying his rent and rallying his spirits. But in the autumn of 1851, while on a sketching trip through the Northern Mines, Martin succumbed to disease and discouragement, leaving behind a sad estate of unrealized hopes, unpaid bills, and unsold pictures, many of them held as security by creditors.

Among the paintings was *Mountain Jack and a Wandering Miner* (plate 5), a large elliptical canvas, measuring more than three feet by six feet in size. Although the miner's cradle, pick, and other equipment are curiously small and out of scale, the picture is a handsome, luminous work of art, at once decorative and symbolic of the meaning of the Gold Rush in American life. Mountain Jack, described in the press as "the wild mountaineer of California," sits near the edge of a rocky precipice in the Sierra Nevada and confidently points to the valley far below. The miner—archetypal with his heavy beard, red shirt, and rough boots—rests on his rifle and gazes at the prospect spread beneath him, dreaming, like Martin and thousands of other Argonauts who had rushed west, of the infinite riches, the success, the happiness that El Dorado promised.[18]

With its large dimensions and self-evident symbolism, *Mountain Jack and a Wandering Miner* eloquently testifies that from the outset Californians recognized the historic significance of the Gold Rush and sought to celebrate it on a scale commensurate with its importance in the unfolding pageant of the national experience. The picture's size also suggests it was painted to hang in a public room, and, in fact, at the time of the artist's death it was on display in the chamber of the Sacramento city council. Although the city fathers did not purchase Martin's work, local governments, as well as the state, did occasionally encourage the growth of art by commissioning or buying pictures. Official tastes inevitably ran to portraits of pioneers venerated as empire builders, such as the heroic canvas of John Sutter by William S. Jewett, which in 1855 the state of California acquired for $2,500 by act of legislature. For the most part, however, it was not the concerns of high-minded government officials that led to the decoration of public spaces with art but rather the pursuit of profits by enterprising entrepreneurs. As the former Argonaut Benjamin Avery observed in 1868 in one of the earliest histories of California art, "the first introduction of fine pictures had a purely commercial motive." With few exceptions, he lamented, they were purchased "to lend another attraction to the vicious 'saloons' wherein fortunes were won or lost on the turn of a card or the toss of a die."[19]

William Johnston, who crossed the continent with the first gold-rush wagon train to reach California, noticed on a visit to Sacramento in September 1849 that the gaming house called the Plains "had its walls frescoed with scenes familiar to overland emigrants, as 'Independence Rock,' 'Devil's Gate,' passes in the Rocky Mountains, and in the Sierra Nevada, etc." Johnston expressed surprise that in Sacramento "the finest and best buildings were those occupied by the black-leg gentry," but as all Argonauts attested, the largest, most elegantly furnished edifices in every town were invariably the gambling halls and saloons (figure 3). Frank Marryat, who acquainted himself with the temptations of San Francisco in the summer of 1850, wrote that upon entering one of the lavishly decorated palaces of masculine pleasure surrounding Portsmouth Square, "the eye is dazzled almost by the brilliancy of chandeliers and mirrors. The roof, rich with gilt-work, is supported

Figure 3. Miners take their pleasure in one of the richly furnished saloons that sprang up in San Francisco during the Gold Rush in an illustration by Frank Marryat that appeared in his *Mountains and Molehills* (1855). Marryat wrote that the walls of the palaces of masculine recreation he visited in San Francisco were invariably hung with paintings "of which female nudity forms alone the subject." Other Argonauts observed that public art throughout California invariably celebrated the female figure. *California Historical Society.*

by pillars of glass; and the walls are hung with French paintings of great merit, but of which female nudity forms alone the subject." If most miners lacked Marryat's confident connoisseurship and failed to distinguish between the European and American canvases staring down at them over bottles of sparkling liquors and boxes of choice cigars, they, nonetheless, responded warmly to the universality of their themes—which Friedrich Gerstäcker nicely summed up, in describing the paintings hanging in the El Dorado in San Francisco, as "calculated to arouse the instincts." Gerstäcker, it should be noted, was somewhat of a student of the pictorial riches of California's "gambling hells," and he informed his readers that as one traveled inland from San Francisco, "the more indecent these pictures became, becoming in the mines the most obscene points."[20]

Whatever the truth of Gerstäcker's assertion, there is little doubt that notwithstanding the landscapes William Johnston admired in the Plains, most public art in California celebrated the female figure. A San Francisco correspondent of the *Alta California* wrote in March 1850 that a striking view of the city of Canton and a fine engraving of the Battle of Chapultepec hung in the Bella Union on Portsmouth Square, but admitted that the images "that most attracted my attention and admiration were the pictures of Cleopatra, the Greek Slave, the Bacchanals and Venus." Six months later, when the saloon of the newly completed Union Hotel opened on the east side of the square, it was reported with some surprise that it was adorned with landscape and marine paintings. "Not the least pleasing feature of the whole arrangement," declared the *Picayune,* in commenting on the room's beauty and elegance, "is the absence of all lascivious pictures, such as decorate the walls of almost every saloon in the city."[21]

At this date, most of the pictures that hung in saloons and gambling halls, as well as in hotels, restaurants, and private residences, were from the East or Europe or Asia, part of the astounding array of luxury goods that came flooding into the port of San Francisco, along with countless crates and barrels of picks and pans, blankets and boots, flour and cheese, coffee and pork. In the spring of 1849 Andrew Jackson Grayson offered a "great variety" of oils and watercolors for sale at his general merchandise store in the City Hotel, and in September a "splendid collection" of more than three hundred Chinese paintings carried to California on the ship *Rhone* was auctioned off at Osborn & Brannan's new salesroom on Montgomery Street. Early the next year "lovers of the fine arts" were encouraged to visit Delmonico's dining saloon on Portsmouth Square, where "several magnificent paintings on copper, by some of the most celebrated German artists," could be purchased. Merchants handled sculptures as well as pictures, and in August 1850 Everett & Co. advertised the sale of "a number of beautiful Parisian statuettes and figurines," all of which were said to be "suitable for public saloons."[22]

Although Benjamin Avery scorned the "commercial" impulses that led to the importation of painting and sculpture, he acknowledged that among the innumerable artworks shipped to California were pieces of real distinction. The first important collection to appear in San Francisco, he asserted, comprised some "thirty or forty old European pictures of merit" that S. J. Gower put up for bid in the winter of 1850 at his auction house on Montgomery Street. Not long afterwards Joseph C. Duncan, whom Avery characterized as one of the first Californians "to introduce and encourage Art in a liberal and critical spirit," began to deal in paintings, importing them both for sale and for his own collection, which at one time was the largest in the state. In the spring of 1854 Duncan returned from a trip to Europe with a huge collection of pictures—including a "magnificent painting of the *Descent from the Cross* after Rubens," a "superb tableau of *Psyche and Amour*," and original works by Teniers, Greuze, and Van Dyck—that he sold, together with bronzes, jewelry, crystal, silver, porcelain, and "the largest diamond in the United States," through a lottery called the California Art Union. In a scheme perfectly suited to the reckless, gambling, go-ahead spirit of the Gold Rush, Californians purchased 100,000 tickets at a dollar each, which in mid-November were drawn from a wheel of fortune at the Metropolitan Theater. Over the course of two days, in a grand spectacle that provided entertainment and promoted culture, some six thousand "superb articles" were distributed to the crush of excited Californians who jammed the theater.[23]

If there was something of the huckster in Duncan, he nevertheless was successful in bringing good examples of European art to California. The scholarly John S. Hittell, a Forty-niner who was sensitive to the shaping power of painting and sculpture on society, mentioned several of these works in 1863 in the first survey of art in San Francisco. Like Avery, who echoed his judgment, Hittell praised an oil of *Prometheus* attributed to Andrea del Sarto that was still in Duncan's own collection and a "magnificent" painting of *Diana Starting for the Chase* by Nicholaes Maes. The best picture in California, and one of the best in the country, he declared, was a huge canvas by Jacobs of Dresden, *The Taking of Samson by the Philistines*. Ironically, though, as a consequence of the triumph of gentility over the raw masculine impulses of gold-rush days, the painting was "condemned to serve as an attraction to the liquor saloon known as the Bank Exchange," because, lamented Hittell, "the squeamishness of American society makes ladies afraid to look at human figures partly nude, even though the general idea be chaste."[24]

The single Argonaut capable of executing the large figural compositions admired by Hittell and Avery on the one hand and by saloon owners and miners on the other was Charles Nahl (figure 4), who indisputably stands as the foremost artist of the Gold Rush. Born in 1818 in the German town of Kassel, Nahl was the son of an engraver and etcher, the scion of several generations of painters, sculptors, and

Figure 4. When William Shew photographed Charles Nahl in the mid-1870s, the celebrated gold-rush artist was near the end of his life and would die a few years later. Like countless other Argonauts, he had come west to gather the golden harvest and then return home. But instead he stayed on, and for a quarter of a century his career perfectly reflected the evolving social and cultural conditions of the Golden State. An accomplished portrait, genre, and history painter, he also created innumerable designs for wood engravings that helped shape the popular image of life in El Dorado. *Courtesy Oakland Museum of California; gift of Robert Neuhaus.*

craftsmen. As a youth he attended the local art academy and gradually acquired the strong draftsmanship and the marvelous ability to reproduce surface textures with a stunning verisimilitude that came to distinguish his finest work. Moving to Stuttgart he achieved his first great success when the King of Württemberg purchased and placed in the state collection a huge canvas from his hand that portrayed a scene from one of Friedrich von Schiller's famed historical dramas of the Thirty Years War. At the age of twenty-eight Nahl went to Paris, where he came under the influence of the immensely popular Horace Vernet, though there is no evidence that he actually studied with him. In 1849 he took ship to New York and two years later came down with gold fever.[25]

Traveling by way of Panama with a small entourage that included his mother and several half-brothers and half-sisters, Nahl arrived at the diggings that spring. In the search for fortune, the family not only endured hardships common to all miners but also had the bad luck to purchase a salted claim that yielded them but nine dollars in gold. By the autumn of 1851, both Charles and his younger brother Arthur having suffered a debilitating attack of malaria—the storied "fever and ague" of the frontier—the Nahls took up residence in Sacramento. A year later, following a conflagration that consumed much of the town, they moved to San Francisco, where for a quarter-century Charles Nahl was a leading figure in the artistic life of the city.

Despite his great gifts as a painter of history and genre, his solid record of achievement in Europe and the East, Nahl undertook a remarkable variety of commissions in California. The range of his endeavors reflected both his own hard-driving ambition to succeed financially and the imperatives of gold-rush society—a society in which the entrepreneurial skills necessary to respond to the demands of a rapidly evolving frontier proved more valuable than the academic training required to create elegant pictures of subjects associated with a cultivated outlook, good taste, and social position. Although Nahl had exhibited at the Paris Salon, he was not above painting a banner of the Mexican War hero and presidential candidate, Winfield Scott, for the Whigs to carry in a parade, or one of George Washington for the Free Masons to wave. More than once he mixed his oils to satisfy the vanity of a patron whose eyes had been blackened in a brawl, carefully coloring the bruised and swollen flesh with perfectly matched tones. He frequently collaborated on projects with his brother Arthur or with August Wenderoth, a family friend who had traveled from Paris with them, and on one occasion all three labored on a moving panorama with scenes of California, the Sandwich Islands, Tahiti, and Australia. Not surprisingly, Charles executed a number of huge canvases for saloons and hotels, often working with incredible speed. In 1854, for example, he wrote of completing two coastal scenes, both seven by five feet, in five days and an even larger picture of a Turkish bath in two days.[26]

The enormous demand for pictures in California, together with his astounding versatility and restless energy, led Nahl to work in a wide range of media. He operated a daguerreotype gallery, developed a method for engraving glass photographic negatives called the Nahlotype, and drew on the lithographic stone, producing not only the archetypal *A Miner Prospecting* (1852) but several notable certificates of membership, including that of the Society of California Pioneers (1859). It was in his designs for wood engravings, though, that Nahl was most prolific. He began to draw on the block in 1852, and over the years he created countless illustrations of local life and color, his work brightening the pages of such newspapers and periodicals as the *Sacramento Pictorial Union, Wide West,* and *Hutchings' California Magazine.* Many of his pictures of the mines were also published as pictorial letter sheets, the popular illustrated stationery that Argonauts often favored for correspondence with friends and loved ones back home. His designs, moreover, appeared in numerous books, among them the widely read moralistic poem attributed to William Bausman, *The Idle and Industrious Miner* (1854), and Alonzo Delano's *Old Block's Sketch-Book* (1856), in which the artist was accurately described as "the Cruickshank of California." Nahl was not only highly successful as an illustrator but tremendously influential as well. His engravings—a half-dozen or so examples of which enliven the present volume—helped to shape the popular conception of life in gold-rush California years before Bret Harte first mined the rich lode of local color, and even today the image of that fabled era as a romantic, rollicking, Dickensian saga is to no small degree a consequence of the wonderful skill and imagination of Charles Nahl.

In addition to commercial work, Nahl produced a marvelous variety of easel paintings, including landscapes, still lifes, animal portraits, and religious compositions, as well as works of genre and history. In 1851 or 1852 he and August Wenderoth turned out a large, evocative picture of four Argonauts washing gold with a long tom, *Miners in the Sierras* (National Museum of American Art, Smithsonian Institution), and in 1856 he collaborated with Arthur on the superb *Fire in San Francisco Bay* (plate 6), one of the first historical paintings on a local theme produced in California. An elegant, luminous picture, filled with authentic detail, it dramatically depicts a blaze that had broken out three years earlier on the *Canonicus* and the *Manco,* two abandoned vessels converted into storeships. As great sheets of flame blossom from the *Manco,* threatening to ignite powder kegs kept in the hold and endangering the city itself, the brigade captain stands at the stern of the ship and oversees the fearless attack of his red-shirted volunteers, who direct streams of water from hoses ferried by rowboats from the Sacramento Street wharf.

For all of his strengths as an artist, most of the paintings Charles Nahl produced in the new El Dorado were portraits. He undertook his first commissions while recovering from malaria in the diggings, producing drawings of the miners at twelve dollars a head, and after settling in Sacramento he and August Wenderoth shared a studio where their work brought them praise on two counts. "Their likenesses," it was reported, "are strikingly correct and possess that important recommendation as to price, which places a domestic luxury within reach of the most moderate means." In San Francisco, Nahl sprang to prominence when an influential businessman asked him to make a portrait of his deceased partner—"who was still fresh in everyone's memory"—from a dark, poorly exposed daguerreotype. "I succeeded beyond expectations," he wrote home, "and soon I had orders to paint rich attorneys, bankers, as well as merchants and court personnel."[27]

Many of these images survive today. For the most part they testify to Nahl's accomplishments as a portraitist and to the genteel aspirations of his sitters, who, staring across a century and a half at us, radiate pride and propriety and who, in dress and appearance, are indistinguishable from Americans of that day who sat to artists in New York, in Boston, in Philadelphia, in Charleston. By contrast, Nahl occasionally produced portraits that were distinctively regional, rooted in the immediacy of the western experience, of which *Peter Quivey and the Mountain Lion* (plate 7) is particularly fine. A striking image of life on the California frontier, it depicts the fearsome "catamount" of the American wilderness lying dead at the feet of the self-assured hunter, a pioneer of 1846, and reveals the artist's considerable talents as an animal painter, as well as his remarkable skill in rendering the "feel" of fur and leather and other surface textures.

The rapid rise of portraiture that helped to assure Nahl's success was not accompanied by significant support for other branches of painting in California. Although the Forty-niners and those who followed in their path were often eager to acquire a picture of mining life, an urban scene, or a scenic view, they rarely showed an interest in owning paintings of the same subjects. Like the Californios and the pioneer families, they purchased portraits and little else, confirming the assertion of Henry Inman, a founder of the National Academy of Design and in the late 1830s reputedly the highest paid painter in the nation, that people always prefer pictures of themselves "in the infancy of the Fine Arts in all countries." In 1857, at the first fair held by the Mechanics' Institute of San Francisco, professional artists overwhelmingly contributed portraits to the fine arts display. The judges, observing that the walls were hung with more paintings of local worthies than of local scenery, remarked in awarding a diploma to the amateur Mrs. A. T. Oakes for her landscapes in oil, "There are but few of this class of picture on exhibition. The luxuries of painting can only follow the introduction of wealth-creating improvements, and it cannot be expected that at this epoch of the development of arts in California, the talents of artists in this class will be duly encouraged."[28]

The same theme was echoed by others who saw the cultural evolution of the Golden State within the larger context of the national experience. Beginning with the

Massachusetts Bay Colony in the seventeenth century and continuing on over successive frontiers, Americans had not turned their attention to the fine arts until they had conquered the wilderness and achieved a modest prosperity. Their first paintings were invariably portraits, stiff likenesses of family members that for generations stared down from parlor walls. Later, with the rise of a broad class of merchants and physicians and lawyers, with the growth of wealth and leisure, the arts blossomed and painters received commissions for a variety of pictures, particularly landscapes. Such was the strength of the pattern that in 1859 a San Francisco newspaper asserted, "California is too young yet to have given birth to any artists; she is almost too young to patronise those who have come hither from abroad. So long as a country is engaged in providing itself with the first necessaries of life, building its homes and fencing its fields, it can scarcely be expected to spend much for the fine arts."[29]

But contrary to precedent and perception, the full flowering of art on the Pacific Slope awaited developments other than settlers securing "the first necessaries of life." For in the sphere of culture, as in so many others realms, California was indeed "the great exception." The Gold Rush created a frontier unlike any other in American history, a frontier where wealth was common at the outset and where the economic and institutional growth of decades was compressed into a few years. But if the material foundation for the support of art was established early, the motives that sent the Argonauts hurtling west delayed the emergence of a society in which painting could flourish. Although many of the miners appreciated pictures and other possessions associated with culture and financial success, they were rarely inclined "to accumulate art objects," as Benjamin Avery observed, "as few of them expected to remain and build homes here." In 1855, for example, well after Charles Nahl had solidly established himself in San Francisco, his mother wrote of the family's unremitting labors and real estate investments, "Every penny that is saved gets us closer to our wish to leave this place." Three years later, in a letter to his uncle, Arthur made it clear that the Nahls had still not come to think of themselves as Californians. "Is this a grand country?" he asked rhetorically. "No, Sir, be sure that he who does not have to stay here, will not stay here."[30]

The Nahls did remain, as did other Argonauts, and as they and newer immigrants worked to suppress the worst legacies of the Gold Rush—the greed and waste, the coarseness and vulgarity, the crime and brutality—the patterns of life associated with long-established communities appeared. The evolution of a reckless, transient population into an increasingly mature and stable society continued through the 1850s and into the 1860s. And though the more spectacular manifestations of the search for order, such as the Vigilance Committees of 1851 and 1856, have traditionally attracted the most attention, the growth of the fine arts speaks more persuasively of sojourners becoming settlers, of their emerging commitment to California and her future.

Despite a lack of substantial encouragement, artists produced a wide range of paintings, particularly landscapes, in the age of gold. Some of these canvases were the work of amateurs, such as the ship chandler Charles D. Shed and the elusive Mrs. A. T. Oakes, about whom little is known, but most came from the studios of painters who earned their living with the brush. In addition to the versatile Charles Nahl, William Jewett executed a variety of pictures, including genre scenes and at least one canvas on a religious theme, but he was best known, apart from portraiture, for his landscapes. As early as the spring of 1850 he received a commission from the enterprising Coloma merchant and hotel owner John T. Little to paint the charming foothill valley celebrated as the site of the gold discovery, and the following year he produced the first of two nearly identical views of the Sutter Buttes from the Feather River.[31]

Jewett, in fact, achieved his greatest prominence for *The Promised Land* (plate 8), a large, handsome composition in which the Sierra Nevada and the Sacramento Valley figure symbolically in the inner meaning of California and the westward movement. In 1846 a St. Louis merchant, Andrew Jackson Grayson, had responded to the call of destiny and, with his wife and infant son, followed the path of empire across plains and mountains to the edge of the American continent. Four years later, having grown wealthy through mining and land speculation, Grayson asked Jewett to commemorate the moment of golden memory when the family broke through the forests of the Sierra Nevada and gazed upon the broad, fertile valley of the Sacramento. Ferdinand Ewer, editor of the literary monthly *The Pioneer*, who saw the painting hanging in the hall of the Society of California Pioneers in 1854, was moved by the beauty of the landscape—the "grandeur" of the mountains, the "magnificent" sweep of the distant plain—and praised the work highly, calling it "truly and exclusively a California picture." Later writers concurred but came to see something more in the canvas, including, as one critic put it, "the high idea of the progress of civilization westward." Benjamin Avery, who composed his history of California art when many a Forty-niner was recasting the meaning of the Gold Rush, perceived that Jewett had portrayed a geography of hope as well as a geography of place, and he drew upon Samuel Johnson's eighteenth-century romance of the Prince of Abyssinia to make the analogy of a Pacific paradise. "This," he declared of the grand vista spread before the Graysons, "is the Rasselas Valley of sober fact."[32]

In giving pictorial form to the California landscape, in *The Promised Land* and in all his other works, Jewett relied less on direct observation than on the conventions of the Hudson River School, the prevailing American tradition of nature painting, which he had mastered as a young artist in New York, where he had come to know the first leader of the school, Thomas Cole. As a consequence Jewett invariably failed to faithfully portray the distinctive character—the light, the color, the atmosphere, and even the flora—of the Golden State. Other artist-Argonauts similarly drew heavily upon the aesthetic of the native movement, or correlative European

Plate 1.
Samuel S. Osgood,
General John A. Sutter, 1849.
Oil on ticking, 29 ⅛ x 23 ¾
in. *Fine Arts Museums
of San Francisco; Museum
purchase,* DY54768.

Plate 2.
William S. Jewett,
*Lieutenant
Washington A. Bartlett,
U.S.N.,* 1850. Oil on
canvas, 22 x 18 in. *Cali-
fornia Historical Society;
Fine Arts Purchase Fund.*

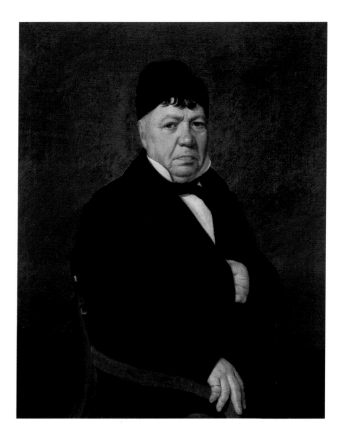

Plate 3.
Leonardo Barbieri,
José de la Guerra y Noriega,
1850. Oil on canvas, 35 x 28 in.
Collection of Santa Barbara
Historical Society.

Plate 4. Thomas Moore,
E. W. McIlhany, 49er,
1850. Oil on canvas,
28 ½ x 23 ½ in. *Oakland*
Museum of California,
Museum Donors
Acquisition Fund.

Plate 5. E. Hall Martin, *Mountain Jack and a Wandering Miner,* 1850. Oil on canvas, 39 ½ x 72 in. *Oakland Museum of California, gift of Concours d'Antiques, Art Guild.*

Plate 6. Charles C. Nahl and Arthur Nahl, *Fire in San Francisco Bay,* 1856. Oil on canvas, 26 x 40 in. *Private collection. Photograph courtesy Montgomery Gallery, San Francisco.*

Plate 7. Charles C. Nahl, *Peter Quivey and the Mountain Lion*, 1857. Oil on canvas, 26 x 34 in. *Fine Arts Museums of San Francisco, Museum purchase, James E. Harrold, Jr. Bequest Fund and gift of Carol W. Casey, 1998.32.*

Plate 8. William S. Jewett, *The Promised Land—The Grayson Family*, 1850. Oil on canvas, 50 ¾ x 64 in. *Daniel J. Terra Collection, 5.1994, Terra Museum of American Art, Chicago.*

Plate 9. Alburtus D. O. Browere, *View of Stockton*, 1854. Oil on canvas, 16 x 28 in. *Oakland Museum of California, Kahn Collection.*

Plate 10. Thomas A. Ayres, *Relief Valley*, ca. 1856–1858. Oil on canvas, 14 ¼ x 20 ¼ in. *Jane and Thomas McLaughlin Collection. Photograph courtesy North Point Gallery, San Francisco.*

Plate 11. George Tirrell, *View of Sacramento, California, from across the Sacramento River,* undated. Oil on canvas, 27 x 47¾ in. *Gift of Maxim Karolik for the M. and M. Karolik Collection of American Paintings, 1815–1865, Museum of Fine Arts, Boston.*

Plate 12. Frederick A. Butman, *Mt. Shasta and Shastina,* ca. 1862–1871. Oil on canvas, 26 x 43 in. *Bancroft Library.*

Plate 13. Samuel M. Brookes, *Still Life*, 1862. Oil on canvas, 34 x 44 in. *Crocker Art Museum, Sacramento, Calif.: E. B. Crocker Collection.*

Plate 14. Virgil Williams, *View South from Sonoma Hills toward San Pablo Bay and Mount Tamalpais*, 1864. Oil on canvas, 30 ¼ x 48 in. *Private collection. Photograph courtesy Montgomery Gallery, San Francisco.*

Plate 15. William Marple, *View of Clear Lake*, 1867. Oil on canvas, 18 x 30 in. *Private collection. Photograph courtesy Montgomery Gallery, San Francisco.*

Plate 16. Albert Bierstadt, *Winter in Yosemite Valley*, 1872. Oil on paper, 14 ¼ x 19 ⅛ in. *Garzoli Gallery, San Rafael, Calif.*

approaches to romantic realism, and their paintings also usually testified as much to the shaping power of established pictorial practices as to the wild beauty of California. In the complex interplay of landscape art and landscape experience, painters gradually responded more creatively to local conditions. But as late as 1868 Benjamin Avery felt compelled to counsel that artistic success would come only to those "who, while painting Californian scenery, grasp not its outlines merely, filling them with the color, tone and details of another clime, or with merely conventional strokes but catch its own atmosphere and sentiment, absorb and reproduce its distinctive individuality."[33]

More active than Jewett in exploring the pictorial possibilities of the California landscape were the artist-Argonauts Thomas Ayres and Alburtus D. O. Browere. Browere, born in Tarrytown, New York, was of Dutch ancestry, sturdy and self-reliant, and in 1852 he made the first of two lengthy trips to California. Though he lacked the astounding technical gifts of Nahl, he possessed a resourceful versatility of his own, proclaiming in an advertisement that he not only painted portraits "in the finest style of art," but was prepared to execute "landscapes, scenes from nature, views of mining claims and operations, farms, and pictures of every kind," as well as "ornamental and decorative painting" and "plain and fancy signs, saloon and house painting." Among his many extant pictures, which include portraits, landscapes, and a series of vigorous genre scenes, is *View of Stockton* (plate 9), a charming, luminous painting distinguished by subtle effects of light and atmosphere. Executed in 1854, it shows a prosperous city of brick and wood buildings bordering a channel of the San Joaquin River, and, beyond, glistening in the warm light of the afternoon sun, the snowy peaks of the Sierra Nevada.[34]

Thomas A. Ayres, a native of New Jersey and a fellow passenger of the ill-starred E. Hall Martin on the ship *Panama*, turned his full attention to the California landscape within a year of his arrival in 1849. He traveled widely through the state and made drawings of characteristic scenery from Mount Shasta to the sparkling shores of the San Diego littoral, which he planned to use in the creation of oil paintings. He was the first artist to enter the Yosemite Valley, a member of the pioneer tourist party assembled in the spring of 1855 by the English-born Forty-niner James M. Hutchings, who the following year published several engravings after drawings by Ayres in the first issue of his literary periodical, *Hutchings' California Magazine*. Enthralled by the glories of the Yosemite, the artist returned the following year and spent some two weeks exploring the valley. While thousands of miners toiled in the dusty foothills far below, he delighted in the sublime beauty of grand vistas and towering granite ramparts and in the silvery song of swift-flowing rivers. On one of his excursions he came upon Illilouette Fall and wrote that the water spilled over the cliff "like a gust of living light from heaven." Though Ayres occupied himself endlessly with drawing from nature, he seems never to have opened a studio in California, and he had

executed no more than a score of paintings when in 1858, at the age of thirty, he
tragically went down with the schooner *Laura Bevan* off Point Dume in a fierce
nor'wester. Among his few extant oils is a picture of *Relief Valley* (plate 10), located
some thirty miles northeast of Yosemite, along the old emigrant trail, near the head-
waters of the Stanislaus River.[35]

In 1854 Ayres collaborated with Thomas H. Smith to produce a panorama titled
California on Canvas, comprising a series of forty-six scenes that mixed images of urban life with scenes of natural wonder and curiosity. Ayres provided the drawings,
which Smith rendered in oil on a long strip of canvas that could be unrolled to reveal the sights one by one. The panorama opened with a view of the Golden Gate
and continued on to show Sacramento, the principal towns of the gold fields, and
such marvels as Mount Shasta, the summit of the Sierra Nevada, and the Big Trees,
and concluded with a dramatic depiction of the San Joaquin River illuminated by
moonlight and the fierce blaze of the surrounding tules on fire. Exhibited in August
at the Musical Hall in San Francisco, *California on Canvas* proved an enormous
success, the audience repeatedly breaking out in applause as the splendid scenery of
the state passed before their eyes.[36]

Panoramas, which combined art with entertainment and, potentially, huge profits
for artists and promoters, had been popular in the United States since the 1830s, and,
not surprisingly, Ayres and Smith's production was but one of a host of works inspired by the discovery of gold and the ensuing fascination with the new El Dorado.
As early as September 1849 a *Grand Nautical Panorama* of a voyage around Cape
Horn to California opened at Stoppani Hall in New York City. Based on the drawings of William Meyers, a naval gunner and amateur artist, the panorama was said
to be particularly popular with women "whose husbands, brothers, lovers, etc. have
gone to California." It was swiftly followed by Emmert and Penfield's *Original
Panorama of the Gold Mines,* Beale and Craven's *Voyage to California and Return,* and
James F. Wilkins's *Moving Mirror of the Overland Trail.* Wilkins first exhibited his
grand work in September 1850 to a packed house in Peoria. As the canvas moved
across the stage, "a stillness deep as the tomb" overcame the audience, it was reported,
"and with open mouths and stretching necks," they watched as prairies gave way to
deserts and mountains, until "anyone with a little imagination would actually believe
that he was on the way to California."[37]

The first panorama shown in California was the work of Paul Emmert, a Swiss-
born artist who was living in New York City when word of gold sent him speeding
west. Said to be nearly a mile in length, Emmert's moving canvas featured representative scenic views and images of the mining districts, as well as a dramatic depiction of the city of Sacramento inundated by the muddy waters of one of the terrible floods that periodically swept the Central Valley. Exhibited in the spring of 1852
at the Theatre of Varieties in San Francisco, it enjoyed a run of several weeks,

confirming that Californians—who for the most part were strangers in a strange land—were as curious as other Americans about the wonders of the Golden State. Emmert's panorama was followed by others, of which the most celebrated was the work of the Boston-born Forty-niner George Tirrell. Although scenic artists were typically limited to broad effects, Tirrell was capable of strong drawing and sensitive, luminous effects of light and color, as can be seen in his *View of Sacramento* (plate 11), which illustrates, as well, the enormous importance of California's great river as a major artery of western travel and commerce. Tirrell first unrolled his huge pano-rama in the spring of 1860 at Tucker's Academy of Music on Montgomery Street in San Francisco. One critic declared it "a beautiful work of art, and worthy the atten-tion of *connoiseurs.*" Among the many Californians who came to see it over the course of several weeks was the governor of the state, John Downey; and, even to-day, reading a description of the panorama's many scenes—"varied by constantly changing natural effects of sunrise, noonday, sunset, moonlight, firelight, rain, snow, etc., and enlivened by upwards of 3,000 characteristic figures"—suggests an enjoy-able evening's entertainment.[38]

The first Californian to earn his living as a landscape painter was Frederick Butman. A self-taught artist, he struck out from his native Maine in 1857 and began his ca-reer in San Francisco inauspiciously, putting in scenic backgrounds for the por-traitist James Wise. Two years later, he sprang to prominence when several of his paintings of Yosemite Valley were exhibited in a shop window on Montgomery Street and received highly favorable notice in the local press. Enterprising and en-ergetic, Butman traveled through the state and up into the Pacific Northwest, mak-ing open-air studies in color of Lake Tahoe, the snowy peaks of the Sierra Nevada, Monterey Bay, the Golden Gate, Mount Hood, and other picturesque scenery, which he used in the execution of his studio paintings. Among his best work is *Mt. Shasta and Shastina* (plate 12), a dramatic depiction of the "King of the Moun-tains," in which a dark rocky foreground contrasts with the golden tones of the up-land plain and leads the eye to the glistening glaciers of the majestic peak itself. But-man's paintings appealed strongly to Californians and until the end of the Civil War "gave him a greater share of popularity and success than was enjoyed by any other painter." His pictures graced the walls of grand houses and fashionable hotels, and he was said to have been paid as much as $8,000 for one of his canvases.[39]

Butman's success as a landscape painter stemmed not only from his skill and en-terprise but from the "rapid, monstrous maturity" of California, which had under-gone enormous changes since the first flush days of gold. At the date of his arrival, the population of the state stood at 300,000, of whom one out of six lived in San Francisco. Many were Argonauts who had stayed on after their dreams of riches died, but most were like Butman, part of the great migration—from the East, from

Europe, from Asia—that continued on year after year. Although a third of Californians still labored in the mines, the state's economy had grown and diversified with commerce, agriculture, and industry all contributing to the wealth of the Golden State. In 1859, the year Butman established his reputation, the Irish prospectors McLaughlin and O'Riley made their fabulous strike in the wastes of western Nevada, and over the following two decades the Comstock Lode yielded four hundred million dollars in silver and gold, much of it flowing to San Francisco, which supplied the men, machinery, and capital for the hardrock mines.

Although San Francisco had been a dusty village of some sixty adobe and frame buildings on the eve of the Gold Rush, it had soon become a major American port, and by the time the state entered the age of silver, it had taken on the appearance of a city far older than its actual years. Substantial brick and stone edifices lined busy thoroughfares of commerce, and elegant houses graced the stylish neighborhoods of rich industrialists, financiers, and merchants—evidence of a prosperity that promised a bright future for the fine arts. "As we increase in wealth and stability," the *Alta California* sanguinely observed in late 1859, "our citizens have more time to devote to matters of taste, and life becomes less a mere scramble for dollars, while what tends to public refinement, and the cultivation of the beautiful, is patronised with increased liberality."[40]

Critical to the growth of patronage was the rise of galleries and exhibitions, which brought public attention to art and promoted sales. As early as the autumn of 1851 a collection of California landscapes was displayed at the Athenaeum on Sacramento Street in San Francisco, and a few years later Marvin & Hitchcock's Pioneer Book Store on Montgomery Street began to advertise engravings and paintings among its stock of goods. But it was not until the appearance of shops devoted to framing, gilding, and the sale of artists' materials—which, by tradition, hung pictures in their windows—that Californians could regularly see paintings by local artists displayed. Particularly prominent among these concerns was the firm of Jones, Wooll & Sutherland, carvers and gilders, established in the mid-1850s. In addition to selling frames and artists' materials, the partners handled engravings, lithographs, and paintings, and it was their exhibition of the Yosemite views of Frederick Butman in 1859 that launched the artist's career in California.[41]

On the evening of 11 January 1865, on the second floor of Jones, Wooll & Sutherland's building at 312 Montgomery Street, the newly founded California Art Union threw open the doors of the first true gallery in the American West. At the gala reception, members and their guests sipped champagne and circulated through the room, admiring the dozens of paintings, both for sale and on loan from private collections, that lined the walls. In one of the many speeches given that night, the gathering was reminded of the remarkable transformation California had undergone since the days of gold, "when nobody intended to make his permanent home

Figure 5. Amidst the hustle and bustle of Steamer Day in San Francisco, a lone passerby admires the paintings hung in the window of Snow & Roos, purveyors of artists' materials, in a broadly humorous lithograph by Edward Jump published in 1866. *California Historical Society; gift of E. G. Schmidell, FN-06083.*

here." "First came the church," declared the speaker, as he traced the rise of civilization on the far edge of the continent, "then the school, then permanent homes, and finally art."[42]

The California Art Union failed by year's end, but by that date there were a half dozen or more picture dealers in San Francisco. Particularly notable were the firms of Adrien Gensoul and Roos & Wunderlich—later Snow & Roos (figure 5)—which at the close of the decade established the first commercial gallery in the city above its shop on Kearny Street. Climbing the stairs on opening day in April 1869, San Franciscans were treated to an exhibition of more than a hundred paintings, chiefly landscapes by local artists, hung beneath an arched ceiling richly ornamented with frescoes after designs by Nahl and others. By day, sunlight streamed through a baffled skylight, washing the walls of the large airy gallery with soft, even light, and

Figure 6. Pedestrians gather outside the pavilion constructed by the Mechanics' Institute in 1865 at the corner of Geary and Stockton streets in San Francisco for its fifth fair. First held in 1857, these popular exhibitions, which customarily opened with a display of fireworks, included works of art among the countless examples of the state's industries, giving Californians the opportunity to view paintings by local artists, as well as by other American and European painters. *California Historical Society, FN-27058.*

at night, gas jets illuminated the room. "There must be much taste for art in a city of 150,000 inhabitants," proudly declared the *Alta California,* "in which dealers in pictures and artists' materials find it profitable to establish a free art gallery full of fine paintings."[43]

For many years Californians had their best opportunity to see works of art, both local and foreign, in the exhibitions sponsored by the Mechanics' Institute of San Francisco (figure 6). First held in 1857, the fairs were enormously popular with Californians, who could spend days wandering the long aisles jammed with displays of mechanical, agricultural, and domestic industry, examining a model of a windmill, a plan for a quartz mill, a white silk embroidered vest. Drawings and paintings were initially hung with little care, but at the fourth fair, in 1864, a separate pavilion was constructed for the fine arts exhibit, with one of the four galleries reserved for the work of California artists. The pavilion proved a huge attraction, particularly the hall devoted to regional art. "The rooms were thronged night and day," recalled Benjamin Avery, and the display "led to the sale of many good pictures, and elicited commissions for more."[44]

Among the artists who contributed pictures to the California section were several of what was becoming the old guard, Forty-niners like the Nahl brothers and Stephen Shaw. But the exhibit's real appeal was the work of the newer men, who, in addition to prudently displaying their skill in portraiture, filled the gallery with landscape, genre, and still-life paintings. In addition to Frederick Butman, this "second generation" included Fortunato Arriola, Gideon J. Denny, E. Wood Perry, Armand Teisseire, and Thomas Hill, who had begun his career in Massachusetts ornamenting carriages but who had recently shown some of the promise that would ultimately make him one of the state's leading landscape painters. Samuel M. Brookes, an English-born artist who had been active in the Midwest before coming to California, also exhibited examples of his work, most notably a selection of still lifes. He had established his preeminence in this field shortly after his arrival in San Francisco in 1862 with the eponymously titled *Still Life* (plate 13), which later entered the huge collection of Judge E. B. Crocker of Sacramento. A large formal composition that testifies to Brookes's expert draftsmanship as well as to his close study of the seventeenth-century Dutch tradition, it portrays a sumptuous selection of fish, fowl, and vegetables from the local market, including the regional delicacies of western meadowlarks and California quail.

The most prominent artist to exhibit at the 1864 fair was Juan B. Wandesforde, who had studied in his native England with John Varley and who had enjoyed the prestige of membership in the Century Association in New York before coming west. Equally talented was the cultivated and cosmopolitan Yankee Virgil Williams, who was then working on a commission that was destined to play an important role in advancing art and shaping public taste in California. In 1862, while living in Rome, he had met Robert B. Woodward, a high-minded westerner on the Grand Tour. Woodward, who owned the well-known San Francisco temperance hotel the What Cheer House, had been "deeply impressed" by the paintings he had seen in Holland and Florence and Rome, and he was eager to establish the beginnings of a gallery of art that would "one day vie with the best collections of the eastern cities." He found an ally in Williams, who quickly assembled a group of some forty canvases, many of which were copies of masterworks from his own hand, and then accompanied Woodward to San Francisco.[45]

Taking a room at the What Cheer House, Williams settled into the rhythms of local life, painting landscapes and genre scenes and overseeing the construction of the art gallery and other attractions at Woodward's estate at Fourteenth and Mission streets. The gallery, designed by the distinguished architect John Gaynor and "frescoed after the Pompeiian manner by Poldemann," was chiefly hung with European pictures and copies of European pictures but included the work of several California artists, most notably Williams himself. A contemporary description of one of these canvases, *Napa Valley,* is highly suggestive of the picture now titled *View South from Sonoma Hills toward San Pablo Bay and Mount Tamalpais* (plate 14). An elegant, spacious composition, the painting is the earliest pictorial work to play upon the Mediterranean analogy first evoked by the explorer John C. Frémont, who delighted in the striking similarities of light and landscape—the earthy, radiant warmth, the bright blue skies—that California shared with Italy. The collection was first viewed by San Franciscans in November 1864 at a benefit for the United States Sanitary Commission, and two years later Woodward permanently opened the gallery (figure 7) and surrounding grounds to the public. Although much of the art was second-rate, as Williams later admitted, the collection nonetheless helped to introduce Californians to the long tradition of European painting, and for years the gallery was a popular resort for culture-conscious San Franciscans.[46]

Following the 1864 Mechanics' Institute Fair, interest in art increased rapidly in California. Decades later the landscape painter William Keith stated that an "art wave" had swept over the state. "Everything and anything in the semblance of a picture sold then," he fondly recalled. "The people had money, had more of it than they needed, so they bought art works generously." In 1866 William Marple, a Forty-niner who had been painting houses and signs in Placerville, was so encouraged by this "art wave" that he came to San Francisco and launched out as an artist. Though self-taught and far out of the artistic mainstream for much of his life, he was a talented painter, as suggested by one of his early works, *View of Clear Lake* (plate 15), and in 1868 he received a medal for the best landscape in oil exhibited at the Mechanics' Institute Fair. The rise of patronage in San Francisco similarly emboldened Harvey O. Young, who in 1867 turned from painting carriages to painting scenery, and the following year the wood engraver William Keith first advertised himself as a landscape painter, as did Norton Bush, a student in his youth of the famed Jasper Cropsey, who despite significant local recognition as an artist had spent fifteen years working at the San Francisco Gas Company.[47]

The remarkable growth of patronage culminated in the early 1870s, when San Francisco emerged as one of the leading art centers in the country. Contributing to this efflorescence was the completion in 1869 of the transcontinental railroad, which brought countless painters west, including such major figures as Martin Johnson Heade, Samuel Colman, James Hamilton, William Bradford, and the master of the "heroic style" of landscape, Albert Bierstadt. Although most were excursionists, eager to paint the storied scenery of the Golden State and then return home, some remained for months, stimulating local painters and helping to create enthusiasm for art at all levels of society. Bierstadt, who arrived in July 1871, apparently contemplated staying not much longer than he had in 1863, when on the eve of his rise to fame he camped for six or seven weeks in Yosemite Valley. But his visit ultimately stretched out to more than two years, as he wandered the state making open-air studies (plate

Figure 7. Youthful art lovers take in the display of paintings and sculpture at the art gallery at Woodward's Gardens in San Francisco. Opened to the public in the mid-1860s by the wealthy Robert Woodward, the gallery was largely composed of European works, and though many of the paintings were copies or of questionable merit, the collection played an important role in the advancement of culture in California. *California Historical Society, FN-00411.*

16), which he worked up into the splendid canvases that added to his already lustrous reputation in America and abroad.

Shortly after Bierstadt arrived in California, he was made an honorary member of the San Francisco Art Association. Founded that spring for "the promotion of Painting, Sculpture and Fine Arts akin thereto," the Art Association proved popular at once, and within two years more than seven hundred Californians had joined. Much of the organization's success sprang from its series of receptions, which united the aspirations of artists and society. Held at the Art Association's rooms several times a year, these festive gatherings gave members and their guests the opportunity to see the newest work of local artists, who, for their part, could meet wealthy and cultivated Californians in a congenial atmosphere of champagne and musical entertainment. By the summer of 1872 the *Overland Monthly* could credit much of "the very noticeable increase of the general interest taken in art matters" to the association's receptions, observing that they not only had "given an enlivening impulse to the *esprit de corps* of the professionals, but tended to make art popular by making it talked about and fashionable."[48]

In February 1874, less than three years after its formation, the San Francisco Art Association realized one of its principal goals, "the establishment of an Academy or School of Design." The curriculum of the school reflected the experience and values of the first director, Virgil Williams, and was modeled on traditional lines, with students beginning their studies by copying engravings and then moving on to drawing from plaster casts of classical Greek and Roman sculpture. The first art academy founded in the American West, the California School of Design affirmed that support for the fine arts had reached maturity in the distant reaches of the young nation.[49]

Not long after the first class of forty students assembled to learn the fundamentals of solid draftsmanship in the school's sunny room on Pine Street, Benjamin P. Avery sat down to compose an article on California art for the New York journal *The Aldine.* As a green youth of twenty-one, Avery had struck out in 1849 for El Dorado, and having experienced firsthand the tumultuous history of the Golden State, it was with no little pride that he wrote of the growth of refinement and taste, of "a very marked aesthetic movement," in San Francisco. In tracing the rise of art, he focused on the School of Design, declaring that nearly two centuries had passed after the first European settlement of New York before the city had an academy of fine art, and that Boston had waited even longer. "Yet San Francisco, which twenty-five years ago was a hamlet of three hundred inhabitants," he wrote, "can already boast that it has done more for art culture than either of the two older cities had done within the early memory of men whose heads are not yet gray." And, indeed, in this lively cosmopolitan city could be found an active colony of painters—some with national reputations—an art association, an art academy, fashionable galleries, and important private collections of American and European paintings. Yet only a quarter century had passed since William Redmond Ryan had pulled out into the harbor in search of the brushes and colors he was unable to find anywhere in the wind-blown, helter-skelter village teetering on the edge of history.[50]

NOTES

1. William Redmond Ryan, *Personal Adventures in Upper and Lower California, in 1848–9*, 2 vols. (London: William Shoberl, 1850), 2:230–35. The quotations are from pp. 234 and 232.

Modern inquiry into the art and artists of the age of gold began with Jeanne Van Nostrand, whose "Sights in the Gold Region and Scenes by the Way" (M.A. thesis, University of California, Berkeley, 1939) formed the basis for much of her *California Pictorial: A History of Contemporary Pictures, 1769 to 1859* (Berkeley: University of California Press, 1948), co-authored with Edith M. Coulter and published on the centennial of the gold discovery. She subsequently continued her study of the period, incorporating her findings and those of other pioneering scholars, such as Elliot Evans, Joseph Armstrong Baird, Jr., and Moreland Stevens, in "Painting in Eldorado, 1849–1859," the longest of four chapters in her book *The First Hundred Years of Painting in California, 1775–1875* (San Francisco: John Howell Books, 1980). Together with the volume's appendix of brief biographies and references, it formed an invaluable contribution to the field, and despite numerous errors of fact, it has long served as a guide and a reference. Unfortunately, for more than a decade the studies begun by Jeanne Van Nostrand have languished, with historians of California art focusing their attention chiefly on the open-air painting of the late nineteenth and early twentieth centuries. Moreover, most discussions of gold-rush art that have appeared in broader studies of California and western art have contributed little that is new to the field, apart from interpretive readings—often highly imaginative and not rooted in historical fact—of paintings and prints. A welcome exception to this neglect is Janice T. Driesbach, Harvey L. Jones, and Katherine Church Holland, *Art of the Gold Rush* (Berkeley: University of California Press, in association with the Oakland Museum of California and the Crocker Art Museum, 1998), published on the sesquicentennial of the discovery. It reproduces both little-known images and familiar works, as well as provides new information, and will perhaps awaken new interest in the subject.

For gold-rush graphics, the standard sources have long been Harry T. Peters, *California on Stone* (Garden City, N.Y.: Doubleday, Doran and Co., 1935), and Joseph Armstrong Baird, Jr., *California's Pictorial Letter Sheets, 1849–1869* (San Francisco: David Magee, 1967). Though in need of updating, a still useful reference for researchers is Joseph Armstrong Baird, Jr., and Ellen Schwartz, *Northern California Art: An Interpretive Bibliography to 1915* (Davis: Library Associates, University Library, University of California, 1977). For biographical information, a recent, if not entirely reliable, compendium is Edan Milton Hughes, *Artists in California, 1786–1940*, 2nd ed. (San Francisco: Hughes Publishing Co., 1989).

My own work is based largely on research among primary materials, as suggested by the notes that follow. Although I cite sources for specific biographical information relating to my narrative and occasionally draw attention to useful biographical sources or to significant errors in secondary studies, I have made no attempt to include comprehensive references for the artists discussed. For bibliographies of this sort, the reader is directed to the works previously mentioned.

2. Quoted in Robert Glass Cleland, *A History of California: The American Period* (New York: Macmillan, 1922), 273; San Francisco *Picayune,* 6 December 1850, in Kenneth M. Johnson, ed., *San Francisco as It Is: Gleanings from the* Picayune (Georgetown, Calif.: Talisman Press, 1964), 97.

3. Ryan, *Personal Adventures,* 1:v, 2:131, 239–40, 241–42. Van Nostrand, *First Hundred Years,* 28–29, 120, has biographical information on this little-known artist, though her account of his California career is inconsistent in many regards with that set forth by Ryan himself.

4. Coit to Harriet Frances Coit, 29 April 1849, in George P. Hammond, ed., *Digging for Gold Without a Shovel: The Letters of Daniel Wadsworth Coit from Mexico City, 1848–1851* (Denver: Old West Publishing Co., 1967), 70. Almost nothing is known of Prendergast. He arrived in 1848, according to Hubert Howe Bancroft, *History of California,* 7 vols. (San Francisco: History Co., 1884–90), 4:291, and was active in California until about 1852.

5. *New York Tribune,* 22 June 1849.

6. Ibid.

7. Bayard Taylor, *Eldorado, or, Adventures in the Path of Empire,* 2 vols. (New York: George P. Putnam, 1850), 1:61; *New York Tribune,* 20 October 1849; Henry W. French, *Art and Artists in Connecticut* (Boston: Lee & Shepard, 1879), 60.

8. J. D. Borthwick, *Three Years in California* (Edinburgh: William Blackwood & Sons, 1857), 162. The public library of Santa Cruz, California, has a first edition of Borthwick's book, formerly owned by the Territorial Pioneers of California, in which an early reader, presumably an Argonaut, wrote in the margin of the page quoted, "One man made $18,000 drawing pictures in the mines." Although J. D., as he liked to be called, wrote that he left for California in 1851, his biographers point out that he actually arrived in September of the previous year. See R. E. Mather and F. E. Boswell, *John David Borthwick: Artist of the Gold Rush* (Salt Lake City: University of Utah Press, 1989), 25.

9. Borthwick, *Three Years in California,* 320–21.

10. Letter of William S. Jewett, 28 January 1850, in Elliot Evans, ed., "Some Letters of William S. Jewett, California Artist," *California Historical Society Quarterly* 23 (June 1944): 160. Jewett was not a good speller.

11. Letter of William S. Jewett, 24 February 1850, ibid., 163, 164.

12. For Barbieri, see Bruce Kamerling, "California's Leonardo: The Portraits of Signor Barbieri," *California History* 66 (December 1987): 262–77.

13. Edward Washington McIlhany, *Recollections of a '49er* (Kansas City, Mo.: Hailman Printing Co., 1908), 9–23, 44–53. Although the artist printed his name "Tom More" on the verso of the canvas, McIlhany uses the spelling Moore, as does David Morris Potter, ed., *Trail to California: The Overland Journal of Vincent Geiger and Wakeman Bryarly* (New Haven: Yale University Press, 1945), 11, who examined his military record.

14. A. Delano, *Life on the Plains and Among the Diggings* (Auburn, N.Y.: Miller, Orton & Mulligan, 1854), 292.

15. Borthwick, *Three Years in California,* 202–203.

16. [Louise Amelia Knapp Smith Clappe], *California in 1852: The Letters of Dame Shirley,* ed. Carl I. Wheat (San Francisco: Grabhorn Press, 1933), 36; letter of William S. Jewett, 28 January 1850, in Evans, "Some Letters," 162; Nahl to his father and stepmother, [1853], trans.

Hermann Friedlander, Charles C. Nahl Letters, Bancroft Library, University of California, Berkeley.

17. George D. Dornin, *Thirty Years Ago, 1849–1879* [Berkeley, 1879], 8; *Alta California* (San Francisco), 7 and 11 January 1850; *Sacramento Union*, 23 December 1851.

18. *Sacramento Transcript*, 20 December 1850. The Forty-niner and amateur artist J. Goldsborough Bruff wrote in his diary on 6 December 1850 that he had made the acquaintance of Martin, whom he characterized as "a very clever artist." He admired several paintings Martin had in his studio, all of which he thought good, making reference to the work reproduced here. Georgia Willis Read and Ruth Gaines, eds., *Gold Rush: The Journals, Drawings, and Other Papers of J. Goldsborough Bruff*, 2 vols. (New York: Columbia University Press, 1944), 2:936.

19. B. P. Avery, "Art Beginnings on the Pacific," Part I, *Overland Monthly*, o.s., 1 (July 1868): 30. On 5 May 1855 Governor John Bigler signed the bill purchasing the painting *Major General John Augustus Sutter* (California Department of Parks and Recreation), which for many years hung in the State Capitol. Although the Assembly bill had been amended in the Senate, requiring Jewett to furnish a portrait of the Mexican War hero General John E. Wool without further compensation, Bigler approved the bill reluctantly, complaining that the amount appropriated exceeded "the value of the labor performed," and warning that "the financial condition of the State precludes the expenditure of large sums." California Assembly, *Journal of the Sixth Session* (Sacramento: B. B. Redding, State Printer, 1855), 853.

20. William G. Johnston, *Overland to California* (Oakland: Biobooks, 1948), 184; Frank Marryat, *Mountains and Molehills, or Recollections of a Burnt Journal* (New York: Harper & Brothers, 1855), 42; Friedrich Gerstäcker, *Scenes of Life in California*, trans. George Cosgrove (San Francisco: John Howell, 1942), 72; Gerstäcker, *California Gold Mines* (Oakland: Biobooks, 1946), 68.

21. *Alta California*, 6 March 1850; San Francisco *Picayune*, 12 September 1850, in Johnson, *San Francisco as It Is*, 44.

22. *Alta California*, 22 March and 6 September 1849, 28 January and 5 August 1850.

23. Avery, "Art Beginnings on the Pacific," 30; *Alta California*, 26 June, 23 September, 16 November and 17 November 1854.

24. John S. Hittell, "Art in San Francisco," *Pacific Monthly* 10 (July 1863): 101.

25. The standard source on Nahl is Moreland L. Stevens, *Charles Christian Nahl: Artist of the Gold Rush, 1818–1878* (Sacramento: E. B. Crocker Art Gallery, 1976).

26. Charles Nahl to his father and stepmother, [1853] and [1854], trans. Hermann Friedlander, Charles C. Nahl Letters, Bancroft Library.

27. Letter of Henriette Nahl, 28 June 1855, Nahl Family Letters, Bancroft Library; *Sacramento Placer Times and Transcript*, 1 January 1852, quoted in Stevens, *Charles Christian Nahl*, 39; Nahl to his father and stepmother, [1853], trans. Hermann Friedlander, Charles C. Nahl Letters.

28. Quoted in C. Edwards Lester, *The Artists of America: A Series of Biographical Sketches of American Artists* (New York: Baker & Scribner, 1846), 43; Mechanics' Institute, *Report of the First Industrial Exhibition of the Mechanics' Institute of the City of San Francisco* (San Francisco, 1858), 97.

29. *Alta California*, 11 January 1850.

30. Avery, "Art Beginnings on the Pacific," 30; letter of Henriette Nahl, 28 June 1855, Nahl Family Letters; Arthur Nahl to uncle, 2 April 1858, Nahl Family Letters.

31. Little engaged the New York firm of Sarony & Major to lithograph Jewett's painting, which he distributed for sale in the spring of 1851 with the title *A View of Sutter's Mill & Culloma Valley*. The two landscapes of the Feather River country, both currently titled *Hock Farm* and dated, respectively, 1851 and 1852, are owned by the Oakland Museum of California and the California Department of Parks and Recreation.

32. Ferdinand C. Ewer, "Editor's Table," *The Pioneer* 2 (August 1854): 113, 112; Mechanics' Institute, *Report of the First Industrial Exhibition*, 98; Avery, "Art Beginnings on the Pacific," 31. Jewett's painting of the Grayson family—invoking, as it does, the American dream of a better life to the west—bears certain similarities to William Ranney's well-known composition of the previous year, *Boone's First View of Kentucky* (Gilcrease Museum, Tulsa), and anticipates in many ways Emanuel Leutze's more theatrical and far more famous mural in the U.S. Capitol, *Westward the Course of Empire Takes Its Way*.

33. B. P. Avery, "Art Beginnings on the Pacific," Part II, *Overland Monthly*, o.s., 1 (August 1868): 119.

34. *Tuolumne Courier*, 14 July 1860. Browere painted several versions of this scene, including a much larger canvas in the collections of the Fine Arts Museums of San Francisco.

35. "The Yo-ham-i-te Valley," *Hutchings' California Magazine* 1 (July 1856): 2–8; Thomas A. Ayres, "A Trip to the Yosemite Valley," *Alta California*, 6 August 1856. The chief sources on Ayres are his obituary in the *Alta California* of 27 May 1858, and Jeanne Van Nostrand, "Thomas A. Ayres, Artist-Argonaut of California," *California Historical Society Quarterly* 20 (September 1941): 275–79.

36. *California! On Canvas!* broadside [San Francisco, 1854], Bancroft Library; *Alta California*, 9 August 1854.

37. *New York Tribune*, 26 September 1849; *Peoria Democratic Press*, 2 October 1850, quoted in John Francis McDermott, "Gold Rush Movies," *California Historical Society Quarterly* 33 (March 1954): 33.

38. *Alta California*, 20 May 1852, 4 May and 22 April 1860.

39. Norton Bush, "Days Gone By," *San Francisco Chronicle*, 14 July 1889; *Alta California*, 31 October 1859; Avery, "Art Beginnings on the Pacific," 33–34. The quotation is from Avery. Despite his importance to California art, surprisingly little work has been done on Butman. Although it is usually said that he was born in Gardiner, Maine, in 1820 and died there on 26 July 1871, he was probably born in 1822 or 1823 in either Dixmont or Bangor, Maine, and didn't arrive in Gardiner until 1849, when he opened an apothecary shop. He died on 22 July 1871 in Shelburne, New Hampshire, while on a fishing trip. *Gardiner Home Journal*, 26 July 1871; *Kennebec Reporter* (Gardiner), 29 July 1871; Henry Sewell Webster, ed., *Vital Records of Gardiner, Maine, to the Year 1892*, 2 vols. (Gardiner: Reporter-Journal Press, 1914), 2:233, 542.

40. *Alta California*, 11 December 1859.

41. *Alta California*, 5 October 1851, 30 and 31 October 1859; *LeCount and Strong's San Francisco Directory for the Year 1854* (San Francisco, 1854), opposite 129. The rise of firms that carried art can be traced through the classified section of the San Francisco city directories, initially under "Carvers and Gilders" and later under "Artists' Materials" and "Pictures and Engravings."

42. *Alta California*, 12 January 1865. Also see *A Classified Catalogue of the Paintings on Exhibition at the Room of the California Art Union* (San Francisco: California Art Union, 1865) and Avery, "Art Beginnings on the Pacific," 117–18.

43. Unidentified newspaper clipping, Bancroft Scraps, 21:4, Bancroft Library; *Alta California*, 11 April 1869.

44. Avery, "Art Beginnings on the Pacific," 116. The fairs were held irregularly for some years, but from 1874 until 1891 they were an annual event.

45. "The Fine Arts," *North Pacific Review* 2 (November 1862): 88. For a biography of Williams, see Ruth N. Post, "The California Years of Virgil Macey Williams," *California History* 66 (June 1987): 114–29.

46. For a full description of the paintings and other attractions at the gardens, see *Illustrated Guide and Catalogue of Woodward's Gardens* (San Francisco: Alta California Book and Job Printing House, 1875). The quotation and the description of Williams's painting *Napa Valley* are on p. 58. John S. Hittell observed in 1863 that Williams had lived for many years in Rome and that he had "brought with him a number of views taken in the Campagna, many similar in general tone, and the form of the plain and distant mountains, to the scenes in the coast valley of this State." Hittell, "Art in San Francisco," 103

47. William Keith, "Future of Art in California," *San Francisco Call*, 25 December 1895, quoted in Brother [Fidelis] Cornelius, *Keith, Old Master of California*, 2 vols. (New York: G. P. Putnam's Sons, 1942; Fresno, Calif.: Academy Library Guild, 1956), 1:275. Bush exhibited at all the early Mechanics' Institute Fairs, winning several awards, and in 1863 John Hittell declared that his *Mount Diablo*, done five years earlier, was "the best picture that has ever been painted of the scenery of the coast valleys of this State." Hittell, "Art in San Francisco," 102.

48. *Constitution, By-laws, and List of Members of the San Francisco Art Association* (San Francisco: Edward Bosqui & Co., 1872), 3; *Alta California*, 1 April 1874; "Etc.," *Overland Monthly*, o.s., 9 (July 1872): 91.

49. *Constitution, By-laws, and List of Members*, 3; "Etc.," *Overland Monthly*, o.s., 9 (June 1874): 575.

50. B. P. Avery, "Art in California," *The Aldine* 7 (April 1874): 72.

8

Romancing the Gold Rush

The Literature of the California Frontier

Michael Kowalewski

California was the first region of the United States to undertake precious metal mining on a large scale, and between 1849 and 1855 some four hundred million dollars in gold was harvested by miners. Yet whatever the economic and political importance of that "harvest," it was not simply a new extractive industry that made the Gold Rush a historical phenomenon. It was the carnivalesque atmosphere of swagger and possibility, heightened expectation and boomtown hokum, that sent fortune seekers from around the world to "see the elephant" in California. Perhaps Mark Twain best captured, as he so often did, the mix of human emotions that helped propel tens of thousands of young Argonauts toward this remote maritime province so recently wrested from Mexico. In *Roughing It* (1872), Twain's narrator describes the volatile state of his feelings at hearing that his brother had just been appointed Secretary of Nevada Territory:

> I was young and ignorant, and I envied my brother. . . . He was going to travel! I never had been away from home, and that word "travel" had a seductive charm for me. Pretty soon he would be hundreds and hundreds of miles away on the great plains and deserts, and among the mountains of the Far West, and would see buffaloes and Indians, and prairie dogs, and antelopes, and have all kinds of adventures, and may be get hanged or scalped, and have ever such a fine time, and write home and tell us all about it, and be a hero. And he would see the gold mines and the silver mines, and maybe go about of an afternoon when his work was done, and pick up two or three pailfuls of shining slugs, and nuggets of gold and silver on the hillside. And by and by he would become very rich, and return home by sea, and be able to talk as calmly about San Francisco and the ocean, and "the isthmus" as if it was nothing of any consequence to have seen those marvels face to face. What I suffered in contemplating his happiness, pen cannot describe.[1]

"The beguiling attraction of California," as James D. Houston puts it, springs from the interplay of geography, social history, and imagination. Perhaps no single historical event exemplifies this attraction better than the Gold Rush. Without the human avalanche, "the noise and spectacle" of the Gold Rush, the legacy of "a few thousand pounds of gleaming metal," Houston says, would have been simply "greed . . . and bank accounts," not "a world-class legend to tickle the memory and stir the blood."[2] This is not to assert that greed—along with vigilantism, violence against "foreigners," and cultural disruption—did not also exist in the Gold Rush. Indian massacre sites, disintegrating gravestones in the Mother Lode, and the scarred hillsides and gravel piles lining rivers in Trinity, Plumas, and Calaveras counties also provide testimonials to the lasting effects of the Gold Rush. Life expectancy was short (within six months of arriving, one in every five Forty-niners was dead), medicine was often primitive, and high rates of suicide and alcoholism (or opium use among the Chinese) testified to the grim, lonely, sick-at-heart side of gold-rush life. So did the miners' recourse to prostitution and their mania for gambling—compulsive gambler's syndrome, we might call it today. Wallace Stegner once recalled seeing the headstone of a young miner inscribed *Nato a Parma 1830, morto a Morfi 1850,* an inscription as significant for its revelation of youth and nationality as for its misspelling of "Murphys," the camp where this boy died.[3]

Initial exuberance about one's golden prospects in California was often quickly tempered by the sobering realities of cholera, sickness, and bad weather, by exorbitant prices, blisters, muscle aches, sunburn, fleas, and the boredom of hard, repetitive labor. Every glowing report of wonder and riches in the Golden State was matched by dispirited letters home from impoverished or homesick miners. "The *greatness of California!* Faugh!" Alonzo Delano harrumphed in 1850. "When the sufferings of the emigrants both on the plains and after their arrival is known at home, our people will begin to see California stripped of her gaudy robes . . . and they will be content to stay at home and reap their own grain."[4] A different kind of emotional void, that created by long absence from loved ones, is revealed in the postscript Forty-niner William Swain's two-year-old daughter scrawled at the bottom of one of her mother's letters: "Poor Pa. See Pa. Love Pa. See Papa. Kiss Pa."[5]

The Gold Rush was assessed in radically divergent and contradictory terms from the moment it started, both by the miners themselves and by outside observers speculating about what it all meant. At first, for instance, Ralph Waldo Emerson, one of the most widely known and respected American intellectuals, saw only "a rush and a scramble of needy adventurers, and, in the western country, a general jail delivery of all the rowdies of the rivers." Two years later, however, he felt a witness to an emerging pattern of history: "Nature watches over all, and turns this malfeasance to good. California gets peopled and subdued, civilized in this immoral way, and on this fiction a real prosperity is rooted and grown. . . . Out of Sabine rapes,

Miners working a claim with a line of sluice boxes strike a pose of studied nonchalance. The Forty-niners and those who followed in their wake wrote voluminously of their adventures and misadventures in the land of gold, recording their experiences and observations in letters, diaries, and books, some few of which achieved the status of literature. *Courtesy George Eastman House, Rochester, N.Y.*

and out of robbers' forays, real Romes and their heroisms come in fullness of time."[6] Emerson's prickly friend Henry David Thoreau, on the other hand, was appalled by the gigantic spectacle of what he considered simple whoring after quick money: "The hog that roots his own living, and so makes manure, would be ashamed of such company. If I could command the wealth of all the worlds by lifting my finger, I would not pay such a price for it. . . . Going to California. It is only three thousand miles nearer to hell."[7]

The Gold Rush embodied America's new sense of itself as mirrored in California, whether the image reflected back was seen as a triumphal exemplification of sunburned American know-how or as a cautionary tale about monetary greed and xenophobia only seventy-five years after the Declaration of Independence. Debated and pondered at the time, the precise significance of the Gold Rush remained (and still remains) open to question. It was filled with contradiction and ambivalence, comic incongruity and tragic irony. It was, in other words, a rich, germinal ground for literature. Seen whole, the Gold Rush has the composite intricacy and scope and the multiple, crosshatching plotlines of a Dickens novel. The writing of the time—in fiction, plays, diaries, essays, letters, song lyrics, and satiric squibs—provided a vivid, on-the-ground response to life in frontier California, one that often embodied imaginative extremes and swung from exultation to roughhewn comedy to sour disillusionment with a verve and variety that are quite distinctive. Yet, despite the continuing fascination in the popular imagination with the *idea* of the Gold Rush, much of this writing has been neglected. Or rather, it has usually been appraised in only one light: its documentary function has been emphasized without a corresponding attention to its aesthetic complexity. A reappraisal of the ingenuity and inventiveness of this work helps us appreciate the unique regional culture that sprang into being in mid-nineteenth-century California. It also helps emphasize the difficulties artists and writers still encounter when attempting to evoke and describe the landscape and multiple cultures of California.

EASTERN AESTHETICS AND "UNREAL" CALIFORNIA

In 1925, in a book entitled *South and Southwest,* the literary scholar Jay B. Hubbell claimed that "our literature has always been less American than our history."[8] This statement, while probably less provocative at the time than it may appear now, raises an interesting question. Would Hubbell have made such an assertion if he had known of the full extent and imaginative richness of gold-rush writing? Few people knew precisely how extensive and multifaceted that writing was until the publication in 1997 of Gary Kurutz's magisterial bibliography, *The California Gold Rush,* which lists over seven hundred individual works published in the five years from 1848 to 1853.[9] There are more written documents about the California Gold Rush than about any other nineteenth-century historical event except the Civil War. As linguistic historians have noted, the gold-rush migrants were "the first—and the last—frontiersmen to have the education and the inclination to describe what they saw and heard."[10] As a collective outpouring of wit, homesickness, self-promotion, and social observation, there was, as Kevin Starr says, an "epic sweep" to the first surge of gold-rush writing, though it is generally "untouched by historical imagination or dramatic art." "Anxious to strike it rich, having risked their lives to do so, miners wasted little time in asking who they were," Starr asserts. What holds the literature together is "a collective return to primary experience" and the narratives of the Forty-niners are filled with moments of stark experience—murder, death, loneliness, the comfort of new companions who could speak your language, food by a fire—that are often "recorded without self-consciousness and yet shot through with mythic power."[11]

Many of the distinctive features of this writing arose out of social and economic factors characterizing frontier California life and publishing. The delegates to the state constitutional convention in 1849 chose well when they selected the image of Minerva, with her spear and Gorgon shield, to serve as the principal figure for the state's Great Seal. The image was a formal acknowledgment of the velocity with which California had sprung, full-grown, Minerva-like, into statehood, thereby bypassing the normal territorial waiting period. The tidal wave of immigration sparked by the Gold Rush created not a typical American frontier, but what Franklin Walker called "the acme of all frontiers, the most concentrated of quickly flourishing societies."[12] The rate of social and material change was so accelerated in gold-rush California as to seem scarcely credible to observers. "The rapidity with which a ready-made house is put up and inhabited" in San Francisco, Bayard Taylor noted in 1850, "strikes the stranger . . . as little short of magic." San Francisco real estate prices set an early standard for exorbitance, and "the very air" in that city, Taylor says in *Eldorado: or Adventures in the Path of Empire*, "is pregnant with the magnetism of bold, spirited, unwearied action": "One knows not whether he is awake or in some wonderful dream. Never have I had so much difficulty in establishing, satisfactorily to my own senses, the reality of what I saw and heard."[13] The Gold Rush permanently altered the cultural adrenaline of the state, creating an electric sense of possibility and a new standard for life in the fast lane. Anything might happen in California, the feeling went, and *very* quickly.

Of signal importance in considering the nature of gold-rush writing is the fact that, as Walker reminds us, no *native* Californian wrote for publication during its frontier period. The writing of the 1850s was done by people translated from conditions of relative stability to social chaos.[14] Thus the novelty of California was largely emphasized for an audience in the East, or at least for an audience with eastern sensibilities. There were discernible social and aesthetic norms implicit in this writing, even when those norms seemed of limited usefulness in depicting western life. Writing in 1866, Bret Harte complained in a series of letters to newspapers in Springfield, Massachusetts, that California offered "quantity instead of quality," "grandeur, sublimity and picturesqueness," but not "bucolic and pastoral comfort":

> [California's] rains are deluges—her droughts are six months long. What she loses in delicacy she makes up in fibre—whether it be strawberries that look as if they had been arrested on their way to become pine-apples, or a field of wild oats, whose every stalk is a miracle of size, but whose general effect is most unpastoral and unmeadow-like. The effect on the inhabitants may be readily conceived. We have *ranchos* instead of farms, *vaqueros* for milk-maids; the "neat-handed Phillis" is apt to be a Chinaman, and our gentle shepherds are swarthy looking Mexicans.[15]

Traditional pastoral imagery was inadequate in California, Harte implied, partly because of race. Skin color and facial features, as much as abnormal farm products, defeated conventional forms of literary expression. Yet his jaunty exaggeration itself suggested less a genuine lament for the pastoral than a spirited sense of its inappropriateness in the first place.

In his letters intended for publication in the East, Harte repeatedly deplored the bragging and local puffery he found in California that demanded compliments "with the air of a footpad [robber]." He told of visiting Japanese diplomats, for instance, being "haled out of their beds" in San Francisco by local boosters and "driven frantically hither and thither, and asked to be astonished."[16] But Harte also saw such boosterism as almost inevitable given the extremes of landscape, climate, and behavior in the West. Commenting on winter in the Sierra Nevada, he intimated that comic skepticism alone proved insufficient in adequately representing this landscape:

> You have an idea that snow of ten and fifteen feet in depth represents a pretty severe winter blockade. Why, our Pacific Railroad goes through snow thirty and forty feet deep. The smoke of the locomotive as you approach the summit of the Sierras, rises between snow banks sometimes one hundred feet above the track. Looking back on the foot-hills the road seems to pass through a canal of white marble whose walls vary from fifteen to twenty feet in height. . . . Think of cabins entirely hidden, with their chimneys melting a small crater around their tops as they smoke on the roadside. . . . You will say you have read something like this in Munchausen, but these are facts. Imagine what ought to be the fiction of such a people.[17]

Harte's tone of unembarrassed wonder here suggests strongly that he understood how such out-of-scale western landscapes beggared conventional description. The most engaging gold-rush writing allowed California's new landscapes and the new behavior and idiomatic speech of its inhabitants to challenge the aesthetic and social criteria eastern readers might bring to a work. The writing of Harte, Twain, and Louise Clappe often establishes a complex bilingualism, as it were: one that attempts to include both the language of eastern convention and the expressive possibilities of western landscape and idiom.[18] Mediating between the East and the West, the narrative voice in such writing, Stephen Fender says, "has news that will surprise the East but, as an initiate to the West, it must not betray excitement about the news. . . . it may deprecate something it calls romance, but it manages to convey a sense of romance nevertheless."[19]

The compelling strangeness of contemporary life in California thus often called forth remarkable moments of description, as when Harte wrote of the adobe buildings of Mission Dolores, "with tiled roofs, like longitudinal strips of cinnamon," and the view from Telegraph Hill, from which one could see "long twinkling parallelograms" of gaslights on opera nights.[20] Some fifteen years earlier, Bayard Taylor too had searched for the proper terms with which to describe what he saw in the new city from a vantage point on San Francisco Bay:

The appearance of San Francisco at night, from the water, is unlike anything I ever beheld. The houses are mostly of canvas, which is made transparent by the lamps within, and transforms them, in the darkness, to dwellings of solid light. Seated on the slopes of its three hills, the tents pitched among the chaparral to the very summits, it gleams like an amphitheatre of fire. . . . The picture has in it something unreal and fantastic; it impresses one like the cities of the magic lantern, which a motion of the hand can build or annihilate.[21]

Such descriptions—sometimes extended, sometimes fleeting and parenthetical—are scattered throughout gold-rush writing and are to be appreciated not only for their artfulness. They should also be seen as experimental attempts to find a descriptive vocabulary adequate for the unprecedented experiences of gold-rush California, which could often seem "unreal and fantastic."

POETRY, FICTION, AND DRAMA

The boom-and-bust mentality of San Francisco, along with its rapid settlement and polyglot mixing of cultures, all helped sponsor an art and literature that tended to stress the novel and the picturesque. As Harte put it, "Californians, like the Arabian Prince, prefer their cream tarts with pepper."[22] Walker has pointed out that the emphasis was on lawlessness rather than law; gambling rather than the slow accrual of a fortune; the prostitute with a heart of gold rather than the pioneer mother; the abandoned orphan rather than the extended family with solicitous relatives in China, Mexico, or New Jersey. The trials of the patiently grubbing, homesick "honest miner" did not tend to captivate writers' imaginations. As Joseph Henry Jackson said, "a hero hip deep in an icy mountain torrent is a chilly hero at best; there is . . . little greatness in subsisting on moldy pork and soggy biscuit in order to get rich. A dyspeptic shaking with ague is not the stuff of which legends are built."[23]

The jostle of competitive publishing venues open to writers on the California frontier also undoubtedly contributed to the sensationalistic or melodramatic cast of much gold-rush writing. As early as 1850, some fifty printers worked in San Francisco, and the city boasted that by the mid-1850s it published more newspapers than London (many in languages other than English). Writers could see print quickly in reputable journals like *The Pioneer*, the *Golden Era*, and, after 1868, the *Overland Monthly*, as well as in ephemeral local publications with names like *Hombre, Satan's Bassoon*, or the *Wine, Women, and Song Journal*.

Poetry tended to be an undistinguished genre in early California. It was characterized by either belabored dialect poems or overly lush and self-consciously literary celebrations of the landscape by California "songsters" (the kind of poetry Mark Twain would later satirize in the figure of Emmeline Grangerford in *Huckleberry*

One of the illustrations by Charles Nahl for *The Idle and Industrious Miner*, published in 1854 and believed to be from the pen of William Bausman. Bausman's moralistic poem, inspired by William Hogarth's *The Rake's Progress*, met with wide acclaim in California. The success of the work, which first appeared in the *Sacramento Pictorial Union*, was in no small measure due to the imaginative designs of Nahl, who knew firsthand a miner's life. "Embittered at his low estate—unmindful of its cause—the sluggard mopes away his hours, indifferent to applause." *California Historical Society, FN-31551.*

Finn). Nevertheless, the sheer abundance of such sentimental work suggests its popularity with male miners, who went heavily armed by day and night but could weep openly over the picture of a wife or child.

In fiction, the one notable work that was inspired by the mining camps was John Rollin Ridge's sensationalist romance, *The Life and Adventures of Joaquín Murieta, the Celebrated California Bandit* (1854). The first novel published by an American Indian (Ridge was half Cherokee), *Joaquín Murieta* is primarily remembered for establishing Murieta's image as what Richard Rodriguez calls "a matinee idol among bandits,"[24] an unjustly persecuted Mexican miner who is forced to become an outlaw by gold-hungry Anglos motivated by "the prejudice of color, the antipathy of races, which are always stronger and bitterer with the ignorant and the unlettered."[25] Ridge seems to have been torn between writing a moralizing indictment of Anglo imperialism and an action-filled potboiler sure to make money. Given his own biracial identity, Ridge also displays a complex ambivalence about his hero Murieta. Having himself been dispossessed of Cherokee land by the U.S. government, as Blake Allmendinger observes, "Ridge identified with Murieta as a member of a persecuted racial minority; but having relocated and invested in mainstream society, Ridge also disapproved of Murieta's repeated attacks on white frontier communities."[26]

Ridge suggests the uneasy, often indiscriminately violent interracial relations of miners on a polyglot frontier. The tensions were not only between whites and nonwhites but between minority groups as well. The California Indians are treated as subhuman by Murieta's gang and Chinese miners are repeatedly brutalized by the Mexican desperadoes, especially Murieta's sadistic sidekick, Three Fingered Jack. "I can't help it," Jack declares, "somehow or other, I love to smell the blood of a Chinaman." At one point 150 Chinese miners are left scattered "along the highways like so many sheep with their throats cut by the wolves."[27] Ridge portrayed the mining camps as rough but bustling communities where a romantic landscape of isolated arroyos and dusty canyons matched the sensationalistic plot twists of daring disguises and quick getaways—followed, ultimately, by the decapitation of the novel's hero and the public display of his severed head in a jar.[28]

Gold-rush drama embodied the love of melodrama and action displayed in *Joaquín Murieta*. The Gold Rush captured the imagination of playwrights who had never been to California, such as the Englishman J. Stirling Coyne. Coyne wrote a farce entitled *Cockneys in California* in 1849; it was joined by similar efforts on the British stage and in the eastern United States. One of the first eyewitness dramas about the Gold Rush was David G. ("Doc") Robinson's *Seeing the Elephant* in the early 1850s. The manuscripts of this and other plays by Robinson have been lost, but contemporary accounts of the play indicate that it dealt with gullible miners who head west with overblown hopes of striking it rich, only to encounter bad weather, hunger, and bandits.

Amongst the popular melodramas and farces of the day, such as *Bombastes Furioso* (many given raucous unisex performances in the predominantly male camps), a number of plays dealt with mining life in California: Warren Baer's musical satire, *The Duke of California* (1856), Alonzo Delano's sentimental melodrama, *A Live Woman in the Mines; or, Pike County Ahead* (1857), Charles E. B. Howe's romantic melodrama, *Joaquin Murieta de Castillo, the Celebrated California Bandit* (1858), and Joseph Nunes's *Fast Folks; or the Early Days of California* (1858). These were followed

Miners cheered the arrival of women in their community, as depicted in *A Live Woman in the Mines,* one of the illustrations by Charles Nahl for Alonzo Delano's delightful collection of stories of gold-rush California published in 1853 under the title *Pen-Knife Sketches.* Several years later, in 1857, Delano wrote a play titled *A Live Woman in the Mines,* which was loosely based on an assortment of characters he had known in his mining days. When the heroine of the melodrama approaches the diggings, an advance contingent of miners borrows one of her petticoats and returns with it to camp in order to prepare the boys for the appearance of a real, live woman. *California Historical Society, FN-19803.*

by later reminiscent plays about the mines, such as Bret Harte's *Two Men of Sandy Bar* (1876) and Joaquin Miller's *The Danites in the Sierras* (1877) and *'49: The Gold-Seeker of the Sierras* (1884).[29]

Often more historical curiosities than fully realized plays, many of these works nevertheless have a kind of rough-and-ready impudence that can still beguile. Delano's *A Live Woman in the Mines,* for instance, features characters with names like Sluice Box and High Betty Martin (who wears men's clothes and carries a gun: "a specimen of a back-woods western Amazonian," Delano notes, "who is indomitably persevering and brave under difficulties, but withal with woman's feelings when difficulty is over").[30] The play is insensitive in its portrayal of California Indians, but it still manages to include fresh portraits of miners yearning for feminine company or news from home. The characters speak a wild and woolly western vernacular that is indebted to the Southwest humorists, as when an express rider recounts his latest journey:

> Run the gauntlet between a pack of cayotes, three grizzlies, and a whole tribe of Digger Indians—killed two horses and jumped a ledge a hundred feet—hung myself by the heels in the bushes—turned forty somersets down a canyon—slept three nights on a snow bank—froze three legs stiff, had 'em amputated and climbed the hill next morning on crutches, and have brought lots of letters for the boys. . . . Please take the bags, and give me a glass of brandy and water without any water in it.[31]

Delano's farce focuses not only on the excitement caused by the arrival of a woman in the mines, it also comically presents the miners' starvation. When the food runs out, the men dine on rats and boots. They also tie the last piece of pork to a string; each man swallows the pork, then pulls it out and passes it on.

NONFICTIONAL PROSE

Whatever attention is due gold-rush poetry, fiction, and drama, however, the true imaginative wealth of the Gold Rush resides in its nonfictional prose: diaries, letters, journals, memoirs, government documents, and personal narratives. Gold-rush letters and diary entries often consisted of simple, unrefined, sometimes ungrammatical prose. ("The schoolmaster certainly was abroad," John Banks wryly commented about handwritten notes he saw along the California trail.)[32] The writing frequently addressed practical matters such as the price of meals or hardware, mining techniques, and claim disputes. Yet in the best works, this very emphasis on the demands of everyday life—on the mud, heat, and fleas in the camps—contributes to the roughhewn piquancy of these memoirs. Gold-rush chronicles mix pedestrian detail with a sudden sense of wonder. Listen, for instance, to William Lewis Manly's observation of what he saw on the California trail outside of Fort Laramie in *Death Valley in '49* :

> We crossed one stream where there were great drifts or piles of hail which had been brought down by a heavy storm from higher up the hills. At one place we found some rounded boulders from six to eight inches in diameter, which were partly hollow, and broken open were found to contain most beautiful crystals of quartz, clear as purest ice. . . . I have since learned that such stones are found at many points, and that they are called geodes.[33]

Weather and geology blend into one general realm of strangeness in Manly's account, as if it has been hailing geodes, "clear as purest ice." Later, after trying his hand at mining, Manly shipped out of San Francisco on a steamer headed for the eastern United States via Panama, and marveled at the marine life he observed near Acapulco. His ship "went through a hundred acres of porpoises, all going the same way. The ship plowed right through them, but none seemed to get hurt by the wheels. Perhaps they were emigrants like ourselves in search of a better place."[34]

The best mining camp narratives blend satire and affection in unanticipated ways. In *The Shirley Letters*, arguably the finest firsthand account of the Gold Rush, Louise Clappe (using the *nom de plume* "Dame Shirley") wrote a series of twenty-three letters from two high-country camps in the upper reaches of the Feather River to her stay-at-home sister in Massachusetts. The primitive living conditions startled her eastern notions of decorum: "How would you like to winter in such an abode?—in a place where there are no newspapers, no churches, lectures, concerts or theaters; no fresh books, no shopping, calling nor gossiping little tea-drinkings; no parties, no balls, no picnics, no *tableaux*, no charades, no latest fashions, no daily mail (we have an express once a month), no promenades, no rides, nor drives; no vegetables but potatoes and onions, no milk, no eggs, no *nothing?*" Yet just when conditions seem most crude and unredeemable, Clappe adds a characteristic sparkle of candor and mischief. "Now I expect to be very happy here. This strange, odd life fascinates me."[35]

"Dame Shirley" remained a playful role Louise Clappe assumed in gaining distance not only on life in the camps but on her own responses to that life, which might otherwise have become too somber or too easily discouraged. "I wish that you could see *me* about these times," Clappe wrote when picturing herself as a whimsical figure of melancholia in the cold winter rains of 1852: "I am generally found seated on a cigar-box in the chimney corner, my chin in my hand, rocking backwards and forwards . . . casting a picturesquely hopeless glance about our dilapidated cabin."[36]

Clappe's tolerance for rough living conditions in the camps did not compromise her sensitivity to the social tensions of an ethnically diverse frontier. She did, like many Americans in California at the time, see the Indians she met (probably of the Maidu tribe) as degraded savages who fell disappointingly short of "the glorious forest heroes that live in the Leatherstocking Tales."[37] But she was exhilarated by the cultural heterogeneity of the mining camps. She was fascinated with the original Spanish names for rivers, towns, and mountains; she freely sympathized with the Hispanic miners, who were unjustly abused in the hot summer of 1852 by violent Yankee bigots; and she was quick to call the hanging of a Swede for an alleged theft "a piece of cruel butchery."[38] In other words, finding life in the camps to be scented with "that fine and almost imperceptible *perfume* of the ludicrous"[39] did not mean Clappe glossed over the ugliness and the prejudice she encountered. Her letters offer a unique blend of sympathetic social portraiture and literate satire. (Both Harte and Mark Twain seem to have found inspiration in Clappe's letters for some of their best known stories without acknowledging the source.) In her last letter, Clappe states that she has moved from being a "feeble and half-dying invalid" to a "perfectly healthy" woman who will miss the mines: "I *like* this wild and barbarous life; I leave it with regret."[40]

A parallel process is at work in *The Diary of a Forty-Niner* (1906), a gold-rush memoir purportedly written by one Alfred T. Jackson. Little is known about Jackson; in fact his authorship of the book cannot be authoritatively confirmed. Originally from Connecticut, he spent just over two years, from 1850 to 1852, on Rock Creek near Nevada City. His diary details his life with his friend and mentor, "Pard," and his romance with his French sweetheart, Marie. In disarmingly simple but responsive prose, Jackson chronicles his own transformation of character. He starts out as a timid, morally censorious greenhorn, homesick—"way off here out of the world"[41]—for the safety of the New England countryside, and ends up a more adventuresome and broad-minded Californian, at home in the stimulating environment of the foothill mines. Though headed out of the mines at the end of the book, Jackson is unwilling to return to Connecticut to "vegetate" on a farm.[42] He has discovered the pleasures of good friendship and of reading Byron's poetry out loud. At their farewell dinner in a Nevada City hotel with "a couple of baskets" of champagne, Marie expresses the crowd's general sentiments when she exclaims, "Oh! zey are ze good boys, and in our hearts we will nevair, no nevair, forget zem."[43]

A number of other gold-rush narratives are worthy of note. Many are by Americans: Walter Colton's *Three Years in California* (1850); Edward Gould Buffum's *Six Months in the Gold Mines* (1850); Leonard Kip's *California Sketches With Recollections of the Gold Mines* (1850); Alonzo Delano's *Life on the Plains and Among the Diggings* (1854), which was later supplemented by a collection of thirty-six letters to newspapers in *Alonzo Delano's California Correspondence* (1952); Eliza Farnham's *California In-Doors and Out* (1856); Mrs. D. B. Bates's *Incidents on Land and Water, or Four Years on the Pacific Coast* (1858); J. Ross Browne's *Crusoe's Island* (1864); Franklin A. Buck's *A Yankee Trader in the Gold Rush* (1930); *The Life and Adventures of James P. Beckwourth* (1856), the as-told-to autobiography of an African American fur trapper and mountain man; Sarah Royce's later reminiscences in *A Frontier Lady: Recollections of the Gold Rush and Early California* (1932); J. Goldsborough Bruff's journals and drawings in *Gold Rush* (1949); John Letts's *California Illustrated* (1852); Mary Jane Megquier's letters from 1849–1856, collected in *Apron Full of Gold* (1949); and Joaquin Miller's later autobiographical account of his time in the Shasta and Siskiyou county mines, *Life Amongst the Modocs: Unwritten History* (1873). Others are by Latin American writers like the Chilean Vicente Pérez Rosales, whose memoir, *Viaje a California: Recuerdos de 1848, 1849, 1850,* was published in 1878; the Mexican rancher Ygnacio Villegas's *Boyhood Days* (1895); and the native Californio Mariano Guadalupe Vallejo's five-volume autobiographical text, *Recuerdos históricos y personales tocante a la alta California* (1875). Still others are by Europeans: the Polish physician Felix Wierzbicki's *California as It*

Miners try their luck in a game of faro with professional gamblers, the "blacklegged gentry," in one of the charming, evocative illustrations that enliven the pages of John D. Borthwick's *Three Years in California*, published in 1857. As talented a writer as he was an artist, the young Scots adventurer arrived in El Dorado in 1850 and produced one of the classic books of the Gold Rush, a luminous, instructive, and entertaining account of a frontier society without parallel in American history. *California Historical Society, FN-31544.*

Is, and as It May Be (1849), the first English-language book published in California; the French nobleman Ernest de Massey's *A Frenchman in the Gold Rush* (1927); the English sportsman Frank Marryat's *Mountains and Molehills, or Recollections of a Burnt Journal* (1855); the Scottish artist and writer J. D. Borthwick's *Three Years in California* (1857); and the Belgian landscape gardener Jean-Nicolas Perlot's account of his experiences in the Southern Mines, collected in *Gold Seeker* (1985).

Realistic prose accounts of the Gold Rush were often less well known at the time in California than the work of frontier humorists like Alonzo Delano and George Horatio Derby. Delano published *Life on the Plains* and other works under his legal name in the East, but he presented himself as the long-nosed character Old Block in San Francisco. He wrote popular whimsical sketches, or "whittlings from his penknife," of western types like the miner and the gambler, for San Francisco's *Pacific News*. These articles were collected in two books: *Pen-Knife Sketches, or Chips from the Old Block* in 1853 and *Old Block's Sketch Book, or Tales of California Life* in 1856. Delano was a productive author who never considered writing his exclusive occupation. He moved to Grass Valley later in his life, opened a bank, invested in quartz mines, and was an enthusiastic Grass Valley promoter.

George Horatio Derby was a caricaturist and U.S. Army topographical engineer assigned to California in the early 1850s, after service in the Mexican War. He wrote under the pseudonyms John Phoenix and John P. Squibob and became famous as a wag and practical joker. His letters, squibs, and burlesques appeared in various California papers. His most notorious escapade occurred in 1853, when he was left in charge of editing the San Diego *Herald* while its editor, Derby's friend, was away. Derby changed the political alliance of the paper from Democratic to Whig and turned the weekly into a comic journal complete with mock-advertisements and mock-editorials. The audacity of the stunt gained statewide attention. It was the comic culmination of Derby's previous satires of phrenologists, land speculators, pompous politicians, and pretentious literary reviewers. His occasional prose was collected in two volumes, the popular *Phoenixiana; or Sketches and Burlesques* (1855), which went through some twenty-six printings, and the posthumous *Squibob Papers* (1865).

Striking a pose of boisterous urbanity, Derby's writing is full of a racy, irresponsible humor and comic earnestness. After writing a droll exposé of the treeless, flea-bitten town of Benicia (which served as the California state capital from 1853 to 1854), for instance, Derby expressed his mock sorrow about being "unhonored and unsung, and, what is far worse, unrecorded and untaxed" in Benicia: "How sharper than a serpent's thanks it is to have a toothless child, as Pope beautifully remarks in his *Paradise Lost*. One individual characterized my letter as a 'd . . . d burlesque.' I pity that person and forgive him."[44] Like a cross between Mrs. Malaprop and Groucho Marx, Derby's energetic burlesques of contemporary topics prompted Twain to call him "the first of the great modern humorists."

TWAIN, HARTE, AND THE *OVERLAND MONTHLY*

Full of raillery, literate satire, and vivid social comment, the writing of Derby, along with that of Delano, Ridge, Clappe, and others helped lodge the California Gold Rush in the American imagination. Their work anticipated a second generation of authors in the 1860s and 1870s—including Twain, Harte, Joaquin Miller, Charles Warren Stoddard, Ina Coolbrith, and Prentice Mulford—who transformed the Gold Rush into mythic history and eclipsed the work (except for Clappe's letters) of those who had preceded them. The central vehicle for that literary transformation was the monthly magazine the *Overland Monthly,* probably the most important literary periodical ever published in California. Founded in San Francisco in 1868 by a local bookseller and former miner named Anton Roman, the *Overland Monthly* was designed to encourage immigration to California. The magazine was made possible by the economic boom preceding the arrival of the transcontinental railroad (which would soon be carrying copies of the journal to appreciative eastern readers). Yet as Franklin Walker pointed out, the designs of the covers of *The Pioneer* magazine, which had published Clappe's letters, and the *Overland Monthly* strikingly highlighted the change in mood between the 1850s and the late 1860s. On the masthead of *The Pioneer,* exultant pioneers looked confidently westward toward the promised land on the Pacific. By contrast, the cover of the *Overland Monthly* (which had been collaboratively designed by its first editor, Bret Harte, and the artist Arthur Nahl) featured a grizzly bear turning its snarling face down a section of railroad track, as if to meet an approaching locomotive. Paradoxically dependent upon the very economies that had so drastically altered the California now eulogized within the magazine, the grizzly, Walker noted, "symbolized the last stand for independence on the part of a pioneer society. . . . Near the end of its frontier days, the West, having passed from naïveté to satire, reached the stage in which its early days became romantic."[45]

Although he never actually published in the *Overland Monthly,* Mark Twain warmed up his eastern audience to the local color of California subject matter in November of 1865, when he published his now well-known story "The Celebrated Jumping Frog of Calaveras County" in *The New York Saturday Press.* A parody of a tall tale, in which a nameless confidence man outwits the con man Jim Smiley in one of the animal contests of which miners were so fond, Twain's story made literary capital out of subliterary frontier humor and established his talent for simultaneously embracing and satirizing the entertaining, misspelled western slang of the mining frontier and the characters who so inventively used it.

Although he never went as far as Twain with satire and hoax, Harte did quickly learn what Patrick Morrow has called "the power of California to 'customize,' to modify material from other eras, locations, and cultures and imprint this material with a Golden Gate stamp."[46] Harte's story "The Luck of Roaring Camp," which was published without a signature in the second issue of the *Overland Monthly,* was an overnight sensation. It "reached across the continent and startled the Academists on the Atlantic Coast," Kate Chopin later recalled, and helped make Harte the country's highest-paid author and a household name in the early 1870s.[47] More than any other writer, Harte was responsible for creating the legendary, larger-than-life image of the Gold Rush. He did so by transforming squalid mining camps like Roaring Camp, Poker Flat, and Red Gulch into mythical towns inhabited by a society that now, in the mist of memory, looked, as Walker put it, "as romantic and unusual as Camelot or Bagdad": "Harte created the land of a million Westerns, a land in which gun-play was chronic, vigilante committees met before breakfast, and death was as common as a rich strike in the diggings."[48] Stories such as "The Luck of Roaring Camp" (1868), "The Outcasts of Poker Flat" (1869), and "Tennessee's

Born in Albany, New York, Bret Harte arrived in California in 1854, when the grand adventure of placer mining was becoming a memory, and the corporate enterprises of hydraulic and quartz mining were fast gaining ascendancy. After working variously as an apothecary, an expressman, and a typesetter, he turned to writing. In 1863 he published a tale of Spanish California in the *Atlantic Monthly*, but it was the appearance five years later of "The Luck of Roaring Camp," in the pages of the *Overland Monthly*, that launched his career as a writer of local-color stories. *California Historical Society, FN-26875.*

Partner" (1869), to mention but the most familiar, are peopled, in most readers' memories, by grizzled sentimentalists (Kentuck and Stumpy), debonair gamblers (John Oakhurst and Jack Hamline), young innocents (Piney Woods and the Luck), and golden-hearted, but fallen, women (Mother Shipton and the Duchess).

The presence of such endearing characters might at first seem odd, for Harte's gold camps were also filled with violence and degradation. Little Tommy Luck's mother, Cherokee Sal, for example, was an Indian prostitute who died during childbirth. At the end of "The Outcasts," John Oakhurst committed suicide and the story ended with the images of the corpses of two frozen women. Even the ostensible forces of law and order in Harte's world were of doubtful origin. The citizens of Poker Flat were indiscriminately "after somebody" when they banished the outcasts. They were motivated only by "a spasm of virtuous reaction, quite as lawless and ungovernable as any of the acts that had provoked it."[49] Harte's pine and cedar forests were, as David Rains Wallace notes, "usually well stocked with blue jays and squirrels, [and] can have a sentimental sweetness approaching the Disney cartoon."[50] But his stories could also convey an effective sense of impending violence and isolation, as on a warm night before a lynching in "Tennessee's Partner," when a "little canyon" stood "stifling with heated, resinous odors, and the decaying driftwood on the Bar [sent] forth faint sickening exhalations."[51]

What kept Harte's stories from becoming truly terrifying or morally ambivalent was his ability, in Kevin Starr's words, to create mythic history by depicting the Gold Rush as "quaint comedy and sentimental melodrama, already possessing the charm of antiquity."[52] That "antique" charm stemmed as much from Harte's narrative voice as from his subject matter. No matter what Harte described, the voice in his fiction established a warm-hearted, civilized verbal buffer meant to absorb and detoxify the worst that human nature or natural disaster could throw at it. Even when presenting readers with ostensibly realistic details, Harte managed to keep his narrative authority intact. The town of Roaring Camp, he wrote, "numbered about a hundred men":

> One or two of these were actual fugitives from justice, some were criminal, and all were reckless. Physically they exhibited no indication of their past lives and character. The greatest scamp had a Raphael face, with a profusion of blond hair; Oakhurst, a gambler, had the melancholy air and intellectual abstraction of a Hamlet; the coolest and most courageous man was scarcely over five feet in height, with a soft voice and an embarrassed, timid manner. The term "roughs" applied to them was a distinction rather than a definition. . . . The strongest man had but three fingers on his right hand; the best shot had but one eye.[53]

The references here to Raphael and Hamlet and the narrator's curatorial care about how to use the term "roughs" might have distanced another author from his vernacular subjects. But Harte used this descriptive aside as a means of establishing his insider's knowledge of the true character of Roaring Camp. He inverted conventional notions that a scamp should look degenerate, that a courageous man should have a commanding physique, and so forth, the better to insist that tender emotions lurk unseen within his characters, ready for the moral transformations his stories enact. "The Luck of Roaring Camp," a student once aptly suggested, might well be retitled "Sixteen Men and a Baby."

LITERARY LEGACIES

Harte's image of the stout-hearted, red-shirted Forty-niner was gradually drained of its melancholy and unruliness in the late 1870s and made into the entrepreneuring pioneer of the California boosters, which partly explains why later writers who dealt with the Gold Rush would not follow his example. Josiah Royce, Clarence King, and John Muir all variously expressed reservations about the refashioning of the Argonauts as pioneer entrepreneurs basking in the glow of civic rectitude. Naturalist writers at the turn of the century like Frank Norris, Jack London, and Ambrose Bierce used mining camps (often in deserted towns with dank mine shafts) to create a spooky, surreal atmosphere for dark parables about violence and psychic collapse. Their legacy can be seen in a contemporary writer such as Roy Parvin, whose stories in *The Loneliest Road in America* (1997) use the hardscrabble mines of the Trinity Alps as the backdrop for haunting tales of violent misfits and solitary dope growers. Other writers would be drawn to the darker side of historical figures, like John Sutter, the Swiss entrepreneur upon whose land gold was first discovered. In his novel *Gold* (1925), the Swiss writer Blaise Cendrars painted an unforgettable portrait of an elderly and destitute Sutter in Washington, D.C., a loner, down-at-the-heel, flecked with dandruff, and petitioning Congress to be reimbursed for his loss of property and wealth in California.

Contemporary writers concerned with nature and ecology such as David Rains Wallace and Gary Snyder have followed the lead of earlier writers such as John Muir and Mary Austin in studying both the human and natural history of California mining. The paucity of firsthand accounts of the Gold Rush (at least translated into English) by Native Americans, Asians, and Latinos has also inspired rich revisionist imaginings of what it must have been like for marginalized groups to participate in the Gold Rush. Literary attempts to resurrect the lost lives of, say, a widowed Maidu mother surrounded by her dying children in Janice Gould's poem "History Lesson" (1990), or a young Chinese woman unexpectedly forced into prostitution, in Ruthanne Lum McCunn's *Thousand Pieces of Gold* (1981), have added a fresh, challenging complexity to our understanding of the California frontier.

The fact that the Gold Rush continues to fascinate contemporary writers should come as no surprise. As Stephen Birmingham asserts, this epic event created a new version of California élan: "a special doughtiness, a certain daring, a refusal to be fazed or put off by bad luck or circumstances, an unwillingness to give up."[54] Of course, it is sometimes a fine line between daring and derangement, open-spiritedness and short-sightedness, risk-taking and irresponsibility. But the Gold Rush ensured that Californians would henceforth be willing to walk that line. The variety of opinions about the meaning and desirability of the Gold Rush has been rich and contradictory since the moment it began and has helped make western mining an irresistible literary subject for a century and a half. The sheer profusion of gold-rush literature powerfully reminds us—in its roughhewn panoply of various forms—that, as with any complex phenomenon, the composite truth of this historical event cannot be found in any single story, new or old. Like many of the literary works that take it as their subject, the Gold Rush continues—as all engaging literature and history does— to enlighten, entertain, and inform us, and to surprise us out of our own responses.

NOTES

A portion of this chapter appeared first in *Gold Rush: A Literary Exploration* (Berkeley: Heyday Books, 1997).

1. Mark Twain, *Roughing It* (1872; New York: Penguin, 1985), 49–50.

2. James D. Houston, "From El Dorado to the Pacific Rim: The Place Called California," *California History* 68 (Winter 1989/90): 174.

3. Wallace Stegner, *Where the Bluebird Sings to the Lemonade Springs: Living and Writing in the West* (New York: Random House, 1992), 58.

4. Alonzo Delano, Letter, 20 October 1850, in *Gold Rush: A Literary Exploration,* ed. Michael Kowalewski (Berkeley: Heyday Books, 1997), 173.

5. Quoted in J. S. Holliday, *The World Rushed In: The California Gold Rush Experience* (New York: Simon & Schuster, 1981), 387.

6. Ralph Waldo Emerson, *The Conduct of Life* (1860), in Kowalewski, *Gold Rush,* 299.

7. Henry David Thoreau, Journal Entry, 1 February 1852, in Kowalewski, *Gold Rush,* 297–98.

8. Jay B. Hubbell, *South and Southwest: Literary Essays and Reminiscences* (Durham: Duke University Press, 1965), 273.

9. Gary F. Kurutz, *The California Gold Rush: A Descriptive Bibliography of Books and Pamphlets Covering the Years 1848–1853* (San Francisco: The Book Club of California, 1997). For additional listings of primary (and secondary) sources, see Robert LeRoy Santos, *The Gold Rush of California: A Bibliography of Periodical Articles* (Denair, Calif.: Alley-Cass Publications, for California State University, Stanislaus, University Archives, 1998).

10. Robert McCrum et al., *The Story of English* (New York: Penguin, 1987), 252.

11. Kevin Starr, *Americans and the California Dream, 1850–1915* (New York: Oxford, 1973), 50–52; Starr compares the Gold Rush, as an "epic experience," to both the *Iliad* and the *Odyssey,* 52–68.

12. Franklin Walker, *San Francisco's Literary Frontier* (1939; New York: Alfred A. Knopf, 1943), 14.

13. Bayard Taylor, *Eldorado: Or Adventures in the Path of Empire* (1850; Lincoln: University of Nebraska Press, 1988), 84, 88, 44.

14. Walker, *San Francisco's Literary Frontier*, 27.

15. Bret Harte, 28 April 1866 Letter to *Christian Register*, in *Bret Harte's California: Letters to the "Springfield Republican" and "Christian Register," 1866–67*, ed. Gary Scharnhorst (Albuquerque: University of New Mexico Press, 1990), 26–27.

16. Ibid., 116.

17. Ibid., 122.

18. See my essay, "Quoting the Wicked Wit of the West: Frontier Reportage and Western Vernacular," in *Reading the West: New Essays on the Literature of the American West*, ed. Michael Kowalewski (New York: Cambridge University Press, 1996), 82–98.

19. Stephen Fender, "'The Prodigal in a Far Country Chawing of Husks': Mark Twain's Search for a Style in the West," *Modern Language Review* 71 (October 1976): 741. Also see Fender's *Plotting the Golden West: American Literature and the Rhetoric of the California Trail* (Cambridge: Cambridge University Press, 1981).

20. Harte, *Bret Harte's California*, 33, 74.

21. Taylor, *Eldorado*, 90.

22. Harte, *Bret Harte's California*, 140.

23. Joseph Henry Jackson, Introduction to John Rollin Ridge, *The Life and Adventures of Joaquín Murieta, the Celebrated California Bandit* (1854; Norman: University of Oklahoma Press, 1986), xix–xxx.

24. Richard Rodriguez, "The Head of Joaquín Murrieta," in his *Days of Obligation* (New York: Penguin, 1992), 133.

25. Ridge, *Joaquín Murieta*, 9–10.

26. Blake Allmendinger, *Ten Most Wanted: The New Western Literature* (New York: Routledge, 1998), 48.

27. Ridge, *Joaquín Murieta*, 64, 97.

28. Rodriguez tells of seeing what may be this severed head in contemporary Santa Rosa, in "The Head of Joaquín Murrieta," 133–48.

29. For an excellent overview of the early history of the performing arts in San Francisco, see Misha Berson, *The San Francisco Stage: From Gold Rush to Golden Spike, 1849–1869* (San Francisco: San Francisco Performing Arts Library and Museum Journal, 1989).

30. Alonzo Delano, *A Live Woman in the Mines, or Pike County Ahead* (1857), in *California Gold-Rush Plays*, ed. Glenn Loney (New York: Performing Arts Journal Publications, 1983), 66.

31. Ibid., 90.

32. John Banks, *Two Buckeye Rovers in the Gold Rush*, ed. Howard L. Scamehorn (Athens: Ohio University Press, 1965), 72.

33. William Lewis Manly, *Death Valley in '49* (1894; Ann Arbor: University Microfilms, 1966), 69.

34. Ibid., 416.

35. Louise Amelia Knapp Smith Clappe, *The Shirley Letters: From the California Mines, 1851–1852*, ed. Marlene Smith-Baranzini (Berkeley: Heyday Books, 1998), 50.

36. Ibid., 175.

37. Ibid., 12.

38. Ibid., 80.

39. Ibid., 54.

40. Ibid., 178.

41. Chauncey L. Canfield, *The Diary of a Forty-Niner* (1906; New York: Turtle Point Press, 1992), 3. Some historians suspect that Canfield may himself have invented Jackson's narrative, but the evidence is not conclusive.

42. Ibid., 173.

43. Ibid., 183.

44. George Horatio Derby, "Squibob in Sonoma" (October 21, 1850), in *Squibob: An Early California Humorist,* ed. Richard Derby Reynolds (San Francisco: Squibob Press, 1990), 32.

45. Walker, *San Francisco's Literary Frontier,* 256, 261.

46. Patrick D. Morrow, "Harte, Twain, and the San Francisco Circle," in *A Literary History of the American West,* ed. J. Golden Taylor et al. (Fort Worth: Texas Christian University Press, 1987), 349.

47. Kate Chopin, *St. Louis Republic,* 9 December 1900, quoted in *Selected Letters of Bret Harte,* ed. Gary Scharnhorst (Norman: University of Oklahoma Press, 1997), 6.

48. Walker, *San Francisco's Literary Frontier,* 264.

49. Bret Harte, "The Outcasts of Poker Flat," in *The Outcasts of Poker Flat and Other Tales,* ed. Wallace Stegner (New York: New American Library, 1961), 112.

50. David Rains Wallace and Morley Baer, *The Wilder Shore* (San Francisco: Sierra Club Books, 1984), 98.

51. Harte, "Tennessee's Partner," in *The Outcasts of Poker Flat,* 126.

52. Starr, *Americans and the California Dream,* 49.

53. Harte, "The Luck of Roaring Camp," in *The Outcasts of Poker Flat,* 102.

54. Stephen Birmingham, *California Rich* (New York: Simon & Schuster, 1980), 29.

9

From Indifference to Imperative Duty
Educating Children in Early California

Irving G. Hendrick

Thinking about formalized schooling in gold-rush California requires immediately at least three important—if obvious—caveats. The first is that there was formal schooling taking place in California before the American period under Spanish and Mexican rule. The second is that the American common school had already experienced some important, if brief, success in eastern and midwestern states before American political and educational leaders attempted to adapt it to California soil. Finally, there is always in history the issue of whose history is to be told. Given the racial history of mid-nineteenth-century America and California, most stories are not completely balanced according to racial, ethnic, and religious considerations.[1] These issues, particularly the racial one, are not ignored here, but the central focus is on the adoption and extension of the American public school system to California soil.

The demands of a self-governing republic practically required that universal education eventually would be necessary. The federal ordinances of 1785 and 1787 provided that public land for the support of schooling would accompany the development of the West. This is not to suggest that the forces of localism, provincialism, parochialism, and private endeavor did not dominate formal schooling during the early years of California statehood. Indeed, they did. Yet because major early battles for free, publicly supported schooling were fought—and won—in states well east of California, the national model of public schools was established before 1848 and would eventually apply to California as well.

For most of the first half of the nineteenth century, leaders promoting state-supported schooling had to persuade a doubting citizenry of at least three major principles: (1) that public schools needed to be free and available to all children, (2) that states rather than local communities needed to guarantee the quality of the education provided, and (3) that the public schools needed to be separated from sectarian religious control.[2] By the time California's earliest leaders in the American period assumed office, much progress in winning national adherence to those ideals had been achieved. Still, the issues and disagreements continued to be active. Thus, the rise of a California public school system is explained by earlier similar successes in other states, by referring to provisions for school support in the California Constitution of 1849, by early legislation, and by the sheer leadership of powerful educational and government officials.

For the most part, state officials and state legislation had little to do with either the presence or absence of schools during the 1850s. The California of the gold-rush era was a very different place—in the literal geographic sense—from California today. Persons thinking of public education during the late twentieth century likely think first of the educational challenges facing students, parents, and educators in Los Angeles, San Diego, San Jose, San Francisco, other large urban centers, the suburbs, and the great Central Valley. During gold-rush days, Los Angeles hardly deserves mention. Los Angeles County was not to be found among the ten most populous counties in California. During the 1850s the most populated counties included El Dorado, San Francisco, Yuba, Nevada, Calaveras, Tuolumne, Sacramento, Placer, Mariposa, and Butte. Of these, San Francisco was in a class by itself in trade, commerce, finance, culture, and education, albeit early in the decade its population had not yet exceeded that of El Dorado County.

One can imagine that a rush to acquire nearly instant wealth by persons new to the state, most of them single men, did not provide the best social and economic environment for attending to the building of institutions, including schools. Yet, the American patterns were present and not that difficult to take advantage of by the men who participated in framing the first state constitution. The provisions for education were a case in point. While education was not one of the more powerful immediate concerns, it did receive enough attention to establish an adequate basis for the state's assuming subsequent financial responsibility for operating schools and for future enabling legislation. Five sections of Article IX of the 1849 Constitution established the office of superintendent of public instruction, provided a basis for founding a state university, and established a system of common schools partially supported by a general school fund derived from the sale or rental of the state's public land.[3] Previously, only four states, including Michigan, Iowa, Wisconsin, and Vermont, had provided for an elected chief school officer through the constitutional process.

The school fund issue was somewhat controversial, but all attempts to add a limiting proviso on its size were defeated.[4] Gold was at the heart of the controversy. While the tradition of federal land sales in other states had established a clear example for the framers of the state constitution to follow, Sacramento attorney Winfield S. Sherwood argued that some of the acres might be located on gold

Students apply themselves to their studies at Saint Vincent's Orphan Asylum, San Rafael, in a photograph by the famed California photographer Eadweard Muybridge. Established in 1855 by the Sisters of Charity of St. Vincent de Paul, and for a period administered by the Christian Brothers, it is now St. Vincent's School for Boys. *California Historical Society, FN-31530.*

mines, thus becoming too rich a source to be devoted to education. Happily, the Sherwood proviso was defeated by a vote of 18 to 17.[5]

Constitutional provision for schooling notwithstanding, the legislature gave only slow and grudging support to providing a state tax levy and assuring a minimum length to the school term. Indeed, the first state legislation pertaining to education provided only for the election of a state superintendent of public instruction. Leadership from governors and most members of the legislature was conspicuously absent in the 1850s, although all of the early state superintendents of public instruction did advocate for a publicly supported school system. When the first state superintendent, Judge John Gage Marvin, came to the capital at San Jose in December 1850 to assume his post, there literally was no job to perform.[6] He could do nothing about schooling until he had some legislative direction, and that was slow in coming. While the first and second legislatures were lethargic in regard to school legislation, the popular press was generally supportive and critical of the political leaders for their inaction. To be sure, certain members of the legislature were supportive of public schools. Early in the first session, Senator Elcan Heydenfeldt of San Francisco attempted to translate the constitutional plan for common schools into a functioning law. His and a few other futile efforts notwithstanding, the dominant attitude of the earliest governors and legislators was to wait. Governor Peter Burnett's attitude was stated as follows:

> Under existing circumstances, before any of the public lands to which the State will be entitled have been assigned to her, and while we have so few families in the State, and our population is so unsettled, it may not be practicable to establish any general system of free schools, or endow any university. But the time must soon arrive when we shall have both the families and the means to adopt and carry out such a system. In the meantime, it might be made the duty of the Superintendent to collect useful statistical information to be reported annually to this body.[7]

Private subscription, not tax support, constituted the means of furthering schooling during the 1850s. Legislation approved in 1851 and 1852 helped the schools very slightly in that it provided that funds obtained from the sale of school lands and the apportionment of interest collected from the state school fund be distributed among private, religious, and sectarian schools on the basis of attendance. The provision of state funds for private religious schools produced a good deal of criticism. Notwithstanding the vigorous—and largely successful—national efforts to separate church from state as part of the public school fight, California's early history with the apportionment of state school funds gave a pro rata share of those funds to religious and sectarian schools. Catholic schools especially benefited.

Initially, as implied in Governor Burnett's recommendation, the state superintendent's role was largely to gather statistics concerning the extent of schooling in

the state. The results did not yield an admirable picture, particularly from the mining districts. From Calaveras County came the report: one hundred children, no
school. From San Luis Obispo County, two hundred children were reported, along
with the news that "a school was kept open last summer by a Spanish teacher, but
was so grossly neglected that it was abolished." The report from San Juan in Monterey County was only slightly more hopeful. The postmaster there reported that 179
children were present, including 44 "English or American," and 135 "Native Californians." His report continued that "Morality and society are in desperate condition. I have built a house 20 x 32, a half mile from the mission, which I offer free of
rent for a school house, but they appear to be very indifferent about the education of
their children."[8]

In the larger towns, the picture was more hopeful, although not uniformly so.
From Sacramento came a report from one James A. Rogers that there were about
four hundred children in the county, but that there were no schools outside Sacramento City, which maintained two primary schools and one academy. "This city has
never spent a cent for elementary instruction," he added. "There have been three attempts to get up a school, which have failed after two or three month's trial. . . . My
sympathies are with the Common or Free Public School System. In their absence I
started a private school."[9] Catholic schools maintained by the Sisters of Charity
and other religious orders were operated at Monterey, San Rafael, and San Jose. The
cities of Napa, Santa Cruz, Sacramento, and Stockton each had schools supported
by tuition ranging from four to eight dollars a month. Outside of San Francisco, only
Benicia maintained a school at public expense, and even there tuition was charged.

Although state leadership and action lagged, the record of school support was decidedly better in San Francisco. City legislation immediately influenced the establishment of schools in that growing city, and eventually in the state. In September
1851, a Free School Ordinance was enacted by the city council for the creation of a
school board and the establishment, regulation, and support of free common schools.
The population of children and youth was growing rapidly and action was demanded. Earlier, during 1849 and 1850, a semipublic operation was initiated by the
council, thanks to the leadership of John C. Pelton.[10] Pelton was enraptured by the
appeal of California, though not necessarily its gold. In 1849 he left his position as
principal of the Phillips' Free School at Andover, Massachusetts, and soon found
himself to be the most influential schoolmaster in San Francisco.[11]

By 1851 there were already four schools serving four districts of the city. Each enrolled from about 60 to 160 students.[12] Many features of that San Francisco ordinance are still recognizable today. Then as now, the board was given authority to appoint a superintendent of schools, purchase property, build schools, prescribe a
course of study, and hire teachers. The last task was particularly challenging in the
absence of any form of state standards. Pelton, more than State Superintendent

Students and teachers gather outside Lincoln Grammar School on Fifth Street in San Francisco for a photograph by Carleton Watkins. Strong support for public education arose early in San Francisco, and by 1859 more than six thousand students were enrolled in the city's seventeen public schools, including a separate school for Chinese and one for blacks. Despite the importance laid on academic studies, especially mathematics, physical exercise was also part of the curriculum. According to *Hutchings' California Magazine,* exercise gave "boys strong muscles to fight their way in the world," and girls "erect forms, well developed chests, grace of movement, and ease of carriage." *California Historical Society, FN-31675.*

Marvin, was the most visible early public school leader in California. As author of an official report, "The First Public School in San Francisco," he was widely quoted in the press. It was for this reason that Marvin was urged to consult with Pelton about state legislation, which he did.

Appraising the quality of schools during gold-rush California must be done with an eye on contemporary values. Even mindful of that, it is hard to speak well of the earliest efforts of the legislatures and governors. At first blush, the grassroot communities appeared to be doing quite well. By the start of 1854, Californians were supporting forty-seven common schools, enrolling 4,052 students who were attending class at least three months a year.[13] The discrepancy in perception is important. The history of early nineteenth-century America included a powerful tradition of individual responsibility, family responsibility, and church responsibility. Notwithstanding the significant public school precedents that had already been established in New England and the Midwest, the notion that taxation should be enacted on land for the support of public schooling was still controversial. Repeated admonitions to the legislature for public school support by early state superintendents of public instruction had little effect. To the credit of those men, they did speak out. State Superintendent Paul Hubbs, the second person to hold that office, complained bitterly in 1855 about the legislature's inactivity and asserted that "no government is worthy of the name of civilization that refuses to educate, and to educate properly, the children of the state."[14] Hubbs claimed that three-fourths of California children were growing up unable to read and write.

In 1856 Andrew J. Moulder, a southern Democrat, was elected state superintendent of public instruction. In 1859 he was reelected overwhelmingly. Perhaps it is in the career accomplishments and racist views and deeds of Andrew Moulder that contemporary students of California's educational history can appreciate the complexity of interpreting California's past. More than any of his predecessors, Moulder brought experience, training, and leadership to the office. More than any of his predecessors, he helped to establish a viable system of public schooling for children of the state, as well as normal schools to prepare teachers for the public schools. After leaving his state office in 1863, he went on to serve as a member of the University of California's first Board of Regents and even at the time of his death in 1895 he served as superintendent of schools in San Francisco. Fifty years ago, educators might have celebrated Moulder's high achievements without comment concerning his racial and segregationist views. Not today; such is the complexity of the human experience and the evolving perceptions of democracy and equality under the law.

Moulder advocated strongly for the financial support of public schools each year he was in office and, after two years of failure, experienced modest success in 1858. The school law of that year provided only the most minimal amount of state support and then only conditionally. A school district could levy a district tax for maintaining a school or for building a schoolhouse with the approval of the district's voters, but only if it had maintained a school for at least four months during a year, and had insufficient funds to defray one-half the cost of continuing that school for another term. Moulder was incensed that fewer than 21,000 students had attended school in 1857–58, and slightly more than 29,000 had received no schooling at all. The latter he described as "neglected" children who well could grow up to become "benighted men and women." He continued:

Damning as the record is, it is yet lamentably true, that during the last five years the State of California has paid $754,193.80 for the support of criminals, and but $284,183.69 for the education of the young. In other words, she has paid nearly three times as much for the support of an average of 400 criminals as for the training and cul-ture of thirty thousand children. To make the point more forcible, the figures show that she has expended $1,885 on every criminal, and $9 on every child![15]

As the election of Lincoln and the Civil War approached, California was in seri-ous jeopardy of splitting almost as the nation was splitting. A significant faction of southern sympathizers populated California's southern section, but with Moulder serving as state superintendent, this was not particularly disadvantageous to the cause of public schooling. Moulder was at the peak of his influence, having been elected overwhelmingly in 1859 on the Democratic ticket. The 1860 legislature was the last to be controlled by the Lecomptonite, or pro-slavery wing, of the Demo-cratic Party. It had no difficulty supporting Moulder's call for cutting off state funds to any public school daring to admit blacks, Asians, or Indians. Yet the body reacted positively to Moulder's recommendations that the county school tax be raised from ten cents to twenty-five cents, that the state superintendent be authorized to appoint an examining board to issue teaching certificates, that school funds must be used during the same school year in which they were appropriated, and that the state board of education be authorized to select a series of textbooks for compulsory adoption by all districts. All of this had not yet led to a full legislative commitment in favor of free public education, but that day appeared to be getting closer.[16]

Moulder had help during his last term as superintendent, likely the result of the match that existed between his political orientation and that of the legislature. Per-haps the most notable contributor to his success was Assemblyman John Conness, who later became a United States senator from California. Conness led the fight against sharing state school funds with parochial schools, mainly Catholic schools. By 1855, opposition to parochial education, particularly public assistance to Catholic schools, resulted in a repeal of the Religious Aid Bill of 1853 and produced a virtual ending of financial assistance for private and religious schools.[17] On the public school front, legislation introduced by Conness in 1861 permitted implementation of the federal ordinances of the 1780s by providing that the proceeds from the sale of the sixteenth and thirty-sixth sections of each township's public lands could be des-ignated for the state school fund. By 1861, nearly 200,000 acres of federal land had been sold and the monies placed in that fund.[18]

Perhaps the greatest of Superintendent Moulder's legacies was the establishment in 1862, his last year in office, of a state normal school for the preparation of teach-ers. Interestingly, a decade-long delay in establishing a normal school did not seem particularly inappropriate. The supply of teachers in California exceeded the demand during the 1850s, and while the good teachers were concentrated in San Francisco and were not distributed well throughout the state, that city was also the first to rec-ognize the need for a normal school. The actual school was established under city

The old schoolhouse at Murphys, Calaveras County, constructed in 1860. Built by volunteer labor in the Greek Revival style, it has served the community as an educational institution for nearly a century and a half. During the age of gold, one-room schools sprouted up throughout the mining districts, which composed the most populous counties in the state. *Photograph by Anthony Kirk.*

authority five years prior to its designation as a state-supported institution. Moulder had pleaded for the school at his teachers' institutes and at other educational meetings and had helped to organize educator support for it. Notwithstanding the differences in their political parties, Governor Leland Stanford approved the legislation on May 23, 1862, and on July 3, 1862, the new state normal school in San Francisco commenced work with five students in attendance. This humble beginning established the early small roots for additional normal schools and, eventually, state teachers' colleges, state colleges, and ultimately the largest comprehensive university system in the world, the California State University.

When Moulder left office after the 1862 election, he did so with some notable achievements, led by the ones that have been identified above. That said, a critical interpretation of his work from a human rights perspective presents a less generous story of his legacy. Moulder was not above attempting to advance the cause of public education by playing on the racial fears of legislators. Attitudes and policies of racial discrimination in California may be explained in large measure by the legacy

of slavery in America, although by midcentury the northern experience in that regard was already much different from the southern experience. Efforts by black
people in the northern states during the early national period to interpret equality
and freedom quite literally according to the language of the Declaration of Independence had met with some success. Yet, progress in that regard had been painfully
slow, as white intellectual and government leaders continued through the first half
of the nineteenth century to proclaim one set of principles and act on a different set.

Perhaps Moulder's most outrageous recommendation to the legislature in regard
to race was the one contained in an 1858 bill to prohibit local school districts from
admitting persons of "inferior races," especially blacks, to schools attended by whites.
In his annual report to the legislature that same year he lashed out against the
"Negrophilist school of mock philanthropists" who had found their way to California and were attempting to "introduce children of Negroes into our public schools
on an equality with whites." Moulder feared amalgamation, and described his worry
as follows:

> Until our people are prepared for practical amalgamation, which will probably not be
> before the millennium, they will rather forego the benefits of our schools than permit
> their daughters—fifteen, sixteen, and seventeen years of age plus—to affiliate with
> the sons of Negroes. It is practically reduced to this, then, that our schools must be
> maintained exclusively for whites, or they will soon become tenanted by blacks alone.[19]

In the same report Moulder urged legislators to withhold funds from any district
"that permits the admission of the inferior races into their schools." The affected
races he defined as African, Mongolian, and Indian. He denied prejudice, maintaining that he had no prejudice "against a respectable Negro in his place."

Moulder and his successor, the much heralded and respected John Swett, shared
a common commitment to free, publicly supported, nonsectarian schooling for the
children of California. The one crucial difference, of course, was that Moulder was
a committed segregationist. Although Republicans were only slightly more the ad-
vocates of racial equality than were Democrats, there were significant differences between the two parties, all of which added up during the Civil War to some improved
treatment of blacks under a Republican governor, legislature, and state superintendent of public instruction. For other nonwhites, particularly the Chinese, there was
little perceptible difference between the parties.

As secession by southern states began, California Democrats had control of the
governor's chair, the legislature, and all four seats in Congress. The Democratic split
between pro- and antislavery forces, combined with a dominant loyalist sentiment
in the state, assured success for the fledgling Republican Party and the carrying of
California by Abraham Lincoln in the presidential election of 1860. Success continued with the election of Republican gubernatorial candidate Leland Stanford in

1861 and with the easy election in 1862 of John Swett as state superintendent of public instruction. In 1863 Republicans gained control of the California legislature for the first time.

Although they lacked political and social equality during gold-rush days, the black leadership of California, ardently committed to education and cultural advancement of their people, campaigned vigorously for equal treatment under the law. They had some slight encouragement from Republicans, nearly none from Democrats. Republicans did give overwhelming support to approving the Thirteenth Amendment to the national constitution on ending slavery in 1865, and in 1867 favored granting blacks all civil rights under the Fourteenth Amendment. It was Republican State Senator Robert F. Perkins of San Francisco who in 1863 successfully steered through the legislature a bill giving blacks the right to testify in court. Success on that front had been the number one priority of blacks throughout the 1850s. For their part, politically active blacks experienced no difficulty perceiving where their support was coming from and backed Republicans virtually without a blink of an eye until the 1880s.

If the right to testify in court and gaining the franchise to vote were the first two political aspirations of blacks, a desire for improved educational opportunities followed closely. On numerous occasions during the 1860s and 1870s, black spokesmen called attention to inequalities within the segregated public school system. During the early part of that period their focus was on achieving public education on terms of approximate equality with whites. All legal impediments to realizing this goal were objected to. At the State Convention of Colored Citizens of California held in 1865, attention was directed toward a section of the school law that permitted, but did not require, local school commissioners to establish schools for blacks even if fewer than ten black children resided in the area. Of the twenty-four resolutions approved at the 1865 convention, two had to do with education. One recommended "our brethren to aim at the same high order of education developed among the white race, and to make such persistent claims on the public educational provisions, and to establish such institutions, where necessary and practicable, as will insure to us and our children that desirable condition." The second resolution was aimed at practical education, it being "the imperative duty of parents, or guardians of children to have them, as far as possible, educated in some branch of business pursuits, by which they may be producers."[20]

There are many indications that California citizens valued education, albeit the commitment to those values differed a good bit, depending on the extent to which children were present in a community. Both white and black Californians appear to have promoted schooling in the interest of advancing the well-being of their families and communities. For blacks, the challenge and obstacles were markedly greater, owing largely to the racist views and policies of most whites. Of the several black leaders who emerged in early California, Jeremiah B. Sanderson was the one who focused his major efforts on education.[21] As a native of New Bedford, Massachusetts, with African, Indian, and Scottish ancestry, Sanderson had obtained a good education, presumably in non-segregated schools. In 1854 he arrived in California, intending only a short stay to improve his financial position before returning home. Shortly after arriving in San Francisco, he left for Sacramento, assuming his leadership and teaching role there in 1855. He was next heard from in San Francisco, where he served as a teacher between 1859 and 1866, with the exception of the 1864–65 term, when another teacher was appointed and Sanderson was made principal of the Broadway Colored School. The advancement of Sanderson lasted only as long as the new assistant, a black woman, remained in her position. When she resigned and was replaced by a white assistant, the school board felt compelled to replace Sanderson with a white principal, lest a black person be placed in a position of authority over a white person. Sanderson was then transferred to a second Negro school in a different part of the city. Not outwardly embittered by his experience in San Francisco, Sanderson in 1869 moved on to Stockton, where he taught for five years in a newly organized school for blacks prior to culminating his career with pastoral duties in Oakland. According to one account, Sanderson's school at Stockton became something of a center of learning for black youth, attracting several students from as far away as Los Angeles.[22] In any case, it seems evident that the small but highly motivated black community in California demonstrated a keen interest in obtaining an education.

The election of John Swett as superintendent of public instruction in 1862, coupled with increasing influence from San Francisco and other emerging urbanized areas, produced new and important support for public schooling.[23] On the issue of race, Swett was decidedly pro-Union and antislavery. His public statements and behavior seemed to indicate that he believed in extending free school opportunities to blacks as well as whites. Dominant racial values of the day, however, seemed to constrain even what Swett was prepared to advocate.

At long last, by 1863 a law was enacted that authorized local school boards to call elections for levying taxes for the purpose of furnishing school facilities or lengthening the school year. The following year, thanks again to Swett's leadership, another major advance occurred. In his first report to the legislature for the previous year, Swett pointed out that while California claimed 754 public schools, only 219 of them were fully "free schools." In the tradition of effective legislative advocacy, Swett drew on more favorable records in other northern states where the schools were all free. He informed the legislators that California raised by taxation only $4.42 per child, and that the total derived from all sources, rate bills included, was only $7 per child. Drawing on contemporary historical developments, including rapid population expansion attributable to the arrival of the railroads, Swett pointed out that the general social and economic fate of California rested with the mass of the population, not with a few brilliant minds.

Swett and his supporters circulated petitions for a state school tax sufficient to meet the educational needs of the state, declaring that it was "the duty of a representative government to maintain public schools as an act of self-preservation."[24] The petitions reportedly received widespread support and only rarely did a citizen decline to sign one. A successful bill followed from this petition effort, one that made provision for an annual state school tax of five cents on each one hundred dollars of taxable property. Each county was required to levy a minimum county school tax equal to two dollars for each child between the ages of four and eighteen years. It increased the maximum rate of county tax allowed by law from twenty-five to thirty cents. Fortuitously, the bill experienced no opposition in the Assembly, but a determined—though unsuccessful—fight to defeat it was met in the Senate. The victory of this legislation effectively assured the future of tax-supported public school education in California. A year later, the state ad valorem tax was increased from five cents to eight cents, and the minimum county tax was raised to three dollars per child.

Swett's crowning achievement was the school law of 1866. In that year the Senate Education Committee formally resolved that the state superintendent prepare a "Revision of the State School Laws." Such an invitation gave to Swett a magnificent opportunity to include every progressive element in support of public education that he believed could meet with legislative approval. Much of the work only amounted to a reenactment of the laws, but the comprehensive nature of the undertaking permitted the resulting bill to be named "An Act to Provide for a System of Common Schools." This legislative achievement established California in the front ranks of progressive states so far as a *full system* of free public education was concerned. The major points were summarized well by Roy W. Cloud nearly a half-century ago. Among the features of this legislation were the following:

1. Provision for a reorganization of the state board of education to consist of nine members and the formation of a separate board of normal school trustees of eight members.

2. Authorization of the state board of education to adopt rules and regulations for the conduct of the schools; to establish a course of study for district schools and to adopt a uniform state series of textbooks for such schools.

3. Provision for the payment of necessary expenses for teachers' institutes from the county school fund.

4. A requirement that all school districts furnish at district expense, school supplies, ink, chalk, pens, and stationery for use by the pupils.

5. Limit school hours for children under eight years of age to four hours a day, exclusive of intermissions.

6. Establishment of school libraries paid for by 10 percent of the state school apportionment.

7. Provision for the granting of life diplomas, i.e., certificates to teach, for teachers having ten years' experience; recognized normal school diplomas from other states and required that city, state, and county boards of examination be composed of professional teachers only.

8. Authorize and require school trustees to levy district school tax sufficient to keep a free school open five months in a year.

9. Provision for a state tax of 8 cents on each $100 of taxable property; a minimum county school tax of $3 per census child; and a maximum tax of 35 cents on each $100.[25]

When Swett left office in 1867, the state's public school system was enrolling approximately 46 percent of California's white children and 40 percent of its black children, but fewer than 1 percent of the Indian and Asian children.[26] Blacks clearly had asserted some influence and acquired some power. How far they had come is reflected in the statistics cited above. How far they still had to go in order to achieve equality is revealed in the debate and terms of the 1866 legislation. For the first time, the new legislation did permit a local school board, by majority vote, to admit into schools for whites "half-breed Indian children and Indian children who live with white families or under the guardianship of white persons." Other nonwhites would be allowed to attend school with whites only if a school district could not provide for their instruction in any other way. Under that circumstance local trustees would have to approve the idea by a majority vote, whereupon their decision would stand unless a majority of white parents objected in writing.[27]

A Senate amendment to the bill giving trustees authority to admit nonwhites into the schools passed by a vote of 25 to 5. The Assembly, however, refused to concur, thereby temporarily endangering the entire bill. Doubtlessly Swett could have lived with the amendment himself, but it was not something he viewed as worthy of fighting for at the risk of endangering his landmark legislation. The people of California were, he reported in 1867, "decidedly in favor of separate schools for colored children."[28] The amendment was deleted from the final version of the bill. The near absence of state-provided schooling for Indian and Asian children is explained by their own cultural orientation, by their lack of power, and by white prejudice. The harshest days of Chinese exclusion and discrimination against other minority groups still lay ahead.

If John Swett appears to Californians at the end of the twentieth century as a leader who was prepared to place pragmatic considerations ahead of principle on the issue of race, such a conclusion would be hard to refute. At the same time, it is not difficult to understand. Events soon confirmed that his social and political worries were warranted. By the end of the Civil War, improved unity in the Democratic Party and the arrival of numerous new residents, including many Chinese, led to defeat for the Republican ticket in 1867. Swett too was a casualty, losing to the southern sympathizer Reverend O. P. Fitzgerald, the same Breckenridge Democrat who had finished third and last in the 1862 election. The voters did, indeed, prefer "separate schools for colored children." As innocuous as the 1866 school law was on the race issue, it was too progressive for a majority of state legislators in the years immediately ahead. By 1870 two changes of note occurred. First, sparked by racist attitudes against an increasing number of Chinese, no reference at all was made in Section 56 of the school law to "Mongolian" children, the clear implication being that they should be excluded from participating in the benefits of public schooling. Second, no reference was made to the possibility, remote though it was, that blacks and Indians might he admitted to school with whites if local trustees chose to accommodate them in that manner.

The significance of educational legislation passed between 1863 and 1866 cannot be overemphasized. Professor Benjamin Silliman of Yale College, one of the nation's most eminent educators of his day, spoke of it in his graduation address at the private College of California in 1867. Silliman referred to Californians' having laid the foundations and set up the framework for "the best system of general common-school education for the whole people that existed in any state or country where the English language was spoken."[29] Setting up an institution of public schooling was of primary importance, but the quality of that institution would be defined by the quality of teachers serving in the schools, by the instructional programs offered in the schools, and by the materials that students and teachers had to work with. Early school leaders in California attended to all three needs as best they could, but the scarcity of dollars and qualified teachers seemed inevitably to make the challenge greater than the means to meet it.

State law during the early years of statehood made no restrictions on the level or subject that a teacher could teach, and local school committees were not about to enforce any restrictions themselves. Teachers in gold-rush California enjoyed closeness to their pupils and communities that they gradually lost in later years. In a technical and legal sense, the only qualification for teaching in those years was a willingness to teach and an ability to pass the scrutiny of a local school committee. As was the case with nearly all nineteenth-century occupations, a college education was not required. Local school committees were not infrequently made up of illiterate persons who were not above applying capricious standards in favor of hiring their friends and relatives for the low-status job of teacher. Yet, no matter how low the salary or the status, the occupation always held an attraction for some, particularly women, whose own nineteenth-century identities were closely associated with child-rearing.

Interestingly, the growing feminization of teaching in California was not evident until the years after 1860. In that year, 560 men teachers and 218 women teachers were believed to be working in California. By 1876, the gender majority had reversed dramatically to 1,167 men and 1,983 women. Salary discrimination seems always to have existed, albeit the differential during the 1860s was less dramatic in California than in the eastern states. For example, in 1864 the average woman teacher received $62 per month; the average man $74. Over the next half-century there grew in California and the nation the virtual truism that "women were admirably suited to the classroom," an observation that has invited to this day a mix of positive and negative analyses of gender roles and salaries.[30]

Beginning in 1863 with legislation written by John Swett, the state board of education became fully responsible for teacher examinations at all levels. However, the triumph of state authority was more apparent than real, as local school boards continued to hire and rehire teachers according to criteria they approved. Even as early as the 1860s, there was some modest advantage for teachers to pass the state examination, as contrasted with a county examination. While the locally prepared examinations generally were valid for just one year, the examinations established by the state authorized service for two, three, or four years, depending on the teacher's score. From the 1860s forward into the twentieth century, the counties exercised authority to issue certificates to elementary teachers.[31]

An obvious consequence of minimal preparation of teachers and easy access to the occupation was low status and little teacher independence from school committees in the management of schools. Established by state legislation passed in 1862, the State Normal School, a subcollegiate institution specifically designed for the preparation of teachers, constituted the first line in the training of teachers. The law provided that the state board of education, together with the city superintendents of schools in San Francisco, Sacramento, and Marysville, should be the board of trustees for the new school. What had changed, however, were only the governance structure and the funding source. The actual fledgling institution had existed since 1857 under San Francisco authority. In 1871 the institution moved to what was to become its permanent site in San Jose. Not until 1881 was the second such school authorized by the legislature, this one for Los Angeles.[32]

What has recently become known as "staff development" also began at an early date. Beginning in late December 1854, State Superintendent Paul Hubbs assumed initiative for convening the first state convention of teachers. The event was held in San Francisco and drew approximately one hundred teachers from most of the northern settlements of California. The program consisted of inspirational addresses, the sharing of stories about practice, discussions of ways to secure support for schools, and expressions of concern about salaries. Less than two years later, a second teachers' convention was held at Benicia, this time with about sixty teachers in attendance. Among the speakers was John A. Monroe, a United States commissioner at San Francisco,

The young women of Mills' Seminary, as Mills College was formerly called, gather for a delightfully informal portrait beneath the spreading limbs of an oak tree on the school grounds. Established in 1852 as the Benicia Seminary by Mary Atkins, and later purchased by Cyrus and Susan Mills, who moved the institution to Oakland, it was the first women's college in the Far West. *California Historical Society, FN-29897.*

who spoke about the need for "thorough training" as an essential for success in life. Others talked about the mission of females as teachers and about courses of study.

By 1861, the early staff-development approach received legislative support when State Superintendent Andrew Moulder received $3,000 to put on the first state teachers' institute, a three-day event attended by 250 teachers. Featured topics included a speech stressing the need for uniform state textbooks, a gymnastics demonstration, a discussion of school discipline, and a lecture on methods of teaching. This meeting, and similar institutes held in 1862 and 1863, emphasized the continuing need for greater public school funding. The symbolic sign of professional success was to be a publication, *The California Teacher,* which was published under various sponsorship between 1863 and 1876. By 1875, roughly the end of the gold-rush period, California teachers and principals were becoming numerous enough, resolute enough, and well organized enough to form the California Teachers Association (CTA), an organization that would become a potent force in the state's educational history from its first day to this.[33]

If the legislative session of 1866 may be thought of as producing the capstone achievement for the advance of elementary education late in the gold-rush days of California, the capstone event in higher education may be thought of as coming only a bit more than a year later. On March 21, 1868, a bill sponsored by Assemblyman John W. Dwinelle of Alameda County received legislative approval for the state to acquire the small, private College of California and to transform it into the public University of California. A week later, an appropriation bill followed, which made it possible for the university to operate, and a year after that, in 1869, it began operation at the College of California's site in Oakland.

The university brought with it a legacy rooted in the history of American higher education, including the classical traditions of the seventeenth and early eighteenth centuries. Late eighteenth- and early nineteenth-century influences produced greater egalitarian values in society and in higher education, but change was slow in coming. Such colleges as were established nationally until beyond the mid-nineteenth century favored the traditional liberal arts curriculum and the study of law and religion. Eventually, however, the practical necessity of forging a new nation based on a strong agricultural economy created a need for practical studies as well. Soon these contested for a place in the college curriculum. Congressional passage in 1862 of the first Morrill Act for the advancement of higher education in agricultural and mechanic arts granted public land to support state universities emphasizing that curriculum.

The Morrill Act was intended to change dramatically the focus of American higher education in favor of more practical studies. While it was largely successful in that regard over time, the power of classical education could not be set aside easily. The fate of state universities was not necessarily linked with practical studies. Although the University of California was founded shortly after passage of the Morrill Act, it patterned its early curriculum as much, arguably more, after the private colleges of the East. The leading western state university at the time was the University of Michigan, an institution that emphasized Greek and Latin, the natural sciences, mathematics, philosophy, and morals.

The experience of English influence on higher education in America dated back virtually to the founding of Harvard College in 1636. Thus, the desire and expectation for higher learning in America was well established prior to the American period in California. By 1850 the U.S. census reported 119 colleges, along with 44 theological seminaries, 36 medical schools, and 16 law schools.[34] Like its experience with elementary education, the state's establishing of private and public colleges hardly could be described as pioneering. However, they were substantial, and in less than a hundred years after its founding, the state university's new campus at Berkeley, first occupied in 1873, was described by objective observers of American higher education as, in the words of the American Council of Education, the "best balanced, distinguished university in the country."[35]

The story of the University of California's founding in 1868 starts at the beginning of the American period. Samuel H. Wiley, a Monterey Protestant clergyman, proposed in 1849 that a public university be established.[36] Soon Wiley acted on his ideals. An influential chaplain at the first constitutional convention, he may have influenced the authorization in the first constitution of funds from the sale and rental of state lands to support a university. Clearly, though, this constitutional authorization did not have an immediate impact. The legislature did in its first session in 1851 establish a university board and mandated that a site valued at no less than $20,000 be acquired. Almost immediately the new trustees acquired an offer of land in San Jose, but the Supreme Court found that offer unacceptable. The failure of this initial effort essentially ended the public effort until after passage of the first Morrill Act.

Private efforts to found colleges succeeded during the 1850s even as public effort failed. Wiley transferred his pastoral services from Monterey to San Francisco, where he established a close friendship with Henry Durant, a Yale graduate and Congregational minister. Together, in 1853, they and several other Congregational and Presbyterian clergy founded an academy-level institution offering classes for three students at a house in Oakland. Two years later they won a legislative charter and founded Contra Costa Academy, known after 1860 as the College of California. Notwithstanding that they appeared to have more space than students at their site in Oakland, Durant, Wiley, and their small band of sponsors sought to acquire a site that in the future would be worthy of an institution of moral and intellectual greatness. The pursuit was successful, and in 1858 they purchased a magnificent 140-acre site on both banks of Strawberry Creek in the Berkeley hills. The college remained in Oakland for more than a decade, however.

Durant became the college's first professor. The second was Martin Kellogg,

Joseph Le Conte, professor of geology and natural history, lectures to his class in South Hall at the University of California on a spring day in 1874. A student of Louis Agassiz's at Harvard, he arrived in California in 1869 and was for some years the only scholar with an international reputation to teach at the new university. Popular with his students—inspiring both Josiah Royce and Frank Norris in their formative years—he was not only an innovative scientific thinker but a great outdoorsman, who in 1870 made the first of many trips into the High Sierra. *Courtesy Bancroft Library.*

pastor of the First Congregational Church at Grass Valley and, beginning in 1868, professor of Latin and Greek at the newly transformed university. Both men went on to become important presidents of the University of California. Durant was the founding president and served until July 30, 1872, a year before the completion of the first building on the Berkeley campus. Kellogg was the seventh president and presided over the increasing growth of the institution during the 1890s.

Even as the college and later university's faculty was often resistant to the practical influences of the Morrill Act, the eventual transformation of the private College of California into a state-supported university was made possible by that act. It provided to each state 30,000 acres of public lands to public higher education

Sometime in the 1860s the San Francisco photographer Carleton E. Watkins traveled to the south end of the bay and made this rather forlorn image of Santa Clara College. Established in the old buildings of Mission Santa Clara de Asís in 1851 by the Jesuit priest John Nobili, it was the first institution of higher learning in the Golden State—though the nearby California Wesleyan University (University of the Pacific) was the first to receive a state charter. Four years earlier, an overland immigrant, Olive Mann Isbell, had opened the first American school in California at Santa Clara Mission. *California Historical Society, FN-05859.*

institutions, presumably devoted to the establishment of agriculture and mechanical arts. In 1868 Henry Durant was able to convince a state commission to merge the university with the College of California and to relocate it on the site of the college's recently acquired acreage in Berkeley. For the college's part, its board voted to convey to the University of California all its assets and debts, including the Berkeley land, and then to disincorporate. The approach worked, and California gained an institution with at least a semblance of maturity. When the new university opened in the fall of 1869, thirty-eight students began their study.[37] Agriculture and classical studies shared the curriculum.

Not only the College of California, but all efforts to begin collegiate-level instruction during California's gold-rush period were initiated from a religious influence. Even prior to the efforts of Congregationalists and Presbyterians to found the College of California, Methodists in 1851 had founded California Wesleyan College at San Jose, and later in the same year renamed it the College of the Pacific. In spite of significant financial challenges during its early years, the institution managed to stay open and thus deserves the distinction of being the longest-surviving college in California. Within the next two decades Catholics established four colleges in northern California—Santa Clara (1851), San Francisco (1855), St. Mary's (1855), and Notre Dame (1855). They also established a college in southern California, St. Vincent (1865), now Loyola Marymount University.

During their first twenty years under statehood, California citizens had created the initial and fledgling educational institutional structures that would serve them and succeeding generations for the balance of the nineteenth century and through the entire twentieth century. A public system of free elementary education was initiated and was gaining support. A normal school had been created for the training of teachers. A state university that would become the envy of the world was begun. The beginnings of a state-mandated curriculum were in evidence. Teachers were being tested and certified. Even as progress seemed slow and plodding to early public school activists, it looks more impressive to students of the state's history. If there is any other lesson in this story it is probably this: History flows in an ever-changing continuum, even as human needs and human nature seem to remain remarkably constant. Education in gold-rush California was the product of what went before and what was occurring at the time. The achievements were notable. So were the lapses and inequalities. The story is a continuing one, and one where hope and optimism have most often outdistanced despair and pessimism.

NOTES

1. Over the past twenty-five years there have been numerous doctoral dissertations and articles written on racial discrimination in California and the West. Among the most comprehensive, general, and accessible to the general reader are Charles M. Wollenberg, *All Deliberate Speed: Segregation and Exclusion in California Schools, 1855–1975* (Berkeley: University of California Press, 1976), and Irving G. Hendrick, *The Education of Non-Whites in California, 1849–1970* (San Francisco: R & E Research Associates, 1977).

2. Virtually all general histories of American education tell the story of the founding of the system of common schools. Likely the most comprehensive and objective of these is Lawrence A. Cremin, *American Education: The National Experience, 1783–1876* (New York: Harper & Row, 1980).

3. California, *Constitution*, 1849, Article IX.

4. William B. Spring, "The Influence of Interest Groups on Educational Legislation in California" (Ed.D. diss., Stanford University, 1963), 45.

5. Irving G. Hendrick, *California Education: A Brief History* (San Francisco: Boyd & Fraser, 1980), 7.

6. The first hundred years in the development of the California state department of education is told in Leighton H. Johnson, *Development of the Central State Agency for Public Education in California, 1849–1949* (Albuquerque: University of New Mexico Press, 1952).

7. California Legislature, *Journal of the Senate*, First Session, December 20, 1849, p. 20. A full discussion of this earliest period for public education is found in two excellent sources: David F. Ferris, *Judge Marvin and the Founding of the California Public School System*, University of California Publications in Education, vol. 14 (Berkeley: University of California Press, 1962), 51–52; and William W. Ferrier, *Ninety Years of Education in California, 1846–1936* (Berkeley: Sather Gate Book Shop, 1937).

8. California Superintendent of Public Instruction, *First Annual Report of the Superintendent of Public Instruction* (1852), 45. This source is also quoted in Ferris, *Judge Marvin and the Founding of the California Public School System*, 72.

9. Ferris, *Judge Marvin and the Founding of the California Public School System*, 138.

10. See Ferris, *Judge Marvin and the Founding of the California Public School System*, 55.

11. Ferrier, *Ninety Years of Education in California*, 35–40. This was the first, and arguably is still the best and most comprehensive, narrative history of early California education yet written.

12. California Superintendent of Public Instruction, *First Annual Report*, 45.

13. John Bigler, "Governor's Special Message to the Senate and Assembly of California, Benicia, January 31, 1854," *Appendix to Assembly Journal* (Sacramento, 1854).

14. Roy W. Cloud, *Education in California* (Stanford: Stanford University Press, 1952), 27. No book published to date about education in California contains as much detailed information for the period between 1849 and 1949 as this book by a former executive secretary of the California Teachers Association.

15. Cloud, *Education in California*, 38.

16. Spring, "Influence of Interest Groups on Educational Legislation," 58.

17. Ibid., 54.

18. John Swett, *History of the Public School System of California* (San Francisco: A. L. Bancroft, 1876), 31.

19. Hendrick, *California Education*, 10; California Superintendent of Public Instruction, *Annual Report* (1858), in *Appendix to Senate Journal* (Sacramento, 1858), 7.

20. *Proceedings of the California State Convention of Colored Citizens held in Sacramento on the 25th, 26th, 27th, and 28th of October, 1865* (San Francisco: Office of *The Elevator*, 1865), 78–81, 95, 99, 100, as cited in Irving G. Hendrick, *Public Policy Toward the Education of Non-White Minority Group Children, 1849–1970: Final Report* (Riverside: School of Education, University of California, Riverside, 1975), 33.

21. Rudolph M. Lapp, "Jeremiah B. Sanderson: Early California Negro Leader," *Journal of Negro History* 53 (October 1968): 321–33; Sue Baily Thurman, *Pioneers of Negro Origin in California* (San Francisco: Acme Publishing Co., 1952), 37–40.

22. Thurman, *Pioneers of Negro Origin*, 40.

23. Although cases have been made for the first state superintendent of public instruction (John Gage Marvin) and the third (Andrew Moulder) being honored as the founders of California's public school system, that honor is most frequently assigned to the fourth state superintendent, John Swett, owing to the significance of the school law of 1866. In addition to his biennial reports as state superintendent of public instruction and numerous contributions to state education journals, Swett also wrote *Public Education in California* (New York:

American Book Co., 1911). Biographies about him include William G. Carr, *John Swett: The Biography of an Educational Pioneer* (Santa Ana: Fine Arts Press, 1933), and Nicholas C. Polos, *John Swett: California's Frontier Schoolmaster* (Washington, D.C.: University Press of America, 1978).

24. Ferrier, *Ninety Years of Education in California*, 12.

25. Cloud, *Education in California*, 42.

26. Hendrick, *Education of Non-Whites in California*, 17.

27. California, Statutes, chap. 342, sec. 56 (1866), and quoted in Hendrick, *Education of Non-Whites in California*, 16.

28. Rudolph M. Lapp, "The Negro in Gold Rush California," *The Journal of Negro History* 49 (April 1964): 85–86.

29. Ferrier, *Ninety Years of Education in California*, 12.

30. Kathleen Weiler, *Country Schoolwomen: Teaching in Rural California, 1850–1950* (Stanford: Stanford University Press, 1998), 36–38.

31. The long and often changing state experience with credentialing teachers has been told in numerous doctoral dissertations over the past five decades. The most detailed and comprehensive explication is found in Ralph E. Brott, Jr., "The Cyclical Nature of Education Reform: A Case Analysis of Educator Certification in California" (Ph.D. diss., University of California, Berkeley, 1989).

32. Cloud, *Education in California*, 49–50, 80.

33. Ibid., 63.

34. Cremin, *American Education: The National Experience, 1783–1876*, 400.

35. Hendrick, *California Education*, 55.

36. Likely still the best source of information concerning the earliest history of the University of California is one of the oldest: William W. Ferrier, *Origin and Development of the University of California* (Berkeley: Sather Gate Book Shop, 1930).

37. Hendrick, *California Education*, 50–52; Ferrier, *Ninety Years of Education in California*, 177–87.

10

Phelan's Cemetery

Religion in the Urbanizing West, 1850–1869,
in Los Angeles, San Francisco, and Sacramento

Steven M. Avella

A tremendous explosion shook the bustling city of Sacramento at about noon on January 27, 1854. Within a few hundred feet of docking at the city wharves, the steamer *Pearl*, en route from Marysville, blew up, hurling bodies and debris into the air. Fifty-five people died in the blast, and most of the one hundred or so passengers sustained some sort of injury. The power and frightfulness of the explosion shook the city to its foundations. "Our city is overshadowed by gloom," wrote Sacramento physician Gregory J. Phelan as he related the tragedy to readers of the *New York Freeman.* On the day of the burial of the victims, businesses closed and the streets were draped in black bunting. The legislature adjourned to attend the funeral and more than three thousand marched to the Sacramento city cemetery. In the procession were the Sacramento Pioneer Associates, members of the legislature, fire companies, Hebrew Society, temperance societies, Odd Fellows, Free Masons, and Chinese immigrants. Phelan related:

> All the dead were buried in the City Cemetery. Perhaps in no country could a similar scene be exhibited. Christians of various denominations and Pagans, each with their peculiar rites and ceremonies, placed in the earth almost side by side.
>
> While the voices of the choir resounded through the air, the sounds of the strange strains of Chinese music fell upon the ear. And while the ministers of various denominations were discoursing of the sad event which caused this vast assemblage, and were offering up prayers to the one only God, the disciples of Confucius were chanting their services, providing a feast for the departed spirits, and preparing them for that unknown journey [from] whence no traveler returns. . . .[1]

The imagery of this powerful cemetery scene evokes so many realities of early American California: the fragility of life, the heterogeneity of the population, and the spontaneity with which the highly individualistic community came together in the wake of a common tragedy. The funeral services also encapsulated a unique moment in the religious world of Californians, and one could reasonably speculate as to what was running through their minds as they beheld these rituals. To the strongly Roman Catholic Phelan, the strangeness of it all is clear from the tone of his writing. No doubt practitioners of the other religious traditions represented at the grave site were similarly bemused or intrigued by the behavior of those around them. Among the mourners were certainly those who had no particular religious affiliation at all, and the state of their minds would not find its way into any denominational journal dedicated to reporting on the state of religion in the West. Whatever the people's reactions, in Phelan's cemetery, with its cacophonous rituals for the dead, we have a snapshot of the realities of religion in the American West.

ELEMENTS OF RELIGION IN THE AMERICAN WEST

To some degree, regional realities have always defined the meridian of religious life in America.[2] Puritanism subsisted within a New England shell. Evangelical religion is often best understood against a southern backdrop. In the American West, this is also the case, for as historians Ferenc Szasz and Margaret Connell Szasz observe, "The vastness of this immense territory, with its many ecological subregions, provided a multitude of homes for native belief systems, as well as for the diverse faiths brought by European, African, and Asian immigrants."[3] Into this diverse geographical and cultural container, with its extensive spatial distances and peculiar patterns of migration, poured a plethora of religious beliefs, customs, rituals, and institutions.[4] Without exhausting the list of regional variables, one can note the distinctiveness of some: the diversity of native tribal cultures; the spatial distances that provided shelter and isolation for religious outsiders, such as the Mormons; and the presence of Latino, Asian, and even Russian communities, with their religious traditions. In the cyclotron of these conditions, these groups constantly collided with one another, jarring each other's sensibilities and carefully constructed theologies, cosmologies, and philosophies. The collision among these competing realities sometimes evoked negative reactions, but more often than not, and to the dismay of many co-religionists in the East, it created a live-and-let-live mentality that made the West a natural home to a wide spectrum of religious beliefs and philosophies.[5] No doubt this was also facilitated by the sheer distance that separated settlers from the social controls of their home nations or cities, weakening denominational ties and producing some of the lowest rates of church membership and attendance in America. "When I left home in Missouri," one miner told Methodist William Taylor, "I hung my religious cloak on my gate-post until I should return."[6]

A northern Maidu binds a corpse as part of a ritual used both in burial and cremation. The diversity of religious customs among the native tribes of California anticipated the complex mosaic of beliefs and ceremonies brought to El Dorado by peoples of different faiths from every quarter of the globe. *California Historical Society, FN-31549.*

CALIFORNIA

In California many of these larger regional trends were concentrated, and all of them had a bearing on its religious development. The state's geographical diversity provided a multitude of different settings and backdrops for religious expression.[7] California's cultural geography was equally complex, including Native American, Hispanic, a myriad of European American groups, and Asian communities, all of which produced a bewildering (at least for an easterner) array of religious systems.

What especially distinguishes California's regional environment were the conditions of its population growth. Here, not only the massive influx of people brought by the Gold Rush, but also the materialism that undergirded this movement, provided an important challenge to traditional religious values.[8] "The Americans think only of dollars, talk only of dollars, seek nothing but dollars," wrote one Catholic priest of the Argonauts; "they are the men of dollars."[9] The disgusted cleric noted not only the material preoccupation of the Argonauts, but also their overwhelming male gender and perhaps their youth as facts significantly affecting the shape of religion in the Golden State.

California's peculiar, pioneer religious pattern has been a hearty perennial interest of denominational historians.[10] More recently, historians anxious to provide a "thick(er) description" of California life have attempted to ascertain the interplay of California's distinctive environment with the religious experience of its various inhabitants and to "write in" the religious component of California's larger past.[11] One of the earliest examples of this was William Hanchett, whose unpublished 1952 doctoral dissertation examined the role of Christian churches in the Gold Rush. Hanchett's research sought to determine whether religion either brought about social stability on the gold mining frontier, or was a beneficiary or product of a gradual process of "civilization." Hanchett concluded the latter, but his work provided an early example of attempts to intersect religion with the wider sphere of life in California.[12]

In that same vein, Tamar (Sandra) Sizer Frankiel's slender volume, *California's Spiritual Frontiers* (1988), used the realities of geography and climate to offer some provocative suggestions about the spiritual and denominational liberation many religiously strait-jacketed Argonauts and seekers of health experienced when they came to the sunny climes of the West Coast.[13] Kevin Starr and Laurie Maffly-Kipp have used the social and cultural backdrop of gold-rush California to explain why, despite the prodigious efforts of an erudite, eloquent, and well-heeled ministry, the New England Protestant establishment was unable to build a new "city on a hill" on the shores of the Pacific.[14] Historians of the Asian American experience, such as Sucheng Chan, testify to the importance of religious institutions in establishing a foothold for these "exotic" faith traditions on California soil.[15] All of these historians grasp the same essential insight: namely, that religion in the West is indeed, according to Kevin Starr's term, the "Great Exception."[16] Some have suggested that the study of California's dynamic diversity and distinctiveness, paradigmatic of the entire Pacific Slope, might very well stimulate a major reinterpretation of the controlling narratives of American religious history.[17]

Deeply indebted to the work of those historians, the essay at hand seeks to integrate California's religious heritage into the wider framework of the state's social and cultural history by examining the role of religion in shaping the urban cultures of Los Angeles, San Francisco, and Sacramento.[18] Each of these cities would merit a monograph on the subject of religion and urban culture, and here the limits of space provide the opportunity for only the proverbial "lick and a promise." Nonetheless, urban communities provide the best laboratories to examine the interplay of religion with the environment. Within their boundaries the full spectrum of religious activity—indeed the sacralization of the soil—took place. The chronological boundaries of this essay take us from the flux of the gold-rush era to a moment of "settling" symbolized by the completion of the transcontinental railroad in 1869, a defining moment in California's history.

Religious communities and institutions in these cities played an important role in rooting culture in the barbarous soil of California. First and foremost, they reflected the deepest beliefs and aspirations of the men and women who adhered to them. In this essay, religion and religious sensibilities are not treated as epiphenomena that served as a substitute for "real" underlying economic or social concerns. Rather, it takes seriously the claims of the devotees and faithful practitioners that these religious beliefs helped them make sense of life's most profound questions and transitions and connected them to the supernatural. In early California, religion was often the only framework of meaning in a sometimes confusing and chaotic world. Witness, for example, the sentiments of some who thought the discovery of gold in California was a providential event with millennial implications. "Why sir," asked E. L. Cleaveland writing in *Home Missionary*, "were the immense treasures of California hidden from all the world, even the keen-scented Spaniard, until she was annexed to this Republic? And tell me, if anyone can, why it was that the title deed of transference had no sooner passed into our hands, than she gave up her mighty secret, and unlocked her golden gate. Is it possible not to see the hand of God in all this?"[19] Religion also provided an important impetus for moral and ethical conduct and a spur to action. William Hanchett suggests the intensity of the spiritual motivation of gold-rush-era clergy when he notes, "the concern of the Christian Churches, both Protestant and Catholic, to get missionaries into Gold Rush California, was in direct proportion to the eagerness of Argonauts all over the world to get there."[20]

Yet, in their essentially spiritual quest, religious institutions and communities were not hermetically sealed from the world around them, and the distinctions between the sacred and the secular were often erased. Although often undertaken for the highest spiritual purposes, the activity of religious people had a significant impact on the urban milieu. For example, religious institutions invested in city property by building schools and hospitals, helped to create social peace, and occasionally attempted to influence local politics.[21] One San Francisco businessman expressed the social importance of religion perfectly when he welcomed a newly arrived minister in 1849 by observing that "Property is worth more under the Gospel, life is safer, community is happier—we can't do without it."[22]

A comprehensive history of religion and life in California has yet to be written, but a review of city-booster publications, monographs, articles, and dissertations suggests similar patterns of religious development in most of California's cities with the onset of the Gold Rush. Native American and Hispanic Catholic religious worlds were overwhelmed by the rush of new settlers and gold miners and were either pushed aside or forced out of existence, although in some places, like Los Angeles, Hispanic Catholicism held on. Enthusiastic evangelical Protestants, funded by mission societies in the East, dispatched missionaries to California, determined to make the West a new "city on a hill." San Francisco provided the common port of entry for most of them (although a few came overland), and these doughty men of God began their work by preaching in the Bay City and quickly moved to establish temporary and later more permanent houses of worship.[23] Boarding river steamers, missionaries next moved to the supply cities of the gold country—Sacramento, Stockton, and Marysville—replicating these same patterns of preaching, organizing, and building. From there they moved to the more remote mining camps or cities, preaching and exhorting as conditions warranted. Catholic missionaries appeared simultaneously, recruited along with Catholic immigrants from a variety of countries, and determined to revivify, modify, and assume control of the remnants of Hispanic Catholicism. Jews, Mormons, and Chinese religious communities mobilized as well to carve out their respective niches in the burgeoning El Dorado. Like their Protestant counterparts, these "outsiders" made their collective presence felt as they too preached, organized congregations, and built churches. All religious groups experienced the same process of interaction with California's polyglot population: initial transitory encounters with interested or homesick Argonauts, which ultimately evolved into more stable and permanent relationships within settled and financially secure congregations. When the gold fever ended and urban life became more settled, a greater institutional visibility for religious communities resulted in new, permanent (and sometimes very impressive) church buildings, Sunday schools, benevolent societies, elementary schools, separate academies for boys and girls, and social welfare institutions. Virtually all of these patterns are to be found in the case studies of this essay: Los Angeles, San Francisco, and Sacramento.

Yet, we must again remind ourselves, important differences exist among these cities that make sweeping generalizations highly perilous. Since the regional culture around each of them was so different, the role and function of religion in city-building varied from place to place. What follows is a sample of some of the ways religious belief systems and institutions affected the development of these communities.

LOS ANGELES: RELIGION AND CULTURAL PERSISTENCE

Much changed with the American takeover of California in 1848. In southern California, the new American administration brought about significant changes to the land-holding and economic life of the powerful Spanish/Mexican rancheros who had so defined and controlled the order of things in earlier times. These grandees of the old order felt quickly the effects of the American regime—especially in redefining their relationship and rights to the lands they had accumulated under Mexican rule. Lured by soaring gold-rush-era food prices, rancheros were weaned from largely subsistence activities to market farming and large-scale cattle ranching, were compelled for the first time to pay property taxes on their holdings, and ultimately found their rights to the land challenged by American property and boundary regulations.[24] These changes also dramatically altered the relationship between the once mostly self-sufficient ranchos and the sleepy pueblo of Los Angeles. As the ranchos dissolved into commercial enterprises and small farms with even greater productivity, the importance of the city as a processing and commercial center increased proportionally. Los Angeles's population grew steadily from 1,610 in 1850 to 5,738 in 1870, with most of this increase coming from an influx of American settlers. Los Angeles was then fixed on the path of urbanization, a process that would culminate with the arrival of a transcontinental railroad in 1876. These developments ultimately relegated the community's distinctively Hispanic elements to "picturesque" status. However, as much as the world shifted around them, the older Californio culture would persist, to some extent, through a continued adherence to Roman Catholic folk religion. Catholicism's rituals and way of life provided one avenue of cultural resistance to the onset of Americanization. The proof of this was the inability of mainline evangelical churches, often seen as agents of Americanization, to gain much beyond a toehold in the city of the Angels.

"It is important to bear in mind," writes historian Michael Engh, "that southern California was a frontier that stood as an exception to the patterns of religious pioneering in the United States."[25] Indeed, Protestant evangelical groups had tried in vain since the 1850s to thrive in Los Angeles. Part of the reason for this was, of course, the lure of the gold fields of the north. This made it difficult for early Los Angeles to attract and retain a permanent Protestant presence through the 1850s and 1860s. Few Anglo-Americans wished to live in Los Angeles at this time, and the Protestant denominations, even those with strong records of adaptability to frontier locations, such as the Methodists, did not have a critical mass of men and women to sustain worship and institutional growth. Moreover, Protestant ministers who did come with any hopes of converting the locals (and this was never a priority with Anglo-Protestants) were hampered by their inability to speak Spanish. As a result, there was no permanent Protestant establishment in Los Angeles until Old School Presbyterian minister James Woods succeeded in incorporating a church in 1854. However, even Woods was unable to sustain the fledgling congregation and it languished, unable to finish a church building until 1862. Woods's experience was not unique, for as Engh observes, "Methodist, Baptist, Presbyterian church leaders had dispatched dedicated clergymen to serve the spiritual needs in Los Angeles, only to see one divine after another give up the demoralizing field."[26] What demoralized Protestant evangelicals even more was the visible presence of Roman Catholicism in the city. The discomfit that church brought to the traditionally anti-Catholic Yankees who visited the community is evident in a letter of a federal land commissioner from Vermont, Hiland Hall. Hall wrote of a Sunday festival in honor of the Virgin Mary that he witnessed in September 1852. "This is Sunday morning, and the manner in which the day has been spent in the City of the Angels forms such a contrast with that which I have been accustomed in North Bennington. . . . In the first place there is no church in this city except a Catholic one, and in the second Sunday is regarded by everybody here only as a day of exemption from labor and devotion to amusements and frolicking." Hall related the noises and sounds of the festal celebrations in the city plaza and his attendance at a celebratory bull fight. Some of it seemed to have intrigued him, but to his correspondent he wrote, "The ringing of bells and firing of cannon as a part of religious worship on Sunday seems rather odd to me."[27]

What was the nature of the Catholic presence in Los Angeles that so repelled Hall, and how was it able to mount such a spirited resistance to Protestant migration? European religion had entered California with the Spanish mission chain in 1769. These proto-religious institutions have been discussed at length in any number of publications. The culture of Hispanic Catholicism that emanated from these highly successful evangelical centers, with the support of the secular state, infused itself into the bloodstream of Los Angeles for years to come. This culture, a variant of the dynamic Counter-Reformation Catholicism of Spain, included not only doctrinal formulations but also Catholic notions of sacramentality, public celebration, and syncretic practice.[28] Even after the collapse of Spanish colonial power in 1821, the secularization of the missions in the 1830s, and the subsequent importation of a native Mexican clergy into California, the Catholic ethos and holding power persisted over the Californios, who dominated California until the American takeover.

The persistence of Hispanic religion as a counterweight to Anglo-American domination is not accepted by all. Some have suggested that Hispanic religious practices, because they were so integrated into daily life, lacked the same intensity as evangelical religions.[29] The fact is, however, that the vibrancy and depth of this religious culture was not always evident in statistics of sacramental activity, or even in financial contributions. Rather, it manifested itself in other cultural expressions characteristic of Hispanic Catholics: devotion to the Virgin, participation in religious fiestas, and a strong home-based practice of religion, exemplified by home altars and private devotion. Historian Leonard Pitt discussed the complexity of the religious world of the Californios, who benefited directly from the collapse of the mission system and had never reattached to a new religious organization with secular clergy and a local bishop. Moreover, Californios did not attend Mass and disdained priests. Indeed, Catholicism was perhaps in a "medium state" as Pitt suggested, but its popular and cultural expression (which drove Protestants such as James Woods to distraction and mutterings of "idolatry, idolatry, idolatry") was very much alive. "Most of their [the Californios'] enjoyments," wrote Pitt, "were formalized and communal. Saint's days and other religious holidays took a great deal of planning."[30] The city plaza continued to be the site of public religious display, including the elaborate Corpus Christi processions with benedictions given at three altars, the Christmas reenactment of *Los Pastorales,* and celebratory bull fights on the August 15th cele-

The Church of Nuestra Señora la Reina de los Angeles, located on the west side of the dusty, sun-soaked Los Angeles Plaza, about 1869, not long after the Gothic bell tower was constructed. Designed by the carpenter José Antonio Ramirez and built by neophytes from the missions of San Gabriel, San Diego, and San Luis Rey, the church was completed in 1822. Still used today, it has dominated the heart of old Los Angeles for the better part of two centuries. *California Historical Society/Title Insurance and Trust Photo Collection, University of Southern California.*

bration of the Assumption of Mary.[31] In fact, one might argue that the symbolic power of these Catholic symbols was so pervasive that the Protestant establishment resurrected them, pruned of their creedal elements, as tools in marketing the region.[32]

It is important to note that even the Catholic Church was not immune to the forces of Americanization sweeping other areas of Los Angeles life. Religious reorganization of the pueblo in the American period had already begun with its former Mexican bishop, Francisco Garcia Diego y Moreno. In 1853, Vincentian Thaddeus Amat, a Spaniard who had served in Philadelphia, was appointed to the new bishopric of Monterey, and by 1859, he had moved his episcopal headquarters to the heavily Catholic city of Los Angeles.[33] Amat, according to historian Jeffrey Burns, was hardly sympathetic to the folkways of the residual Mexican religion and sought, through the creation of institutions such as schools, hospitals, and orphanages, to "Americanize" the pueblo world around him, to make it more in keeping with the diverse immigrant Catholics—Irish, Germans, French, and Italians—moving into Los Angeles. However, Amat, like other American bishops confronting strong ethnic groups, came to realize the limits of his episcopal power. Burns further observes that fiestas and other ancient practices went on despite his opposition.[34] Hispanic Catholic practice, like many other forms of popular religion, did not die because of clerical opposition.

Ultimately the ethos of Hispanic Catholicism would wane as the supporting Mexican civilization weakened. The community was eventually detached from its former cultural moorings as new demands for public order, sanitation, and education began to be voiced by increasing numbers of American and European settlers who sought consciously to Americanize and improve the backwards pueblo. The new social and political structures of the city were responsive to these demands, and local leaders and others eager to move Los Angeles along the path of greater urban development lamented the absence of a visible Protestant establishment. Evidence of this is historian Robert Fogelson's observation that the local press "appealed to missionary groups for assistance and at the same time urged the residents of Los Angeles to form their own religious institutions."[35]

Interestingly, the Jews and Chinese appeared to fare better in making headway in establishing their presence in Los Angeles. Judaism had been able to carve itself an early place in the religious world of the emerging city. In 1854, a Hebrew Benevolent Society was founded that gave the first institutional expression to the "Israelites" of Los Angeles. Lay rabbi Joseph Newmark, from Poland, was the catalyst for the growing religious identity of the small group, and under his leadership, dietary laws were able to be observed, weddings and funerals could be conducted, and the high holy days could be observed. Newmark and others took the initiative to invite Wolf Edelman to become the first permanent rabbi and teacher for Congregation B'nai B'rith in 1862. Los Angeles's small Jewish community, which had only numbered eight in the 1850 census, was by the 1860s well over two hundred. A closely knit group, this community intersected with larger Los Angeles life through business relationships, fraternal organizations, politics, and public charity.

Chinese Angelenos also figured into the mixture of religious identity in the emerging city. The numbers were small. The 1860 population of Chinese was only 16—14 men and 2 women. By 1870 that number had grown to 170. Huddled together in a small residential district south of the plaza, most of the Chinese were manual laborers—doing laundry, cooking, and cleaning. Inferences about their religious systems suggest that they continued to practice the traditional folk religion of their region of China. This did not include weekly worship services, but did involve the lighting of joss sticks or the burning of paper money to attract the favor of a particular deity. Occasionally, Asian faith spilled out onto the streets with celebrations of the lunar New Year and other calendar festivals.[36]

In the 1860s, the culture of early American Los Angeles was to some extent still determined by the strength of popular Hispanic Catholicism. Yet the power of these symbols was also reinforced by the relatively slow growth of population in the former pueblo. A very different set of circumstances developed north of the Tehachapis where the "world rushed in" in quest of gold.

SAN FRANCISCO: SOCIAL SERVICES, CULTURAL CONFLICT, AND AMERICANIZATION

Northern California was the cockpit of early California's growth and the heartland of its later religious diversity. The cities of the Gold Rush share a common historical trajectory, all of them springing into being virtually simultaneously in response to the intense commercial needs generated quickly by the Gold Rush. The representatives of at least forty nations gathered in these "instant cities" and in them were the visible representations of California's early culture—its public facilities, bars, brothels, commercial houses, and its churches. In these cities, we see even more vividly the role of religious bodies as agents of urbanization. They provided important social welfare functions, enhanced the value of urban property through the construction of churches, schools, and colleges, raised the moral and intellectual tone of the communities, created outlets for cultural expression, and provided anchors for the forces of development. San Francisco and Sacramento especially embodied these developments. Greater or lesser variations on these themes could be found in other gold-rush cities such as Marysville and Stockton and even larger towns in the heart of the mining activity such as Grass Valley and Nevada City.

San Francisco was a commercial village of about 1,000 denizens in 1848. Two years later, the seekers of El Dorado caused the village to blossom into a city of 34,776. Ten years later, the number had arisen to 56,802 and by 1870, to 149,473. The city rapidly developed a strong economic base, becoming the most important financial center of the American West and a transportation hub for ocean-bound and inland-bound trade, as well as the source for supplies to the ever increasing demands of the mining frontier. Manufacturing and other forms of commercial activity secured the city's economic hegemony not only over the economy of northern California, but over the entire Pacific Coast and the inland West as far as the Rocky Mountains. The composition of its population made it one of the most cosmopolitan cities in the nation. By 1860 it was the third largest center of immigration in the United States. Out of its 57,000 residents, nearly 3,000 were Chinese and 2,000 were African

Americans. By 1870 one out of every three San Franciscans was a native of Ireland, Germany, China, or Italy. The Irish would dominate the immigrant mix of the city for much of the nineteenth century, followed by the Germans and the Chinese. The massive influx of people to San Francisco, many of them in transit to the Mother Lode, created for a time a climate of social disorder, or at least instability. In this turbulent context, religion and religious institutions rendered important civic functions that assisted the processes of city stabilization and building.

Like Los Angeles, San Francisco "was born Catholic," as the former Mission Dolores formed the core of a pueblo.[37] Indeed, the Catholicity of the missions initially so thoroughly penetrated the local culture that a visiting Russian characterized the city's inhabitants as "religious fanatics."[38] The first infusion of American religionists were two hundred Mormons under Samuel Brannan, who landed in Yerba Buena in 1846, doubling the population of the community. California, with its burgeoning gold-rush populations creating critical masses of potential churchgoers, stimulated not only the appetites of those who sought gold, but also of the minions of evangelical and apostolic-minded Christian denominations.[39] Imbued with the zeal of reforming evangelical Protestantism, home missionary societies carried the torch for ministerial action in the land of El Dorado.[40] San Francisco was the first port of call for those who were sent to organize the pioneering foundations of the thriving churches of the East.

Among the first missionaries was Timothy Dwight Hunt, a New School Presbyterian who arrived from Honolulu in 1848 and accepted the post of "city chaplain." He was followed in 1849 by a veritable galaxy of ministers. The America Home Missionary Society sent Samuel Hopkins Willey and John W. Douglas. The Baptists dispatched Osgood Church Wheeler, while Sylvester Woolbridge represented Old School Presbyterians. A second Old School Presbyterian, Albert Williams, came to San Francisco in March 1849. Flavel S. Mines, Episcopalian, opened a church in response to private appeal, while Jean L. Van Mehr succeeded in his wake and opened Grace Episcopal in December 1849. Northern Methodist missionaries William Taylor and Isaac Owen showed up in September 1849, Taylor coming by sea and Owen by oxcart overland. Southern Methodists Jesse Boring, D. W. Pollock, and A. M. Wynn made their appearance in April 1850. In 1860, San Francisco's Unitarian pulpit was filled by one of the state's most eloquent and dynamic clergymen, Thomas Starr King.[41]

Institutional maturity came quickly. The Presbyterians formed the Presbytery of San Francisco in May 1849, retaining an attachment to the Synod of New York and New Jersey until 1857. In 1851, Old School Presbyterians organized the Presbytery of California, and a group of Cumberland Presbyterians established a presbytery in April of the same year. The Congregationalists formed an association in 1852, and in August 1850, the Episcopalians organized the Diocese of California under the leadership of the refined William Ingraham Kip. A San Francisco Baptist Association

Worshipers gather outside the first Baptist church erected in San Francisco, a simple foursquare frame meeting house on Washington Street, which might have been prefabricated in the East and shipped 'round the Horn. One Argonaut wrote home from San Francisco in December 1849 that "heaven is not quite forgotten here in this worldly place." He noted that numerous churches had sprung up in the gold-rush boomtown and, attending an Episcopal Christmas service, was pleased to find it "filled with a most respectable audience who responded well and sang the songs in harmony." *Courtesy Huntington Library, San Marino, Calif.*

followed in October 1850.

Roman Catholics did not have homegrown missionary societies, but many Catholic missions were supported by the French-based Society for the Propagation of the Faith and other European fund-raising enterprises. More importantly, the church had a centralized system of missionary endeavors in Rome, the *Propaganda Fidei,* which monitored and coordinated global Catholic missionary enterprises. *Propaganda* had long known about California's spiritual conditions through the comprehensive reporting of priests and prelates in the East. Locally, the Franciscan order's administrator of the old Mexican diocese, Gonzales Rubio, hearing of the rapid increase of the population in the north, petitioned various bishops and religious communities to dispatch priests to California. Three missionaries of the Sacred Hearts of Jesus and Mary, known popularly as Picpus Fathers, arrived in San Francisco in

March 1850. By the end of the year, they were joined by four other clerical comrades. Catholicism had already carved out a place for itself through the presence of Mission Dolores, founded in 1776. In 1850 the Spanish Dominican, Joseph Sadoc Alemany, was appointed the first bishop of Alta California. His headquarters were initially at the old colonial capital of Monterey; however, three years later Alemany moved to San Francisco and became the first archbishop of that city. Alemany built the infrastructure of Catholic life in San Francisco during the 1850s and provided his rapidly growing flock with parish churches, schools, orphanages, and hospitals. Catholic churches made this growing presence visible. A network of ethnic parishes developed that attempted to accommodate the diverse, but heavily Irish, population. St. Francis (1849), St. Patrick's (1851), St. Mary's (1854), St. Joseph (1861), St. Brigid's (1863), and St. Peter's (1867) were for the Irish. Notre Dame des Victoires (1856) was for the French, and St. Boniface (1860) served the Germans.[42]

Chinese Argonauts began to appear in large numbers in 1850 and San Francisco's Chinese population grew thereafter. Their cultic life included an observance emerging from South China, a devotion to the Queen of Heaven, who assumed the role of a female protector of sailors and was worshipped in many parts of China.[43] Even more important was the cult of Guan Yu, also known as Guan Gong, a male heroic figure of the Three Kingdoms who was "honored and worshiped by people across China for his courage, his loyalty, and faithfulness." To the Chinese, Guan Gong's red-faced and black-bearded image was "the most popular of all Gods. Few white visitors to Chinatown failed to notice his existence." Chinese visitors recognized the importance of Guan Gong to the local San Francisco Chinese population. When the Burlingame delegation came to San Francisco in 1868, its Chinese officials paid their respects at the temple of Guan Gong.[44]

Mormons also established a presence in the city (despite the defection of Sam Brannan) when Parley P. Pratt, president of the Mormon Pacific Mission, organized a church in 1851. Jews from Poland and Germany established Congregation Sherith Israel in 1850, and later that year southern German Jews established Temple Emanu-el. Spiritualism as well made serious inroads in San Francisco's population; twenty Spiritualist circles were reported in 1852. By 1856, there was a total of two Jewish, six Catholic, and twenty-two Protestant houses of worship in the city. San Francisco's rapid growth and sometimes tumultuous urban culture provided the context for the development of these religious institutions and communities.

All of this religious development occurred as the city itself was struggling to forge its urban culture. This complex process included a great deal of struggle and a sorting out of winners and losers, as diverse citizens determined who would rule the economic, political, and social life of San Francisco. Religious issues and sensibilities played a role in this process, especially during the stormy decade of the 1850s. Evangelical Protestants in particular were determined to make San Francisco the test ground for the replication of the religious values of New England, and initially they had the upper hand. However, as the balance of immigration began to tip more in favor of the Irish and the Germans, and San Francisco's population took on more of a Catholic tone, social conflict developed.

The rise of anti-Catholic Know Nothingism in California between 1854 and 1856, although somewhat altered from its manifestation elsewhere, was felt in the emerging urban politics of San Francisco.[45] Know Nothingism enjoyed significant electoral success in California in the mid-1850s even though its anti-Catholic message was somewhat blunted in San Francisco. Nonetheless, it had the effect of galvanizing Protestant opposition to rising Catholic power in the city. These feelings were brought to expression in the revival of vigilantism in 1856. Although the motivation for this movement admits of a variety of interpretations, Patrick Blessing argues convincingly that the tactics and violence of the 1856 vigilantes were motivated in large measure by evangelical Protestants anxious to challenge the rising presence of the Catholic Irish, whom they detested. Congregational and New School Presbyterians from New England in particular, Blessing argues, had an "anti-Catholic obsession . . . that filled the pages of the two newspapers of the American Home Mission Society, *The Pacific* and *The Home Missionary*."[46] Ultimately the victory for dominance would go to the more numerous Catholics.[47] Protestant historian Douglas Firth Anderson observes that indeed "native born Protestant merchants exercised hegemony in early San Francisco society, first economically, then politically through the Committee of Vigilance of 1856, and the consequent People's Party." "Yet," Anderson asserts, "this hegemony was permeable, and it was singularly muted religiously as time went on."[48] Protestantism would be a minority faith in San Francisco well into the twentieth century.[49]

By contrast with Hispanic Los Angeles, San Francisco's Catholicism was heavily Hibernian and was strongly drawn toward assimilation with the larger culture.[50] Historian R. A. Burchell noted the importance of the church for the Irish community. "The Church itself recognized its social roles that ran beyond its religious one and symptomatically became the center of a system of associations that revolved around it."[51] Sodalities—devotional, fraternal, and benevolent—were all part of a thriving Catholic culture and exercised a sphere of influence within the larger community. San Francisco did not lay down any bars against Catholic upward ascendancy in either the political or commercial realm. Frank McCoppin, the first Irish-Catholic mayor, was elected in 1867. The number of seats in Catholic churches grew from 6,050 in 1860 to 21,000 in 1870.[52] "Our Countrymen need not fear," said the Irish-Catholic *San Francisco Monitor* in 1869, "that they will have to encounter the prejudices against their race or religion, that are such drawbacks to their settlement in many parts of the Eastern states." The editor further noted that "Catholicity, too has struck as firm a root in California as in any part of the United States . . . and as probably over a third, if not a full half of the population of our State belong to her

Constructed in 1865 on Sutter Street in San Francisco from designs by the English-born architect and Forty-niner William Patton, a former associate of the famed Sir Gilbert Scott, the Gothic-Byzantine Temple Emanu-el dominated the skyline of Union Square in San Francisco for many years. The congregation of Temple Emanu-el had been established in 1850 by German Argonauts not long after the organization of Congregation Sherith Israel, which held the first Jewish services in the city. *Courtesy California State Library.*

fold, Catholics here need not fear the loss of their faith for want of Church and Catholic associations, even in the more thickly settled districts."[53]

Religious institutions contributed substantially to the city-building process in other ways, such as the use of urban space, literary endeavors, educational and social welfare provisions, and ethnic accommodations. Church buildings, although of varying architectural styles and degrees of sophistication, were nonetheless a reassuring sign to community developers that order and propriety were gaining the upper hand in San Francisco. The establishment of a viable religious press was yet another hallmark of the advance of civilization. The Presbyterian/Congregationalist *Pacific* and the Roman Catholic *Monitor* were papers of high quality and broad appeal. Benevolent societies among the city's Jewish and Catholic communities provided succor to those struck by the illness or sudden death of a member of the family. Even the development of the network of public and private schools had religious overtones. When transplanted New Englanders created the first San Francisco schools in the image and likeness of the public schools in the East (replete with Bible reading and hymn singing), Catholic Californians protested and demanded their share of public monies to form their own schools.[54] The vigor of the Catholic school system was made possible by the ranks of religious women who taught in them. Convent school education, such as that conducted by the Sisters of Notre Dame in San Jose, had a broad appeal even to non-Catholics. Italian Jesuits arrived as well and opened successful colleges in Santa Clara and San Francisco.[55] The Catholic Sisters of Mercy opened St. Mary's Hospital in 1857 and rendered signal service during the city's recurrent health crises.[56] Religious forces compelled a cessation of gambling on the Sabbath and were the source of serious contention over the use of public funds for hospitals and schools. Social reform ministers, reports historian Roger Lotchin, "condemned the barbarities practiced against Indians; led in establishing schools, libraries, orphan asylums, and sailor's homes."[57]

Perhaps a more critical function were the efforts of churches in service to the ethnic diversity of the period. Churches here seemed to serve a two-fold function: as a preserver of ethnic identity or as a bridge to other cultural groups. Lotchin hailed the significance of churches "in defending the immigrant's heritage," noting specifically the positive role multiple synagogue creation played in accommodating the different nationalities of Jews in San Francisco. Similar observations were made regarding the importance of Catholic ethnic parishes for Irish, Germans, and French.[58]

Equally important were the contacts made between Christian churches and the growing Chinese population. Although this interaction was primarily for the purpose of converting the "heathen Chinee" to Christianity, there was nonetheless a social utility to these contacts, at least from the vantage point of those interested in integrating the Chinese into American society. Gunther Barth notes that "In the absence of larger social organizations in the unstable gold rush society, church groups guided the attempt to make the Chinese Americans."[59] Specifically, Barth cites the work of the Canton-based Presbyterian missionary William Speer, who arrived in San Francisco on November 6, 1852, and began preaching to the Chinese the next February in the Presbyterian Church on Stockton Street. Catholic efforts to convert the Chinese were more sporadic (and perhaps less enthusiastic, given the growing hostility of the Irish toward the "Celestials"). Various priests and religious made efforts; one notable example was the native Chinese priest Father Thomas Cian of

Chinese worshipers assemble in the Buddhist temple on Pine Street in San Francisco in a wood engraving designed by Charles Nahl. Established by the Sze Yap Company, a mutual-benefit society of some nine thousand Chinese Argonauts scattered through the state, the temple was part of a large complex that included business offices, a storehouse, and an asylum for the sick and poor. *Courtesy Huntington Library, San Marino, Calif.*

Hunan Province, who endeavored to proselytize his fellow Chinese in San Francisco and throughout northern California. However, his mission was ultimately unsuccessful, and he ended his days in Italy.[60]

Cian's failure to make many inroads among his countrymen was the common result of all these proselytizing efforts. Historian Yong Chen suggests that Christianization efforts among the San Francisco Chinese fell short and notes that, from the inception of Chinese immigration, various Chinese communities built their own temples: "Chinese immigrants were not overwhelmed by white American culture, not only because they experienced discrimination, but also because they had their own rich and distinctive cultural heritage."[61] Alexander McLeod wrote that "The local missionaries offered them our God, our heaven, and our religion, but they had scores of their own manufacture better and cheaper."[62] Nonetheless, despite the fact that few Chinese actually converted to Christianity, it appears that the missionary efforts of Protestant denominations were among the few structured opportunities for cultural exchange that existed in San Francisco and elsewhere. Indeed, dedicated ministers like Speer devoted themselves to combating the rising anti-Chinese animus that would build in the 1870s.

San Francisco was the point of debarkation for many headed for the gold fields and to the next tier of instant cities that developed along the strategic points of the inland rivers that ultimately emptied into San Francisco Bay. The interplay of religion and urban culture in the interior is best seen in the city of Sacramento, destined to become the state capital.

SACRAMENTO: THE DOMINANCE OF THE ENTREPRENEURS

Sacramento grew up as a pure gold-rush city, literally rising from the nucleus of Sutter's Fort. Its population surged from 6,820 in 1850 to 16,283 in 1870. Although the city possessed certain advantages because of its position at the confluence of the American and Sacramento rivers as well as the remarkable richness of its surrounding agricultural lands, Sacramento was a community that faced considerable obstacles in its quest to remain at its founding location. Historian Mark Eifler provides important detail regarding the earliest years of Sacramento's existence.[63] After the 1848 gold discovery, the city quietly bloomed as a commercial entrepôt as miners descended upon it, thronging its embarcadero and setting up a tent city along the banks of the Sacramento. Sacramento was a veritable labyrinth of tents and make-do stores and shops; its popularity augured well for a prosperous future. Shrewd real estate speculators, with the compliance of John A. Sutter, Jr., son of the community's founder, carved up the lands from the Sacramento River east to Sutter's Fort and began to market the city to all comers. The decision to locate the city along the low land on the banks of the Sacramento with the American River embracing its northern boundary was done largely to edge out rivalry from the elder Sutter, who had plans of his own to create a new city on higher ground south of the present site. This decision to locate Sacramento had important implications for the city's historical development, largely because it nearly proved to be disastrous. Floods nearly wiped the city from the face of the earth in 1850, 1852, and again in winter 1861–62. In addition, the scourge of frontier communities, fire, also flattened the community on several occasions. After the flood of 1862, and after nearly ten years of existence, the San Francisco *Morning Call* opined, "it is simply an act of folly for the people of the town of Sacramento to endeavor to maintain the city on its present location."[64]

As a result of these disasters though, hard-driving entrepreneurs, who had invested heavily in the fledgling city, and enterprising residents who were also aware of the economic potential of the community made a decision that ultimately shaped the heart and soul of Sacramento. They determined to maintain the site and do whatever it took to ensure that Sacramento survived. Rather than move the city from its poor location vis-à-vis the river, city builders determined to build stronger and more durable levees and, in the tradition of Chicago and other western cities, to raise the entire level of the city anywhere from six to twelve feet above the river banks.[65] To prevent fires from wiping out their gains, city fathers decreed in 1854 that Sacramento's public buildings had to be of brick. To secure their city's future they bargained hard and built wisely in order to attract the state capital.[66] In this they were successful. This single-minded will to survive is perhaps the most important element that defined early Sacramento society. Builders, developers, and merchants exercised a powerful influence over the shape of the city's emerging culture, and this was the prevailing ethos in which the religious realities of the city also developed. Indeed, with no preexisting Hispanic residents and culture to erase or supplant, Sacramento truly was a tabula rasa on which the energetic forces of urban development could write their story.

Following the Argonauts who plied river steamers and small drought boats up the Sacramento River, a series of San Francisco ministers made for the bustling entrepôt that was the point of departure for the mines of central California. Docking at Sacramento's crowded embarcadero, ministers such as Presbyterians J. W. Douglas, A. Williams, and S. Woolbridge had begun a small preaching mission in Sacramento as early as March and April 1849. However, it would be some years before they separated from the Congregationalists to form their own organization. Flavel Mines, who had founded the Episcopalian church in San Francisco, held services in August 1849 in a blacksmith shop on Third and J streets. The Congregational Church, destined to be Sacramento's leading church for many years, held its first meeting a month later on the northwest corner of Third and I streets. J. A. Benton, one of the pioneer clergy of the Anglo-Protestant tradition, drew together for a brief time Congregationalists and Presbyterians and was the presiding figure and the leading Sacramento clergyman for many years. Northern Methodists (under the missionary "Father" Owen) began their churches by the end of that same year. The next year, the Methodist Episcopal Church South was established by W. D. Pollock. The year 1850 as well saw the establishment of the Catholic St. Rose congregation in August and St. Andrew's African Methodist Episcopal Church in the fall. Two years later, the city's Jewish community opened Congregation B'Nai Israel, and in

1855 the Presbyterians established their own separate community. In 1865, the Mormons set up their first organization as did the German Lutherans. Sacramento's Chinese population, with its traditional rites, grew dramatically as well.

Sacramento's decision to stay put provided the backdrop for the formation of religious institutions. The city's religious benefactors included Peter Burnett, not only the first American governor of California, but also a major land speculator in early Sacramento. Burnett donated the lot on which the city's first Roman Catholic Church was erected. Church construction demonstrated one means by which the growing religious denominations contributed to the informal decision of the city that Sacramento was to stay put. The early Sacramento churches grew up with the city, but most were huddled near the city's main business arteries stretching east from the river, along J and K streets. The 1854 city government decree that future buildings in the city be constructed of brick posed a problem for many of Sacramento's churches, which had slender financial resources. Nonetheless, since the brick was a visible symbol of the decision for permanence, churches complied, and sometimes magnificently. Indeed, two of the city's major churches led the way in constructing brick church buildings of ample size and architectural elegance.

The First Christian Church (Congregational/Presbyterian) on Sixth and I streets served in the best New England tradition as both worship site and community meeting house.[67] "Mr. Benton's Church" as the locals called it, was a handsome brick structure designed by one of its own members, Albion Sweetser. Benton, the first Congregational minister ordained in California, exercised considerable sway over the city's moral tone through his eloquent pulpitry, which consistently set a high tone for moral influence. His three-hundred-seat church served Sacramento in other ways. The city's gridiron pattern had effectively packaged its lots for purchase, but left it lacking a distinct central gathering place or communal center. Moreover, for many years there were no halls or meeting rooms of sufficient size for various civic events. Benton's large church stepped into the gap, serving, in the best New England tradition, as Sacramento's first meeting hall. The church hosted widely attended cultural and social events that lifted the tone of the developing city. Moreover, it was also used as a gathering place for urban politicians, providing a neutral space for the evolution of the city's politics.

Catholics, on land donated by Peter Burnett at Seventh and K streets, attempted to match the elegance of Congregational Church at Third and I streets and managed to raise enough money to build a large brick structure designed by the San Francisco architectural firm of Crain and England. A handsome building of classical design, St. Rose Church held six hundred worshipers, and its dedication in August 1856 by Archbishop Alemany was a major civic event.[68] St. Rose never attained the level of urban prominence that the Congregational Church achieved, and it soon fell into disrepair as its mostly working-class Irish parishioners refused to

Designed by William Crain and Thomas English, who also drew the plans for old St.
Mary's in San Francisco, the handsomely proportioned classical brick church erected in
1856 at Seventh and K streets in Sacramento for the Roman Catholic parish of St. Rose
of Lima was long a local landmark. *California Historical Society, FN-19581.*

put up the money to lift the building to the new level of the city streets. However,
in 1886, as evidence of the long-standing nature of church/community cooperation,
Sacramento Catholics built the magnificent Cathedral of the Blessed Sacrament on
the corner of Eleventh and K; the building competed with the nearby state capitol
for architectural elegance.

Brick churches were one visible sign of the citizens' concurrence with the decision
to root Sacramento in its "barbarous soil." As in San Francisco, city developers were
also anxious to provide the element of stable urban life that made the city a desirable
place to live and work. Here too, religious bodies rendered important assistance by
creating schools and academies that appealed to a broad spectrum of Sacramento's
population. Catholics took the lead. Shortly after St. Rose Church was established,
a parochial school was opened by Father John Ingoldsby. This institution floundered
until 1857, when the Sisters of Mercy arrived from San Francisco. These religious
women would play an important role in the creation of Sacramento's urban culture
through their educational and health care institutions.[69] By 1860, the sisters secured

a plot of land on Eighth and G streets, wherein they established a convent and opened a school for girls in honor of St. Joseph. St. Joseph's Academy, as it came to be known, was fairly typical of Catholic schools for young women. It consisted of both boarding and day facilities for girls from elementary classes to those in their late teens. Course work included academic subjects, as well as music, sewing, and other "feminine" skills. Graduates of St. Joseph's received a high-quality education, and the school itself represented an important asset for the community at large.

Even though the school was Irish-Catholic in its orientation, Catholics did not, and indeed for financial reasons, could not exclude others not of their faith. While the enrollment at St. Joseph's included a preponderance of Catholic girls, most of Irish extraction, a substantial portion of its pupils were from various other denominations—including the daughters of local Jewish Sacramentans.[70] The attractiveness of the education for a wide diversity of Sacramento's young women redounded to the steady improvement of the city, and St. Joseph's Academy itself was one of the city's cultural symbols of the rising numbers of female citizens that brought stability and settlement to the community.[71] It also redounded to the benefit of the Sisters of Mercy, whose various endeavors relied heavily on the benefactions of a large number of people in the community, not just the Catholics. St. Joseph's would become one of the main providers of teachers for Sacramento's growing school system. The sisters would ultimately branch into health care in the 1890s with the establishment of Mater Misericordiae Hospital.

A similar dynamic of accommodation existed between the church and the growing business class of the city. As Sacramento matured and an increasing level of sophistication attended business practice, local firms required more trained office workers, clerks, and middle-level managers. Sacramento lacked any institution of higher learning for young men. Into this void stepped Father Patrick Scanlan, pastor of St. Rose's, who diverted money from church improvement to the creation of a school for boys that would be a counterpart to St. Joseph's Academy. In 1876, the San Francisco-based Christian Brothers opened a school on Twelfth and K streets. Enrollments were strong from the outset with a spectrum of boys from every religious group in the city. The order offered both boarding and day school classes, and ultimately provided the kind of commercial courses that businesses of the city needed to fill their growing work needs.[72]

CONCLUSION

"Perhaps in no country could a similar scene be exhibited," wrote Dr. Phelan of the sad scene at the Sacramento city cemetery in 1854. The competing rituals were indeed symbolic of the different views of life and death that reposed in the hearts and minds of those thrown together by the social dynamics of California life, and life in the American West. While this essay can only suggest dimensions of the urban experience affected by religious communities and institutions, further study will no doubt reveal richer veins of information and a more complete picture of the multiple forces shaping society in early American California. Just as important is an awareness of how much distance separates our own time and Phelan's. Indeed, our reactions to the cemetery scene would probably avoid characterizations of other religions as "pagan," or somehow as culturally inferior. Over one hundred and fifty years of experience with growing religious toleration, as well as the increasing secularization of our society (and the consequent marginalizing of religion from public life) have given us a different mindset. The nature of California's early religious diversity, and the people's reaction to it, can tell us much about this evolution and thus, much about our national culture.

NOTES

1. "Our California Correspondence," *New York Freeman's Journal and Catholic Register,* 10 March 1854.

2. The relationship between region and religion is outlined in some of the following: Wilbur Zelinsky, "An Approach to the Religious Geography of the United States: Patterns of Church Membership in 1952," *Annals of the Association of American Geographers* 51 (June 1961): 139–93; Edwin S. Gaustad, *Historical Atlas of Religion in America* (New York: Harper & Row, 1976); "Regionalism in American Religion," in *Religion in the South,* ed. Charles Reagan Wilson (Jackson: University Press of Mississippi, 1985), 155–72; "Geography and Demography of American Religion," in *Encyclopedia of the American Religious Experience: Studies in Tradition and Movements,* ed. Charles H. Lippy and Peter W. Williams, 3 vols. (New York: Charles Scribner's, 1988), 1:71–84; James R. Shortridge, "Patterns of Religion in the United States," *Geographical Review* 66 (1976): 420–34, and "A New Regionalization of American Religion," *Journal for the Scientific Study of Religion* 16 (June 1977): 143–52; Catherine Albanese, "Research Needs in American Religious History," *CSR Bulletin* 10 (1979): 101, 103–105; Martin E. Marty, "Interpreting American Pluralism," in *Religion in America: 1950 to the Present,* ed. Jackson W. Carroll et al. (New York: Harper & Row, 1979); John B. Boles, "Religion in the South: A Tradition," *Maryland Historical Magazine* 77 (Winter 1982): 388–401; Richard E. Wentz, "Region and Religion in America," *Foundations* 24 (1981): 148–56; Roger W. Stump, "Regional Migration and Religious Commitment in the United States," *Journal of the Scientific Study of Religion* 23 (September 1984): 292–303, "Regional Divergence in Religious Affiliation in the United States," *Sociological Analysis* 45 (1984): 283–99, and "Regional Variations in the Determinants of Religious Participation," *Review of Religious Research* 27 (1986): 208–25; Jerald C. Brauer, "Regionalism and Religion in America," *Church History* 54 (September 1985): 366–78; Eldon C. Ernst, "American Religious History from a Pacific Coast Perspective," in *Religion and Society in the American West: Historical Essays,* ed. Carl Guarneri and David Alvarez (Lanham, Md.: University Press of America, 1987); Thomas W. Spalding, C.F.X., "Frontier Catholicism," *Catholic Historical Review* 77 (July 1991): 470–84; Laurie F. Maffly-Kipp, "Eastward Ho! American Religion from the Perspective of the Pacific Rim," in *Retelling U.S. Religious History,* ed. Thomas A. Tweed (Berkeley: University of California Press, 1997), 127–48.

3. Ferenc Szasz and Margaret Connell Szasz, "Religion and Spirituality," in *Oxford Encyclopedia of the American West,* ed. Clyde Milner et al. (New York: Oxford University Press, 1994), 359–60.

4. The only bibliography of religion in the West is Richard W. Etulain, comp., *Religion in the Twentieth Century West: A Bibliography* (Albuquerque: Center for the American West, 1991). Various religious topics are covered in Howard R. Lamar, ed., *The New Encyclopedia of the American West* (New Haven: Yale University Press, 1998) and Alan Axelrod and Charles Phillips, *Encyclopedia of the American West* (New York: Macmillan, 1996). D. Michael Quinn, "Religion in the American West," in *Under an Open Sky: Rethinking America's Western Past,* ed. William Cronon et al. (New York: W. W. Norton, 1992), 145–66, offers some interesting insights. See also Gary Topping, "Religion in the West," *Journal of American Culture* 3 (1980): 330–50; and Ferenc Szasz, "The Clergy and the Myth of the American West," *Church History* 59 (December 1990): 497–506. Other sources are cited throughout the essay.

5. Patricia Nelson Limerick, "Believing in the American West," in Geoffrey C. Ward, *The West: An Illustrated History* (Boston: Little Brown and Company, 1996), 207–13.

6. William Taylor, *California Life Illustrated* (New York, 1858), 204.

7. For the best treatment of California's geographical variety, see Philip Fradkin, *The Seven States of California* (Berkeley: University of California Press, 1997).

8. Regarding religion and the gold rush, J. S. Holliday, *The World Rushed In: The California Gold Rush Experience* (New York: Simon & Schuster, 1981), contains vignettes of religious observance recorded in letters and diaries. He also deals with moral conditions on the mining frontier, a cause of much concern for religious leaders. Malcolm J. Rohrbough, *Days of Gold: The California Gold Rush and the American Nation* (Berkeley: University of California Press, 1997), also weaves religious issues and themes into his narrative. Laurie F. Maffly-Kipp's *Religion and Society in Frontier California* (New Haven: Yale University Press, 1994) is a good study of the impact of Protestantism on the mining frontier. Harland E. Hogue has written *Prophets and Paupers: Religion in the California Gold Rush, 1848–1869* (Bethesda, Md.: International Scholars Publications, 1996). An older but still very helpful doctoral dissertation is William Francis Hanchett, "Religion and the Gold Rush, 1849–1854: The Christian Churches and the California Mines" (Ph.D. diss., University of California, Berkeley, 1952). See also William Mead Muhler, "Religion and Social Problems in Gold Rush California: 1849–1869" (Ph.D. diss., Graduate Theological Union, 1989).

9. Hanchett, "Religion and the Gold Rush," 54.

10. Catholic sources are extensive and include William Gleeson, *History of the Catholic Church in California,* 2 vols. (San Francisco: A. L. Bancroft Co., 1872); Henry L. Walsh, S.J., *Hallowed Were the Gold Dust Trails* (Santa Clara: University of Santa Clara Press, 1946). Jesuit John McGloin was one of the leading historians of his church. His works include *Eloquent Indian: The Life of James Bouchard, California Jesuit* (Stanford: Stanford University Press, 1949); *California's First Archbishop: The Life of Joseph Sadoc Alemany, O.P.* (New York: Herder and Herder, 1966); *Jesuits by the Golden Gate: The Society of Jesus in San Francisco, 1849–1969* (San Francisco: University of San Francisco, 1972). See also John T. Dwyer, *Condemned to the Mines: The Life of Eugene O'Connell* (New York: Vantage Press, 1976); James Culleton, *Indians and Pioneers of Old Monterey* (Fresno: Academy of California Church History, 1950). Francis J. Weber has been a prolific scholar of Catholicism in California, especially the Southland. See his *Century of Fulfillment: The Roman Catholic Church in Southern California, 1840–1947* (Mission Hills: The Archival Center, 1990) and *Thaddeus Amat: Cal-*

ifornia's Reluctant Prelate (Los Angeles: Dawson Book Shop, 1964). Helpful as well are Weber's *A Bibliographical Gathering: The Writings of Msgr. Francis J. Weber, 1953–1993* (Mission Hills: The Archival Center, 1995) and *The Catholic Church in California* (Mission Hills: St. Francis Historical Society, 1997).

Protestantism in California has been discussed in the following works: Douglas Firth Anderson, "California Protestantism, 1848–1935: Historiographical Explorations and Regional Method in a Nascent Field" (paper, Graduate Theological Union Library, 1983); Methodist Leon L. Loofbourow tells the story of his denomination in *In Search of God's Gold: A Story of Continued Christian Pioneering in California* (Stockton: The Historical Society of the California-Nevada Annual Conference, 1950); see also Edward D. Jervey, *The History of Methodism in Southern California and Arizona* (Nashville: Parthenon Press, 1960). Presbyterian history is recounted in Clifford M. Drury, "The Beginnings of the Presbyterian Church on the Pacific Coast," *Pacific Historical Review* 9 (June 1940): 195–204, and *The Centennial of the Synod of California, 1852–1952* (pamphlet, San Francisco: Synod of California Presbyterian Church, 1952); James L. Woods, *California Pioneer Decade of 1848: The Presbyterian Church* (reprint, Fresno: Pioneer Publishing, 1981). For Lutheranism, see Richard T. DuBrau, *The Romance of Lutheranism in California* (Oakland: Concordia Publishing House, 1959). On the Baptists see Sanford Fleming, *God's Gold: The Story of Baptist Beginnings in California, 1849–1860* (Philadelphia: Judson Press, 1949) and Floyd Looney, *History of California Southern Baptists* (Fresno, 1954). On the Unitarians see Arnold Crompton, *Unitarianism on the Pacific Coast: The First Sixty Years* (Boston: Beacon Press, 1957). For African American churches see Philip M. Montesano, "San Francisco Black Churches in the Early 1860s: Political Pressure Group," *California Historical Society Quarterly* 52 (1973): 145–52; Kenneth Wilson Moore, "Areas of Impact of Protestantism upon the Cultural Development of Northern California, 1850–1870" (M.A. thesis, Pacific School of Religion, 1970). For Judaism see Fred Rosenbaum, *Architects of Reform: Congregational and Community Leadership, Emanu-El of San Francisco, 1849–1980* (Berkeley: Western Jewish History Center, 1980), and *Free to Chose: The Making of a Jewish Community in the American West: The Jews of Oakland, California, From the Gold Rush to the Present Day* (Berkeley: Judah L. Magnes Memorial Museum, 1976).

11. A good contemporary synthesis of a new religious history approach to California religion is Sandra Sizer Frankiel, "California and the Southwest," in Lippy and Williams, *Encyclopedia of the American Religious Experience,* 3:1509–23.

12. Hanchett makes this point in his dissertation, "Religion and the Gold Rush." A synthesis of the argument is found in his article "The Question of Religion and the Taming of California, 1849–1854," *California Historical Quarterly* 32 (1953): 49–56.

13. Sandra Sizer Frankiel, *California's Spiritual Frontiers: Religious Alternatives to Anglo Protestantism* (Berkeley: University of California Press, 1988).

14. Kevin Starr, *Americans and the California Dream, 1850–1915* (New York: Oxford University Press, 1973); Maffly-Kipp, *Religion and Society.*

15. These general works contain information about the role of religion in Asian communities: Gunther Barth, *Bitter Strength: A History of the Chinese in the United States, 1850–1870* (Cambridge: Harvard University Press, 1964); Sucheng Chan, *Asian Americans: An Interpretative History* (Boston: Twayne Publishers, 1991); Yong Chen, "China in America: A Cultural History of Chinese San Francisco, 1850–1943" (Ph.D. diss., Cornell University, 1993); see also Robert Seager II, "Some Denominational Reactions to Chinese Immigration to California, 1856–1892," *Pacific Historical Review* 28 (1954): 49–66.

16. Starr, *Americans and the California Dream,* 93–97.

17. Maffly-Kipp, "Eastward Ho!"

18. Significant discussions of cities and the American West include Gunther Barth, *Instant Cities: Urbanization and the Rise of San Francisco and Denver* (New York: Oxford University Press, 1975); Donald W. Meinig, "American Wests: Preface to a Geographical Interpretation," in *Re-Reading Cultural Geography,* ed. Kenneth Foote, Peter J. Hugill, Kent Mathewson, and Jonathan M. Smith (Austin: University of Texas, 1994), pp. 111–38; Carl Abbot, "The Metropolitan Region: Western Cities in the New Urban Era," in *The Twentieth Century West: Historical Interpretations,* ed. Gerald D. Nash and Richard W. Etulain (Albuquerque: University of New Mexico Press, 1989), 71–98; Bradford Luckingham, "The Urban Dimensions of Western History," in *Historians and the American West,* ed. Michael P. Malone (Lincoln: University of Nebraska Press, 1983), 323–43; Lawrence H. Larsen, "Frontier Urbanization," in *American Frontier and Western Issues: A Historiographical Review,* ed. Roger L. Nichols (Westport: Greenwood Press, 1986), 69–88; Carol A. O'Connor, "A Region of Cities," in *The Oxford History of the American West,* ed. Clyde Milner et al. (New York: Oxford University Press, 1994), 535–64.

19. E. L. Cleaveland in *Home Missionary* 26 (July 1853): 65.

20. Hanchett, "Religion and the Gold Rush," 30.

21. Religion's role in the shaping of city culture has become a matter of intense interest among urban historians. Kathleen Neils Conzen has suggested ways in which the role of organized religion can be more effectively integrated into our understanding of the wider processes of city-building. For example, religious people and institutions have played important roles in the urban process by their occupation of space, their provision of social services and their contributions to the overall development of urban communities. See "Forum: The Place of Religion in Urban and Community Studies," *Religion and American Culture* 6 (Summer 1996): 107–30.

22. Quoted in Hanchett, "Religion and the Gold Rush," 28.

23. Clifford M. Drury, "A Chronology of Protestant Beginnings in California," *California Historical Society Quarterly* 26 (June 1947): 163–74.

24. Robert M. Fogelson, *The Fragmented Metropolis: Los Angeles, 1850–1930* (Cambridge: Harvard University Press, 1967), 10–23.

25. Michael E. Engh, S.J., *Frontier Faiths: Church, Temple, and Synagogue in Los Angeles, 1846–1888* (Albuquerque: University of New Mexico Press, 1992), 2. See also Francis J. Weber, ed., *The Religious Heritage of Southern California: A Bicentennial Survey* (Los Angeles: Interreligious Council of Southern California, 1976).

26. Engh, *Frontier Faiths,* 19

27. June Barrows, ed., "A Vermonter's Description of a Sunday in Los Angeles, California, in 1852," *Vermont History* 38 (1970): 192–94.

28. Jeffrey Burns alludes to the nature of this popular Catholicism in "The Mexican Catholic Community in California," in *Mexican Americans and the Catholic Church, 1900–1965,* ed. Jay P. Dolan and Gilberto Hinojosa (Notre Dame: University of Notre Dame Press, 1994), 136. Timothy M. Matovina refers to the same dynamic among the Tejanos of San Antonio. See *Tejano Religion and Ethnicity: San Antonio, 1821–1860* (Austin: University of Texas Press, 1995), 4, 20–22. For further descriptions of Hispanic Catholicism in California see Moises Sandoval and Salvador E. Alvarez, "The Church in California," in *Fronteras: A History of the Latin American Church in the USA Since 1513,* ed. Moises Sandoval (San Antonio:

Mexican American Cultural Center, 1983), 209–21; Michael C. Neri, *Hispanic Catholicism in Transitional California: The Life of Jose Gonzalez Rubio, O.F.M.* (Santa Barbara: American Academy of Franciscan History, 1995); Antonio Soto, "The Chicano and the Catholic Church in Northern California, 1848–1978: A Study of an Ethnic Minority Within the Roman Catholic Church" (Ph.D. diss., University of California, Berkeley, 1978).

29. Gregory H. Singleton, *Religion in the City of Angels: American Protestant Culture and Urbanization, Los Angeles, 1850–1930* (Ann Arbor: UMI Research Press, 1979), 10.

30. Leonard Pitt, *The Decline of the Californios: A Social History of the Spanish-Speaking Californians, 1846–1890* (Berkeley: University of California Press, 1966), 13.

31. Ibid., 218.

32. For the evolution of the mission myth and the recapturing of the ethos of Spanish Catholicism by Los Angeles's boosters, see James J. Rawls, "The California Mission as Symbol and Myth," *California History* 71 (Fall 1992): 342–61. See also Valerie Sherer Mathes, "The California Mission Indian Commission of 1891: The Legacy of Helen Hunt Jackson," *California History* 72 (Winter 1993/94): 338–59.

33. Weber, *Thaddeus Amat.*

34. Burns, "Mexican Catholic Community," 135–37.

35. Fogelson, *Fragmented Metropolis,* 27.

36. Engh, *Frontier Faiths,* 24–26, gives a good summary of Chinese religious rituals in Los Angeles.

37. Glenna Matthews, "Forging a Cosmopolitan Civic Culture: The Regional Identity of San Francisco and Northern California," in *Many Wests: Place Culture and Regional Identity,* ed. David C. Wrobel and Michael C. Steiner (Lawrence: University of Kansas Press, 1997), 216.

38. William Issel and Robert W. Cherny, *San Francisco, 1865–1932: Politics, Power, and Urban Development* (Berkeley: University of California Press, 1986), 8.

39. Bradford L. Luckingham, "Religion in Early San Francisco," *The Pacific Historian* 17 (Winter 1973): 56–74.

40. In 1826, the American Home Missionary Society was formed on an interdenominational basis, but was largely under the aegis of Congregationalists and New School Presbyterians. Old School Congregationalists had had a mission board since 1816. A Methodist Mission Society was formed in 1819, and after the 1846 schism, a Southern Methodist Board was created. In 1821, the Episcopalians formed a Domestic and Foreign Mission Society, and in 1832, the Baptists created the American Baptist Home Mission Society.

41. William Day Simonds, *Starr King in California* (San Francisco: P. Elder, 1917); see also Starr, *Americans and the California Dream,* 97–105; Frankiel, *California's Spiritual Frontiers,* 18–31. For the early history of Episcopalians in San Francisco, see William Ingraham Kip, *Early Days of My Episcopate* (New York: Thomas Whittaker, 1892); D. O. Kelly, *History of the Diocese of California: 1849–1915* (San Francisco: Bureau of Information and Supply, 1915); and Edward Lamb Parsons, *The Diocese of California: A Quarter Century, 1915–1940* (Austin, Tex.: Church Historical Society, 1958).

42. The significance of the ethnic parish in western cities is described in Jeffrey M. Burns, "Building the Best: A History of Catholic Parish Life in the Pacific States," in *The American Catholic Parish: A History from 1850 to the Present,* ed. Jay P. Dolan, 2 vols. (New York: Paulist Press, 1987), 2: 49–78.

43. Chen, "China in America," 139.

44. Ibid., 141–42.

45. The standard work on the rise of the Know Nothing movement is Ray Allen Billington, *The Protestant Crusade: A Study in the Origins of American Nativism* (New York: Macmillan, 1938); for the California version of this national movement see Peyton Hurt, "The Rise and Fall of the 'Know Nothings' in California," *California Historical Society Quarterly* (1930): 16–49.

46. Patrick Blessing, "Culture, Religion and the Activities of the Committee of Vigilance, San Francisco, 1856," *Cushwa Center Working Papers Series* 8 (Fall 1980): 5. For a fuller description of the variety of interpretations given to the vigilantism of 1856, consult the appendix of Robert M. Senkiewicz, S.J., *Vigilantes in Gold Rush San Francisco* (Stanford: Stanford University Press, 1985), 203–31.

47. Issel and Cherny observe that by 1860, "San Francisco stood not only as one of the nation's leading immigrant centers but also as a particularly Irish—and Roman Catholic—city" (*San Francisco, 1865–1932*, 14).

48. Douglas Firth Anderson, "Through Fire and Fair by the Golden Gate: Progressive Era Protestantism and Culture" (Ph.D. diss., Graduate Theological Union, 1988), 4.

49. Although he discusses a period of time after the chronological parameters of this essay, Douglas Firth Anderson notes the minority status of Protestantism in the Bay Area in "'We Have Here a Different Civilization': Protestant Identity in the San Francisco Bay Area, 1906–1909," *Western Historical Quarterly* 23 (1992): 199–221.

50. For a good treatment of Irish Catholicism, see Emmet Larkin's *The Historical Dimensions of Irish Catholicism* (Washington, D.C.: The Catholic University of America Press, 1984); and also Lawrence J. McCaffrey, *The Irish Catholic Diaspora in America* (Washington, D.C.: The Catholic University Press of America, 1997).

51. R. A. Burchell, *The San Francisco Irish, 1848–1880* (Berkeley: University of California Press, 1980), 91. The Irish in California are also the subject of Patrick Blessing's "West Among Strangers: Irish Migration to California, 1850 to 1880" (Ph.D. diss., University of California, Los Angeles, 1977). A venerable work worth citing as well is J. Quigley, *The Irish Race in California and on the Pacific Coast* (San Francisco: A. Roman & Co., 1878). Patrick J. Dowling has provided a series of interesting, if sometimes factually flawed, mini-biographies in *Irish Californians: Historic, Benevolent, Romantic* (San Francisco: Scottwall Associates, 1998).

52. Burchell, *San Francisco Irish*, 5.

53. Quoted in ibid., 4.

54. For additional information regarding Catholic schools in San Francisco see Catherine A. Curry, "Shaping Young San Franciscans: Public and Catholic Schools in San Francisco, 1851–1906" (Ph.D. diss., Graduate Theological Union, 1987).

55. Gerald McKevitt, S.J., *The University of Santa Clara: A History, 1851–1977* (Stanford: Stanford University Press, 1979); see also McGloin, *Jesuits by the Golden Gate.*

56. Mary Aurelia McCardle, *California's Pioneer Sister of Mercy: Mother Mary Baptist Russell (1829–1898)* (Fresno: Academy Library Guild, 1954).

57. Roger Lotchin, *San Francisco, 1846–1856: From Hamlet to City* (New York: Oxford University Press, 1974), 326.

58. Ibid., 121.

59. Barth, *Bitter Strength*, 159.

60. John B. McGloin, S.J., "Thomas Cian: Pioneer Chinese Priest in California," *California Historical Quarterly* 48 (March 1969): 45–58.

61. Chen, "China in America," 134.

62. Alexander McLeod, *Pigtails and Gold Dust* (Caldwell, Idaho: Caxton Printers, 1947), 40, 98.

63. Mark Anthony Eifler, "Crossroads City: Culture and Community in Gold Rush Sacramento, 1849–1850" (Ph.D. diss., University of California, Berkeley, 1992).There are very few full-scale studies of the history of Sacramento. Joseph McGowan's three-volume *History of the Sacramento Valley* (West Palm Beach: Lewis Historical Publishing Co., 1961) is dated but still the best source available. Two additional books are Thor Severson, *Sacramento: An Illustrated History: 1839–1874* (Sacramento, 1973), and Joseph A. McGowan and Terry Willis, *Sacramento: Heart of the Golden State* (Woodland Hills: Sacramento County Historical Society, 1983). Another helpful source is Susan Wiley Hardwick, "Ethnic Residential and Commercial Patterns in Sacramento with Special Reference to the Russian-American Experience" (Ph.D. diss., University of California, Davis, 1986).

64. Quoted in Severson, *Sacramento: An Illustrated History,* 108–109.

65. These herculean efforts are recorded in Barbara Lagomarsino, "Early Attempts to Save the Site of Sacramento by Raising Its Business District" (M.A. thesis, Sacramento State College, 1969).

66. The decision to situate the state capital in Sacramento is related in June Oxford, *The Capital That Couldn't Stay Put* (Fairfield: James Stevenson Publisher, 1995), 61–66.

67. Paul Freye, "A History of The Pioneer Church of Sacramento, California, 1849–1949" (pamphlet, Sacramento Room, Sacramento City Library).

68. "Church Dedication," *Sacramento Daily Union,* 18 August 1856.

69. The work of the Sisters in Sacramento is described in Mary Evangelist Morgan, *Mercy, Generation to Generation: History of the First Century of the Sisters of Mercy, Diocese of Sacramento, California* (San Francisco: Fearon Publishers, 1957).

70. "Records of St. Joseph Academy, 1861–1868," Archives of the Sisters of Mercy, Auburn, Calif.

71. For an overview of the history of women in Sacramento, see Elaine Connolly and Dian Self, *Capital Women: An Interpretative History of Women in Sacramento, 1850–1920* (Sacramento: Capital Women's History Project, 1995).

72. See Ronald Isetti, *Called to the Pacific: A History of the Christian Brothers of the San Francisco District, 1868–1944* (Moraga: St. Mary's College of California, 1979), 46–48; evidence of the good rapport built up between the Brothers and the local business community, who contributed handsomely to the construction of a new school building in the 1920s, is on pp. 249–50. See also Sister Marie Vandenbergh, R.C., "Attitudes and Events Leading up to the Establishment of Christian Brothers School in Sacramento, 1871–1876" (M.A. thesis, Sacramento State College, 1968).

11

Popular Culture on the Golden Shore

Gary F. Kurutz

> The Sabbath in California is kept, when kept at all, as a day of hilarity and
> bacchanalian sports, rather than as a season of holy meditation or religious
> devotion. Horse-racing, cock-fighting, cony-hunting, card-playing, theatrical
> performances, and other elegant amusements are freely engaged in on this day.
> —Hinton Helper, *The Land of Gold*

The California Gold Rush and the harvesting of millions of dollars worth of gold
dust gave the Argonauts an unprecedented level of discretionary income and plenty
of ways to burn it. Miners who had made their pile and those who made a living off
the Argonauts enjoyed a multitude of diversions provided by the cities, towns, and
camps of this new El Dorado. Out of this caldron of chaos developed the gambling
"hells" and drinking saloons referred to by just about every major journal keeper and
letter writer. Short on the heels of these infamous institutions grew other forms of
popular culture reflecting the educational levels and the incredibly diverse nature of
the mining population. While hunting for gold was a rugged and dangerous business
bringing out the worst features of many personalities, the stereotype of rough, carousing, cursing, crude miners quickly gave way to a population that appreciated the
finer things of life.

A large number of highly literate, sophisticated individuals poured into California during this rough and ready era, and they wanted and demanded diversions
other than swilling liquor and playing monte and faro. Seemingly overnight, theaters, music halls, circuses, literary societies, bookstores, lending libraries, and other
forms of wholesome recreation blossomed. Californians, too, enjoyed a variety of
contests ranging from bull-and-bear fights to billiards, thus laying the foundation for
the state's love affair with sports. Those who realized that California's streets were
not paved in gold saw a need to develop forms of amusement that would not only
improve the mind but also create a stable social foundation conducive to permanent

settlement. By the early 1850s, Californians began to worry about their reputations, and with this concern, on an unparalleled scale were importing the civilizing influences of their former homes.[1]

The first manifestation of popular culture in gold-rush California centered on Sunday. Reflecting the American roots of many of the gold seekers, this traditional day of rest turned out to be a day of merriment and money-making opportunities, a veritable institution of the Gold Rush. It was on this day that the population not only tended to chores and reflected on the Sabbath, but also "let loose" after a hard week of physical toil. Sunday represented a chance to socialize and enjoy life, and the Argonauts, without any real rules of social behavior but with bags of gold, often turned to games of chance and the comfort found in a bottle. But it was also on this day that miners held balls, went to the theater, sang songs, read newspapers, whooped it up at foot races, thought of home, and wrote letters.[2]

Sundays, like Saturday nights, gave others a "golden" opportunity to turn a profit. The professional gambler, barkeeper, thespian, musician, and the owners of these establishments happily relieved gold-rushers of their hard-earned gold dust. Others, too, who supplied services to the Argonauts, found this alternative use of the "Lord's Day" most pleasing. Jared Brown, a young blacksmith at Coloma, for instance, boasted that Sunday was his most profitable. It also happened to be horse-racing day. Brown wrote his father: "I plate a horse Sunday morning for running and he run right away from the others. Sunday is the day all racing is done. I do as much work on Sunday as all the rest of the week."[3]

This essay surveys the rapid development of popular culture and amusements during the first years of that fast-paced era. Many of these later developed into solid, long-lasting institutions; while others, like the bacchanalian sports described by Hinton Helper, died off as a result of public pressure.

"All gamble to a frightful extent"

GAMING HOUSES AND DRINKING SALOONS

Without doubt, gambling turned out to be the most popular, most remarked about, and most condemned form of popular culture.[4] As *New York Tribune* journalist Bayard Taylor remarked, "Wherever there is gold, there are gamblers."[5] All the great contemporary chroniclers of the gold-rush era penned extensive and colorful descriptions of the gambling "hells" and the drinking saloons, the men who bet a bagful of gold on the turn of a single card, and the utter dissolution and ruination of young men who lost their moral compasses in these hells. Pioneer directory publisher Samuel Colville, when describing Marysville's gambling saloons, remarked that "Hogarth and Cruikshank might look upon the picture, and wonder where to

Sunday in the California Diggings, a wood engraving after a design by the artist-Argonaut Charles Nahl, appeared both as an illustration to the April 1857 issue of *Wide West* and as a pictorial letter sheet. On their day of rest, the miners occupy themselves with horse racing, gambling, brawling, and drunken dissipation, as well as with washing clothes, writing letters, and Bible study, reflecting the varied character and needs of the men who toiled in the

gold fields. Fifteen years after its publication, Nahl painted a monumental canvas of the same scene, *Sunday Morning in the Mines* (Crocker Art Museum, Sacramento). Exhibited in San Francisco, it awakened fond memories for many a graying Argonaut, one of whom declared that the scene would "be recognized as truthful by those who have witnessed similar ones." *California Historical Society, FN-31251.*

begin and be bewildered to know where to leave off. Here, naked, and unmasked depravity, daily, nightly, and unblushingly manifested itself."[6]

Gambling also caught the attention of just about anyone who took the trouble to write a letter home or make a diary entry. Frequently these letters and diaries struggled with the notion of miners willing to risk all, in the context of the responsibilities they had to loved ones at home. New England preachers warned gold seekers of the immorality found in the gambling saloons of California. The self-righteous condemned the squandering of hard-earned labor, while others, perhaps disingenuously, stated that they merely watched miners gambling and did not wager themselves. "During all this excitement and apparent chance to get rich, I never made a single bet or took a chance," wrote a sanctimonious Charles Ross Parke about the rampant gambling in Sacramento.[7] But, as writers of *The Annals of San Francisco* more realistically observed, "*Every body did so,*"[8] and William Perkins pointed out in his journal that "Merchants, Lawyers, Politicians, Judges, Governors, all gamble to a frightful extent."[9] In Sacramento, Stockton, and Marysville even ministers of the Gospel could be seen "piously engaged in dealing monte" and other games of chance.

Gambling did not draw a boundary, either, when it came to age, sex, or race. Journalist Enos Christman noted that he found himself "surrounded with crowds of persons of all ages, sex and color, from the pale-faced Frenchman to the ebon Ethiopian [African American]."[10] Artist John David Borthwick wrote: "Seated round the same [gambling] table might be seen well-dressed, respectable-looking men, and alongside of them, rough miners fresh from the diggings . . . and little urchins . . . ten or twelve years of age, smoking cigars as big as themselves."[11] John Banks, a Buckeye, was disgusted at seeing a handsome woman drinking, gambling, and swearing (just like the men!).[12]

The Gold Rush has been described as the "great lottery," and it only stands to reason that those who participated in the run for riches would be willing to take a chance at the gaming tables. Away from the moral constraints of home, the saloon gave gold-rushers a playground without restriction. Further, during the early days of gold, gambling provided the primary source of diversion, a relief from the arduous task of making a living, and a place for socializing.[13] For many, especially in isolated camps, there was no other place to go and nothing else to do. Daniel Woods, in his *Sixteen Months at the Gold Diggings*, illustrates the paucity of amusements and rationale for wagering with the following story:

> I saw, to my surprise, a young man who had come from one of the most religious families in his native city placing down his money upon the table. I stepped to his side. In a moment the card was turned, and a small amount of silver was added to that already in his hand. He looked anxiously at me and said, "I would not have my mother know what I am doing for all the money in this room." "Why then do it?" I asked; "have you

The El Dorado, one of the most famed gaming houses in San Francisco, stands next to the city hall on the east side of Portsmouth Plaza. Possibly designed by the French Argonaut Prosper Huerne and one of the first examples of fireproof construction in the city, it replaced the older "gambling hell" of the same name, which was destroyed by one of the periodic conflagrations that swept San Francisco. By 1852, when this pictorial letter sheet was published, San Francisco was becoming increasingly respectable and the riotous days of the city's opulently furnished pleasure palaces lay largely in the past. *Courtesy California State Library.*

thought to what the first step may lead?" "But what can I do," he said, earnestly; "I came not here to gamble, but to find amusement; and can you tell me what other amusement is within my reach?"[14]

Very quickly California became the gambling capital of the world, with San Francisco leading the parade. As portrayed in *The Annals of San Francisco,* "Gambling . . . was *the* amusement—the grand occupation of many classes—apparently the life and soul of the place. There were hundreds of gambling saloons in the town."[15] The Chilean Benjamin Vicuña MacKenna wrote that "Gambling houses, open day and night, were the actual churches of San Francisco, and gold was the only God worshiped."[16] William Kelly added: "The Francisco gaming-houses are never closed, morning, noon, or night."[17] The El Dorado, Verandah, Denison's Exchange, Bella Union, and Aguila de Oro became some of the most infamous names in the world.

The Chinese started their own gambling houses on Sacramento and Dupont streets. So lucrative did this pastime become, that "knights of the green cloth" paid thousands of dollars in annual rent just to set up a table.[18]

What applied to San Francisco applied on a smaller scale everywhere else. Marysville's first saloon consisted of a series of poles planted in the earth and covered with canvas in the center of town. Its owner, James Wharton, called it the "Round Tent."[19] James Lee set up a similar affair, called the "Stinking Tent," made of foul-smelling sailcloth in Sacramento, which in turn was followed by another "Round Tent," then the "Gem," and a score more. In this town, adjacent to perennially flooding rivers, reported John Letts, men stood up to their knees in mud to play monte.[20] Stockton boasted its El Dorado, Nevada City its Empire, Grass Valley its Alta, Sonora its Long Tom, and by 1852, forty saloons and gambling halls lined Columbia's streets.

The gaming houses must have been absolutely incredible, elegant affairs, especially in the larger population centers. One can only imagine what it must have been like for a young Forty-niner from an isolated, protected New England village to enter into a place like the Big Tent in Sacramento or the El Dorado in San Francisco. Bright lights, mirrors with gilded frames, lascivious paintings, tables loaded with buckskin bags of gold dust, painted jezebels with enticing smiles and siren voices, dense clouds of tobacco smoke, a cacophony of swearing and cursing in multiple languages, liquor flowing like water, and the blare of music all combined to create a heady, irresistible atmosphere capable of shattering the staunchest moral spirit.[21] An early San Francisco city directory provided this word picture of the dizzying attraction of the gambling saloon in 1849:

> Almost the only comfortable places of resort were the gambling saloons, which were warm and dry, though fetid with the fumes of tobacco, gin, and other liquors, and the poisonous air which has done its duty in turn to a hundred sets of lungs. In such places men needed not drink as a prelude to intoxication. They could absorb it through nostrils and pores of their skin, and, in addition, bands of music helped the excitement and diverted the self-examination and reflection of those who stood within those alluring hells. Few could see the heaps of gold upon the gambling tables and breathe the air, and resist the influences around and before them. Men entered to avoid the rain and get warm, or through curiosity, saw, bet, and were ruined.[22]

Women, both real and imagined, offered an irresistible attraction. While professional gamblers dominated, owners of saloons exploited the lack of women by placing them behind the gaming tables and liquor bars. William Perkins in Sonora, for example, noted the presence of "a pretty and handsomely dressed Frenchwoman behind the counter." Offering a candid view, he went on to admit that "Even a staid and sedate man like myself will at times spend a few quarters for the enjoyment of a genial smile from a pretty face, or perhaps the still greater stimulus of a flirtation."[23]

Albert Benard de Russailh reported that French girls charged an ounce of gold just to sit next to a customer at a bar or card table. "I may add," wrote the French traveler, "that the saloons and gambling-houses that keep women are always crowded and are sure to succeed."[24]

Owners of these establishments seemingly spared no expense in creating a heady atmosphere even though the structure itself was no more than a large tent. Music was a great enticement, and all kinds of bands and varieties of instruments could be found. Gambling saloon musicians made upwards of an ounce of gold per performance. According to the Marysville directory for 1856, "Musical talent [in the early years] commanded the most Utopian prices. Any amateur that could torture horse hair and cat-gut into any consecutive sounds reasonably endurable, found the gambling saloon a much more remunerative field for his labor, than the richest laden placer or gulch."[25] A Swiss lady, working as an organ grinder in the gambling saloons, made $4,000 in a few short months.[26]

While faro and monte proved to be the most popular, every game of chance known to the gambling fraternity was represented, including roulette, rondo, keno, twenty-one, chuck-a-luck, rouge-et-noir, lansquenet, poker, tub and ball, thimble rig, and strap and pin. Much has been written by contemporary observers of the sums of coin and gold dust bet and the demeanor of those who wagered. Stakes ranged as high as $1,000 to $5,000 a pop, but sums as small as a single dollar stake— still nearly a half-day's wages—were commonplace. Players treated losses with a range of emotions: some cursed, others went so far as to draw out a revolver or knife, and still others showed remarkable equanimity. Miners were notorious for coming into town and gambling away their hard-earned *oro*.[27] William B. Peter in 1851 wrote: "A sailor came back from the mines just a while ago with $6,000 piasters in gold. He ran to a gambling hall, threw his bag of gold on a Monte table shouting 'here's for Panama or back to the mines!' Thus gambling on *one* card the fruit of his labor for the year—fortunately, luck smiled on him. He returned to New York with $12,000."[28]

Drinking saloons, or tippling houses, served as the Siamese twins of the gambling hells, offering many of the same amenities including music, women, bright lights, expensive furniture, and alluring wall decorations. More often than not, drinking took place in gambling hells and gambling took place in the saloons. Hubert Howe Bancroft noted that "There were all grades and descriptions of saloons, from the lowest 'bit' house, where 'rot-gut' whiskey, 'strychnine' brandy, and divers other poisonous compounds with slang names were sold, to the most gorgeous drinking palaces" serving the best bourbon and champagne.[29] Most amazingly, the press reported that in 1853 San Francisco supported 537 liquor vendors and employed 743 bartenders![30] To supply the trade and the Forty-niner's thirst, merchants imported tremendous quantities of spirits. For example, an advertisement in the *Alta California* for

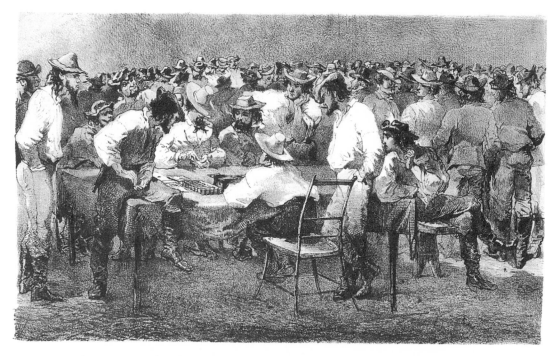

Argonauts try their luck at monte, one of the simplest and most popular games of chance in the diggings, in a lithographic illustration to *Three Years in California* (1857), by the artist-Argonaut John D. Borthwick. The great national game of Mexico at the time of the Gold Rush, monte was quickly taken up by Yankee gamblers. *California Historical Society, FN-31550.*

February 8, 1849, offered for sale 400 boxes of champagne, 100 boxes of cherry brandy, 600 cases of brandy, and 200 cases of gin. "The annual consumption of beer, wines and liquors in this State exceeds five millions of gallons," wrote California basher Hinton Helper in 1852.[31]

These saloons offered two other popular and more respectable forms of diversion: billiards and bowling, or ten-pin alley. Robert Brownlee recorded that a friend bought seven ten-pin alleys and sent one to him at his saloon in Agua Fria. "It was in great demand," he said, "as everybody wanted amusement, and this seemed to fill the bill."[32] At Coloma, James Delavan was astonished that scarce lumber was diverted to building bowling saloons with individuals "preferring to make their *ten strikes* there than to delve in the placers."[33] Apparently, these alleys attracted enough patronage to pay enormous rents. Taylor reported that a single bowling establishment in the Ward House (hotel) in San Francisco pre-paid its rent of $5,000 a month. The El Dorado, in addition to its many gambling tables, in its basement boasted four alleys that were rarely empty. On its first floor, patrons could also amuse themselves with billiards, and in the back, a shooting gallery.[34] As the German Friedrich Gerstäcker summed it up, these diversions offered "A very nice variety of well-meant devices to get the money out of people's pockets as pleasantly as possible."[35]

By 1854, these gambling hells began to die out, giving way to more socially acceptable forms of amusement. The influx of families was putting unrelenting pressure to eliminate or at least segregate the Forty-niner's gambling hell. In 1856, the state legislature outlawed gambling altogether, thus ending perhaps the wildest chapter in California history.

"The only civilized distraction"

THE ARGONAUTS' THEATER

The theater emerged as the most enduring and appreciated form of popular entertainment to survive the Gold Rush. Actors and actresses of note came early to the land of gold, performing before easily satisfied and deeply interested audiences. Some of the most memorable names associated with this era—Lola Montez, Lotta Crabtree, Tom Maguire, Edwin Forrest, Junius Booth and his sons—all provided amusement ranging from renditions of Shakespeare to vaudeville. Theater represented an uplifting, respectable pastime that countered the degrading, debilitating atmosphere of the gambling hells. Those who saw California as their home worried about its reputation, and the theater, along with the church and atheneum, meant respectability.[36] As French traveler Albert Benard de Russailh remarked in 1851, the theater provided "the only civilized distraction."[37] The San Francisco *Daily Alta California,* in a sermon-like editorial, talked of the "Dramatic Temple" as an institution where lessons in morality are imparted and "where great truths are inculcated by the immortal language of the great bard."[38]

Despite the virtuous tones articulated by these editorials, the first theater of the Gold Rush hardly represented a place to impart moral lessons. When Sacramento's Eagle Theatre opened on October 18, 1849, its patrons entered the canvas and wood affair through a saloon, the infamous Round Tent. Before and after the performance, theatergoers could gamble and swill spirits. As journalist Bayard Taylor pointed out, "It would have been taken for an ordinary drinking-house, but for the sign: 'Eagle Theatre.'"[39]

The Eagle achieved lasting fame as the first California structure built for dramatic performances. Its short life, however, illustrates the vicissitudes of operating a palace of entertainment during that fast-paced, makeshift era. Like most businesses constructed in Sacramento in 1849, it consisted of a wood frame with canvas sides and roof. Carpenters fashioned its stage out of packing boxes. Costing a staggering $75,000, the flimsy playhouse measured approximately 30 by 95 feet with a capacity for 400 seats. Expenses did not end there. Actors, doorkeepers, orchestra, scenery, painted drop curtain, posters, and programs drove up the overhead to $600 a night. To pay for all this, managers charged $5 for a box seat and $3 to sit in the pit.[40]

Opening night drew a large and joyous crowd. Miners, dressed in "heavy overcoats and felt hats," poured out their gold dust at the Round Tent saloon and filed into the theater. A number of "well-costumed ladies" sat in a special place known as "dress circle." Taylor and Stephen C. Massett, the celebrated composer and vocalist, witnessed the performance of the first play, *The Bandit Chief; or, The Forest Spectre.* Massett noted that a howling wind and pouring rain put the tent theater to a real test. A group of thespians led by J. B. Atwater and Mr. and Mrs. Henry Ray acted out the medieval tragedy before the packed house. Taylor, somewhat skeptical, wrote: "Several acts are filled with the usual amount of fighting and terrible speeches." Mrs. Ray, Taylor derisively reported, threw herself on the stage several times for no apparent reason other than to prove a woman was indeed part of the play. Her impromptu appearances caused the miners to "applaud vehemently."[41]

Sacramento's inclement weather and flooding rivers challenged the fortitude of spectator and actor alike. During one performance, flood waters seeped through the wooden floors, and by the time the second act began, the audience, rather than fleeing, stood on benches. Apparently the defiant miners loved sloshing to their seats. Pioneering theater historian John B. McCabe reported: "On several occasions when the company were 'piling on the agony' on the stage, one of these miners would appear to be roused to enthusiasm, and while shouting his approbation, would throw his arms open, striking his neighbors on each side, and precipitating them backwards into the water. This practical joke sometimes caused a laugh, sometimes a fight."[42]

The Eagle Theatre lasted just two and one-half action-packed, flood-ravaged months before closing on January 4, 1850. Atwater and his colleagues headed for San Francisco and opened at Washington Hall on January 16, 1850, to a jammed house with Sheridan Knowles's *The Wife.* In short order, a succession of theaters followed, including the National, American, Phoenix, and Adelphi, offering a venue for great tragedians and comics alike. This flurry of activity inaugurated a long and fruitful San Francisco theater history that continues to this day.[43]

While Sacramento fought off floods, San Francisco contended with a series of fires that burnt down one "histrionic temple" after another. Out of these ashes emerged two frontier impresarios, Dr. D. G. "Yankee" Robinson and Tom Maguire. The irrepressible Dr. Robinson had his "Dramatic Museum" burn twice before opening on July 4, 1850, with an original gold-rush farce entitled *Seeing the Elephant.* Success and a craving for new audiences took Dr. Robinson on the road, where he carried the dramatic arts to places like Marysville and Nevada City for the first time. Robinson also brought to California the first professional singer, the beautiful coloratura soprano Elisa Biscaccianti. Saloon keeper Tom Maguire rose to the top as the greatest showman. Arriving in California in 1849, he erected on Portsmouth Square a series of Jenny Lind Theaters. Fire consumed the first two, but the third, the stubborn barkeeper made of brick and stone. It was so substantial that he sold it to officials for a city hall. Like Dr. Robinson, Maguire branched out and operated theaters throughout the mining country. The impresario possessed that rare ability to attract topflight entertainers and keep his audiences loyal with an assortment of acts ranging from vaudeville to musicales to grand opera.[44]

Although San Francisco dominated in numbers and elegance of theater buildings, the mining cities and towns all prized theatrical amusements and raced to build their own dramatic temples. Theaters represented respectability and put communities on the map of civilization. As the *Placer Times* so aptly put it, the theater served as an "oasis in a great desert of the mind." Newspapers carried scores of notices of theatrical offerings, reporters penned tediously detailed reviews, and printers struck gold by churning out posters and programs.[45] The tiny but rich mountain town of Downieville illustrates the determination to lure wholesome entertainment. Just three months after citizens lynched a Mexican woman named Juanita, the town opened up a thousand-seat theater; and in June 1852, it proudly inaugurated the National, with a capacity for 1,500 persons. The National even boasted a drop curtain with a view of Tyrol in Switzerland.[46]

With talented impresarios pulling the levers, just about every famous entertainer came through San Francisco and the mining towns. A bevy of famous actresses dazzled the miners, including Alexina Baker, Matilda Heron, and Catherine Sinclair. None achieved more lasting notoriety, however, than Lola Montez. She stormed through California, dazzled the miners with her alluring "spider dance," fought with them when they failed to show proper appreciation, kept a pet bear at her Grass Valley home, and "discovered" the child star Lotta Crabtree. At the tender age of eight, and under the tutelage of Lola, Lotta captivated audiences with her singing, dancing, mimicking, and acting. Eventually, this California darling became the highest paid actress in America, and loving San Franciscans named a fountain in her honor. Adah Isaacs Menken, who cavorted on a horse wearing flesh-colored tights in *Mazeppa* and did nothing more than smile, created a sensation. Versatile thespians like Edwin Forrest, James Stark, Uncle Willy Chapman, and Junius and Edwin Booth also won rave reviews.[47]

The California theater that entertained the Forty-niners did not lack for variety. This in part reflected the amazing sophistication of theatergoers. Despite the crudeness of California and roughness of its miners, many were well read, and pioneer bookstores and lending libraries carried hundreds of printed plays. Over one thousand theatrical pieces were presented during the 1850s, including 907 plays, 48 operas, 84 extravaganzas, ballets, and pantomimes, and 66 minstrel specialties. Twenty-two plays by Shakespeare led the way.[48] Chinese and French theaters added a true

Reared in the town of Grass Valley, where at an early age she was encouraged by the celebrated actress Lola Montez, Lotta Crabtree began her theatrical career as a child, singing and dancing for the miners. As her career blossomed, she became a national sensation, touring the country with her own company. At the height of her fame, she was the highest-paid actress in the United States. *California Historical Society, FN-04331.*

international flare.[49] The incredible saga of the Gold Rush also stimulated its own productions. Bulbous-nosed Alonzo Delano, known as "Old Block," wrote *A Live Woman in the Mines,* a two-act play based on people he had met in the diggings. The antics of the legendary outlaw Joaquín Murieta inspired Charles Howe to write the melodrama *A Dramatic Play Entitled Joaquin Murieta de Castillo, the Celebrated California Bandit.* To create authenticity, Howe wove in such scenes as a miners' meeting, a miners' court, and an emigrants' camp. The shocking desert massacre of the Oatman family and captivity of Olive and Mary Oatman by Apache and Mohave Indians led to the production of a "beautiful and thrilling" three-act play, *The Oatman Family,* written by C. E. Bingham.[50]

A number of more obscure forms of entertainment found their way to the gold-country theaters, ranging from juggling acts to ventriloquist performances. The Argonauts demonstrated over and over that they were hungry for any form of amusement and would willingly be hoodwinked. A parade of wizards, magicians, mimics, and delineators of eccentricities happily took the miners' gold dust. The *Sacramento Daily Union* for December 29, 1852, for example, reported on what it called the "best treat of the season," which consisted of an exhibition of ventriloquism, legerdemain, and puppets. Its performance brought down "earthquakes of applause and protracted laughter."[51] Signor Giovanni Rossi was a popular magician who toured the major cities giving demonstrations of necromancy, sleight of hand, and ventriloquism. The Italian magician even mimicked animals and insects.[52] William Bickham describes the large crowd that turned out at the Illinois House in San Francisco to see a magician; the performance apparently made a lasting impression on "green'uns" from the backwoods of Missouri and Illinois, who had never witnessed anything like this before.[53]

The titillating performances of the *tableaux vivants,* or artistic models, represented yet another form of entertainment in this competitive, anything-goes environment. A showing of women dressed only in "flesh-colored silk" and "transparent gauze" seemed like a good idea in female-scarce northern California. San Francisco and Sacramento newspapers of 1850 ran frequent notices of "Splendid Living Pictures." Ostensibly, Dr. Collyer, the owner of one of these troupes, claimed that they were merely reproducing historical scenes from classical artists. The editors of the *Alta California* stated that the moment the models began "to pander to depraved tastes" they would be terminated.[54] In Stockton, "Model Artists" "clothed in nature's robes" and sitting on a revolving platform won unbounded applause.[55] As more respectable forms of amusement developed and tastes and morals became more rigorous, patronage for performances like Dr. Collyer's beauties dissipated, and the *tableaux vivants* did not live out the decade.

When the famed Joseph Andrew Rowe opened his Olympic Circus in San Francisco on October 29, 1849, he brought to the gold country a lively, breathtaking show. Known as "the celebrated equestrian and domesticator of the horse," Rowe, along with his wife, formed a company that included a clown, several riders, rope dancers, musicians, and a ringmaster. They gave dozens of performances before enthusiastic audiences at an amphitheater on Kearny Street. On May 2, 1850, Rowe opened his equestrian act in Sacramento and again met with success. After performing for several months, Rowe's thirst for travel and adventure took hold and the circus shipped out to Hawaii and Australia in the spring of 1851. Rowe, however, was not alone in providing high-wire acts, stunts with cannon balls, and clever gymnastic maneuvers on the backs of galloping horses. William H. Foley, Rowe's best clown, formed his own troupe, and the National Circus of H. C. Lee and John R. Marshall enjoyed great popularity.[56]

"The violin shrieked"

MUSIC AND DANCE

Music played a vital role in bringing amusement and comfort to the pioneers. In an astonishingly short time, high-class professional performers flocked to this El Dorado on the Pacific Coast. The saloons and theaters featured an assortment of handsomely paid musicians. Well-established performers like pianist Henri Hertz and vocalist Stephen C. Massett came to the mining region and were treated like royalty. Elisa Biscaccianti, "the American Thrush," and Kate Hayes, "the Swan of Erin," and a succession of female singers regaled adoring crowds of women-starved men. Soon music halls became a feature of most of the larger towns and cities, and the larger cities even supported music stores selling sheet music, violin and guitar strings, instruments of all kinds, and how-to books.[57]

Stephen Massett deserves special mention as the first "star" of the Gold Rush. On June 22, 1849, San Franciscans stuffed themselves into a tiny schoolhouse on Portsmouth Square to see the English-born talent put on a one-man show of singing and skits. For his efforts, Massett took in over $500. This represented the first regular entertainment in the city by the bay. He then proceeded to Sacramento and Marysville. Massett later recorded his theatrical experiences in his autobiography, *"Drifting About," or What "Jeems Pipes of Pipesville" Saw-and-Did.*[58]

Out in the wilderness and in the camps, however, the miners experienced a less sophisticated, but more spontaneous, form of musical entertainment. Luther Schaeffer, throughout his diary, paints a memorable picture. Around campfires or in their tents and log cabins, gold hunters would engage in singing hymns or favorite songs, depending on their country or place of origin. This singing would sometimes counteract the screams, firing of guns, and other hideous noises that emanated from the saloons.[59] At Rough and Ready, one Argonaut noted how a group of Frenchmen

pitched their tents nearby, and when plied with liquor, "would make the woods re-
echo with their French songs and boisterous merriment."[60] On Sundays, they quite
naturally sang the "Marseillaise." The musical charms of the French likewise impressed William Perkins in Sonora. They formed an amateur company and gave
weekly concerts, which Perkins pronounced the only amusement worth the en-
trance money.[61]

Schaeffer, in search of better mining prospects, moved to Grass Valley and took
with him his musical interests. In April 1851, he recalled how his companions met at
each other's cabins and sang "old fashion, plaintive tunes." "Old Virginia Shore,"
"Yankee Doodle," "Susanna," and "Auld Lang Syne" were particular favorites. Singing
dispelled gloom and sadness and helped assuage that sense of deprivation. So powerful did this singing become that large numbers of miners congregated around
them. "Even the most boisterous, the most careless and indifferent, would stop to listen and occasionally wipe away an unbidden tear," Schaeffer recorded.[62]

This casual singing inspired one of his companions to propose putting on a concert for the benefit of Grass Valley. With grand enthusiasm, these rough miners
plunged into their work. Lacking a printing press, they wrote out their programs and
posted them throughout the town, advertising: "Great Vocal and Instrumental Concert by the Grass Valley Minstrels. Cards of admission only 50 cents. The choicest
gems from the most popular operas will be performed."[63]

On a Monday evening, April 7, before a packed house, the Grass Valley Minstrels
gave their one and only concert. The minstrels consisted of two professional musicians, a dentist, a banker, and Schaeffer. They began inauspiciously as Schaeffer, going onto the stage, tripped and fell, causing an embarrassing domino effect. After
much laughter, the musicians regained their composure and played and sang away.
"The violin shrieked," he humorously recalled, "the guitar was out of tune; the
hideous bones rattled; the abominable triangle gave forth about as sweet music as a
tin-pan, and the flute chimed in." When the curtain finally rang down, a thunder-
ous applause rewarded them. Schaeffer, with justifiable pride, noted that their concert was long remembered in the Grass Valley area.[64]

Beginning with the fall of 1848, minstrel troupes became a regular form of entertainment. Painting their faces black and calling themselves "Ethiopian," groups disguised as African Americans went from saloon to saloon with their tambourines,
banjos, bones, violins, accordions, and triangles, singing songs and telling jokes.
Billy Birch, Charlie Backus, The New York Serenaders, Donnelly's (formerly of
Christie's Minstrels) Ethiopian Serenaders, Tyrolese Minstrels, and Stockton Minstrels, among others, brought smiles to thousands.[65]

Of all the forms of popular entertainment, none surpassed the miners' ball, or
cotillion. Whereas gambling drew self-righteous rebukes, dancing seemed to in-
spire approbation. Accounts of these terpsichorean conclaves appear numerous times

in gold-rush literature.[66] As J. D. Borthwick pointed out, "Wherever a fiddler could be found to play, a dance was got up."[67] Christmas, New Year's, the Fourth of July, the opening of a theater, or just plain Saturday night, were all excuses for getting up a dance.

One of the most unforgettable images of the Gold Rush is a lithographed plate in Borthwick's great narrative showing miners dressed in their heavy boots and flannel shirts dancing arm-in-arm. This womanless event he simply entitled "A Ball in the Mines." Equally as memorable, though, is a Kurz & Allison 1887 rendition of *The Miners' Ten Commandments,* which shows a man dancing in the frame of a hoop skirt.[68] Miners found imaginative ways to make up for the lack of female dance partners. A large square of canvas placed on a "certain part of his inexpressibles" would designate a "lady" for that particular dance.[69] Perhaps the most bizarre account of making-do appears in John M. Letts's *California Illustrated:* "At a certain point in the mineral regions, part of a lady's hat was discovered, which caused so much excitement and joy, that it was immediately decided to have a ball on the spot, in honor of the event." The miners then passed out invitations and over 300 celebrants appeared, each with a bottle of brandy. Inspired by a simple female hat, the ball lasted two days![70]

As more women came to California, these pioneer soirées were proportionately enlivened. But there were still not enough female partners to go around. Dr. Morse told how Sacramento prepared for a Fourth of July dance. Reflecting the biases of the day, he wrote "it was essentially important that every Caucasian descendent of Eve in this section of the State should be present."[71] The men of Sacramento scoured the countryside in search of female dance partners, and when the ball began, 200 plain-looking men faced 18 women. Because of the presence of so many ladies, the men paid an astonishing $32 per ticket. Up at Murderer's Bar, William Bickham and fellow miners became so excited at the prospect of attending a ball with women present that they threw off their old mining clothes and put on "new Toggery." Some even shaved, and all wore clean shirts.[72]

In the more diversified Southern Mines and in more cosmopolitan places like San Francisco, women of various nationalities gathered at "fancy-dress balls," or as many miners called them, *fandangos.* "The pretty damsels" and "graceful nymphs" who tended the gambling tables and served the drinks helped considerably to increase the ratio of women to men. A *fandango* in Sonora featured a variety of dances ranging from polkas to Hispanic steps. Musicians playing a piano (a rarity in the mines), violoncello, harp, violin, and two guitars set the pace. Singing in French and Spanish added an international flare to the event.[73]

Most of these balls or *fandangos* contemporaries portrayed as reasonably respectable. But an abundance of alcohol combined with an abundance of lonely men must have resulted in some raucous moments. The writers of *The Annals of San Francisco* observed: "There the most extraordinary scenes were exhibited, as might have been expected where the actors and dancers were chiefly hot-headed young men, flush of money and half frantic with excitement, and lewd girls freed from the necessity of moral restraint."[74]

Free-flowing liquor, quantities of food, and long duration typified these festivities. To keep everyone fortified, most included a large meal or supper. Occasionally, dances lasted until dawn and sometimes even for several days. Dame Shirley, writing as an observer rather than as a participant, left this memorable picture of how miners celebrated the Saturnalia at Indian Bar:

> At nine o'clock in the evening they had an oyster and champagne supper in the Humboldt [hotel], which was very gay with toasts, songs, speeches, etc. I believe that the company danced all night; at any rate they were dancing when I went to sleep and they were dancing when I woke the next morning. The revel was kept up in this mad way for three days, growing wilder every hour. Some never slept at all during that time. On the fourth day they got past dancing, and, lying in drunken heaps about the barroom, commenced a most unearthly howling.[75]

By the time Dame Shirley sent this letter to her sister in 1852, the dance was becoming commonplace. "Such balls were becoming too numerous to be all chronicled," remarked *The Annals of San Francisco,* "while amidst the general brilliancy it is difficult to select any one as a specimen to show forth the times."[76]

"The gold of the mind"
READING AS A PASTIME

While the gambling hells and drinking saloons overflowed with customers, the miners and those who supplied the miners with services also followed much tamer and more civilized pursuits. Reading and writing were chief among them. Writing letters home and making diary entries was one of the most talked-about pursuits, and every Californian eagerly awaited a letter from a loved one. Californians sent thousands of letters around Cape Horn or across the Isthmus of Panama, and they waited for hours in long lines at the post offices for the chance of a letter from home. Sunday, the great day of rest, served as writing day. It is no accident that Charles Nahl's heroic painting, *Sunday Morning in the Mines,* has as its central figure a self-portrait of the artist writing a letter that begins "Dear Mother." Likewise, John Banks, while in the mines, made almost all of his diary entries on Sunday.[77] Certainly, a major pastime of Californians consisted of savoring those communications to and from home. Luther Schaeffer beautifully and eloquently captured the preciousness of those letters:

There is one source of happiness to the Californian, which can never be fully understood by friends at home: I allude to letters—to a sheet of paper, scribbled over, perhaps, carelessly by a friend, who little thinks how each word, each crossing of the T, or
dotting of an I, will be dwelt upon; how every sentence is remembered, and how the
rough miner throws his body down on his hard pallet, with his letter secreted in his bosom, and dreams, perchance, of the writer, or of the pleasure of returning home, and
embracing friends from whom he had so long been absent.[78]

Reading served as a pastime eagerly enjoyed. Despite the rough and tumble of the
Gold Rush, a highly literate group of people occupied the territory. While reading
Scripture led the way, newspapers from the home states were not far behind. Newspapers sold for a premium. Bayard Taylor wrote with astonishment of how a man
from New York arrived with 1,500 copies of the *Tribune* and sold them all within two
hours for a dollar apiece, causing Taylor to search his valise for newspapers.[79] And,
it did not matter if the paper was terribly out of date.

Taylor provided another wonderful, yet realistic, picture of reading, or the lack
thereof, when visiting Sacramento. He pointed out that after a long day of work,
people were simply too tired to read and that candles cost so much that "reading was
out of the question." He went on to say, "I saw many persons who had brought the
works of favorite authors with them, for recreation at odd hours, but of all the works
thus brought, I never saw one read. Men preferred—or rather it grew, involuntarily,
into a custom—to lie at ease instead."[80]

Others, like William Perkins, complained of the lack of books and reading material in 1849 and 1850; but by 1851 Perkins noted a rapid turnaround, reporting that
"literature of all kinds is abundant," which he believed caused a great improvement
in society.[81] Reading also had a curative effect on some. John Marshall Newton, a
sickly but determined young man trying to regain his health from the mines, wrote
from San Francisco: "I passed my time—a couple of months—in eagerly devouring
all the books I could get from the stalls in the streets. As I was quite weak I used to
read all day long propped in bed."[82]

San Francisco pioneered the way with reading. Squeezed into Portsmouth Square,
the same plaza that supported the gambling center of the world, stood an oasis of
civilization, the bookstore of John Hamilton Still of Florida. He set up shop in
September 1849 and supplied his customers with "the latest novels, magazines and
newspapers." Others such as Charles Kimball (the "Noisy Carrier"), Anton Roman,
J. M. Hutchings, and Hubert Howe Bancroft followed. Within a short time, Epes
Ellery became the first to deal in secondhand books.[83]

Despite the constant threat of fire, Fryer and Hullburd opened a private library in
a suite of rooms on Clay Street at the early date of April 1850. The enterprising partners offered a wide array of fictitious, historical, and scientific works, and several

The What Cheer House on Sacramento Street, near Montgomery, in San Francisco, 1865. Established in 1852 as a temperance hotel by Robert B. Woodward, the What Cheer came to have a well-stocked library for the intellectual stimulation of its lodgers, who disdained drinking and gaming. By 1861 the well-patronized Library Room contained two to three thousand volumes, including fiction by Charles Dickens, Washington Irving, Nathaniel Hawthorne, and others, as well as historical works, biography, and weighty tomes on farming and stock-raising. *California Historical Society, FN-02365.*

foreign language newspapers. Additionally, the proprietors made available a service whereby visitors could dictate notes and letters. The *Daily Alta California* proudly reported that San Francisco now had a place for "the gold of the mind."[84]

As northern California and the mining region progressed in the early 1850s, the number of books, magazines, and newspaper vendors likewise multiplied. Newspapers and city directories frequently carried advertisements for books. Columbia and Sonora serve as examples of the popularity of books and reading. Charles J. Brown in Columbia combined a circulating library with his jelly and jam shop, and at the

Broadway Book Store, customers could purchase books in many languages. Sonora supported a circulating library and three bookstores boasting a variety of books, newspapers, and periodicals.[85]

The most amazing instance of the love of reading may be found in the mining camp of Hawkins Bar in Tuolumne County. Howard Gardiner tells of how Morgan Davis, a Yale graduate, established a circulating library in 1852. Davis acquired books by soliciting subscriptions from miners and offered mainly works of fiction but included many standard publications to suite all tastes. Gardiner later recalled that: "In the long winter evenings, the boys would gather in some tent, appoint one of their number reader, while they sat by, smoked their pipes, and listened interestedly. Woe to the man who made a disturbance at these sessions; he was ejected summarily, sans ceremony."[86] Such a scene provided a stark contrast to the stereotype of the swarthy, carousing, swearing, gambling, drunken Forty-niner.

A further example of the civilizing influence of the printed word occurred with the founding of the Mercantile Library Association in San Francisco on January 24, 1853. Located on the second floor of the California Exchange, it opened its doors on March 1 and featured a 1,500-volume library, as well as current newspapers and periodicals. Most importantly, the library offered an option to the many "degrading influences" and gave San Franciscans a "means of mental improvement." As *The Annals of San Francisco* stated, "It is the best substitute for a portion of the comforts of home."[87] The African American San Francisco Atheneum, Hebrew Young Men's Literary Association, and Seaman's Reading Room and Library also provided similar opportunities for intellectual attainment.

Additionally, the mining region and its supplying cities began to support lectures, literary and dramatic essays and readings, and debates on important topics of the day. With many well-educated and talented people flooding into California, it would seem only natural that such intellectual diversions developed. Subjects for visiting lecturers included discourses on mining, mesmerism, and religion and, not surprisingly, the evils of intemperance and gambling.[88]

"Depraved lust for the sordid and sensational"
SPORTS IN THE GOLDEN ERA

A variety of sports and other contests provided an alternative to the saloons for amusement in this wild, reckless environment. Bull-and-bear fights, bull fights, cock fights, horse racing, prize fights, foot races, and walking contests also satisfied the never-ending desire for excitement. Sports helped to relieve the tedium of work and gave the lonely Forty-niner a place to go and something to do.

No activity attracted greater attention or invited more curiosity and comment than the gruesome bull-and-bear fight, in which grizzlies and long-horned bulls fought each other to the death. This legacy of California's Hispanic past continued well into the 1860s, and virtually every major town hosted these contests. The great chroniclers of that era described in gory detail this primitive yet popular form of mortal combat. Local newspapers likewise provided full accounts.[89]

Tracy Storer and Lloyd Tevis in their thorough study, *California Grizzly*, document a marked change in the sport during the American period. "The fights, which had been rooted in the traditions of Spain and were an integral part of the fiestas and religious holidays of Spanish California, now were cheapened and commercialized for the benefit of the newcomers."[90] Curiosity and a "depraved lust for the sordid and sensational" lured many non-Hispanics to these spectacular, bloody contests. In the violent milieu of the Gold Rush, the Forty-niners admired the strength of the bear and bull as much as the skill and determination of the prize fighter.[91]

Recalling the glory days of the Roman coliseum, these four-legged gladiatorial bouts were accompanied by appropriate fanfare. Like most other leisure activities, these fights took place on Sundays, and at the surviving missions, following Mass. Conducted in a carnival-like atmosphere, parades, music, horse racing, cock fighting, and other more benign forms of amusement preceded the main event. Managers promoted the contests in a variety of ways. Hinton Helper, for instance, said he was shocked to hear a drum, fife, and clarinet on the Sabbath, and when he looked out his window, saw a caged grizzly being paraded through the streets of San Francisco. Large posters on the cage announced: "Fun Brewing—Great Attraction! Hard Fighting to Be Done! Two Bulls and One Bear."[92]

Bull-and-bear fights proved to be tremendous bonanzas for the animals' owners. Contemporaries reported crowds as large as six thousand, with spectators paying from $2.50 to $10 admission. When bruin and taurus entered the arena men, women, and children whooped, shouted, and stamped their feet in happy unison. These contests seemed to attract all races and nationalities. Many, particularly Hispanics, came dressed in their finest attire. Most of these affairs took place in makeshift amphitheaters that consisted of a circular pen surrounded by a sturdy, high wooden fence behind which rose tiers of rudely constructed seats.[93]

The *dramatis personae* consisted of beasts bestowed with such colorful names as Lola Montez, Behemoth, Hercules, Trojan, and—recalling the recent Mexican War—Generals Scott and Santa Anna. While the Spanish and Mexican tradition matched a bull against a matador (human), the Californios had modified this by capturing the native grizzly from the Sierra and pitting it against a wild bull. Strong and immense, old bruin usually proved more than a match for the fiercest adversary. The Americans, however, when staging these contests, sometimes mistakenly captured the more passive black bear and enraged spectators when the frightened bear seemed less than enthusiastic when facing a snorting, pawing bull with its rapier horns.[94]

J. D. Borthwick, the Scottish artist, provided a vivid account of one of these deadly contests. Held at Mokelumne Hill, he noted that promoters plastered the town and roadside with signs reading "War! War!! War!!! / The celebrated Bull-killing Bear," / GENERAL SCOTT, / will fight a Bull on Sunday the 15th inst., at 2 P.M.." Borthwick went on to describe the conditions of the contest: "The Bear will be chained with a twenty-foot chain in the middle of the arena. The Bull will be perfectly wild young, of the Spanish breed, and the best that can be found in the country. The Bull's horns will be of their natural length, and '*not sawed off to prevent accidents.*' The Bull will be quite free in the arena, and not hampered in any way whatever."[95]

Managers, in an effort to please the crowd and depending on the willingness of the beasts to fight, used a variety of formats. Sometimes one would be chained to a post, sometimes the hind legs of both were tied together, and other times it would be two bulls against one bear or even a mountain lion or buffalo against a bear. Occasionally, too, the combatants would have to be goaded into fighting. Twisting a bull's tail usually produced the desired effect. The winner would be "rewarded" by facing another foe. The bull's horns and the bear's paws and jaws inflicted horrible wounds, which frequently brought about the death of one or both.[96]

When women, children, and churches had arrived, public revulsion ultimately pressured authorities into putting an end to this blood sport. The San Francisco *Daily Alta California* used such words as "disgusting," "depravity," "sickening," and "brutality" when describing these contests and called them "a disgrace to our city, to society, to our laws and to humanity." Further, the fact that these contests mostly took place on Sundays revolted the pious. By the late 1850s and early 1860s, lawmakers legislated out of existence these brutal confrontations.[97]

Reflecting an Hispanic population that was not Californian, but came primarily from Sonora (in Mexico) and South America, the Southern Mines also enjoyed the more traditional bull fight as a pastime. Both Enos Christman and J. D. Borthwick recorded the practice of this ancient sport at Sonora. Christman, a journalist, told how the contest began with an impressive procession of two gaudily dressed Mexican horsemen carrying long spears, followed by footmen with red flags. After their deep bows and strains of inspiring music, a large wild bull stormed triumphantly into the arena charging both horsemen and footmen. Once things calmed down, all eyes turned as the matador, disguised as "a dusky Mexican señorita, magnificently dressed," bravely entered with sword in hand. The matador parried with the bull, let him make several passes, and then coldly administered the coup-de-grace amid "a shower of silver dollars and a shout of applause."[98]

Borthwick, after witnessing such a contest, noted two unusual features. One was the performance of an athletic and brave man, who brought the crowd to a frenzy by actually riding the bull while it furiously tried to buck his tormentor.[99] He then went on to describe the performance of the celebrated "Señorita Romana Perez," the featured matador at a bull fight at nearby Columbia. The artist wryly noted that the matador was "very well got up as a woman, with the slight exception of a very fine pair of moustaches." When Romana curtseyed, laughter, hisses, and curses greeted her/him. Nonetheless, the bull fighter exhibited much feminine grace and adroitly whisked his petticoats at the bull before giving it the cold steel.[100]

While bulls tried to gore bears with their horns, human beings entertained audiences by pummeling each other with their fists. Bare-knuckle prize fighting was already heavily patronized in the eastern United States and it only made sense that it would come to a brawling, carousing, jumping place like California. In this male-dominated society, prize fighting became a natural companion and extension to the many fights that broke out over mining claims and in the drinking and gambling saloons. As John Boessenecker points out in his study of violence in the Gold Rush, the great champions all came to California during this rambunctious era, including Chris Lilly, Yankee Sullivan, John Morrissey, William "Woolly" Kearney, and Billy Mulligan, among others.[101]

Many boxing matches were held during the early 1850s and drew enormous crowds. The most famous, a bout between Irishman John Morrissey and Britisher George Thompson, did much to create interest in the sport. Morrissey challenged Thompson to a fight to be held on August 20, 1852, the winner to receive a $3,000 prize. On the appointed day, thousands of spectators poured into Mare Island by riverboat and steamer and placed their bets. A *Daily Alta California* reporter, following the fight, noted that "The Sacramento boys bet houses and lots very freely against horses and other livestock." The two pounded each other for eleven rounds, until Morrissey's supporters cried foul and a near riot ensued. The judges agreed with Morrissey and awarded him the fight. That tussle created a keen interest in the sport. "Within a short time every little mining town had a gymnasium, with its professor teaching the young and old how to strike out from the shoulder."[102]

Not all sporting activities involved the spilling of blood. Foot races, with bets ranging from a handful of cigars to $1,000, delighted the miners. William Bickham, an obviously well-coordinated individual, knew how to enjoy himself with his free time at Murderer's Bar. On one Monday, he mentioned that he played a game of foot-ball, and at other times, track and field gave him a welcome diversion. He did not mention, however, placing a wager on any of these activities. He proudly wrote his sisters at home that "I have had much sport upon the clear days, skylarking with my companions of this neighborhood, running races, jumping, &c. I have proven to be the best Jumper on the Bar and am believed to be as good at running as the best. To-morrow I try my speed with *one* of the best. Rivalry."[103]

Another popular American and European pastime that crossed the continent to California was pedestrianism. A short article in the *Daily Alta California* for June 6, 1852, carried the following: "A man named Kelly commenced on Sunday morning,

Gymnasts exhibit their athletic abilities before a huge crowd assembled at Russ's Gardens in San Francisco for the annual May festival of the local Turnverein, established in 1853 by German-born Argonauts. Among the many physical-culture enthusiasts in the city were the artists Charles and Arthur Nahl, who were ranked among the best gymnasts in California. In 1860 Arthur helped form the San Francisco Olympic Club, the first athletic club in America, and three years later the brothers published their illustrated *Instructions in Gymnastics,* which included exercises "suitable for the female sex." *California Historical Society, FN-06037.*

at Selby's ranch, below Sacramento, the arduous feat of walking a thousand miles in a thousand consecutive hours, on a wager of $2,000. He came in at the end of the tenth mile last evening, as fresh as when he started on his long journey."[104] On June 30, the paper reported that Kelly had completed 710 miles despite having to endure badly blistered feet. Remarkably, the *Alta* for July 15 related that this endurance walker had completed the feat and presumably won the bet.[105]

The many Germans who came to California brought with them their love of gymnastics. In 1853, San Francisco Germans established a *Turnverein,* or gymnastic society, and built a gymnasium on Battery Street. To share this respectable pastime with their fellow countrymen, they held an annual May Day exhibition at Russ's Gardens. Attired in brown linen coats and pantaloons, "They leaped, balanced and twirled, danced, sang, drank, smoked and made merry."[106] As depicted in a pictorial letter sheet, a large throng witnessed this happy demonstration of athletic skill. Following the lead of San Francisco, the Turnverein soon spread throughout the region, bringing a healthy alternative to games of chance.

Many other sports entertained the gold-rush population. Horse racing and the development of race courses throughout the state aroused much interest. Hunting and shooting clubs gave many an opportunity to show off their marksmanship. Less savory forms of competition involving cock and dog fights appealed to those with violent dispositions.

"A jaunt of recreation"

ENJOYING NATURE

Gold-Rushers, once they settled into a routine, began to notice what pioneer publisher James M. Hutchings would call "scenes of wonder and curiosity."[107] To be sure, mining and its supporting activities wreaked havoc on the environment, but long before John Muir arrived in 1868, some were appreciating the beauty and geographic diversity of the region. The awesomeness of the Sierra and its powerful rivers; the magnificence of San Francisco Bay and its Golden Gate; the sublime foothills and stately oaks; and the great Central Valley with its wildlife elicited comment from the travel writers of the early 1850s. California, as the newcomers found out, offered more than the sparkle of a golden nugget.

This sense of place gradually led Californians to take "jaunts of recreation" and to delight in its natural surroundings. Leisurely excursions gave people relief from the hurly-burly atmosphere of the cities and camps. San Franciscans, for example, found that Sunday trips out to Mission Dolores, the Presidio, and the ocean gave them a cheap and convenient form of recreation. Traveling by foot, horse, and carriage, and later by omnibus, they would take the Old Mission Road over the sand dunes on their way to quiet adventure. Along the way, they would see numerous homes with well-cultivated vegetable and flower gardens. By the mid-1850s, such places as the Golden Gate, United States, and Sonntag's nurseries gave pleasure to all passersby.[108] Just as Victorian England and its urban masses awakened to the delights of natural history, so did California. As the *Alta California* noted, the green fields and flowering shrubs gave relief to those who have "long been pent up in the cheerless city."[109]

Mary Jane Megquier penned several letters home describing the fields of flowers that could be found on the way to the mission. Such scenes made her think of home. On April 4, 1856, Megquier described such a pleasurable outing:

Yesterday Mrs. Robinson, Emily and myself started for a walk out of town, took a lunch at a friend of Ems from New York with the addition of two ladies from there and two gents, we walked to the mission, visiting a number of private gardens which are perfectly splendid now: roses, verbenas fucias and gillyflowers seem to predominate but the verbenas surpass any thing I ever saw, clusters as large as a teacup, of every shade covering quite an extent of ground, you could be happy while gazing upon them. We went and took an ice cream came home well satisfied with the days adventure.[110]

To celebrate May Day in 1853, Emanuel Russ opened his sprawling gardens to fellow Germans. Located at Sixth and Harrison streets near the Mission Road, Russ's Gardens, as mentioned earlier, hosted a meeting of the Turnverein Association with a variety of events including gymnastic demonstrations, singing, and dancing. Flags and garlands, an amphitheater, and a gaily decorated pavilion greeted the guests. Following this success, the kindly Russ made his comely gardens available for a multitude of celebrations, military exercises, and picnics. It soon became a favorite place of resort.[111] In many respects, this sanctuary of leisure foreshadowed the founding in 1866 of northern California's most famous place of amusement, Woodward's Gardens.[112]

To the south and west of Russ's Gardens stood a collection of adobes redolent with the culture of a bygone era. Mission Dolores attracted many curiosity seekers on Sundays. Its exotic architecture and quiet cemetery evoked a sense of romanticism and nostalgia. "It seems as though we could never weary in looking upon these interesting scenes," publisher J. M. Hutchings wrote.[113] However, the gruesome and noisy bull-and-bear fights held at the mission on Sundays occasionally broke the serenity Hutchings so admired.

A Sunday alternative consisted of an eight-mile ride out to the ocean. The pounding surf, bark of the sea lions, bracing wind, and incredible vistas presented a distinct contrast to city life. Excursionists could also admire the vegetable gardens that supplied their supper tables. By mid-decade, entrepreneurs saw an opportunity and established roadside destinations such as Ocean House, Beach House, Lake House (on Lake Merced), and Rockaway House. These seaside inns gave visitors a place for refreshment before making the trek back to the urban center.[114]

While certainly charming and convenient, these peninsular recreation spots paled when compared to the fantastic natural wonders found in the interior. Long known to Native Americans, the finding of geysers, caves, caverns, natural bridges, giant waterfalls, and leviathan trees by Caucasian newcomers added a dramatic new dimension to California. None created more astonishment than the discovery of the Big Trees Grove near Murphys in Calaveras County. Augustus T. Dowd stumbled upon the grove of *Sequoia gigantea* in May 1852 and lured his companions to the spot by saying he had killed the largest grizzly bear he ever saw. These "vegetable giants," as they were dubbed, apparently could not be believed. Within a short period of time "the trumpet-tongued press proclaimed the wonder to all sections of the State, and to all parts of the world."[115] A tourist attraction had been found.

The reaction to this discovery typified the American view at midcentury. On the one hand, Californians expressed awe and respect for nature, comparing these "patriarchs of the forest" to man-made monuments like European cathedrals or the tomb of Mohammed at Mecca or the Juggernaut of Hindostan.[116] On the other hand, some gold-rush Californians, in characteristic fashion, reacted to these redwood grizzlies as if they had found nature's version of P. T. Barnum's freak show or as something that could make their promoters rich. First, they bestowed names on these 3,000-year-old trees, such as "Three Graces," "Old Maid," "Mother and Son," "Siamese Twins." Next, they cut one down, Dowd's "Discovery Tree." It took a crew of five men over twenty days to fell this noble tree, which measured over 300 feet in height and 96 feet in circumference. Later, a crew polished its stump into a dance floor and its trunk was hollowed out into a two-lane bowling alley.[117]

To convince nonbelievers and those who could not visit the grove and its new hotel, promoters decided to take the trees to the world. California now had its own "wonder of the world." Workmen crated up the twelve-inch-thick bark of the Discovery Tree and a two-foot section of the trunk for exhibition first in San Francisco and then in New York City and Europe. Proclaimed as "The Vegetable Wonder of the World," the bark of this three-millennia-old tree was reassembled to a height a sixty feet and went on display on Bush Street in September 1853. The bark tower delighted crowds for about a month before going on tour.[118] Another, "The Mother of the Forest," was, as John Muir later put it, "skinned alive." Promoter George L. Trask hired workmen to strip its bark to a height of 116 feet and carefully packed it up for show in New York and London. A London broadside touted this bark cylinder as the "greatest curiosity in the world!"[119]

While the discovery of big tree groves in the Sierra and along the coast brought worldwide attention, Californians found other outdoor attractions. Boat trips to the Farallon Islands, hikes up Mount Tamalpais in Marin County or across the bay on Mount Diablo, or an excursion to the hissing geysers in Sonoma County, confirmed that there was much to do and see in natural California. Not too far from the Calaveras Big Trees and located on a creek know as McKinney's Humbug, a Captain Taylor in October 1850, while target shooting, "discovered" the "Great Cave of Calaveras County." Proclaimed as "one of the greatest natural curiosities of California," its owners responded in that typical way by opening a hotel and leading tours into subterranean chambers picturesquely titled "Cathedral," "Bishop's Palace," "Cataract," and "Bridal Chamber." A settlement grew up around this attraction bearing the appropriate name of Cave City. Other caves in the area were discovered, and to this day, lure the curious.[120]

The infusion of tens of thousands of new faces into California in the 1850s led to

In the spring of 1855 James M. Hutchings, having heard rumors of a waterfall a thousand feet high, organized the first tourist party to visit Yosemite, and upon his return, he engaged the pioneer lithographic firm of Britton & Rey to prepare a print of *The Yo-Hamite Falls*. Derived from a drawing by the artist Thomas A. Ayres, who had accompanied Hutchings into the mountains, it was the first image of the valley published and helped to popularize the wonders of the valley. By the end of 1855 three other parties had made their way to Yosemite, the simple beginnings of tourism at what would become one of the greatest scenic attractions in the Golden State and the nation. *California Historical Society, FN-31560.*

the greatest tourist find: Yosemite Valley. Although first entered by explorers in 1833, the glacial chasm did not become widely known until the punitive expeditions of Major James D. Savage and his Mariposa Battalion against the Indians in 1851. One of its members let it be known that the valley boasted a thousand-foot waterfall. This report intrigued J. M. Hutchings, who was planning to publish a monthly magazine on California. He brought along artist Thomas A. Ayres, and in June 1855, the Hutchings party toured Yosemite, enjoying "five days of scenic banqueting." The subsequent combination of Hutchings's writings and his publication of Ayres's drawing in October 1855, opened the valley to the world. Its remoteness, however, made a visit more than a leisurely "jaunt of recreation," and consequently, Yosemite had little impact on the gold-rush population. Pack trails and then a hotel opened in 1859, but not until the completion of the transcontinental railroad in 1869, or even the building of a branch railroad to the edge of the valley in the early 1900s, did Yosemite attract significant numbers of tourists.[121]

Once the Forty-niners had a chance to look around and not worry about making a pile or surviving, they found an abundance of ways to while away their free time. Considering that California, prior to the great discovery in 1848, consisted of a few pueblos and scores of ranchos, it is nothing short of astonishing that it could, by the early 1850s, lead the world in gambling and consumption of spirits and boast first-rate theaters, music halls, and lending libraries. These newcomers also found delight in nature and appreciated California's many "scenes of wonder and curiosity." Popular culture was indeed well established on its golden shores.

NOTES

1. Virtually every narrative history of the Gold Rush contains a section on amusements and popular diversions.

2. For more detail on this day of rest see Hinton Helper, *The Land of Gold: Reality Versus Fiction* (Baltimore: by the author, 1855), 109–15; Charles B. Gillespie, *A Miner's Sunday: From the Writer's California Journal 1849–50*, reprinted from *Century Magazine*, 1891 (Golden, Colo.: Outbooks, 1981); and Elizabeth Margo, *Taming the Forty-Niner* (New York: Rinehart, 1955), 43–53. Charles Nahl's great painting at the Crocker Art Museum in Sacramento, *Sunday Morning in the Mines*, is the best visual reference.

3. Jared Comstock Brown to Charles Brown, Coloma, August 11, 1851, Small Manuscript Collections II, Box 10, California State Library.

4. For a general history of gambling in the Gold Rush, see Thomas R. Jones, *You Bet': How the California Pioneers Did It* (Sacramento: News Publishing Co., 1935); John Philip Quinn, *Fools of Fortune; or Gambling and Gamblers* (Chicago: G. L. Howe & Co., 1890), 438–52; Editors of Time-Life Books, *The Gamblers* (Alexandria: Time-Life Books, 1978), 82–94. Eyewitness accounts of gambling and drinking are too numerous to mention here. Among the best are by Bayard Taylor, Hinton Helper, J. D. Borthwick, William Kelly, William Perkins, Enos Christman, and John F. Morse.

5. Bayard Taylor, *Eldorado, or, Adventures in the Path of Empire*, 2 vols. (New York: George P. Putnam, 1850), 1:87.

6. Samuel Colville, *Colville's Marysville Directory for the Year Commencing November 1, 1855* (San Francisco: Monson & Valentine, 1855), vii. Colville's preface provides one of the most vivid descriptions of a gaming house.

7. Charles Ross Parke, *Dreams to Dust: A Diary of the California Gold Rush, 1849–1850*, ed. James E. Davis (Lincoln: University of Nebraska Press, 1989), 102.

8. Frank Soulé, John H. Gihon, and James Nisbet, *The Annals of San Francisco* (New York: D. Appleton & Co., 1855), 248; hereinafter *Annals of San Francisco*. H. H. Bancroft, in *California Inter Pocula* (San Francisco: The History Company, 1888), 677, supports this view.

9. William Perkins, *Three Years in California: William Perkins' Journal of Life at Sonora, 1849–1852* (Berkeley: University of California Press, 1964), 344; hereinafter *Journal of Life at Sonora*.

10. Enos Christman, *One Man's Gold: The Letters & Journal of a Forty-Niner* (New York: Whittlesey House, 1930), 189.

11. J. D. Borthwick, *Three Years in California* (Edinburgh: William Blackwood & Sons, 1857), 58. William Kelly, *A Stroll through the Diggings of California* (London: Simms and M'Intyre, 1852), 49, describes Indian gambling in Sacramento.

12. H. Lee Scamehorn, Edwin P. Banks, and Jamie Lytle-Webb, eds., *The Buckeye Rovers in the Gold Rush* (Athens: Ohio University Press, 1989), 167.

13. Bancroft, *California Inter Pocula*, 677.

14. Daniel B. Woods, *Sixteen Months at the Gold Diggings* (New York: Harper & Brothers, 1851), 188–89.

15. *Annals of San Francisco*, 248.

16. Benjamin Vicuña MacKenna, in *We Were 49ers! Chilean Accounts of the California Gold Rush*, trans. and ed. Edwin A. Beilharz and Carlos U. López (Pasadena: Ward Ritchie Press, 1976), 196.

17. Kelly, *A Stroll through the Diggings*, 181.

18. *Annals of San Francisco*, 382. Taylor, *Eldorado*, 1:57, recorded that the Parker House paid $110,000 yearly, of which gamblers paid at least $60,000 for use of the second story.

19. Colville, *Marysville Directory*, vi.

20. John Letts, *California Illustrated* (New York: William Holdredge, 1852), 131. For a description of gambling in Sacramento none is better or more colorful than Dr. John F. Morse, "History of Sacramento," in *The Sacramento Directory for the Year 1853–54* (Sacramento: Samuel Colville, 1853), 6–7.

21. For descriptions of the inside of gaming houses, see for example Borthwick, *Three Years in California*, 57; Taylor, *Eldorado*, 1:118–19; Kelly, *A Stroll through the Diggings*, 181–83; Woods, *Sixteen Months*, 74–75; Helper, *Land of Gold*, 70–71; and Albert Benard de Russailh, *Last Adventure: San Francisco in 1851*, trans. Clarkson Crane (San Francisco: The Westgate Press, 1931), 12–17.

22. Samuel Colville, "History of San Francisco," in *Colville's San Francisco Directory* (San Francisco: by the compiler, 1856), xvii.

23. Perkins, *Journal of Life at Sonora*, 218–19.

24. Russailh, *Last Adventure*, 29–30.

25. Colville, *Marysville Directory*, vi.

26. Taylor, *Eldorado*, 2:31. Taylor provides as equally colorful a picture of music as Colville.

27. See Quinn, *Fools of Fortune*, for the rules of the various games. Susan Lee Johnson, "Bulls, Bears, and Dancing Boys: Race, Gender, and Leisure in the California Gold Rush," *Radical History Review* 60 (1994): 27–29, tells of the violence associated with gaming: "Indeed, no other activity in the diggings, aside from mining itself, provided as much rancor as gambling."

28. William B. Peter to Emile Holland, San Francisco, January 1, 1851, Small Manuscript Collections II, California State Library.

29. Bancroft, *California Inter Pocula*, 675. Bancroft also noted: "The saloon-keeper was one of the dignitaries of the town."

30. *Annals of San Francisco*, 452. Liquor, according to this report from the *San Francisco Herald*, was sold in 144 tavern restaurants, 154 groceries, and 46 gambling houses. This number of bartenders included reserves. There were actually 556 working at the time of the report.

31. *Daily Alta California* (San Francisco), February 8, 1849; Helper, *Land of Gold*, 67.

32. Robert Brownlee, *An American Odyssey: The Autobiography of a 19th-Century Scotsman*, ed. Patricia A. Etter (Fayetteville: The University of Arkansas Press, 1986), 118.

33. James Delavan, *Notes on California and the Placers: How to Get There, and What to Do Afterwards* (New York: H. Long & Brother, 1850), 52.

34. Taylor, *Eldorado*, 2:57.

35. Friedrich Gerstäcker, *Gerstäcker's Travels* (London: T. Nelson and Sons, 1854), 274.

36. Invaluable for the study of the theater are the publications of the Northern California Writers' Project: *San Francisco Theater Research*, vol. 1 (San Francisco: Works Projects Administration, 1938), and *Theatrical Annals of Sacramento* (Sacramento: Works Projects Administration, 1939–1940). The following also provide background information on theater: George R. MacMinn, *The Theater of The Golden Era in California* (Caldwell, Idaho: Caxton Printers, 1941), 366–445; Pauline Jacobson, *City of the Golden 'Fifties* (Berkeley: University of California Press, 1941), 166–221; Thor Severson, *Sacramento: An Illustrated History: 1839 to 1874* (San Francisco: California Historical Society, 1973), 149–52; and Margo, *Taming the Forty-Niner*, 89–110.

37. Russailh, *Last Adventure*, 18.

38. "The Drama in San Francisco," *Daily Alta California*, January 24, 1850.

39. The best account of the Eagle appears in Taylor, *Eldorado*, 2:29–31. See also *History of Sacramento County, California* (Oakland: Thompson & West, 1880), 119–20. *Theatrical Annals of Sacramento*, compiled by the Northern California Writers' Project, is a transcription of theater articles and notices from the *Sacramento Placer Times*, August 1, 1849 to June 3, 1850.

40. *History of Sacramento County*, 120; MacMinn, *Theater of the Golden Era*, 28–31.

41. Taylor, *Eldorado*, 2:30–31.

42. Quoted in MacMinn, *Theater of the Golden Era*, 33.

43. The *Daily Alta California* extensively covered the opening of theaters, the various plays, and players; MacMinn, *Theater of the Golden Era*, 38. See also Charles Lockwood, *Suddenly San Francisco: The Early Years of an Instant City* (San Francisco: California Living Books, 1978), 100–104.

44. MacMinn, *Theater of the Golden Era*, 41–45, and Jacobson, *City of the Golden 'Fifties*, 263–71.

45. Ibid.

46. MacMinn, *Theater of the Golden Era*, 57–58.

47. Biographies exist of many of the pioneer actors and actresses. See, for example, Bruce Seymour, *Lola Montez: A Life* (New Haven: Yale University Press, 1996). See also Jacobson and MacMinn for short biographies of individual actors and actresses.

48. MacMinn, *Theater of the Golden Era,* 84 and 196.

49. Vicuña MacKenna, in *We Were 49ers!*, 197–98.

50. Glenn Loney, ed., *California Gold-Rush Plays* (New York: Performing Arts Journal Publications, 1983). In addition to a fine introduction, Loney reproduces the plays of Delano and Howe. See also MacMinn, *Theater of the Golden Era,* 243–52.

51. *Sacramento Daily Union,* December 29, 1852; MacMinn, *Theater of the Golden Era,* 489–90.

52. *Sacramento Transcript,* May 18, 1850 and *Daily Alta California,* April 29, 1850.

53. William Dennison Bickham, *A Buckeye in the Land of Gold: The Letters and Journal of William Dennison Bickham,* ed. Randall E. Ham (Spokane, Wash.: Arthur H. Clark Co., 1996), 161–62.

54. The pioneer newspapers of Sacramento and San Francisco carried numerous advertisements for artistic models. See, for example, *Daily Alta California,* April 3, 1850, and *Sacramento Transcript,* September 28, 1850. MacMinn, *Theater of the Golden Era,* 253–59.

55. George H. Tinkham, *A History of Stockton* (San Francisco: W. M. Hinton & Co., 1880), 177.

56. For more on Rowe, see *California's Pioneer Circus,* ed. Albert Dressler (San Francisco: by the editor, 1926), and "Joseph A. Rowe," in *San Francisco Theater Research,* 1:74–117.

57. The following provide background information on music: MacMinn, *Theater of the Golden Era,* 366–445; Jacobson, *City of the Golden 'Fifties,* 166–221; Corinne Swall, "Elisa Biscaccianti, The 'American Thrush' in Gold Rush California," *The Californians,* vol. 11, no. 1 (n.d.): 8–17; and Margo, *Taming the Forty-Niner,* 89–110.

58. Stephen C. Massett, *"Drifting About," or What "Jeems Pipes of Pipesville" Saw-and-Did* (New York: Carleton, 1863). See also "Stephen C. Massett: Singer, Writer, Showman," in *San Francisco Theater Research,* 1:1–73.

59. Luther Melancthon Schaeffer, *Sketches of Travels in South America, Mexico and California* (New York: James Egbert, Printer, 1860), 36. For examples of gold-rush songs see M. Taylor, composer, *The Gold Digger's Song Book* (1856; with an introduction by Sister Mary Dominic Ray, San Francisco: The Book Club of California, 1975). Original gold-rush sheet music may be found in such repositories as the Bancroft Library, California State Library, Huntington Library, and North Baker Research Library, California Historical Society.

60. Schaeffer, *Sketches of Travels,* 69.

61. Perkins, *Journal of Life at Sonora,* 219.

62. Schaeffer, *Sketches of Travels,* 127.

63. Ibid., 130.

64. Ibid., 130–31.

65. For a discussion of minstrels, see Eugene T. Sawyer, "Old Time Minstrels of San Francisco. Recollections of a Pioneer," *Overland Monthly* 81 (October 1923); MacMinn, *Theater of the Golden Era,* 421–45; and "Minstrels," in *San Francisco Theater Research,* vol. 13 (San Francisco: Works Projects Administration, 1939).

66. Gretchen Adel Schneider, "Pigeon Wings and Polkas: The Dance of the California Miners," *Dance Perspectives* 39 (Winter 1969): 4–57, provides a detailed study of the subject.

67. Borthwick, *Three Years in California,* 321.

68. Kurz & Allison's Art Gallery, *The Miners' Pioneer Ten Commandments of 1849* [chromolithograph] (Chicago, 1887).

69. Borthwick, *Three Years in California*, 320–22.

70. Letts, *California Illustrated*, 89–90.

71. Morse, "History of Sacramento," 9–10.

72. Bickham, *A Buckeye in the Land of Gold*, 134–41.

73. Perkins, *Journal of Life at Sonora*, 244.

74. *Annals of San Francisco*, 248.

75. Louise Amelia Knapp Smith Clappe, *The Shirley Letters from the California Mines, 1851–1852*, ed. and introduced by Marlene Smith-Baranzini (Berkeley: Heyday Books, 1998), 87.

76. *Annals of San Francisco*, 355.

77. See Banks's entries for April 5, 1851, forward, in Scamehorn, Banks, and Lytle-Webb, *The Buckeye Rovers in the Gold Rush*.

78. Schaeffer, *Sketches of Travels*, 188.

79. Taylor, *Eldorado*, 1:56.

80. Ibid., 2:27.

81. Perkins, *Journal of Life at Sonora*, 290.

82. John Marshall Newton, *Memoirs of John Marshall Newton* (Cambridge, N.Y.: Washington County Post, 1913), 42.

83. For a history of early book-selling, see Robert E. Cowan, *Booksellers of Early San Francisco* (Los Angeles: The Ward Ritchie Press, 1953), and Hugh Sanford Cheney Baker, "A History of the Book Trade in California 1849–1859," *California Historical Society Quarterly* 30 (1951): 97–115, 249–67, 353–67.

84. *Daily Alta California*, April 25, 1850. For a superb history of pioneer libraries in California, see Hugh S. Baker, "'Rational Amusement in Our Midst': Public Libraries in California, 1849–1859," *California Historical Society Quarterly* 38 (December 1959): 295–320.

85. Edna Bryan Buckbee, *The Saga of Old Tuolumne* (New York: The Press of the Pioneers, 1935), 111, 202–203. Pioneer newspapers and directories are loaded with advertisements for books.

86. Howard C. Gardiner, *In Pursuit of the Golden Dream: Reminiscences of San Francisco and the Northern and Southern Mines, 1849–1857*, ed. Dale L. Morgan (Stoughton, Mass.: Western Hemisphere, 1970), 213 and 350–51.

87. *Annals of San Francisco*, 428–29; see also *San Francisco Directory for the Year Commencing October, 1856* (San Francisco: Harris, Bogardus and Labatt, 1856), 129–30, for a listing of cultural institutions.

88. Perkins, *Journal of Life at Sonora*, 304; Schaeffer, *Sketches of Travels*, 137, 141.

89. See, for example, Helper, *Land of Gold*, 116–30; Borthwick, *Three Years in California*, 289–99; Perkins, *Journal of Life at Sonora*, 273–77; Christman, *One Man's Gold*, 198–200; and Frank Marryat, *Mountains and Molehills; or Recollections of a Burnt Journal* (London: Longman, Brown, Green, and Longmans, 1855), 251.

90. Tracy I. Storer and Lloyd P. Tevis, Jr., *California Grizzly* (Lincoln: Bison Books, 1978), 152. Storer and Tevis in their chapter, "Bear-and-bull Fights," present a superb overview of these contests. For a different analysis see Johnson, "Bulls, Bears, and Dancing Boys," 30–32.

91. John Boessenecker, *Gold Dust and Gunsmoke* (New York: John Wiley & Sons, 1999), 166–67.

92. Helper, *Land of Gold*, 117.

93. Storer and Tevis, *California Grizzly*, 153.

94. Boessenecker, *Gold Dust and Gunsmoke*, 161.

95. Borthwick, *Three Years in California*, 290.

96. City rats would sometimes be let loose in the arena to arouse the combative spirit in the animals. Storer and Tevis, *California Grizzly*, 161. See also "The Bear Fight at Brighton," *Sacramento Union*, September 14, 1851, and A. A. Sargent, "An Historical Sketch of Nevada County," in *Nevada, Grass Valley and Rough and Ready Directory* (San Francisco: Brown and Dallison, 1856), 30, for examples of uncooperative bruins.

97. Storer and Tevis, *California Grizzly*, 161–62.

98. Christman, *One Man's Gold*, 199–200.

99. Borthwick, *Three Years in California*, 334–39.

100. Ibid., 357–58.

101. Boessenecker, *Gold Dust and Gunsmoke*, 167–78. Contemporary newspapers provided ample coverage of prize fighting.

102. Quoted in Boessenecker, *Gold Dust and Gunsmoke*, 174. See also Margo, "Pugilists and Ponies," in *Taming the Forty-Niner*.

103. Bickham, *A Buckeye in the Land of Gold*, 147.

104. *Daily Alta California*, June 6, 1852.

105. Ibid., June 30 and July 15, 1852.

106. *Annals of San Francisco*, 445. *The May Festival of the Turnverein Association, San Francisco* [pictorial letter sheet] (San Francisco: W. W. Kurz & Co., n.d.).

107. James M. Hutchings, *Scenes of Wonder and Curiosity in California* (San Francisco: Hutchings & Rosenfield, 1860), provides an excellent overview. Much of the text and illustrations originally appeared in various issues of *Hutchings' California Magazine*. A native of Scotland, Hutchings came to California in 1849 as a gold seeker. For a powerful interpretation of outdoor life see Kevin Starr's chapter entitled "Sport, Mountaineering, and Life on the Land," in his *Americans and the California Dream, 1850–1915* (New York: Oxford University Press, 1973), 172–78.

108. "A Jaunt of Recreation from San Francisco, by the Mission Dolores, to the Ocean House and Seal Rock; Returning by Fort Point and the Presidio," *Hutchings' California Magazine* 3 (June 1859): 530–34.

109. *Daily Alta California*, May 2, 1853.

110. Mary Jane Megquier, *Apron Full of Gold: The Letters of Mary Jane Megquier from San Francisco, 1849–1856*, ed. and introduced by Polly Welts Kaufman (Albuquerque: University of New Mexico Press, 1994), 159.

111. *Annals of San Francisco*, 663, and *Daily Alta California*, May 2, 1853. The Willows, another public garden, opened in the late 1850s.

112. Robert B. Woodward founded on Mission Street in San Francisco an amusement park that included gardens, aquarium, art gallery, library, and museum (Lockwood, *Suddenly San Francisco*, 109–14).

113. "A Jaunt of Recreation," 533–34.

114. Ibid., 534–35.

115. "The Mammoth Trees of California," *Hutchings' California Magazine* 3 (March 1859): 387. For a detailed discussion of the big trees see Dennis G. Kruska, *Sierra Nevada Big Trees: History of the Exhibitions, 1850–1903* (Los Angeles: Dawson's Book Shop, 1985).

116. "Mammoth Trees of California," 387.

117. Francis P. Farquhar, *History of the Sierra Nevada* (Berkeley: University of California Press, 1965), 84–85.

118. Kruska, *Sierra Nevada Big Trees*, 20–21.

119. Ibid., 33–39.

120. "The Great Cave of Calaveras County," *Hutchings' California Magazine* 1 (January 1857): 296–98. See also "The Alabaster Cave, of El Dorado, Co., Cal'a," *Hutchings' California Magazine* 5 (December 1860): 242–49. Ann Whipple in "Cave City," *California Gold Rush Camps*, Annual Keepsake (San Francisco: The Book Club of California, 1998), states that a hotel was built in 1850, burned down twice, and in 1853, Messrs. Magee and Angels erected a longer-lived inn.

121. The literature on Yosemite is so vast that it could literally fill a library. See for example, Lloyd W. Currey and Dennis G. Kruska, *Bibliography of Yosemite, the Central and the Southern High Sierra, and the Big Trees, 1839–1900* (Los Angeles: Dawson's Book Shop; Palo Alto: William P. Wreden, 1992). Most useful for this article is Peter J. Blodgett, "Visiting 'The Realm of Wonder': Yosemite and the Business of Tourism, 1855–1916," *California History* 69 (Summer 1990): 118–20.

12

"My own private life"

Toward a History of Desire in Gold Rush California

Susan Lee Johnson

One afternoon in the autumn of 1850, a native woman and man happened upon an encampment of white miners near the Merced River. Gold had been discovered only eighteen months before, but already nonnative immigrants had poured into the Sierra Nevada foothills, setting up towns such as Sonora and Nevada City, as well as ephemeral camps such as the one these Indians encountered near the Merced. The woman carried a small child in her arms. The man, her husband, once had been a resident of one of California's coastal missions, but now lived among the Miwok peoples of the foothills. His wife also may have resided at a mission, or she may have grown up among upcountry Miwoks.

When this native family stopped at the white men's camp, the miners served them a meal. At least one of the miners spoke some Spanish, and the Indian man was fluent, so the assembled diners conversed as best they could using this common language. They also seem to have consumed a good amount of whiskey. When it came time for the travelers to depart, the man was, as one of the miners recalled in his diary, "extremely lavish of his 'mil gracias senores.'" Then the couple headed off down the trail with their babe in arms. The white men watched them leave, and noticed that the Indian man kept stopping to embrace and kiss his wife as they walked. So the miners decided to follow them. Soon enough, the woman and man stepped off the trail into a cluster of willows. The white men crept as close to the couple as they could without being noticed and, as one of them remembered, "stood almost breathless lest we should be discovered and spoil our fun!" This is where the historical record ends, with the diarist's remark, "Perhaps here it would be well to let drop the curtain, rather than incur the displeasure a description of after scenes might bring down upon my poor head—and allow imagination to fill up the remainder!"[1]

With a few notable exceptions, such scenes and "after scenes" have not captured the attention of historians writing about gold-rush California, and so readers are left to "allow imagination to fill up the remainder."[2] This is an unfortunate turn of events, since scholarly inquiry into the history of sex and sexuality has exploded over the past two decades. John D'Emilio and Estelle Freedman's *Intimate Matters: A History of Sexuality in America,* the first interpretive overview of the history of sexuality in the geographic area that is now the United States, is over a dozen years old and already has appeared in a second edition.[3] The University of Chicago Press began publishing the *Journal of the History of Sexuality* a full decade ago—a sure mark of the maturation of the field.[4] And, since the late 1970s, both university presses and trade publishers have been turning out a steady stream of histories of sex and sexuality. The 1990s alone witnessed the publication of works as diverse as Ramón Gutiérrez's *When Jesus Came, the Corn Mothers Went Away: Marriage, Sexuality, and Power in New Mexico, 1500–1846;* Timothy Gilfoyle's *City of Eros: New York City, Prostitution, and the Commercialization of Sex, 1790–1920;* George Chauncey's *Gay New York: Gender, Urban Culture, and the Making of the Gay Male World, 1890–1940;* Elizabeth Kennedy and Madeline Davis's *Boots of Leather, Slippers of Gold: The History of a Lesbian Community;* and Rickie Solinger's *Wake Up Little Susie: Single Pregnancy and Race Before Roe v. Wade.*[5] In light of this explosion of scholarship, the relative silence about sex and sexuality in gold-rush California—indeed, in the history of the North American West generally—is especially striking.[6] Like the white voyeur who watched a native couple having sex among the willows but refused to commit his observations to paper, present-day historians seem content to let imagination satisfy our curiosity about sex and sexuality during the Gold Rush.

This may be because some question the legitimacy of the field. Indeed, skepticism is often the first scholarly response to new areas of intellectual inquiry. When it comes to the history of sex and sexuality, that skepticism often takes two forms. First, doubters maintain that the historical record is silent on sexual matters. More than one historian intent on studying the sexual past has approached an intellectual mentor or an archivist with great enthusiasm, only to be told that no documents exist that shed light on such questions. The diligent and determined researcher, of course, can satisfy such doubters by uncovering the vast range of primary source materials that provide evidence about sexual concerns in times past. A second group of skeptics is far less easily mollified. Such scholars argue that studying the history of sex and sexuality is a trivial pursuit, a prurient waste of intellectual energy that only detracts from the production of historical knowledge that "matters." Besides, these critics sometimes contend, sex does not really have a history; it is a "natural" aspect of human existence that has changed little, if at all, over time, and as such is not a proper topic for historical inquiry. Some go on to add that sex and sexuality are "private," and thus are more suited to psychological than historical analysis.

Historians of sex and sexuality disagree. They argue that sexual concerns have infused historical transformations far more often than skeptics admit. They also maintain that relegating sex to the realm of the "natural" and the "private" distorts our understanding not only of obviously sexualized experiences such as marriage, prostitution, and homosexuality, but of such matters as war, diplomacy, politics, and economics as well. Then historians of sexuality go further to argue that contemporary ideas about sex are themselves products of history. There are many examples of this, but prime among them are the dual notions that sexuality itself is a separate, discrete aspect of human existence, and that people "have" sexualities—that each of us as individuals can be defined and categorized by our sexual proclivities. Following the work of French intellectual Michel Foucault as well as the archival research of a generation of scholars, historians of sexuality have identified such ideas as modern notions, rooted deeply in the cultural, social, and economic history of the North Atlantic world, though now disseminated unevenly about the globe.[7] If we are to understand older meanings and practices of sex, historians of sexuality contend, we must begin by trying to suspend our present-day assumptions about what sex is or what it ought to be, the better to make sense of what it has been in the past. While people in all times and places and cultures have felt sexual desire and engaged in sexual practices, the meanings and significance of that desire and those practices have varied wildly.

Gold-rush California is a particularly rich historical context in which to explore such sexual desires, practices, and meanings.[8] First, the Gold Rush occurred sufficiently long ago that whatever assumptions we now have about sexuality are inadequate guides to understanding how sex happened and what sex meant to participants. Second, the Gold Rush brought together an extraordinarily diverse cast of characters, and thus an extraordinarily diverse array of customary ideas about and practices of sex. Even a partial list of gold-rush participants suggests the stunning variety: Miwok and Nisenan women, Chinese men, enslaved African Americans, Chilean peons, independent Sonoran prospectors, Anglo American artisans, French prostitutes, Californio *patrones*—and the list could go on and on. Third, among these varied gold-rush populations, only native peoples lived in communities with roughly equal numbers of women and men.[9] Among all immigrant groups, by contrast, men far outnumbered women. In the area called the Southern Mines, for example, the enumerated population in 1850 was less than 3 percent female. Ten years later the same area had seen a 1200 percent increase in the number of women; but the total population was still less than 20 percent female.[10] In immigrant homelands, sex between women and men constituted the most common and culturally sanctioned— though certainly not the only—means of sexual expression, so this unusual sex ratio had profound consequences for sexual relations in the "diggings," as the mining areas were called. And because women of all immigrant groups held less social, cultural, political, and economic power than their menfolk, sexual relations generally took place in a milieu of male dominance—though the scarcity of women in California sometimes gave them leverage in a male-dominated world that they might not have exercised back home.

Finally, sex happened in gold-rush California within a larger geopolitical, economic, and cultural context. Gold was discovered in the Sierra Nevada foothills on January 24, 1848, one week before the signing of the Treaty of Guadalupe Hidalgo, which ended the Mexican-American War and by which Mexico ceded California to the United States. This was the era of Manifest Destiny, the rallying cry of white Americans who believed it their God-given right to overspill the continent—with the blessing of the federal government, and despite the claims of prior residents, both Indians and Mexicans. Such racialized notions of cultural superiority touched every aspect of gold-rush social relations, and sexual relations were no exception to this rule. Furthermore, the gold discovery coincided with a key moment in both the development of industrial capitalism and—because of concurrent transportation and communications revolutions—the growth of a globalizing economy, hence the frenzy that led so many people from so many places to rush to California after 1848. These developments touched different parts of the world—even different parts of the United States—differently, but they invariably linked California to economic systems by which distinct working and middle classes were starting to emerge, with accompanying relations of power and privilege that reverberated back through the diggings as well. Sexual matters during the Gold Rush were shot through with such economic inequities and their varied social and cultural expressions.

In spite of all this, historical scholarship on sex and sexuality in gold-rush California is still in its infancy.[11] Rather than review in detail the sparse existing literature, then, I propose in this chapter to survey one particularly rich primary source in order to illustrate the range of evidence readily available to historians who are concerned with sexual matters.[12] If a single text yields such a wealth of sexual content, then the prospects for a more capacious historiography are very good indeed. The source I have in mind is the very diary that offered up the story of the native couple who stole off into the woods for an erotic interlude, not knowing that two white miners were spying on them through the willows. The diarist was a young white man—just twenty-two as he penned his voyeuristic remarks—who hailed from Edgartown, Massachusetts, on Martha's Vineyard, though he emigrated to California from New York City, where he had worked as a clerk. Christened Timothy Osborn, his friends called him Tim. Like many born and raised on the islands off Cape Cod, Timothy came from a seafaring family that profited from the New England-based whaling industry, though his move to New York and then California and his employment as a clerk and then a miner suggests that he had different visions for his economic future.[13] And like many others from the industrializing Northeast, Timothy was caught up in an era of uncertainty for young white men, for whom cus-

tomary paths to economic independence were eroding. While some such men were
starting to join together to resist the subordination of labor that the shift from a
commercial capitalism to an industrial capitalism seemed to portend, others jumped
at the chance for a more individualist solution to vagaries of economic change—and
the discovery of gold in California provided just such an opportunity.[14] Timothy Osborn was a jumper, not a joiner; one might describe him as aspiring middle class.

In September 1849, Timothy and his cousins, William and James Osborn, left for
California, sailing around Cape Horn and arriving in San Francisco in January 1850.
In June, the trio left the city by schooner for Stockton, and then employed a Mexican teamster to transport their belongings up into the foothills, where they commenced mining at the Merced River in the Southern Mines. All along, Timothy
kept a journal, in which he wrote nearly every day until May 1851, and irregularly
thereafter until 1855. Unlike some gold-rush diaries, which are long on weather reports and mining yields and short on men's thoughts and feelings, Timothy called his
"a journal of my own private life."[15] The diary does not disappoint. Indeed, one of the
"private" aspects of his life that Timothy recorded faithfully was his intense curiosity about sex, as well as the opportunities the Gold Rush offered him to indulge that
curiosity.[16] Each one of these recorded opportunities, understood in historical and
cultural context, opens a window on practices and meanings of sex and sexuality in
the gold-rush era. Taken together, they point the way toward a new history of desire
in nineteenth-century California.

When one pictures Anglo Americans who went to California from the eastern
United States—and there were more Anglo American gold-rush participants than
those of any other immigrant or native group—one generally sees either lonely men
of courting age cut off from the means by which most formed intimate relationships,
or else young husbands bereft of young wives.[17] However myopic, these visions do
not lie. The near absence of women whom white men regarded as potential or actual sweethearts or spouses weighed heavily on such gold seekers' hearts, and tormented their bodies as well. Timothy Osborn, for example, filled his diary with
reveries of women back East. He wrote as well of innumerable, interminable campfire conversations among his white companions about the "girls" at home. Of one
such chat, Timothy noted, "We talked of home and its *girls* until our tongues were
weary of wagging."[18]

The young woman Timothy most missed was his cousin, Annie Coffin, though
the closeness of their familial relationship did seem to give him pause. Much of what
he wrote about Annie—like most of the sexual content of his diary—he rendered in
a shorthand that would have been illegible to all but the most determined reader. In
one encoded entry, for example, Timothy recalled "the bitter tears" Annie had shed
when the two parted. He added, with some defensiveness, "It is by no means strange
that I so often think of her, for had it been any other girl with whom I had been

John B. Colton, a slender, youthful Forty-niner who had been one of the unfortunate Jay-hawker party that stumbled into Death Valley on its way to the mines, strikes a pose on Long Wharf in San Francisco in 1850. The enterprising photographer who made the original daguerreotype was soon producing duplicates, which he titled "a girl miner in boy's clothing" and sold at five dollars each. Hundreds of lonely Argonauts, far from home in a land that was overwhelmingly male, purchased copies of the picture; and for years, historians and curators were as easily fooled as the miners. *Courtesy Huntington Library, San Marino, Calif.*

equally intimate, it would be the same."[19] In another shorthand entry, Timothy described a dream he had had about Annie, set "in the little room made dear to our memories by being the scene of our first affectionate kiss." In this dream, Annie laid her head against Timothy's chest and sobbed because, as he put it, "my father had forbidden our intimacy." Timothy promised Annie that he "was not influenced . . . by either father or mother in the choice of [a] wife." Then, Annie smiled up into Timothy's eyes and, "for further assurance," he noted, "*she kissed me!*"[20] By writing in shorthand and using words like "strange" and "forbidden," Timothy hinted that it was not just modesty which moderated his textualizing impulse, but a sense of moral ambiguity. What did it mean to yearn for so near a relative, and how far should he let that yearning go? By literally underlining moments of physical contact and by naming places for the intimacies shared there, Timothy showed that the pleasure of Annie's touch so far had triumphed over his moral qualms.[21]

Annie Coffin was only one of the "girls" Timothy remembered fondly, however. An evening of singing ballads with Cousin William brought several young women to mind. The song "The Enchantress" reminded him of Bell Udell; "Oh Lud Gals" of Mary Taylor; "Off Said the Stranger" of Annie Butler; and "Good Bye," of course, of Cousin Annie. The song "Lovely Rose" sent Timothy off into a rapture over his boyhood favorite, Eliza Mills, whom he regretted he could never marry because "she did not possess those elements of refinement which I would want a wife to have." He worried that Eliza might have inherited "a good deal of her father's animal passion." Thoughts of Eliza and the others stirred him so much that he confided to his diary, "there's *no sleep to-night!*"[22] Other young women from home danced through Timothy's diary as well—Fannie Tucker, a horseback riding companion; Susan P., whom he remembered for "the *open hand* and *heart* with which she always welcomed me"; nameless girls on snowy days, when he would purposely upset a flying sled "to see the fun and *anything else that might turn up!*"[23] Infused with ecumenical longing and tinged with class anxieties (refinement and passion might be irreconcilable), these diary entries bespeak the physical absence of white women in gold-rush California, and their pervasive presence in white men's minds.

Historians have long noted that absence, and argued that what emerged in the breach was a world of dance halls and brothels, where lonely men followed their frustrated yearnings. What few have realized is that this contention presumes a kind of volcanic theory of male sexuality—that is, the idea that men will be men, and that being a man means experiencing insistent desire that will be satisfied, one way or another. This, of course, was how many nineteenth-century white Americans thought about male sexuality, although those of the emerging middle class sought to harness men's eruptive potential by urging male self-control. Prescriptions for male restraint were linked to racialized and class-specific ideas about female sexuality as well—the assumption that white women of means did not experience sexual longing in the same way or to the same extent as did men, which in turn implied that women by nature embodied purity and virtue.[24] That white, middle-class people in the mid-nineteenth century characterized male desire in a particular way (and that some at the turn of the twenty-first century still hold to these beliefs) is no argument for naturalizing those cultural constructions as ultimate truths. Better to see such ideas as just that—as culturally constructed—and to try to understand how such constructions informed sexual relations in a particular historical context.

In gold-rush California, a world of commercialized leisure evolved in which men's desire was constantly stoked and stroked, thereby reinforcing familiar ideas about male sexuality. Lest we think that this milieu of sex-for-sale was somehow unique to the male world of the diggings, however, we should remember that a similar milieu flourished in the East as well, particularly in cities such as New York.[25] Timothy Osborn, then, moved from one hotbed of illicit desire to another. The chief difference between New York and California was that in the East, white men visited markets in pleasure not far from their homes. Close by, then, female relatives and neighbors provided a constant reminder of emerging middle-class sexual ideologies, within which male self-control and female purity lived in symbiosis. In the West, female purity seemed a long way away, and thus male self-control seemed a good deal less relevant.

But there was a similarity between commercialized leisure in such eastern and western places; East or West, sex-for-sale was largely an urban phenomenon. Timothy Osborn, for example, rarely left the camps he and his mining partners set up in Mariposa and Tuolumne counties in 1850, and thus rarely encountered such markets in pleasure. Had Timothy traveled just twenty-five miles north to the town of Sonora, for instance, he would have found it bustling with saloons, brothels, and dance halls, and he could have spent a bit of the gold he dug viewing "Model Artists"—naked or at least scantily clad women who posed for male onlookers.[26] Men who lived in the region known as the Northern Mines could find the same in towns such as Nevada City.[27]

Timothy, however, saw little of this side of the Gold Rush until he gave up on mining altogether in late December and relocated in the San Joaquin Valley at Stockton, which served as the supply town for the Southern Mines (just as Sacramento served as an entrepôt for the Northern Mines). He had some advance warning that Stockton would be different from remote encampments in the diggings. In November, a friend who had just visited the town told Timothy of "the steady importation of 'Ladies' from the Atlantic side, and an increased immigration of *females* from Australia and China." "Of the latter class," his friend told him, "the market is well supplied and 'trade' is light, with market quotations ranging from $50 [to] $100 *tout la nuit*."[28] When he moved to Stockton himself, Timothy walked about the town, surveying the billiard and gambling saloons, the dance halls, and the

San Franciscans dance at the annual Public School Festival held at the Musical Hall
in an 1854 pictorial letter sheet. Opportunities for Argonauts to enjoy women's company
in the days of '49 were largely limited to saloons and gambling halls, where women of
the demimonde gathered, but gradually social events such as the Public School Festival
emerged, offering an alternative for men to meet women in a "proper" social setting.
California Historical Society, FN-04145.

"houses of general ill-repute," all of which did a particularly booming business on
Sunday, the Christian Sabbath. Thinking back on his months in the diggings, he
noted, "If my home in the mountains was not so *refined* (!) it certainly was a more
moral one than can be found in this city."[29] A quick trip to San Francisco over the
New Year's holiday revealed a similar world of commercialized leisure, and Timothy found himself lingering outside a fandango, gazing in the window to watch
"several senoritas waving their handkerchiefs and dancing merrily to the music of a
guitar." Timothy summed up what he saw in these various urban houses of entertainment: "All the paraphernalia of vice in its various forms was arrayed to attract
and decoy the unthinking."[30]

In these diary entries, Timothy Osborn represents himself as a "thinking" man,
one who could resist the temptations of gold-rush California. But other entries hint

that Timothy sometimes swam happily among the decoys, ready to be shot through with desire. After four months in Stockton, for instance, he confessed to his diary:

> This evening, perhaps for the first time in my life, I attended a Spanish "Fancy Dress Ball" at the "Bella Union." About twenty young *ladies* (?) were present, dressed in every variety of costume. As is customary on such occasions, it is not incumbent upon *gentlemen* to conform to a fancy dress. Waltzed with a black eyed senorita from Market Street, and altho' by far the prettiest girl in the room, she was not a good waltzer, but apologized by a graceful "no puedo valse, senor."[31]

A few days later, he passed a French man on the street calling out, "Ici, il y a vue de Paris!" Timothy paid the asking price and then peered into a viewer, only to see "(*not*) a view of Paris," but of (and here he started writing in shorthand) "Naked men and women in all shapes in the *very act*." Switching back to conventional writing, Timothy noted, "I came to the conclusion that, after all, it *was a very good view of Paris*." And within a month he recorded having spent the evening at a "Madame Bouvier's"—no doubt a gambling saloon or a brothel—playing a "private and social game of euchre."[32]

As each of these diary entries suggests, gold-rush participants such as Timothy Osborn often pursued their passions not with Anglo American women, but among women from Mexico, Chile, France, China, and other lands, including Australia. This was especially true of men who lived and worked in the Southern Mines, that region in the Sierra Nevada foothills tributary to the San Joaquin River, which included such towns as Jackson and Mokelumne Hill in the north, Sonora and Columbia in the mid-section, and Coulterville and Mariposa in the south. (The Northern Mines were located in the drainage of the lower Sacramento River, and included such towns as Placerville in the south, Nevada City and Grass Valley in the mid-section, and Downieville farther north.) Timothy spent his entire gold-rush career in the Southern Mines, by far the most demographically diverse of California's mining areas. At the end of the 1850s, for example, immigrants from outside the United States—along with some African Americans and non-California Indians, such as Cherokees—outnumbered Anglo Americans there. In the early months of the Gold Rush, the Southern Mines were known as a haven for Spanish- and French-speaking gold seekers, and that reputation did not entirely evaporate even after the Foreign Miner's Tax of 1850 drove so many out of the diggings for good. Beginning in 1852, Chinese immigrants began to pour into both the Southern and Northern mines, and even the reimposition of the Foreign Miner's Tax, this time at a lower monthly rate, did not stem that tide. Add to this polyglot population those people native to the foothills—in the Southern Mines these were mostly Miwoks along with refugees from missions along the coast and from disease in the Central Valley—and one begins to get a picture of the social world Timothy Osborn inhabited.[33]

Stockton, as entrepôt for the Southern Mines, attracted a like mix. And the streets of San Francisco, of course, Timothy found "thronged with the representatives of every nation—presenting a scene unequalled by any other city in the Union."[34]

Thus it is no accident that many of Timothy's references to sexual matters involve Mexican, Chilean, French, and Miwok women.[35] Demographics alone, however, cannot fully explain his erotic fixation on these particular female gold-rush participants. Indeed, Timothy felt especially free to think in sexual ways about women who were not white and American. We have seen this already in the way he so easily characterized women from the Atlantic states as "ladies" and others as "ladies (?)" or "females." Such characterizations were hardly unique to gold-rush California. Anglo Americans in the East had long participated in an elaborate discourse that located a voracious and unfettered female sexuality among African American and Native American women, in particular, and among poor and nonwhite women more generally. California simply provided a rich soil in which such discursive seeds could take root.

Like the "black eyed senorita" with whom he tried to waltz at a "Spanish" fancy-dress ball, Mexican and Chilean women—individually and collectively—fascinated Timothy Osborn. His first encounter came in September of 1850, when, as he put it, "a Mexican and his 'chola' senorita" stopped at Timothy's camp. As with the traveling Indians, the white men fed this Mexican couple, offering a repast of antelope meat, pea soup, baked beans, bread, flapjacks, coffee, and wine. "The secret of our extraordinary politeness," Timothy confessed, was the fact that the "fair guest was rather better looking than most 'chola' girls." He was especially taken with the way that, after dinner, she "took from her bosom . . . a little cigarette, and commenced smoking with all that nonchalance peculiar to Spanish ladies." Given that Timothy was new to California and had limited knowledge of Spanish, it is not clear what he meant by the term "chola," though he may have heard it used, derisively, by Californios to describe recent migrants from Mexico.[36] A month later, Timothy visited a tent store kept by a man named Johnson, and then noted in his diary, "Johnson has a Spanish woman whose board he pays for a *private* consideration." Then, as if it was part of the same sexualized thought, he continued, "she *certainly* is one of the best horse-riders I ever saw outside of a circus ring. She wore a large pair of spurs 'a la Mejicana' and rode without a saddle or bridle, with merely a noose around the animal's nose."[37] Such female gestures—drawing a cigarette from a dress bodice, straddling a horse bareback and urging it on with a sharp set of spurs—thrilled men like Timothy Osborn. In fact, it was the very next day that the Indian couple came calling; by that time, Timothy must have been ready to watch more than a horseback ride.

Once he moved down to Stockton, Timothy shifted his attentions from Mexican women clearly involved with other men to a Chilean woman whom he encountered by chance. That first meeting left Timothy enraptured. As he wrote in his diary,

A representation of a Chileno couple strolling arm in arm that in 1857 appeared in *Hutchings' California Magazine*. Chilean women not infrequently worked in the mines, and according to *Hutchings'* their expressive faces suggested the tale: "I am perfectly satisfied with my condition as a woman, with my cigarita in one hand, and my other hand and arm where it should be, whether the rest of man or woman kind are or not." Many American Argonauts, such as young Timothy Osborn, were taken by the beauty and poise of Spanish-speaking women and began to question long-held assumptions on ethnicity and sex. One morning two young Chilenas entered Osborn's store, "and the first glance at one of them," he wrote, "touched me as with a magic wand." *California Historical Society, FN-31546.*

"Today my mind has been uneasy, reminding me of the little canoe so beautifully represented in Cole's celebrated paintings of the 'Voyage of Life,' as it takes its departure from the smooth lake and glides on its way to the bosom of the old ocean." The heaving breast onto which he felt himself embarking was a love affair with a woman who happened by the store where he worked:

> This morning . . . two young senoritas Chilenas entered the store and the first glance at one of them touched me as with a magic wand. *Positively and without any exception, she was the most beautiful girl I ever saw!* Talk to me of "American Belles" no longer, for my beau-ideal of perfect beauty is found at last. In fact I'm head and ears in love! Habited in a pink striped white muslin—white silk hose—and kid slippers—a little *en dishabille* about the bodice of her dress, a 'manta' resting gracefully upon her snow white neck—she looked the picture of innocence and beauty! . . . Of course, in waiting upon my fair customer, my gallantry knew no limit, and the limited knowledge of Spanish I possessed was all brought into requisition.[38]

Significantly, Timothy stressed what he perceived as the whiteness of this woman, signaled not only by her fair skin but by her dress and stockings as well. Perhaps this helped him to justify straying off the Anglo American path of romance. It is unfortunate for the historian, however, that Timothy met his "beau-ideal of perfect beauty" not long before he stopped writing faithfully in his diary. A few more entries suggest that she continued to frequent Timothy's store or at least his neighborhood. One day, for example, he wrote, "Have not seen *mi querida* today—wonder *adonde esta.*" Timothy frequented her neighborhood, too, as another entry shows: "Took a ramble thro' the Spanish part of town, to get a sight if possible of my inamorita."[39] But we cannot know if an intimate relationship eventually developed between the two, since the diary entries taper off shortly after they met.

What is clear, however, is that Timothy Osborn's infatuation with this "senorita Chilena," as well as his contact with other Spanish-speaking women in California, prompted him to question notions of propriety he might not have challenged back home. The very day he met his "inamorita," for example, he protested that "the easy and careless manner in which Spanish girls wear American dresses is often made the butt of ridicule from over-modest old maids and beardless young gents." In reply, he suggested that "honi soit qui mal y pense" might be just the motto for such maids and gents to ponder.[40] And, after touring the southern part of Stockton, where most Spanish-speaking residents lived, he noted, "One prominent objection often urged by the virtuous (?) against the Spaniards is their *loose* idea of *propriety* in their conduct between the sexes! May it not be as liable to be the *too contracted ideas* of the American's view of virtue! It is a difficult matter to decide."[41] It *was* a difficult matter to decide, full of question marks and exclamation points, even if the idea of looseness among Chileans and Mexicans was more Anglo fantasy than Latin reality. Gold-rush California tossed difficult matters onto the table every day, and often those matters were sexual.

Timothy Osborn had less contact with French-speaking than Spanish-speaking women in the diggings. Had he encountered them, he might have learned that many French immigrant women hailed from the demimonde of cities such as Paris. They had left France in the wake of an economic depression that accompanied the Revolution of 1848. In California, and especially in the Southern Mines, French women found work not only in brothels but also in dance halls and especially in gambling saloons. At Sonora, for instance, they seem to have held a monopoly on the local gaming tables. And in the town of Mariposa, a number of women with French surnames ran their own saloons.[42] But Timothy seems to have met few of these women. His most memorable episode with a French immigrant—if we put aside his erotic "view of Paris" and his card-playing at Madame Bouvier's—came on a Saturday night in Stockton when he and his business partner went window-peeping at a local hotel. They stood outside a window where they watched a "pretty young French lady" as she prepared for bed. What they saw says as much about life in vermin-infested gold-rush towns as it does about the history of desire in California. Writing in shorthand, Timothy described how the woman "unbraided her long black hair and stripped herself of all but her undershirt and began hunting *fleas*. How little she thought anyone was seeing her fair proportions as she slipped off the 'shimmy' the better to get at the little tormenters!"[43] How little this woman must have cared about how "fair" her "proportions" were as she battled those bugs.

In what manner might a historian make sense of these references to Spanish- and French-speaking women? Timothy Osborn no doubt grew up thinking that gender was divided into two distinct categories, "woman" and "man." He probably further differentiated these categories by race and class, which were themselves malleable cultural constructions that changed over time. In Timothy's world, the best sort of "women" and "men" were "ladies" and "gentlemen." But these were social categories closed to people who were not understood to be "white" and who seemed not to aspire to the emerging middle class. Furthermore, to many antebellum white Americans, the term "American" was more or less synonymous with the term "white," so that even light-skinned non-Americans fit only uneasily in the category of "whiteness," just as dark-skinned people were often banished from the category of "American." It was this set of overlapping beliefs that allowed Timothy to eroticize and exoticize French, Chilean, and Mexican women in ways he did not white American women. In his moral universe, even the most ladylike among Spanish- and French-speaking women might not really be ladies, and so they did not evoke in Timothy the restraint he was accustomed to exercising with the "girls" back home. But, as we have seen, the Gold Rush began to work a change in Timothy, so that the categories of which he felt so sure when he arrived in California began to blur around the edges just a few months later. What he had thought was the truth about sex might simply be "contracted ideas." It was a difficult matter to decide. In the meantime, not a few French, Chilean, and Mexican women who worked in the gold-rush world of commercialized leisure learned to profit from the deliberations of men like Timothy Osborn.[44]

About one group of California women, Timothy felt even less cause to deliberate. These were the native women of the foothills, who, where Timothy lived, were primarily Miwoks. Living among Miwok peoples were Indians who years before had left the secularized missions along the coast as well as people native to California's great Central Valley, which had witnessed a horrific malaria epidemic in the 1830s that drove many survivors up into the hill country.[45] Timothy and his cousins set up camp among this mixed native population in the summer of 1850. Drawing on an older white American discourse about Indian sexuality, Timothy indulged his erotic curiosity among native peoples with few qualms. He regularly commented in his diary, for example, about those who traveled from place to place nearly naked. Former mission Indians generally wore clothing, but Indians who had grown up in the foothills wore very little, at least in the summer. Timothy paid special attention to the women's bare chests, and often mocked the female elders, whose breasts hung low against their torsos. He found native women who had lived at coastal missions more attractive. Of one group camped nearby, he wrote, "The girls were better looking than any I have seen before, and wore head bands of bright colors, and dresses reaching from the hips to the knees."[46]

However he differentiated among Indians by age or dress or nativity, Timothy felt at liberty to regard them in overtly sexual ways. A mixed band that included some former mission Indians caught his attention, for instance, because the women "were entirely nude, with the exception of a small 'tappa.'" He went on, "Perhaps my curiosity, owing to this fact, was exercised rather more freely than strict propriety would allow under other circumstances, but *their modesty did not seem to suffer much.*"[47] Given his beliefs about native women—that sexual modesty was of little consequence to them—he remained convinced that his gaze was harmless. In another diary entry, Timothy described those beliefs, seemingly reinforced by some experience, with striking candor. In shorthand, he wrote,

> It is said by those who are supposed to know that Indian women, like the beasts of the field, have their certain times for seeking the man, and as far as my own experience goes, I am inclined to believe it to be true. I have seen Indian girls, who, when they were "in heat," would fondle around you and in every possible way would ask you to relieve them, while at other times it would be an impossible thing to get your own wishes gratified.

Indian women grind acorns with heavy stone pestles in a wood engraving published in 1854. Countless Argonauts—including, one suspects, Charles Nahl, who made the drawing for this image—found themselves tantalized by the close proximity of women who wore little or no clothing in the mining country. *California Historical Society, FN-30523.*

But the diary entry, steeped as it was in perverse white assumptions about the animal proclivities of native women, then took a curious turn: "I have seen many Indian girls whose person I have coveted but whose modest appearance forbade me ever attempting to do anything wrong."[48]

This is one of those pieces of evidence that makes the historian wish for the option of time travel. Given that option, one might swoop down on Timothy, his pen still in hand, and demand, What on earth do you mean? Do you think there is a sexual continuum among native women, from those who follow "animal" rhythms to those "whose modest appearance" stops you from trying "to get your own wishes gratified"? What are your wishes? And what do you, resident of the foothills for all of two months, understand of native women's desires? Does it occur to you that Indian women might have their own reasons for wanting sex at one time and not another? That some native women might welcome intimacy with you, for whatever reason, while others might abhor the thought? That another white man might appeal to an Indian woman, while you might repel her?[49]

Unfortunately, we are not time travelers, and Timothy will not answer our questions. Nor is there sufficient information on the meanings of sex among the native peoples of the Sierra Nevada foothills in the nineteenth century to venture an interpretation of such cross-cultural contact from an Indian point of view.[50] At the very least, however, Timothy Osborn's diary entries outline a rich field for historical inquiry, inquiry that must move beyond the discursive constraints of Anglo American assumptions about Native American sexuality. As historian Albert Hurtado has shown, the cultural and demographic cataclysm that the Gold Rush visited upon California Indians was rooted in part in the prevalence of sexual violence against native women and the disruption of native patterns of intimacy.[51] And it is crucial to remember that white Americans were not the only invaders of Indian lands in the foothills, though in the long run they did achieve an uneasy dominance in the diggings. In the meantime, however, native peoples contended with a polyglot influx of immigrants, producing any number of possible cross-cultural interactions, some of which must have been sexual. Today, a few Miwok families, for example, count Chinese or Chileans or African Americans among their forebears.[52] Likewise, one of the foremost artists of California, Harry Fonseca, describes his own ancestry not only as Nisenan-Maidu but also as Chilean and Hawaiian.[53] Scholars have barely begun to make sense of the meetings that produced such contemporary Californians.

Not all erotic moments during the Gold Rush, however, had reproductive consequences—or even reproductive potential. If sexual interactions between women and men in California have received scant attention from historians, then same-sex desire and the individual pursuit of erotic pleasure have been all but ignored. Timothy Osborn's diary, however, alludes to the possibility of both, and thus points the way toward a history of desire in gold-rush California that moves beyond one-dimensional images of lonely, sex-starved young men.

As busy as Timothy kept himself contemplating women of every description, one might reasonably conclude that he had little time to eroticize his fellow man. And indeed, his diary is not the richest available source in documenting same-sex desire in the diggings.[54] But even a man whose sexual thoughts and dreams drifted so decisively to the bodies, gestures, and caresses of women could now and then take sensual delight in the male world he inhabited. One Sunday in August 1850, for example, Timothy and his cousins hosted three New York men at their camp. On such Sundays, Timothy wrote, "we put on our 'best' and try to look as 'fascinating' as possible." One of this week's visitors, a man named Goodall, was a favorite of Timothy's, whom he described as "an excellent companion and a fellow of 'infinite jest.'" Timothy also noted his friend's fetching appearance: "Goodall is a little fellow and on Sunday dresses in white pants *a la matelot,* and looks decidedly 'cunning' as the girls would say."[55]

Read out of historical context, this statement may not seem especially erotic in content. But other sources show that during the Gold Rush, men frequently engaged in a kind of cross-gendering of their relationships with one another, in which variations in size, age, strength, behavior—and sometimes race or nationality—came to be interpreted as gender differences.[56] In another camp, for example, the residents gave a "handsome youngster" the name "Sister Stilwell" because of his "fresh complexion, lack of beard, and effeminate appearance."[57] Given that sexual relations back home were deeply and profoundly gendered—that is, that sex was thought to occur naturally between two radically different kinds of human beings called "women" and "men"—it was not such a long walk from cross-gendered looking to same-sex intimacy in the diggings. Then, too, Timothy's reference to Goodall's appearance as "*a la matelot*" may have had a deeper erotic resonance. Most literally, it meant simply "in the manner of a sailor," and there is nothing particularly sexual about that. But sex between seafaring men in this era was common enough that it had its own name; the "boom cover trade" referred to the sex sailors had with each other under the covering that protected ship masts.[58] A New England man from a seafaring clan, Timothy might well have known this.[59] Read in historical context, then, Timothy's description of his friend Goodall very possibly had sexual meanings.

Likewise, a handful of other diary entries hint at same-sex eroticism. In one, Timothy describes the attire of Mexican men who mined nearby: "Their peculiar dress always excites my attention—the loose bottomed under pants of snow white, and the gay woolen outside, open at the sides with long rows of brass buttons, and their black velvet tunic so short in the waist as unable to reach the top of their pants."[60] We must use care in interpreting a reference such as this. As historian

David Goodman has shown, the idea of "excitement" circulated far and wide during the Gold Rush, referring to the mental and emotional state that gold seeking evoked in men.[61] The connotations of the term "excitement" were not so overtly sexual as they are in our own day. Nonetheless, Anglo American gold-rush participants often linked economic and sexual passions, worrying (or wishing, as the case may be) that one would shade into the other in deleterious (or delicious) ways. So while getting excited about the fit of a man's pants surely did not mean then what it might mean now, neither can we discount the possibility of erotic overtones to the emphasis on "loose bottomed under pants."[62] Similarly, a white American named John Marshall Newton looked with longing upon one of his mining partners, a tall Dane named Hans, whom Newton described as "one of the most magnificent looking young men I ever saw." Hans had "massive shoulders and swelling muscles" that stood out "like the gnarled ridges of an oak tree." Newton remembered himself as a slight, soft-hearted boy who "yearned intensely for a friend" and who at first had so much trouble handling heavy mining tools that he often fainted from exertion. The magnificent Dane, then, was a perfect partner, because when Newton could not budge a boulder with a crowbar, he recalled, "Hans would . . . thrust me aside, take hold of the stone . . . and throw it out of the pit."[63] As these examples suggest, a wide range of differences among men were ripe for the erotic picking during the Gold Rush.

Finally, Timothy Osborn's accounts of men dancing together and sleeping with one another indicate, at the very least, the ubiquitous opportunities the Gold Rush offered for same-sex sexual practices.[64] Timothy's references to bed-sharing and dancing are rather elliptical, but other men's diaries, letters, and reminiscences, along with such as sources as legal records, give firmer evidence of the extent to which some men actually seized the moment (and each other) in the diggings.[65] For example, at least one gold-rush woman who followed her husband west to California after he had relocated there ended up suing her errant mate in part because "of his frequently sleeping with certain men, in the same house then occupied by her as his domicil—for the diabolical purpose of committing the crime of bugery."[66] And fuller descriptions of all-male balls in the diggings indicate that some men assumed what was customarily a woman's stance in close couple dancing, while others took the customary male pose, a practice that must have encouraged at least a few men to see the erotic possibilities in a terpsichorean embrace.[67] Timothy Osborn may not be the best guide to same-sex desire during the Gold Rush. Yet it is notable that even a man whose tongue often wearied of wagging over women's charms was not immune to those of mankind.

Timothy, however, seems to have found as much erotic pleasure in solitude as he did with other people, female or male. While mining along the Merced River, for example, his favorite spot to rest was in a hammock of Peruvian netting that he rigged up beneath an oak tree overhanging a ravine. Here, on a Sunday or after lunch on a weekday, Timothy would nap or read a borrowed novel or let his thoughts drift to women back home.[68] He may also have masturbated. In one diary entry, his description of cigar smoking in the hammock seems full of pre-Freudian double entendres, not to mention male dreams of grandiosity. The entry begins with Timothy "smoking away . . . at a third rate 'short six,'" and imagining women he knew walking to church. In no time, however, he finds himself taking a pleasure "in the curling smoke of an ordinary 'long nine' which the unpracticed do not know." Timothy himself must have been practiced, because he knew that a smoker was a contented man who, "impotent of thought, Puffs away care."[69]

At other times, Timothy counted on sleep to bring him contentment. When he first arrived in California, Timothy was frustrated that dreams of women back home had left him unfulfilled: "I never have had a 'golden dream' yet!"[70] But within a few months slumber began to bring results. One night, he woke a tentmate by calling out, "That's a euchre, [Annie], now pay up." Timothy had been dreaming of playing euchre with Cousin Annie. The rules dictated that for every game Timothy won, he also won a kiss, and for every game Annie won, he had to "*pay back the kiss!*"[71] From there, sleep became more and more sexual. Once, Timothy dreamed that he was in the family parlor with a young woman named Eliza Black sitting on his lap. He "breathed sweet words of love into her ear" until she finally kissed him. In return, he gave her a "*long sweet kiss in the mouth.*" This he wrote in shorthand. The rest he would not commit to paper.[72] And one morning, after dreaming about hours spent alone with a woman in an Edgartown hotel, he awoke uncovered, undressed, and exposed to the December chill—but happy.[73] On yet another occasion, an afternoon nap delivered up "a romantic dream" about a young woman in Mexico City who was wealthy, worldly, and "over-anxious to see '*Los Estados Unidos.*'" Osborn was equally anxious to show her *estadounidense* valor. With sweet regret, however, he noted in his diary, "Had I not awoke by the cry of 'supper!' I should have gratified her."[74] And himself, no doubt.

Gold-rush historians, intent on the relative absence of white women and intrigued by the prevalence of sex-for-sale in California, have virtually ignored such evidence of autoerotic and homoerotic desires and practices. The evidence is often encoded, euphemized, or otherwise indirect. But then, so too is much evidence of nonmarital heteroerotic desires and practices. This is because, for men such as Timothy Osborn, all forms of sexual expression outside of marriage were morally suspect, even if they were utterly common both back home and in California—and on the high seas as well. Nonetheless, the evidence is there, if historians will only learn how to read it. Outside of gold-rush historiography, and U.S. western historiography more generally, scholars have made great strides in interpreting primary sources that document the sexual past, including autoerotic and homoerotic pasts. They

"Sunday Evening on Dupont Street," from J. H. Beadle, *The Undeveloped West* (1873), a scene from a typical San Francisco saloon, suggests that freer relations between women and men were possible on the California frontier in the boisterous years after the gold discovery. *Courtesy California State Library, photo reproduction by Nikki Pahl.*

have been careful to understand such materials within appropriate historical and cultural contexts. Few historians of sexuality, for example, would argue that gold-rush participants who engaged in same-sex intimacy were "homosexuals," knowing full well that California's gold-rush era predated the cultural construction of homosexuality by a good half-century.[75] Concomitantly, the Gold Rush predated the cultural construction of heterosexuality as well, so neither can we call men like Timothy Osborn "heterosexual."[76] And understanding masturbation in context requires a similar willingness to think historically. While there had been proscriptions against autoerotic practices among Timothy Osborn's forebears for many generations, earlier embargoes targeted masturbation because it was nonprocreative. Timothy came of age at a time when reformers were arguing that all sexual arousal was potentially dangerous because it could deplete men's vital energies—hence the call for male self-control.[77] These are among the discursive contexts in which sex and sexuality in gold-rush California must be understood.

But there is so much more. As rich as the diary of Timothy Osborn is in its emphasis on the erotic, there are many sexual concerns that it cannot illuminate. In the same manner, the diaries, letters, and reminiscences of other white American men are of limited use—though not of *no* use—as sources for studying the sexual practices, desires, and meanings prevalent among a wider range of immigrant and Indian peoples in California. Consider again my partial list of gold-rush participants, and think about what little can be learned of most of their experiences from a source like the one I have highlighted here: Miwok and Nisenan women, Chinese men, enslaved African Americans, Chilean peons, independent Sonoran prospectors, Anglo American artisans, French prostitutes, Californio *patrones.* And what of Chinese, Chilean, Mexican, and Anglo American prostitutes? What of married women of all immigrant groups? What of free African Americans, Chilean *patrones,* Mexican peons? What of white Americans from the South? What of French, Miwok, and Nisenan men? What of people who did not fit anyone's definition of "woman" or "man," "*mujer*" or "*hombre,*" such as the "Chileno *hermaphrodite*" one Anglo American gold seeker noted meeting along the Mokelumne River in 1852?[78] To begin to comprehend most of these historical experiences, we must turn, for example, to non–English language sources and to documents written or otherwise generated by women. And we must consult materials that open up social and cultural worlds often obscured in white men's personal writings—newspapers, court records, and the oral traditions of native peoples, to name just a few.[79]

Since this call for a history of sex and sexuality in gold-rush California opened with a story culled from a white man's diary, then, it might best close with a tale drawn from the oral repertoire of those peoples whose roots in the Sierra foothills run the deepest. Timothy Osborn cared about Indian sexual expressions only as a voyeur; he watched a native couple slip into the willows in the interests of *his* desire. Indians, of course, have told their own tales of yearning, tales designed to entertain and instruct members of their own communities. Historians would do well to listen to such tales, whether told by contemporary native storytellers or collected in published volumes sanctioned by contemporary Indian collectivities. At the turn of the twentieth century, for example, Miwok people related a great number of stories to anthropologist C. Hart Merriam, including the legend of Ho-hā'-pe, the river mermaid or water woman. Merriam did not record the names of the native tellers of this tale. But the Indians told him of the beautiful water women who lived in large pools, especially in Wah-kal'-mut-tah, or the Merced River—the same waterway along which Timothy Osborn met his native guests in 1850. At one place along the Merced, Indian men from nearby Bear Valley and Coulterville came to catch salmon. They dropped their net into a deep pool, but when the net was full and the men tried to raise it, they could not pull it out. They did not know that Ho-hā'-pe had tied the net to a rock at the bottom of the pool. When one of the men stepped into the river to try to release the net, Ho-hā'-pe wrapped a piece of the net's rope around the man's toe. He was drawn beneath the surface and drowned. A group of men came to the riverbank and together pulled the fisherman's body out of the water. When they did, they all saw the gorgeous water woman in the pool, "her long hair floating out into the current."[80]

Far from a timeless, placeless legend, this tale was situated in a well-known waterscape at a moment after the discovery of gold in California—hence the names of immigrant settlements such as Coulterville and Bear Valley. It bespoke the power of women, the fears of men, and the dangers of desire, tying them tightly to the means by which native peoples got a living from the land—not just any land, but a particular place southern Sierra Miwoks called home.[81] Both the Indian storytellers and the diary-writing Timothy Osborn found the Merced River, Wah-kal'-mut-tah, a place of both longing and hazard. Only when we learn to read such tales alongside and against one another will we start to flesh out a history of desire in gold-rush California.

NOTES

1. Journal entry, October 10, 1850, Timothy C. Osborn Journal, Bancroft Library, University of California, Berkeley. This journal was transcribed in 1932 by Daniel Harris. The Bancroft Library holds both the original diary and the transcription.

2. The most notable exceptions include three works by Albert L. Hurtado: "Sex, Gender, Culture, and a Great Event: The California Gold Rush," *Pacific Historical Review* 68 (February 1999): 1–19; "When Strangers Met: Sex and Gender on Three Frontiers," in *Writing the Range: Race, Class, and Culture in the Women's West*, ed. Elizabeth Jameson and Susan Armitage (Norman: University of Oklahoma Press, 1997), 122–42; and *Indian Survival on the California Frontier* (New Haven, Conn.: Yale University Press, 1988). Just as this article went to press, Hurtado's new book, which incorporates some of the foregoing, appeared in print: *Intimate Frontiers: Sex, Gender and Culture in Old California* (Albuquerque: University of New Mexico Press, 1999). See also Robert L. Griswold, *Family and Divorce in California, 1850–1890: Victorian Illusions and Everyday Realities* (Albany: State University of New York Press, 1982); Jacqueline Baker Barnhart, *The Fair But Frail: Prostitution in San Francisco, 1840–1900* (Reno: University of Nevada Press, 1986); Benson Tong, *Unsubmissive Women: Chinese Prostitutes in Nineteenth-Century San Francisco* (Norman: University of Oklahoma Press, 1994); Judy Yung, *Unbound Feet: A Social History of Chinese Women in San Francisco* (Berkeley: University of California Press, 1995); Douglas Henry Daniels, *Pioneer Urbanites: A Social and Cultural History of Black San Francisco* (1980; Berkeley: University of California Press, 1990); and Tomás Almaguer, *Racial Fault Lines: The Historical Origins of White Supremacy in California* (Berkeley: University of California Press, 1994). Although the work of Antonia I. Castañeda focuses on California's Spanish and Mexican periods, it nonetheless constitutes essential historical and conceptual background for understanding the gold-rush era. See, for example, the following four articles by Castañeda: "Engendering the History of Alta California, 1769–1848: Gender, Sexuality, and the Family," *California History* 76 (Sum-

mer/Fall 1997): 230–59; "Sexual Violence in the Politics and Policies of Conquest: Amerindian Women and the Spanish Conquest of Alta California," in *Building With Our Hands: New Directions in Chicana Studies,* ed. Adela de la Torre and Beatríz M. Pesquera (Berkeley: University of California Press, 1993), 15–33; "The Political Economy of Nineteenth Century Stereotypes of Californianas," in *Between Borders: Essays on Mexicana/Chicana History,* ed. Adelaida R. Del Castillo (Encino, Calif.: Floricanto Press, 1990); and "Gender, Race, and Culture: Spanish-Mexican Women in the Historiography of Frontier California," *Frontiers* 11, no. 1 (1990): 8–20.

3. John D'Emilio and Estelle B. Freedman, *Intimate Matters: A History of Sexuality in America,* 2nd ed. (1988; Chicago: University of Chicago Press, 1997).

4. Publication of the *Journal of the History of Sexuality* commenced in July 1990. Interestingly, the first issue included an extended critique of D'Emilio and Freedman's *Intimate Matters,* particularly for the book's treatment of issues of racial difference and dominance. See Ann duCille, "'Othered' Matters: Reconceptualizing Dominance and Difference in the History of Sexuality in America," and the response by D'Emilio and Freedman, *Journal of the History of Sexuality* 1, no. 1 (July 1990): 102–27 and 128–30, respectively.

5. This brief list of representative titles shows the range of topics explored by historians of sexuality. A complete list of works published in the 1990s on the history of sexuality in North America would run several pages. Full citations for the five works mentioned are: Ramón A. Gutiérrez, *When Jesus Came, the Corn Mothers Went Away: Marriage, Sexuality, and Power in New Mexico, 1500–1846* (Stanford: Stanford University Press, 1991); Timothy J. Gilfoyle, *City of Eros: New York City, Prostitution, and the Commercialization of Sex, 1790–1920* (New York: W. W. Norton, 1992); George Chauncey, *Gay New York: Gender, Urban Culture, and the Making of the Gay Male World, 1890–1940* (New York: Basic Books, 1994); Elizabeth Lapovsky Kennedy and Madeline D. Davis, *Boots of Leather, Slippers of Gold: The History of a Lesbian Community* (New York: Routledge, 1993); and Rickie Solinger, *Wake Up Little Susie: Single Pregnancy and Race Before Roe v. Wade* (New York: Routledge, 1992). A handful of other important works include: Allan Bérubé, *Coming Out Under Fire: The History of Gay Men and Women in World War Two* (New York: Free Press, 1990); Jonathan Ned Katz, *The Invention of Heterosexuality* (New York: Penguin, 1995); Regina G. Kunzel, *Fallen Women, Problem Girls: Unmarried Mothers and the Professionalization of Social Work, 1890–1945* (New Haven: Yale University Press, 1993); Mary E. Odem, *Delinquent Daughters: Protecting and Policing Adolescent Female Sexuality in the United States, 1885–1920* (Chapel Hill: University of North Carolina Press, 1995); Sharon R. Ullman, *Sex Seen: The Emergence of Modern Sexuality in America* (Berkeley: University of California Press, 1997). For a full bibliography of earlier works in the field, see D'Emilio and Freedman, *Intimate Matters.*

6. Interdisciplinary literary scholar Krista Comer offers an intelligent discussion of the silence about sexuality in western studies generally and advances conceptual tools for speaking about desire in the West in *Landscapes of the New West: Gender and Geography in Contemporary Women's Writing* (Chapel Hill: University of North Carolina Press, 1999), esp. chap. 4, "Queering Heterosexual Love: Trailer Parks, *Telenovelas,* and Other Landscapes of Feminist Desire."

7. See esp. Michel Foucault, *The History of Sexuality,* vol. 1, *An Introduction,* trans. Robert Hurley (New York: Pantheon, 1978); *The History of Sexuality,* vol. 2, *The Use of Pleasure,* trans. Robert Hurley (New York: Pantheon, 1985); and *The History of Sexuality,* vol. 3, *The Care of the Self,* trans. Robert Hurley (New York: Pantheon, 1986). For fine examples of the-

oretically informed scholarship that decenters European and North American histories of sexuality, see the special issue entitled "Circuits of Desire," ed. Yukiko Hanawa, *positions: east asia cultures critique* 2 (Spring 1994); and Hanawa, "inciting sites of political interventions: queer 'n' asian," *positions: east asia cultures critique* 4 (Winter 1996): 459–89.

8. Much of what I argue in these two paragraphs derives from my own work on the Gold Rush as well as the works cited in note 2 above. For my work, see *Roaring Camp: The Social World of the California Gold Rush* (New York: W. W. Norton, 2000); "'Domestic' Life in the Diggings: The Southern Mines in the California Gold Rush," in *Over the Edge: Remapping the American West*, ed. Valerie J. Matsumoto and Blake Allmendinger (Berkeley: University of California Press, 1999), 107–32; and "Bulls, Bears, and Dancing Boys: Race, Gender, and Leisure in the California Gold Rush," *Radical History Review* 60 (Fall 1994): 4–37.

9. I say "roughly equal" in light of Hurtado's argument that violence, disease, and privation during the Gold Rush brought about a measurably larger demographic decline among native women than native men. See Hurtado, *Indian Survival on the California Frontier*, esp. 188.

10. U.S. Bureau of the Census, *The Seventh Census of the United States: 1850* (Washington, D.C., 1853), and *Population of the United States in 1860; Compiled from . . . the Eighth Census* (Washington, D.C., 1864). The Southern Mines encompassed the area of the Sierra Nevada foothills in the drainage of the San Joaquin River. In 1850, the Southern Mines included most of Calaveras, Tuolumne, and Mariposa counties. Later, part of Calaveras County split off to form Amador County. So by 1860, the Southern Mines encompassed Amador, Calaveras, Tuolumne, and Mariposa counties.

11. In addition to the works cited in note 2 above, some useful references to sexual matters appear in the gold-rush scholarship of the 1980s and 1990s. See J. S. Holliday, *The World Rushed In: The California Gold Rush Experience* (New York: Simon & Schuster, 1981); Ralph Mann, *After the Gold Rush: Society in Grass Valley and Nevada City, California, 1849–1870* (Stanford: Stanford University Press, 1982); David Goodman, *Gold Seeking: Victoria and California in the 1850s* (Stanford: Stanford University Press, 1994); and Malcolm J. Rohrbough, *Days of Gold: The California Gold Rush and the American Nation* (Berkeley: University of California Press, 1997).

12. My intended audience for this chapter is a broad range of academic historians, California history enthusiasts, and students. Historians of sexuality and theorists of desire will immediately recognize that I do not engage all of the recent conceptual, theoretical, and historiographical arguments in the field. I offer this chapter as a contribution to contemporary conversations about sex and desire, especially as those conversations deploy historical knowledge, and so I have purposely sacrificed some theoretical complexity in the interests of greater accessibility. I am interested in communication that crosses a variety of boundaries and that works to the benefit of those who historically have been marginalized by their relationship to dominant constructions of sex and desire.

13. For background on the world of Timothy Osborn's youth, see Margaret S. Creighton, *Rites and Passages: The Experience of American Whaling, 1830–1870* (Cambridge: Cambridge University Press, 1995). See also Margaret S. Creighton and Lisa Norling, eds., *Iron Men, Wooden Women: Gender and Seafaring in the Atlantic World, 1700–1920* (Baltimore: Johns Hopkins University Press, 1996); and W. Jeffrey Bolster, *Black Jacks: African American Seamen in the Age of Sail* (Cambridge: Harvard University Press, 1997).

14. Much of the background information on Timothy Osborn appears in an introduction to the transcribed diary written by Emma B. Harris, and in a letter from Henry Beetle

Hough to Emma B. Harris, February 23, 1936, also in the Bancroft Library. The rest comes from the Osborn Journal itself (see note 1 above). The interpretive material derives from Johnson, *Roaring Camp*.

15. Journal entry, January 13, 1851, Osborn Journal. Osborn's diary is particularly rich in its references to desire, but it is hardly unique. For a more complete consideration of such sources and what they suggest about the history of sex and sexuality in gold-rush California, see my *Roaring Camp* and "Bulls, Bears, and Dancing Boys."

16. Some of this material I already have developed in *Roaring Camp*, esp. chap. 3, and "Bulls, Bears, and Dancing Boys." Occasionally, I borrow sentences or phrases from these works, as I have here.

17. I use the term "Anglo American" throughout to refer to white, English-speaking gold-rush participants of northern and western European descent.

18. Journal entry, December 8, 1850, Osborn Journal. For histories of courtship and romance among such white, aspiring middle-class men, see Ellen K. Rothman, *Hands and Hearts: A History of Courtship in America* (New York: Basic Books, 1984); and Karen Lystra, *Searching the Heart: Women, Men, and Romantic Love in Nineteenth-Century America* (New York: Oxford University Press, 1989). For other Americans, see, for example, Christine Stansell, *City of Women: Sex and Class in New York, 1789–1860* (New York: Alfred A. Knopf, 1986; Urbana: University of Illinois Press, 1986), esp. 76–101; and Deborah Gray White, *Ar'n't I a Woman? Female Slaves in the Plantation South* (New York: W. W. Norton, 1985), esp. 142–60.

19. Journal entry, August 24, 1850, Osborn Journal (shorthand restored to prose by Daniel Harris).

20. Ibid., August 18, 1850 (shorthand restored to prose by Daniel Harris).

21. Timothy also sought external approval for his romance with Annie. Once, he found a newspaper article entitled "My Cousins," which he read carefully, underlining those passages that were most meaningful to him, especially the description of the "*lady cousin*": "Here is a charming young lady . . . who will lecture you like a sister, and *treat you like a lover*—and then, when gossip begins to wag her many-tipped tongue, 'Oh, *we're only cousins*, you know.'" Ibid., November 29, 1850.

22. Ibid., July 18, 1850.

23. Ibid., August 13 and December 3, 1850, and January 6, 1851.

24. For an overview of such sexual ideologies, see D'Emilio and Freedman, *Intimate Matters*, esp. 55–84.

25. See, for example, Gilfoyle, *City of Eros*.

26. See Johnson, *Roaring Camp* and "Bulls, Bears and Dancing Boys." For rich primary sources that describe such markets in pleasure at Sonora, see William Perkins, *Three Years in California: William Perkins' Journal of Life at Sonora, 1849–1852*, ed. Dale L. Morgan and James R. Scobie (Berkeley: University of California Press, 1964); and Enos Christman, *One Man's Gold: The Letters and Journal of a Forty-Niner*, ed. Florence Morrow Christman (New York: Whittlesey House, McGraw-Hill, 1930).

27. On Nevada City, see Mann, *After the Gold Rush*, esp. 34–67 passim; and, more generally, Rohrbough, *Days of Gold*, esp. 146–50.

28. Journal entry, November 22, 1850, Osborn Journal.

29. Ibid., December 29 and 30, 1850.

30. Ibid., January 1 and 4, 1851.

31. Ibid., April 21, 1851. This "Fancy Dress Ball" sounds very much like the sexually charged costume balls that were so popular in New York City in the nineteenth century. See Gilfoyle, *City of Eros*, 232–36.

32. Ibid., April 25 (shorthand restored to prose by Daniel Harris) and May 18, 1851.

33. See Johnson, *Roaring Camp.*

34. Journal entry, December 31, 1850, Osborn Journal.

35. The diarist had much less to say about Chinese women because he stopped writing faithfully in his journal in 1851, the year before most Chinese began to arrive in California. I have cited his one mention of Chinese women in note 28 above. Just before Timothy left the diggings for Stockton, he mined alongside a group of early-arriving Chinese men. See journal entry, December 26, 1850, Osborn Journal.

36. Ibid., September 1, 1850. On the term "chola/o" in this period, see, for example, Leonard Pitt, *The Decline of the Californios: A Social History of the Spanish-Speaking Californians, 1846–1890* (Berkeley: University of California Press, 1966), 6, 29, 53, 67, 148; and, for a broader historical context, as well as a more critical reading, see David G. Gutiérrez, *Walls and Mirrors: Mexican Americans, Mexican Immigrants, and the Politics of Ethnicity* (Berkeley: University of California Press, 1995), esp. 13–38, 58.

37. Journal entry, October 9, 1850, Osborn Journal.

38. Ibid., January 15, 1851.

39. Ibid., January 18 and May 21, 1851.

40. The phrase meant literally, "shamed be he who thinks evil of it."

41. Ibid., January 15 and 19, 1851.

42. See Johnson, *Roaring Camp,* esp. chaps. 1, 3, and 6.

43. Journal entry, March 5, 1851, Osborn Journal.

44. For theoretical and historical considerations of all these constructions, see Johnson, *Roaring Camp* and "'A memory sweet to soldiers': The Significance of Gender in the History of the 'American West,'" *Western Historical Quarterly* 24 (November 1993): 495–517, reprinted in *A New Significance: Re-envisioning the History of the American West,* ed. Clyde Milner (New York: Oxford University Press, 1996), 255–78. In the latter volume, see commentary by Albert Hurtado, "Staring at the Sun," 279–83, and Deena J. González, "A Regendered, Reracialized, Resituated West," 283–88. See also Antonia I. Castañeda, "Women of Color and the Rewriting of Western History: The Discourse, Politics, and Decolonization of History," *Pacific Historical Review* 61 (November 1992): 501–33. For historical studies of "whiteness," see, for example, Alexander Saxton, *The Rise and Fall of the White Republic: Class Politics and Mass Culture in Nineteenth-Century America* (London: Verso, 1990), and Neil Foley, *The White Scourge: Mexicans, Blacks, and Poor Whites in Texas Cotton Culture* (Berkeley: University of California Press, 1997). On "whiteness" more generally, see Mike Hill, ed., *Whiteness: A Critical Reader* (New York: New York University Press, 1997).

45. See Hurtado, *Indian Survival on the California Frontier,* and two works by George Harwood Phillips: *Indians and Intruders in Central California, 1769–1849* (Norman: University of Oklahoma Press, 1993) and *Indians and Indian Agents: The Origins of the Reservation System in California, 1849–1852* (Norman: University of Oklahoma Press, 1997). In the Northern Mines, most of the Indians were Nisenans.

46. Journal entries, August 8 and 14, September 17, and October 2 and 4, 1850, Osborn Journal.

47. Ibid., October 2, 1850.

48. Ibid., August 8, 1850 (shorthand restored to prose by Daniel Harris).

49. These questions are adapted from Johnson, *Roaring Camp*, chap. 3, and "Bulls, Bears, and Dancing Boys." One reason a native woman might have pursued sex at one time and not another is suggested by a conversation between a Miwok man and a Belgian immigrant recorded in the Belgian's reminiscences. A native man named Juan explained to miner Jean-Nicolas Perlot that his people tried to conceive children so that they would be born between March and June, and thus benefit in the early months of their lives from the natural abundance of spring, summer, and fall in the foothills. See Jean-Nicolas Perlot, *Gold Seeker: Adventures of a Belgian Argonaut during the Gold Rush Years*, trans. Helen Harding Bretnor and ed. Howard R. Lamar (New Haven: Yale University Press, 1985), 230. Historians studying sexual misunderstandings in other moments of contact between native peoples and Europeans or European Americans are sketching out a way to study such conflicts in cultural meaning. See, for example, James P. Ronda, *Lewis and Clark among the Indians* (Lincoln: University of Nebraska Press, 1984), 36–37, 62–64, 130–32, 208–10, 232–33; and Richard White, *The Middle Ground: Indians, Empires, and Republics in the Great Lakes Region, 1650–1815* (Cambridge: Cambridge University Press, 1991), 60–75.

50. Most of what we do understand of such meanings derives from the crucial, extensive work of Albert Hurtado; see *Indian Survival on the California Frontier*, "When Strangers Met," and "Sex, Gender, Culture, and a Great Event." Hurtado's work is especially important for its analysis of sexual violence, a topic that is underdeveloped in this essay because of scant evidence in Timothy Osborn's diary.

51. See especially Hurtado, *Indian Survival on the California Frontier*, 169–92.

52. Personal communication from Craig D. Bates, Curator of Ethnography, Yosemite National Park, February 25, 1999.

53. Fonseca's family tree also includes a Portuguese and Cape Verdean branch, though this intermarriage came after the gold-rush period. Fonseca gave a presentation on his family and, more generally, on the impact of the Gold Rush on native peoples at a session entitled "The Legacy of the Gold Rush on Diverse Peoples," Gold Fever! Symposium, Autry Museum of Western Heritage, Los Angeles, October 24, 1998. Fonseca's artwork has been exhibited nationally and internationally. Especially relevant here is the exhibit *The Discovery of Gold in California*, Oakland Museum of California, April 18, 1998–January 3, 1999. For a description, see the article by Carey Caldwell, "The Discovery of Gold in California: Paintings by Harry Fonseca," *News From Native California* 2 (Summer 1998): 4–5 (reprinted from *Museum of California Magazine*, Spring 1998). See also Fonseca's marvelous illustrations in *Legends of the Yosemite Miwok*, comp. Frank La Pena, Craig D. Bates, and Steven P. Medley (1981; Yosemite National Park, Calif.: Yosemite Association, 1993).

54. I analyze a wider variety of sources in *Roaring Camp*, chap. 3 and Epilogue, and "Bulls, Bears, and Dancing Boys."

55. Journal entry, August 4, 1850, Osborn Journal.

56. For elaboration, see Johnson, *Roaring Camp*, chap. 3, and "Bulls, Bears, and Dancing Boys."

57. Howard C. Gardiner, *In Pursuit of the Golden Dream: Reminiscences of San Francisco and the Northern and Southern Mines, 1849–1857*, ed. Dale L. Morgan (Stoughton, Mass.: Western Hemisphere, 1970), 216.

58. See discussion in Jonathan Ned Katz, "Coming to Terms: Conceptualizing Men's Erotic and Affectional Relations with Men in the United States, 1820–1892," in *A Queer*

World: The Center for Lesbian and Gay Studies Reader, ed. Martin Duberman (New York: New York University Press, 1997), 216–35, esp. 219. Katz takes the phrase from B. R. Burg, *An American Seafarer in the Age of Sail: The Erotic Diaries of Philip C. Van Buskirk, 1851–1870* (New Haven: Yale University Press, 1994), a crucial piece of scholarship that opens up the study of homoeroticism among nineteenth-century American seafaring men. For the "boom cover trade," see esp. Burg, *An American Seafarer,* 75.

59. What Timothy probably did not know is that the word "matelot" derived from the Middle Dutch word "mattenoot," or, literally, "bedmate," from sailors' practice of sharing beds. This practice did not necessarily imply sharing sexual pleasures. But scholars have begun to study the frequency of same-sex eroticism among seafaring men in a variety of historical circumstances. See, for example, B. R. Burg, *Sodomy and the Pirate Tradition: English Sea Rovers in the Seventeenth-Century Caribbean* (New York: New York University Press, 1984); Arthur Gilbert, "Buggery and the British Navy, 1700–1861," *Journal of Social History* 10 (1976): 72–98, and "Sexual Deviance and Disaster During the Napoleonic Wars," *Albion* 9 (1977): 98–113; and Chauncey, *Gay New York,* esp. 64–97 passim, and "Christian Brotherhood or Sexual Perversion? Homosexual Identities and the Construction of Sexual Boundaries in the World War I Era," *Journal of Social History* 19 (1985): 189–212. For "matelot," see *Oxford English Dictionary,* s.v. "matelot"; [Paul Robert's] *Dictionnaire alphabétique et analogique de la langue de la Française,* s.v. "matelot"; *Merriam Webster's Collegiate Dictionary,* 10th ed., s.v. "matelot." My thanks to historian Martha Hanna for helping me think through this and for reading the French dictionary entry for me.

60. Journal entry, August 25, 1850, Osborn Journal.

61. See Goodman, *Gold Seeking,* esp. 188–219.

62. For elaboration on the conflation of things economic and things sexual, see Johnson, *Roaring Camp,* esp. chaps. 2 and 3.

63. John Marshall Newton, *Memoirs of John Marshall Newton* (John M. Stevenson, 1913), 34, 36, 38.

64. Journal entries, December 22 and 25, 1850, Osborn Journal.

65. For elaboration, see Johnson, *Roaring Camp,* chap. 3, and "Bulls, Bears, and Dancing Boys."

66. *Hanna Allkin v. Jeremiah Allkin* (1856), Calaveras County, District Court, Calaveras County Museum and Archives, San Andreas, Calif.

67. See especially J. D. Borthwick, *The Gold Hunters* (1857; Oyster Bay, N.Y.: Nelson Doubleday, 1917), 303–304.

68. Journal entries, July 7 and 11, August 24 and 25, 1850, Osborn Journal. The material in this paragraph and the next is adapted from and also expands on Johnson, *Roaring Camp,* chap. 3, and "Bulls, Bears, and Dancing Boys."

69. Ibid., September 15, 1850. A "short six" and a "long nine" are types of cigars.

70. Ibid., August 24, 1850.

71. Ibid., November 5, 1850.

72. Ibid., November 16, 1850 (shorthand restored to prose by Daniel Harris).

73. Ibid., December 19, 1850.

74. Ibid., December 10, 1850.

75. Journalists have not been as careful. On September 23, 1994, I presented a paper at the Power of Ethnic Identities in the Southwest Conference sponsored by the Huntington Library in San Marino, California. In that paper, I talked about two Anglo American men

who went to California together in 1849 and ended up living together in Tuolumne County for the rest of their lives; both died in 1903. The two may well have had an erotic relationship. But nowhere did I call these men "homosexual" or "gay." My purpose was rather to point out the historical silence about intimate same-sex relationships—some of which might have been sexual—in the Gold Rush. Nonetheless, the next day I read of my work in the newspaper: "Johnson's mention of the legacy left by a pair of homosexual Forty-Niner gold miners raised some eyebrows among the conference audience of 75. But most seemed to feel that a little eye-opening is appropriate for those who read—and write— American history." Elsewhere in the article, referring more obliquely to my talk, the author mentioned "gays who played a role in the California Gold Rush." *Los Angeles Times,* September 24, 1994. For more on the two men, Jason Chamberlain and John Chaffee, see Johnson, *Roaring Camp,* chap. 1 and Epilogue. For more on the cultural construction of homosexuality, see, for example, Chauncey, *Gay New York;* and, for women, Kennedy and Davis, *Boots of Leather, Slippers of Gold.* See also the essays in Martin Duberman et al., eds., *Hidden From History: Reclaiming the Gay and Lesbian Past* (New York: Meridian, 1989); and, for more recent perspectives, Special Issue, "The Queer Issue: New Visions of America's Lesbian and Gay Past," *Radical History Review* 62 (Spring 1995); and Duberman, *A Queer World.*

76. For this argument, see, for example, Katz, *The Invention of Heterosexuality.*

77. D'Emilio and Freedman, *Intimate Matters,* 68–69.

78. Alfred Doten, *The Journals of Alfred Doten, 1849–1903,* ed. Walter Van Tilburg Clark, 3 vols. (Reno: University of Nevada Press, 1973), 1:116; emphasis in original. At the turn of the twenty-first century, some would call such a person "transgendered," but this might bespeak the kind of anachronism historians of sexuality have tried to avoid. Nonetheless, there is much to be learned from the current literature on transgenderism. For an intelligent theoretical discussion especially applicable to a multinational event such as the Gold Rush, see Nan Alamilla Boyd, "Bodies in Motion: Lesbian and Transsexual Histories," in *A Queer World,* ed. Duberman, 134–52. And see the courageous volume by Leslie Feinberg, *Transgender Warriors: Making History from Joan of Arc to RuPaul* (Boston: Beacon Press, 1996).

79. In *Roaring Camp,* chap. 6, for example, I use divorce cases from the district court records of Amador, Calaveras, Tuolumne, and Mariposa counties to illustrate and analyze women's experiences of intimacy in the 1850s. Although they do not focus on sexual matters, three recent dissertations that study gold-rush-era California within a longer chronological framework suggest the extraordinary potential for work based in a broader range of research materials. See Miroslava Chavez, "Mexican Women and the American Conquest in Los Angeles: From the Mexican Era to American Ascendancy" (Ph.D. diss., University of California, Los Angeles, 1998); Mary L. Coomes, "From Pooyi to the New Almaden Mercury Mine: Cinnabar, Economics, and Culture in California to 1920" (Ph.D. diss., University of Michigan, 1999); and Amelia María de la Luz Montes, "'Es Necesario Mirar Bien': Letter Making, Fiction Writing, and American Nationhood in the Nineteenth Century" (Ph.D. diss., University of Denver, 1999).

80. This story first appeared in print in C. Hart Merriam, *Dawn of the World: Weird Tales of the Mewan Indians of California* (Cleveland: Arthur H. Clark, 1910), now reprinted as *The Dawn of the World: Myths and Tales of the Miwok Indians of California* (Lincoln: University of Nebraska Press, 1993), see esp. 228–29. I have taken it from the *Legends of the Yosemite*

Miwok, 53 (and see Harry Fonseca's accompanying illustration, 52), particularly because this volume has been reviewed by the American Indian Council of Mariposa County (see the Foreword by Les Jaimes, vii).

81. According to Merriam, Nisenans at the turn of the twentieth century told a similar tale, but in the Nisenan version, two young women were walking along the American River when they heard a baby's cry. They found the infant on the riverbank, but when one of them reached for it, the baby became the river mermaid and then dragged the young woman into the water. See *Dawn of the World*, 229–30. This Nisenan version perhaps bespeaks a different set of desires.

Contributors

STEVEN M. AVELLA is associate professor and chair, department of history, Marquette University. He holds a Ph.D. from the University of Notre Dame. He is the author of *This Confident Church: Catholic Leadership and Life in Chicago* (1992). He has devoted considerable attention to the role of religion in shaping urban culture in California.

SUCHENG CHAN received her B.A. in economics from Swarthmore College, her M.A. in Asian studies from the University of Hawaii, and her Ph.D. in political science from the University of California, Berkeley. After participating in the Third World Student Strike at U.C. Berkeley in 1969, which led to the establishment of ethnic studies programs, she became a specialist in the emerging field of Asian American history. She has received more than a dozen awards for her scholarly work, teaching, and community service, including the J. S. Holliday Award given by the California Historical Society.

IRVING G. HENDRICK is professor emeritus of education at the University of California, Riverside, where he has served since 1965. He led the School of Education as its dean through a highly innovative and productive period between 1987 and 1998. Currently he is serving as Assistant Vice Chancellor of Development. Most of Professor Hendrick's historical writings have centered geographically on California, and topically on historical studies of teacher education, minority group education, and special education. A native of Los Angeles, his formal education was all completed in California, including A.B. and M.A. degrees from Whittier College and an Ed.D. degree from UCLA.

SUSAN LEE JOHNSON is an assistant professor of history at the University of Colorado at Boulder. She has published essays in *Western Historical Quarterly* and *Radical History Review*. She is the author of *Roaring Camp: The Social World of the California Gold Rush* (W. W. Norton, 2000).

ANTHONY KIRK, who received his Ph.D. in American history from the University of California, Santa Barbara, is an authority on western art and has written extensively on nineteenth-century California painting. He serves as a consultant to corporations, government agencies, nonprofits, and individuals, providing a range of research, writing, and litigation-support services, particularly in the fields of cultural and environmental history. He has worked for Sony, the U.S. Fish and Wildlife Service, the National Park Service, and the California Historical Society, among others. He is a resident of Santa Cruz, California.

MICHAEL KOWALEWSKI is an associate professor of English and American studies at Carleton College in Northfield, Minnesota. He is the author, among other works, of *Deadly Musings: Violence and Verbal Form in American Fiction* (Princeton University Press, 1993). He has edited a collection of essays entitled *Reading the West: New Essays on the Literature of the American West* (Cambridge University Press, 1996). He is also the editor of the anthology *Gold Rush: A Literary Exploration* (Heyday Books, 1997), which was the centerpiece of the California Council for the Humanities' Sesquicentennial Project. A native Californian who grew up in Redding, he is currently the president of the Western Literature Association.

GARY F. KURUTZ serves as Director of Special Collections for the California State Library and manages the publication program of The Book Club of California. His research interests include the California Gold Rush and the iconographic history of California and the American West. He is the author of *The California Gold Rush: A Descriptive Bibliography of Books and Pamphlets Covering the Years 1849–1853*, *The Architectural Terra Cotta of Gladding McBean*, and *California Books Illustrated with Original Photographs*, along with several articles and keepsakes. He has been the recipient of the Oscar Lewis Award of The Book Club of California and the Award of Merit from the Sacramento County History Society.

RICHARD J. ORSI is professor of history at California State University, Hayward. A graduate of Occidental College in Los Angeles, he received his doctorate from the University of Wisconsin, Madison. He is the coauthor (with Richard B. Rice and William A. Bullough) of *The Elusive Eden: A New History of California*, 2nd ed. (McGraw-Hill, 1996), and coeditor (with Alfred A. Runte and Marlene Smith-Baranzini) of *Yosemite and Sequoia: A Century of California National Parks* (University of California Press, 1993). He is nearing completion of another book, "A Railroad and the Development of the American West: The Southern Pacific Company, 1860–1930." Since 1988, he has been editor of *California History*, the quarterly of the California Historical Society.

ROBERT PHELPS is an assistant professor in United States history at California State University, Hayward, where he specializes in the history of California, urban history, and the history of the United States during the Progressive Era. He received his Ph.D. from the University of California, Riverside, in March 1996, and is currently conducting research on the history of factory towns in southern California. Professor Phelps is author of "The Search for a Modern Industrial City: Urban Planning, the Open Shop, and the Founding of Torrance, California," which appeared in the *Pacific Historical Review* in November 1995, and "The Manufacturing Suburb of Los Angeles: Henry Huntington, Alfred Dolge, and the Building of Dolgeville, California," in *Southern California Quarterly* (forthcoming).

MALCOLM ROHRBOUGH is professor of history at the University of Iowa. His most recent book is *Days of Gold: The California Gold Rush and the American Nation* (University of California Press, 1997).

JAMES A. SANDOS, Farquhar Professor of the Southwest at the University of Redlands, earned his Ph.D. from the University of California, Berkeley, in 1978, where he studied with Woodrow Borah. Within Borderlands history he has had an ongoing interest in Indian-white relations in California since 1769. His essay "Between Crucifix and Lance: Indian-White Relations in California, 1769–1848" appeared in *Contested Eden: California Before the Gold Rush*, the first volume of the California History Sesquicentennial Series.

MARLENE SMITH-BARANZINI, associate editor of *California History* since 1990, is editor of *The Shirley Letters from the California Mines, 1851–1852* (Heyday Books, 1998). She is coauthor (with Howard Egger-Bovet) of the USKids History Series, which includes *Book of the American Indians* (1994), *Book of the American Colonies* (1995), *Book of the American Revolution* (1994), *Book of the New American Nation* (1996), and *Book of the Civil War* (1998), published by Little, Brown.

San Francisco-born KEVIN STARR, State Librarian of California, is also professor of history at the University of Southern California and the author of the notable Oxford University Press history series "Americans and the California Dream," which includes *Americans and the California Dream* (1973) and *The Dream Endures: California Enters the 1940s* (1997).

NANCY J. TANIGUCHI is professor of history at California State University, Stanislaus. Her focus is on American history after the Civil War in a variety of areas, including women, law, the American West, and California. She recently published a legal history, *Necessary Fraud: Progressive Reform and Utah Coal.*

Index

TEXT:	11/14 Adobe Caslon
DISPLAY:	Adobe Caslon Regular, Italic and Small Caps
DESIGN:	Terry Bain
COMPOSITION:	Integrated Composition Systems, Inc.
PRINTING AND BINDING:	Malloy Lithographing, Inc.
INDEX:	Robert A. Clark